WEATHERING
THE STORMS

WEATHERING THE STORMS

Psychotherapy for Psychosis

Murray Jackson

Foreword by
James S. Grotstein

Preface by
Paul Williams

KARNAC
LONDON   NEW YORK

First published in 2001 by
H. Karnac (Books) Ltd.
6 Pembroke Buildings, London NW10 6RE

A subsidiary of Other Press LLC, New York

British Library Cataloguing in Publication Data

A C.I.P. for this book is available from the British Library

ISBN 1 85575 267 0

10 9 8 7 6 5 4 3 2 1

Edited, designed, and produced by Communication Crafts

www.karnacbooks.com

Printed and bound by Biddles Short Run Books, King's Lynn

*This book is dedicated to the Scandinavian
psychotherapists who made it possible and who,
for reasons of confidentiality, remain anonymous*

"I have gathered a posie of other men's flowers, and nothing but
the thread that binds them is my own."

Montaigne

CONTENTS

ACKNOWLEDGEMENTS

My indebtedness to my old friend and mentor, the late Henri Rey, is incalculable.

I am particularly grateful to Jeanne Magagna, who, having collected and edited Rey's work, helped me very much with my own. As a teacher of trainee psychiatrists and child psychotherapists, she scrutinized the manuscript in its several draft forms and made many invaluable contributions and helpful suggestions. Michael Sinason also gave a great deal of his time in studying the text, and his expertise was particularly helpful.

Since this work is the fruit of many years of teaching about psychotic illness and its treatment in collaboration with a large number of Scandinavian psychiatrists and psychologists, I can only name some to whom I am especially indebted.

In Norway, I owe a great debt of gratitude to Anna Leira, to the late Thoralv Nødland, and to the late Endre Ugelstad; in Finland, to Yrjö Alanen and Viljo Rakkolainen; in Sweden, to Gøran André, Ulla Arnell, Johan Cullberg, Magnus Elfstadius, Kina Meurle Hallberg, Rolf Holmqvist, and Tiit Saarman; in Denmark, to Ulla Bartells, Elizabeth Blum, Jens Bolvig Hansen, Anne Viskinge Jensen, Margit Jørgensen, Ulla Just, Ebbe Linnemann, Gert Rasmussen, and Bent Rosenbaum. They opened doors to teaching/learning opportunities and offered warm and generous hospitality.

Pearl King told me long ago that I should write about my psychoanalytic work in hospital and academic psychiatry, and I was extremely fortunate in having the opportunity of learning from psychoanalysts who knew a great deal about psychosis, in particular Henri Rey, Hanna Segal, Betty Joseph, Herbert Rosenfeld, and Leslie Sohn.

Jeremy Holmes, Michael Sinason, and Cesare Sacerdoti encouraged me to write about psychosis, and Paul Williams conceived the idea of *Unimaginable Storms,* which we then wrote together. He pressed me to write the present book, which is a sequel to the first, and offered much support and many good ideas throughout the long period of its gestation.

John Steiner, David Morgan, Brian Martindale, David Bell, and Stanford Bourne read all or part of the manuscript and made many helpful comments. Bill Frosch made some characteristically simple but profound observations and suggestions.

I owe thanks to John Alderdice, Stanford Bourne, and David Morgan for allowing me to quote their work, which is included in Chapter 16. My wife, Cynthia, supported me with patience and understanding throughout, and my daughter Judy Parsons made some fundamentally helpful observations.

I wish to express my profound gratitude to the many Scandinavian psychotherapists, whose work forms the basis of this book, for their generous cooperation and for allowing me to publish these accounts of their work. They, and many others whose work is not recorded here, have given me, themselves, and many others the priceless opportunity of learning more about the psychotic mind and of thereby helping those individuals who have had the misfortune to fall into these catastrophic disorders, as well as helping the families and other relatives who undertake the often awesome and sometimes devastating burden of trying to understand and help them.

My special thanks are due to Graham Sleight and Oliver Rathbone for their enthusiastic support, and to Eric and Klara King of Communication Crafts, whose tireless work has made a most important contribution.

I would have wished to convey something of the structure and vitality of the seminar-workshops, the enthusiasm of all the participants, and the excitement of new learning, but this would have required quite a different book.

Finally, I wish to thank Jens Bolvig Hansen for the generous and invaluable help he has given me from the beginning of the book's conception. His wide psychiatric experience, wisdom, common sense, and dry Danish humour served repeatedly as the Ariadne thread to help me withdraw from the dangers of trying to say everything I wished to in this one volume. Without his dedicated and time-consuming help, this book would never have seen the light of day.

ABOUT THE AUTHOR

Murray Jackson is a psychiatrist and psychoanalyst, formerly a consultant at King's College Hospital and the Maudsley and Bethlem Royal Hospitals in London. He is co-author, with Paul Williams, of a previous book, *Unimaginable Storms: A Search for Meaning in Psychosis*.

A native of Australia, he came to England fifty years ago to train at the Maudsley, where his interest in psychosomatic disorders and psychotic states led him to Jung's work in psychosis and to training as an analytical psychologist. Further experience in child and adult psychiatry brought acquaintance with the work of Melanie Klein and to training in psychoanalysis. He pursued part-time psychoanalytic practice in conjunction with work in the public sector of the British National Health Service. As Consultant at the Maudsley, he directed a unit created for exploring the application of psychoanalytic principles to the severely mentally ill, developing the original work of his predecessor, John Steiner, sharing a general psychiatric ward with the Professor of Psychological Medicine, Robert Cawley. This partnership lasted thirteen years and led to the development of a psychoanalytically based ward milieu and an approach to psychotic illness that sought to integrate psychoanalytic and biomedical knowledge. Long impressed by the work of Yrjö Alanen and his colleagues in Finland, retirement from the NHS in 1987 brought the opportunity to accept teaching assignments in hospital-based psychoanalytic psychiatry and psychotherapy throughout Scandinavia (and briefly in Estonia), which he has continued up to the present, commuting from his home in France.

He is a Member of the British Psychoanalytical Society, a Fellow of the Royal College of Physicians and of the Royal College of Psychiatrists, and a life Member of the Royal Society of Medicine. He is also a member of the British Psychological Society and an Honorary lifetime member of the International Society for the Psychological Treatment of the Schizophrenias and Other Psychoses (ISPS).

PREFACE

It is gratifying to see the birth of Murray Jackson's new work, *Weathering the Storms: Psychotherapy for Psychosis*, which reaps the benefit of his lifetime's work in the study and treatment of patients with psychotic illnesses. This new book is a sequel to *Unimaginable Storms: A Search for Meaning in Psychosis*, which he and I co-authored in 1994. In that first book, we concentrated on providing a demonstration of how psychoanalytic knowledge can be employed as a beacon to guide the multidisciplinary treatment of psychosis. Through clinical case examples, it was possible to convey how Jackson and his colleagues brought an unusual level of understanding to seriously ill patients, something that most public mental health services today could not contemplate in the contemporary climate of fast-food psychiatry. In this new book, Murray Jackson demonstrates, again through detailed clinical examples, how his supervisory and teaching skills have, over years, influenced the many psychiatrists and psychotherapists in Scandinavia with whom he has worked closely in the treatment of seemingly intractable states.

Two characteristics of his work stand out. First, the unusual flexibility of his grasp of theory and technique. He forsakes dogmatism and employs theoretical concepts from a variety of schools when and where he finds them useful in the clinical setting. Undoubtedly his interest the work of Klein, Bion, and Rey underpins much of his thinking, but he gives no impression in *Weathering the Storms* of being dependent on ideas or theories that are not stimulated by the realities of the evolving clinical encounter. This is a useful guide to clinicians: working analytically with psychosis demands tolerance of confusing countertransference states of mind, the capacity to follow multiple (often paradoxical) threads of communication simultaneously, and a resistance to premature closure in order to allay the clinician's anxieties. This "negative capability" does not, of course, preclude the acquisition of knowledge; it is a means of acquiring it through emphasis on the unfolding of the transference–countertransference relationship (which never ceases).

The second characteristic of Jackson's work, which is linked to the first, is his combination of curiosity, persistence, and concern in relation to the patients he discusses. He maintains an alertness to his patients' threshold for mental pain but is neither afraid nor deterred by the extent of their suffering in his pursuit of dialogue in order to render meaningful their internal catastrophe. The restoration of human contact, forsaken for the delusional benefits of psychosis, is Jackson's goal.

Although an expert in his field, he does not advocate restriction of this kind of expertise to psychoanalysts. For many years, he has supported the teaching and supervision of a range of mental health professionals in order to foster a psychoanalytic perspective on mental functioning in psychosis. In this book, he shows how psychotherapists, psychiatrists, and psychiatric nurses in Scandinavia have taken to this way of thinking, with impressive results. Murray Jackson has produced a clinical workbook that will assist and illuminate the work of a great many psychotherapists for years to come.

Paul Williams
Professor, Anglia Polytechnic University

Murray Jackson presents us with the most practical, useful, and sophisticated handbook on the treatment of psychotic and primitive mental disorders to date. He applies psychoanalytic thinking to the practical situation in which patients can be seen only once or twice a week at most, sometimes less so, or even not at all. His setting is the clinic where the therapist and other relevant personnel convene to give vital data on the patient.

He moves with unassuming yet confident ease between different schools of psychoanalytic thinking, psychopharmacology, and other aspects of empirical psychiatry and psychology. What emerges is an effective, multidisciplinary approach to treatment. With indefatigable energy, he struggles to make sense of the lives of these patients, drawing on their past histories and from accounts of the dedicated Scandinavian therapists and clinic staffs who keep alive the conviction that well-selected patients can greatly benefit from psychoanalytic psychotherapy.

Jackson's work is an impressive example of a dialectical process that is currently taking place on the borders between psychoanalysis, psychoanalytically informed psychotherapy, and empirical psychiatry in the treatment of psychotic patients and others suffering from primitive mental disorders. Two generations ago, psychoanalytic thinking was in its heyday in regard to its spirit of enthusiasm about the treatment of schizophrenia and other psychotic states. Along came neuroscience, not only with its arsenal of medications for psychosis, but also with a paradigm-shattering revelation that schizophrenia and manic-depressive illness (now "bipolar" and "unipolar") had undeniable constitutional (inheritable, congenital, or perinatal) substrates. The concept of the "schizophrenogenic mother" became obsolete, along with the time-honoured concept of developmental vulnerabilities (fixations) to trauma. Neuroleptic medication became so successful in the amelioration of psychotic symptoms, particularly hallucinations and delusions, that more subtle personality traits received less attention, and, because of the concurrent change in economics which argued for shorter mental hospitalizations, a whole new trend in the treatment of psychotics resulted: treat the acute positive symptoms with neuroleptics and then send them home. This approach contributes to the high incidence of suicide in schizophrenia and to the large number of homeless people who inhabit every major city in the world.

There are signs that a return to psychoanalytic and psychotherapeutic thinking in the treatment of these disorders is at hand. It has gradually become apparent that schizophrenic, bipolar, and unipolar patients suffer from state disorders as well as from trait disorders, and psychopharmacological agents only address the former, never the latter, whereas psychological treatment addresses the latter and even sometimes the former.

In his theoretical discussion, Jackson gives much weight to Bion's theory of container–contained. In this view, the psychotic person lacks the basic integrative capacity, normally established in infancy, on which mental stability rests. He is unable to dream normally, or to distinguish between sleep and wakefulness, conscious and unconscious, and internal and external worlds. Bion believed that dreaming never stopped, but continued throughout the day and night. This factor is partially responsible for that characteristic of schizophrenia known as over-inclusion of stimuli.

The schizophrenic, cut off from his normal world because of its intolerability, seeks to create another one, a parallel world, but one that obeys different rules. It is essentially a psychic retreat. The cost of the retreat is madness; the reward is a new "meaning" for a virtual life.

Weathering the Storms is about listening to psychotic patients with both a psychiatric and a psychoanalytic ear. In this current work as well as in his other contributions, Murray Jackson provides an admirable model for the new integration that has today at last become possible.

James S. Grotstein
Clinical Professor of Psychiatry, UCLA School of Medicine.

WEATHERING
THE STORMS

Introduction

This book follows a previous one, *Unimaginable Storms: A Search for Meaning in Psychosis* (co-authored with Paul Williams) and is a further contribution to the application of modern psychoanalytic concepts to the understanding and treatment of schizophrenia and related psychotic illness. Although it is addressed primarily to psychiatrists and psychotherapists working with psychotic patients in the public-hospital sphere, I hope that others might find it of interest.

Major psychotic disorders are one of the world's most important health problems, and their cost, in terms of both human suffering and socio-economic burden, is very high. Expert opinion is divided about how they might best be understood, treated, and ultimately prevented. Several different professional disciplines have acquired important knowledge in the field, and the search for comprehensive understanding, and for treatment modes that might effectively integrate what is useful in each, is currently a matter of concern.

Despite recent advances in the understanding of brain function, and the development of powerful anti-psychotic drugs, a high proportion of the schizophrenic psychoses continue to follow a relapsing course, or proceed to early chronicity. Psychoanalytic contributions to the field of psychosis were at their zenith a few decades ago, and many mental health workers looked forward with optimism to a future in which increasing integration of psychoanalytic and psychiatric perspectives would bring greater understanding of people with psychotic disorders, and more effective approaches to treatment. Despite these hopeful beginnings, interest in the psychoanalytic approach to schizophrenia and related disorders, which was extremely active in the post-war period, has subsequently suffered a considerable decline. Polarized thinking and oppositional attitudes still prevail in contemporary psychiatric teaching and clinical practice in much of the Western world. In the United Kingdom, a long-established biomedical tradition has borne much fruit but has, in general, been uninterested in psychoanalytic ideas about psychosis. In the United States, many psychiatrists are worried about "dehumanizing" developments in psychiatry associated with the increasing emphasis on anti-psychotic drug treatments (Fleck, 1995) at the expense of interviewing skills and of understanding psychotic patients in terms of their personal development.

Having worked for all my professional life in public hospitals of the British National Health Service and at the same time in private psychoanalytic practice, I have had considerable personal experience of the merits and limitations of different approaches to the understanding and treatment of psychotic patients. I have also learned something of the heavy demands and responsibilities that may confront workers in each sphere. Writing this book from the point of view of both disciplines, wearing two hats as it were, makes it practically inevitable that I will do justice to neither, but for better or worse it is the only way I can approach the subject. I believe that such an approach is appropriate to the need to build bridges between the two perspectives at the present time, when the dazzling achievements of biomedicine and the emphasis on brief methods of therapy are bringing the risk that the psychological understanding of the individual will be progressively neglected, and at the worst the prospect that psychiatrists' skills in psychological understanding and treatment will eventually atrophy (Holmes, 2000; Reiser, 1988).

There have been many reasons for this diminishing interest, of which the introduction of drugs with powerful symptom-suppressive effects and the remarkable advances in research in neurobiology are perhaps the most important. Nonetheless, psychoanalytically based work has continued to flourish in many centres in Europe and the Americas.

In Finland, the work of Yrjö Alanen and his co-workers has developed, over the last thirty years, a psychotherapeutically oriented "need-adapted" approach to the treatment of schizophrenia (Alanen, 1975, 1997; Alanen, Räkköläinen, Laakso, Rasimus, & Kaljonen, 1986; Alanen, Ugelstad, Armelius, Lehtinen, et al., 1994). This remarkable and highly successful work, associated with the Turku Schizophrenia Project, has offered an ideal model for a comprehensive approach to the treatment of schizophrenia and related psychoses and has increasingly informed research and practice throughout Scandinavia. In the last few years, this approach has begun to receive wider attention, as part of a general increase of awareness of the importance of early detection and treatment (Alanen, Lehtinen, Lehtinen, Aaltonen, & Räkköläinen, 2000).

Kernberg (1992) has outlined some of the reasons for this revival of interest in the psychoanalytic approach to schizophrenic disorders. He points out that the assumption that psychopharmacological treatment of psychotic illness would render psychotherapeutic approaches obsolete has proved illusory. He remarks that the pioneer work of a few psychoanalysts has profoundly improved our understanding of the psychodynamics of psychosis and of treatment procedures, and that it has been increasingly recognized that study of psychotic patients greatly illuminates the psychodynamics of less severe disorders and, indeed, of the development and functioning of the normal mind.

These concepts offer important contributions to the understanding of psychotic illness and help to make sense of the incomprehensible and apparently meaningless thinking and behaviour commonly associated with psychotic states of mind. In this way, the concepts can provide a guide for workers with different skills and perspectives and contribute to the formulation of treatment plans appropriate to the patient's needs, psychological disabilities, and assets at any particular time.

A psychoanalytic perspective can help the clinician decide what type of psychological treatment might be most helpful to a particular patient, and when long-term individual psychoanalytically based treatment might be an important mode of treatment and when it might not. Severely ill psychotic patients usually require advanced psychiatric resources in the public mental health services in hospital and community, and skilled coordination of a team of mental health specialists with different but complementary skills. Such a team can provide a necessary network support for the psychotherapist who is conducting individual psychotherapy, and without this his work may prove impossible.* These resources are relatively rare in the United Kingdom, but they are much more available in the Scandinavian and some other European countries.

The uses and misuses of theory

Psychoanalytic concepts can help explain *how* some psychotic patients improve in the course of treatment (in the sense of defining what constitutes "improvement"), *why* they improve (in the sense of defining the "agents" of change), and why some fail to improve.

In trying to understand psychosis, it is important to be guided by theory and not driven by it. But this resolve may not be so easy to follow, because there is much that will remain undiscovered if the investigator lacks the knowledge of what to look for, and how to go about discovering it. A procrustean procedure of forcing observations into preconceived theories may be difficult to avoid. Theory can, for better or for worse, serve as a "transitional object" to reassure inexperienced therapists. An exclusive preoccupation with the deepest roots of psychosis, which are to be found in the highly sensitive, as yet only partially understood, and psychobiologically complex mother–baby relationship, may lead to neglect of matters that may sometimes be of more practical importance for the future psychotic individual, such as the role of the father and of life experiences after leaving the nursery. The branches may sometimes be more relevant and important than the roots.

The source of the case material

All the case studies in the book have been made available by Scandinavian psychotherapists with whom I have had the privilege of working over many years in their individual psychotherapy with seriously ill psychotic patients, work conducted within a publicly

---

*In the interests of simplicity, I have not attempted correct gender attribution.

funded hospital context, usually on the basis of once- or twice-weekly therapy sessions. Over a period of fifteen years work in fifteen hospital centres throughout Scandinavia, some 200 psychotic and severely borderline patients were discussed in depth, and of these about 60 were receiving some form of individual psychotherapy. Some of these teaching events were sufficiently frequent to ensure a degree of continuity of contact with some individual cases. These took the form of supervisory seminars discussing ongoing psychotherapeutic work with psychotic patients in groups of various sizes, meeting at intervals of several months over a year or more. Other events were concerned with the exploration of the psychopathology of a particular patient on one or more occasions, and many events were consultations with large groups of staff of acute psychiatric wards about very disturbed and difficult patients.

From these patients, I have selected fifteen cases who illustrate, in separate chapters, a wide range of psychotic conditions; in addition, in Chapter 16 I have included fifteen brief vignettes (some from my own practice) that focus on particular psychotic processes. Some of the patients were receiving long-term individual psychotherapy, mostly on a once- or twice-weekly basis, and these were discussed in the ongoing seminars. In these cases, some discussion of the process of the psychotherapy and follow-up of the long-term outcome was possible. In other cases the material is less detailed and the presentation is focused on the exploration of possible meanings of psychotic phenomena. The vignettes in Chapter 16 derive mostly from the consultation work and from my own clinical experience.

Much of what follows will be familiar to psychodynamically oriented psychiatrists, psychologists, and social workers. Some of it, in particular in the application of Kleinian and Bionic concepts and formulations, may be less familiar, and I hope that the case illustrations will bring some clinical substance to often difficult concepts.

Theoretical background

I have not aimed to present the contributions of different psychological, psychosocial, or psychotherapeutic approaches but, rather, have tried to show how the concepts that I will use can contribute to them all. Neither have I aimed at providing a detailed description of other important streams of psychoanalytic thinking. The omission of Harry Stack Sullivan and the Washington school associated with the Chestnut Lodge Hospital is a major one. Searles (1965a), Pao (1968a, 1968b, 1979), Jacobson (1967), Feinsilver (1986), and many others working in that "interpersonal" tradition have made fundamental and enduring contributions. Developments in the field of ego-psychology and self-psychology—Kohut's "interactive" model of infancy and his views on narcissism (Kohut, 1977; Kohut & Wolf, 1978)—and the influential work of Lacan (1997) and other French writers have all added to the understanding of psychotic disorders, sometimes in conflict with Kleinian views. (Details of the works of these authors can be found at the beginning of the References.)

To try to do justice to these weighty contributions would take me beyond my particular theme—and indeed beyond my competence— and I have often needed to remind myself that this book is not meant to be a treatise on psychoanalysis, but an exercise in psychoanalytic psychiatry aimed at the integration of psychoanalytic knowledge within clinical psychiatry and psychotherapy.

Learning from experience

It has sometimes been remarked that psychoanalytic concepts only become believable when some experience of personal individual psychotherapy has been acquired. Although I think that this is an unduly pessimistic generalization, there is much truth in it. Many readers may find Kleinian writing opaque and incomprehensible on first acquaintance. Although some intuitive mothers may readily appreciate the explanatory power of Klein's theories about the minds of babies and small children, or even see the beauty and logic of her vast and complex theoretical structure, many beginning readers are likely to be baffled and discouraged.

Contact with psychotic patients can be emotionally disturbing, even for experienced professionals, and this is one reason why psychosis treatment is usually best conducted as work within a multidisciplinary psychiatric team. Individual psychotherapy with such patients requires special interest and training and is therefore not a path for everyone. Those who choose it will find that a sufficiently long period of personal psychoanalytically based psychotherapy will help them in their work (Mace & Margison, 1997).

The structure of the book

Each of the first fifteen chapters is based on the study of one individual psychotic patient and is self-contained, as were the seminars. Sufficient theory is presented in each chapter to make the case understandable, perhaps with the help of the Glossary, and the reader will therefore meet a degree of repetition of concepts and overlapping of themes. Some chapters offer a certain amount of detail of the process of psychotherapy over a long period, where issues of transference, countertransference, and working-through can be considered. Others offer less detail, and some are based on a single session of case discussion. Follow-up reports, formal and informal, of various lengths of time have been available in several of the cases.

Because of the central importance of the psychodynamics of obsessional processes of impulse and defence, these are introduced in the early chapters. The next chapters illustrate the psychodynamic relation between hysterical neurosis and schizophrenia, and the possible pathogenic consequences of severe primitive sibling jealousy. Paranoid, phobic, and manic-depressive states are then described.

Fifteen brief vignettes offer further illustrations of psychotic processes, and some theoretical and practical issues are considered in the light of the foregoing case material. The final chapter offers some concluding comments, and three appendices add further reflections. The Glossary may help readers find their bearings in what some may experience as a conceptual jungle, and at the start of the References and Bibliography there are details of relevant psychiatric and psychoanalytic texts that I have personally found particularly helpful.

My emphasis on Kleinian and "neo-Kleinian" concepts, as I have understood them, does not imply a lack of recognition of the important work of psychoanalysts with different theoretical orientations. Rather, it is the expression of my personal experience that these concepts are useful tools for understanding and making sense of the complex clinical data that psychotic patients present. This psychotic material forms the substance of the book, providing a resource for critical discussion.

Some readers will already be quite familiar with the concepts that have been employed in the case studies. Others may wish to know where they came from, what are the most important, and where they seem to be going, a matter that is addressed in Chapter 17. Psychoanalysts have often been regarded as being poor communicators with

non-analysts. The detailed and lucid presentations of the evolution
of psychoanalytic theory in general by Bateman and Holmes (1995), of
psychotherapy by Bateman, Brown, and Pedder (2000), and in particular of Kleinian concepts by Hinshelwood (1989, 1994) are therefore
particularly welcome models of clarity and accessibility. I have at
times relied heavily on these texts, and on that of Sandler, Dare,
and Holder (1992), in my own expositions. Those readers who are
acquainted with the work of Henri Rey will recognize the origin of
some of my own formulations.

Aims

My main aim is to illustrate the application of psychoanalytic theories
of psychosis and to draw attention to their practical relevance as
helpful tools in the everyday clinical work of psychiatrists and other
mental health professionals. I also wish to show that if the necessary
setting can be provided, properly conducted individual psychoanalytic psychotherapy can help very many psychotic patients; and that
psychoanalytic thinking can make an important contribution to the
formulation of treatment plans by the psychiatric multidisciplinary
psychiatric teams who are usually involved in the management of
severely ill psychotic patients. The proper and secure setting for individual psychotherapy requires the therapist to arrive promptly for set
times of sessions, relatively little change in times or room, advance
warning to the patient of unplanned separations, and as few external
changes to the regular routine of meetings as possible.

I hope that reading about these patients will encourage mental
health professionals to persevere in their struggles to understand
psychotic patients better and to further their interest in the powerful,
strange, and confusing world of psychological reality.

I also hope that the material presented in this book speaks for
itself and illustrates my conviction that psychotic patients bring the
work of Klein to the therapist, and not the other way round. There are
many other ways of thinking about these patients and their psychotherapists' work, but the theoretical concepts I have used have been
the most effective for my purposes. Their emphasis on the "primary"
pre-oedipal traumas and emotional deprivations in the mother–baby
relationship which influence the later and more familiar oedipal ones
can add depth to the understanding of psychotic thinking.

I also wish to demonstrate that the practice of psychoanalytic psychiatry and psychology is a model for the future, and that psychoanalytic theory of psychosis is more than merely one of the theoretical systems available to eclectically minded practitioners.

I use the terms "psychoanalytic" and "psychodynamic" as being equivalent, and the term "psychotherapy" to imply "psychoanalytically based" psychotherapy, unless specified as referring to other modes of psychological treatment, such as cognitive-behavioural psychotherapy.

The "unimaginable storms" of psychosis draw many more than the disturbed individual into its net of confusion and misery. Relatives trying to help and understand psychotic patients may sometimes be forced to live with an intolerable burden of despair, frustration, and guilt. I hope that this book will provide a navigational aid in understanding and "weathering the storms" of psychosis.

CHAPTER ONE

Psychotic features
in obsessive-compulsive neurosis:
"Ada"

Obsessive-compulsive neurosis provides an illustration of the frequent differences between the psychiatric and psycho-analytic approach to understanding severe mental illness, and of the fact that psychotic features may be found in non-psychotic individuals.

Obsessive-compulsive neurosis, now commonly classed as "obsessive-compulsive disorder" (OCD), is a relatively uncommon illness, but obsessional symptoms and mental mechanisms are often encountered as a feature of other forms of illness. Melanie Klein was so impressed by the ubiquity and importance of obsessional mental processes that she originally referred to them as expressions of a universal developmental organization, the "obsessional position", linking them to a later "manic position" (see Chapter 15).

Obsessional *traits of personality* are common in the normal population, taking the form of minor, often hidden, phobias; the tendency to ruminate about unanswerable questions; irrational indecisiveness; doubting; superstitiousness; "out-of-character" mental images; and rituals in minor degrees. A large proportion of the population experiences intrusive thoughts and images at times, but these are easily dismissed and do not cause the distress accompanying true obsessions.

Such features can only be regarded as obsessional *symptoms* if they are experienced as persistently intrusive, alien to the self, unwanted, and resisted ("ego-dystonic"). Obsessions are usually associated with compulsions, namely irrational impulses to perform some unwanted action, usually feared to be sexually or aggressively destructive and struggled against in various ways—realistic (such as avoiding contact with knives) or symbolic (such as repetitive hand-washing).

Many *phobias* are not obsessive-compulsive and are considered by some as learned habits. True obsessional phobias have the characteristics of compulsive repetitiveness, provoking distress and unsuccessful attempts to banish them from the mind.

Psychiatrists have long recognized the association of obsessional features with severe (psychotic) depression, hypochondriasis, depersonalization, phobias, and perhaps schizophrenia (Lewis, 1936; Rosen, 1957). Obsessional symptoms may appear following brain injury or organic lesions, a phenomenon suggesting a neuropathological substrate to the psychogenesis of obsessive-compulsive disorders and a rationale for the now largely abandoned treatment by surgical lobotomy.

Psychoanalysts have studied obsessional disorders in great detail ever since Freud originated the term "obsessional neurosis" in 1895 (A. Freud, 1966) and published his famous "Rat Man" commentary (Freud, 1909d). The results of psychotherapy with adult patients have been generally disappointing, and behavioural methods of treatment have been developed which frequently offer effective control of symptoms (Marks et al., 2000). However, reports of psychoanalytic work with very young children who show obsessional mechanisms with associated persecutory anxiety (Joseph, 1966), and disturbance of bowel and speech function (Grinberg, 1996; Ramzy, 1966), suggests that early treatment might be more effective.

Although minor obsessional symptoms may often respond to supportive psychotherapy, major disorders generally remain intractable. A possible explanation may be sought in the power of psychotic mechanisms underlying severe cases, which are much nearer to psychotic than neurotic disorders. The following case illustrates the features commonly involved.

Ada

Ada had been in psychiatric treatment for over twenty years for an illness, diagnosed as obsessive-compulsive neurosis, which involved severe anxiety, ritualistic symptoms, and inhibitions characteristic of this illness. It had proved resistant to all psychiatric treatment, and eventually Ada had begun psychotherapy, one session weekly, with a social worker. Two years later, he brought the case to the seminar, where she was discussed on two occasions.

Evolution of the illness

Ada had been an anxious and vulnerable person since her early childhood but had been much worse since she left the parental home and married. After some years of an apparently successful marriage, she started to become increasingly concerned that her husband, who was actually in good health, would die and that she would not be able to survive the loss. This anxiety had been joined by other severe and irrational preoccupations, in particular a recurring belief that she must be suffering from cancer or some other life-threatening disease. Her belief had been so firm that she insisted on repeated diagnostic medical investigations. Because these investigations had always proved negative, her insistence was regarded as an expression of hypochondriacal preoccupations, and phobic-obsessive anxieties of near-delusional proportions.

These preoccupations included the fear that she would be killed by masonry falling from buildings undergoing repair, or would be fatally hit by a car when crossing the street. They were of such severity that she was obliged to take extreme precautionary avoidance measures. So real did these dreaded possibilities feel to her that she regularly requested an emergency appointment with her general practitioner to reassure herself that she had not actually sustained injury and thus that the event had not really happened.

Along with internal dangers, Ada was constantly preoccupied with threats from the outside world. She believed that her home was being invaded by vermin. This fear of vermin was so severe that she regularly compelled the health authorities to send pest-control specialists to investigate. Reassurance that there were no vermin had had only temporary effects. This characteristic of obsessional neurosis was first explained by Freud (1909d) in his "Rat Man" study.

On one occasion, she was lent an electrocardiograph machine to check her cardiac function over a long period. The recordings continued to be normal, and it was noticed that the possession of the machine gave her such a sense of security and comfort that when the time came to return it to the hospital she was extremely reluctant to give it up.

She had found some transient relief from psychiatric support and medication but had become dependent on tranquillizing drugs, a complication that had required several hospitalizations over many years before she could succeed in renouncing the drugs.

Her personal history

No detailed record of her background was to be found in earlier psychiatric notes, but the intractability of her condition was fully recognized. When the psychotherapy began, the characteristics of her thinking, the details of her complaints, and her personal history became more clear.

She was the older of two children, her brother being four years younger. Although no detailed record of her early development was available, it was clear that her relationship with her mother was insecure, and that she had always held strong feelings of being rejected by her and in her frequent moments of anxiety had turned to her quiet and supportive father for love and comfort. Panic attacks during her third and fourth years, at the time of her mother's pregnancy and the birth of her brother, required her father's comforting presence. She suffered from recurring bouts of anxiety during her school years and brief episodes of palpitations when she had to talk in class in front of other pupils.

Her later childhood and adolescence passed without overt psychiatric manifestations or obvious obsessional personality features, although subsequent exploration revealed a great deal of suppressed, but quite conscious, resentment of her mother. She married a supportive and understanding man whom she hoped would provide her with a sense of security that she had previously found only with her father.

Her mother took an intense dislike to her future son-in-law and made this very clear to Ada. However, she eventually became reconciled to the marriage, which had proved to be quite successful. There was no evidence that Ada had had any difficulty with her pregnancies or with her role as a mother. Her two children were healthy and independent, and she had acquired a poodle puppy which, at the time of the reporting, was ten months old.

The psychotherapy

The therapist's strategy in the once-weekly treatment was based on his understanding of the meaning of the patient's obsessive thoughts and repetitive ritualistic attempts at seeking reassurance from others. He regarded her illness as a typical and severe example of this apparently neurotic condition, whose essential psychopathology consisted of unconscious hostility of great intensity towards one or both parents, a hostility with its origins in childhood, which was in intolerable conflict with her need for and love of them. Anxiety attacks at the time of the birth of her brother could be understood as springing from her feelings of guilt and her fear that her hidden feelings about this intruder would be found out. The therapist thought it likely that her later panic attacks in the classroom may have had similar roots.

He saw this complex of feelings as having undergone a process of repression, a defensive manoeuvre that removed them from conscious awareness but burdened her with unconscious guilt. Being aware of the possibility of a hereditary contribution to this particular disorder, the therapist had established that there was no family history of any formal psychiatric illness. Neither was there evidence that Ada had had any obvious obsessive-compulsive features in her personality prior to the onset of the symptoms at the age of twenty-five years.

Although she had previously told the therapist that her mother had herself had an insecure and unhappy childhood and had at times been severely agoraphobic, it was only later in the therapy that she remembered her mother's reaction to the news that she was intending to get married. Her mother did not like her future husband and had tried to prevent the marriage, repeatedly threatening to kill herself if Ada went ahead with it.

It was clear that Ada's relationship with her male therapist was most important to her. She displayed an attitude of extreme possessiveness towards him, accompanied by an intrusive interest in his personal life. When she learned that the therapist's wife was shortly to have a baby, Ada spent much therapeutic time in expressing her pleasure in a way that the therapist found intrusive and embarrassing.

As the psychotherapy proceeded, Ada gradually experienced some reduction in the level of her background anxiety, and found relief in expressing some of her aggressive feelings towards her mother. However, her basic disabling obsessive preoccupations remained essentially unchanged, and, after two years of psychotherapy and following the death by suicide of a woman friend, new symptoms emerged. She began to fear that she was responsible for the death of this friend, a fear that was entirely without foundation, and she repeatedly requested that her friend's husband reassure her that she was not.

Tenacious substances

She now began to dread that a piece of chewing-gum would contaminate her by sticking to her body in such a tenacious manner that it would prove impossible to remove. This chewing-gum had, she believed, been deposited on the furniture by some guest at her home. Her fear also expressed itself in the therapy sessions, where she felt compelled to examine the chair before she was able to sit in it, lest a previous patient had followed the same disgusting practice.

Since the acquisition of the puppy ten months previously, her fears had become worse. She began to believe that in running through the nearby forest, the puppy had come into contact with the resin of the pine trees which had stuck to her like chewing-gum. Frequent vigorous scrubbing of the puppy produced only temporary relief for the patient, but considerable discomfort to the animal.

Elusive recipes

As these fears of chewing-gum and sticky resin developed, they were accompanied by another obsessive thought, leading to further compulsive repetitive behaviour. She began to believe that she had recently seen a particular food recipe in a magazine, and she felt compelled to retrieve it. She began to accumulate magazines and to spend hours searching through them for the original recipe. Eventually, she would find one that seemed to fit the specification, whereupon she would cut it out and file it away. She did not prepare the food and was only able to discard a magazine when she had succeeded in extracting the item that she valued.

A further feature of this, so far inexplicable, behaviour lay in Ada's insistence that the therapist should take some of the magazines into his possession during the vacation breaks in the therapy, and "look after them". The therapist had found this demand difficult to deal with, because he believed (correctly) that this was manipulative behaviour which he could not yet understand, so he declined to submit to her pressure.

Ada began to fear that if she did not find the recipe, she would be overwhelmed by violent, murderous impulses. She felt that she had no choice but to search for and find the recipes, and that if she failed she would be compelled to stab her children in their hands. She also dreaded that if she did not find them, she would suddenly kill the poodle by throwing it down the steps leading from the house. So real was this threat to the beloved puppy that she forced her husband to have a high wall built in order to make this more difficult to do.

The seminar

As the result of the seminar discussion, the therapist decided to increase the sessions from once to twice weekly and to use some of the new understanding in his work. Over the next three years, a considerable improvement took place. Ada gradually began to realize that her symptoms were protecting her from disturbing impulses and memories hidden since her childhood.

The loss of her most disabling symptoms exposed her to an increased preoccupation with the doubt that she may have been responsible for the death of her friend. This new focus allowed the therapist to concentrate his attention on this symptom. There was no evidence that the relationship with her friend had been an abnormal one, and so its importance seemed to reside specifically in the fact of the loss of a woman towards whom she was close emotionally. Although it seemed likely that such feelings might eventually find their way into the transference, the new focus allowed Ada to become much more aware of her aggressive feelings. She suddenly realized that she would become very anxious whenever she was angry with somebody or if someone was angry with her. This led to the further realization that she sometimes felt that the people with whom she was angry would commit suicide. She was then able to make the connection with her anger about her mother's suicide threats and to start to understand the effect that they had had on her.

Accepting her hostility enabled the patient, with the help of her therapist, to begin to resolve her deepest pathogenic conflicts. Increasing *intellectual* understanding of the reason for her belief that aggression kills the victim had begun to lead to an *emotional* recognition and to consequent considerable relief of her anxiety.

Her obsessional search for reassurance that she had not killed someone with her car or been injured herself gradually receded, and she resumed driving for the first time since the onset of her illness more than twenty years before. The fears of harming her children, and of invading vermin, slowly disappeared, she no longer spoke of chewing-gum or resin, and she stopped the cleansing behaviour towards the poodle. Her new-found degree of freedom from obsessive thinking and compulsive behaviour had brought her a more relaxed and happier life.

Discussion

Psychodynamic explanation—retrospective reconstruction

A search for understanding the nature and origins of her mental illness can begin with the hypothesis that powerful emotional conflicts in relation to her parents, originating in her childhood, had remained unresolved and had come to exert a pathogenic influence on her adult thinking. These conflicts can be considered to have undergone a process of defensive encapsulation in her mind, while persisting unconsciously. Eventually they emerged when the pressure of later emotional stresses became too great for this method of containing intolerable conflict.

Apart from the intensity of the patient's hostility towards her mother, it is not at first clear why these conflicts, not necessarily different from those that may occur in mentally healthy individuals, should have remained so intense. Nor was it clear why the psychodynamic pathway she had followed had ended in this obsessional disorder, rather than, for example, in forms of neurosis, overt psychosis, or sociopathic disorder. The absence of a manifest family history of the disorder does not rule out the possibility of a hereditary factor predisposing to the formation of a vulnerable constitution, a view generally accepted in psychiatry in the case of OCD. However much this may be true, in Ada's case it was the psychogenic factors that proved to be modifiable. The possible influence of parents with obsessional tendencies on the early developmental processes must not be forgotten (Ramzy, 1966).

Ada's intense pathogenic conflicts can be considered to be rooted in the early relation with her mother. Their intensity implies that she had originally succeeded in forming a strong but insecure attachment to her mother, and that the birth of her brother aroused powerful feelings of rejection and of murderous jealousy. These unconscious and conflict-laden aggressive feelings were responsible for her attacks of anxiety at that time. In her childhood, she tried to cope by turning to her father for the security that she needed. This helped her survive throughout childhood and adolescence without further overt psychological disturbance.

Marrying a man with some of the good qualities of her father helped her to fulfil her role as wife and mother. But her unconscious negative feelings towards her parents began to threaten to break through her defences, in the form of unconscious death-wishes towards her husband, experienced as fears that he would die and that she would not survive the loss.

This unstable and "decompensating" situation required the deployment of further emergency defences. She developed the hypochondriacal belief that she was suffering from lethal processes inside her body (such as cancer) and the paranoid belief that her home was being invaded by vermin (explained by Freud, 1900a, p. 357, as the symbolic representatives of unwanted children or rival siblings). Thus the threat of direct impact of the murderous feelings and impulses towards the parents who made the rival baby were further removed by the unconscious use of symbolic disguise, the regressive "de-differentiation" of mental and bodily processes, and the defensive "perceptualization" of thinking. Put in a different way, elements of emotional thought defensively expelled from her mind were now felt to be alien objects trying to invade and colonize her body (the tenacious substances, the vermin) or, by the process of introjection, to be actual dangerous things inside her body, the cause of her hypochondriacal symptoms.

These processes were no longer recognizable by her as *thoughts* that would make her aware of dangerous feelings but were now experienced as *things*, the invading vermin. Her inability to recognize the symbolic nature of her preoccupation provides evidence of a considerable impairment of the capacity for symbolic thinking, an impairment that is characteristic of psychotic disorders.

We can now begin to understand how her original murderous jealousy of her brother—the cause of the panic at the age of 4 years— and of the "bad" mother who was felt to prefer the new baby had continued to seek a place in Ada's consciousness. In order to evade conscious awareness, these feelings and the associated object relationships had been transformed by mental defence mechanisms, finally assuming the form of symbolic derivatives such as the tenacious substances and the elusive recipes, experienced by her to various degrees as "symbolic equations" [see Glossary] and of compulsive and ritualistic behaviour.

Further defensive operations had led to bizarre sequences of thought. We could give these thoughts an imaginative voice, verbalizing the unconscious phantasies [see Glossary] associated with her intolerable conflicts:

> "So dangerous are my (infantile) aggressive feelings towards the ['bad'] mother [of my childhood], without whom I cannot hope to survive, that any relinquishing of control and admission of genuine dependency today is potentially lethal. I have a recurring belief that I have killed my good husband and my mother's baby—but I can reassure myself, in the form of actions aimed at denying my belief in my murderousness, that I haven't. I also have the belief that I have killed my friend. I shall therefore suffer the same fate [in accordance with the psychological law of talion, 'an eye for an eye, a tooth for a tooth'], and be killed [by falling masonry, cancer, or other agencies]. However, the doctor realizes that it is impossible that this has happened without my knowing it, so I must go to him to recover the sanity of judgement that I have lost."

The chewing-gum and the pine resin that cannot be removed and the defensive displacement of mother's new baby to the puppy represent further symbolic derivatives of the same theme. The aggressive thoughts (symbolized by the chewing-gum which she cannot dispose of, however hard she tries), having been evacuated from her mind by projection into a containing object, such as masonry or road traffic, threaten to return to their home in her mind, and to refuse to be ejected again. This dynamic process illustrates the useful dictum that elements of thought that are, in unconscious phantasy, violently ex- pelled from conscious awareness by projection will inevitably strive to seek re-entry into the mind where they belong.

Ada's thoughts now assume yet another form by means of the mental mechanism of displacement, to the resin of pine trees that will adhere to the puppy. Trying desperately to rid her mind of these dangerous murderously jealous thoughts, now felt as physical pro- cesses, she mercilessly scrubs the sibling-puppy.

The meaning of Ada's "irrational" behaviour can thus be under- stood as the expression of mental conflicts involved in unconscious object relationships. But although this intelligent woman might be capable of acquiring an intellectual grasp of such an explanation of the unconscious meaning of her disabling symptoms, it is unlikely that this would make a great difference to her severe anxiety and fore- bodings of disaster. When she is actually experiencing the dreaded thoughts, they have for her the emotional value of actual deeds and their punitive consequences. This omnipotent, "magical" thinking is characteristic of the psychotic and the obsessional, and in lesser de- grees of the "normal" superstitious individual.

It is this sense of the immediacy of such symbolic equations (Segal, 1991) as "chewing-gum = resin = puppy = baby" and "food recipe = good nourishing mother" that accounts for much of the literal, "con- crete" thinking of the psychotic mind [see Glossary], and which can been seen in its most overt form in schizophrenia and other psychotic disorders, as discussed in later chapters.

Thus, recovering the recipe for preparing good food has come to be *equated* with a good relationship between a good feeding mother and a good child (or baby). If she had been able to think of the recipe in a *symbolic* way, she would have been able to enjoy the recipe and the food in a normally appreciative manner. As it is, Ada is driven to hold on to it because it is equated with the good relationship itself. She searches for the recipe, and when she finds it she clings to it desperately. She is compelled to do this in order to prove to herself that her good feelings for the mother of her childhood, who was once her exclusive possession, are more powerful than her concealed hatred of the mother who gave birth to the rival sibling, represented by the puppy. In the transference [see Glossary] she manages to preserve her good (but in this respect idealized) relationship with her supportive therapist, who can then remain as the representative of her good mother.

Her wish that she should only have a good mother about whom she can have only good feelings is doomed to failure because in her unconscious mental life she is still attacking the mother whom she has never forgiven for the displacement by the baby and for her alarming opposition to her marriage. She is compelled to repeat her search for the recipe because if she did not she would lose all hope of recovering the good "feeding" mother in her inner world. What she needs is to find in her therapist a person who can withstand and understand her murderous feelings as they emerge in the transference relationship with him. In this way, the therapist can help her to develop a better understanding of her vulnerable mother and eventually enable her to try to accept her mother's failings, real or imaginary.

If the therapist had attempted to give this patient the attention and emotional gratification that she so persistently demanded, in the belief that he could be a better mother for her than her own mother, the negative feelings would be further split off. The patient's feelings of gratification would not last, and her condition would very likely have deteriorated.

Her wish for her therapist to take the food recipe with him on vacation is a search for reassurance that he will keep her in mind, rather than totally replace her by his other beloved figures, as she believed her mother to have done. This fear of displacement came near consciousness when she felt compelled to examine the chair occupied by the previous patient before sitting down (see the case of Alec, in Chapter 3). By trying to keep the therapist and the food recipes together during a period of absence, the patient unconsciously hopes that she will not have to confront the jealousy evoked by the separation from him as the representative of her good mother.

Ada consciously *knows about* some of her hostile feelings towards her mother, and she feels quite justified in having them. However, the unconscious fears of the destructiveness of her hatred against her mother-of-the-past (her "internal" mother) is operating at a deeper level, and it is the impulses belonging to this level that seek entry into the transference relationship with the therapist. It is in the transference relationship that an individual can best come to *know from experience* the full force of such intense destructive and possessive feelings and thus have the opportunity of integrating them and deriving strength from this "recovery of lost parts of the self" (Steiner, 1993).

Ada's defensive repertoire could be listed in the following manner:

- *Denial*—of the reality of her inner world
- *Splitting*—"good" and "bad" aspects of object and self kept far apart
- *Idealization*—only admitting of good feelings towards the therapist
- *Displacement*—of the endangered object from baby to puppy
- *Projection*—into potentially dangerous external objects such as cars and building masonry
- *"Concrete" symbolism*—equations
- *Condensation*—of different levels of meaning, such as invading insects representing her own aggressive invasive-damaging emotional thoughts and also symbolizing intrusive rivals
- *Introjection*—of "damaged objects", leading to hypochondriasis
- *Reaction formation*—exaggeration of genuinely good feelings in order to exclude bad ones

Several of these mental mechanisms are "immature" ("primitive"), in the sense that they are part of the normal mental equipment of infancy and childhood, used in the service both of defence (the management of conflicting feelings) and of growth. For instance, projection endows the emerging world with familiar meanings, and introjection forms the basis for learning. However, when these primitive defence mechanisms are activated prematurely and excessively in infancy, they can lead to failure in normal development and may come to constitute a vulnerability factor to psychotic illness later in life. In such a case, these "primitive" mechanisms have assumed the significance of "psychotic" mechanisms, as is illustrated and examined in later chapters.

Symbolism is essential to the development of the capacity for increasingly mature and abstract forms of thinking, and it is the impairment of this capacity that led to Ada's inability to appreciate the symbolic nature of her symptoms. In this psychoanalytic view, the roots of this developmental failure are to be found in the "preverbal" period of the first two years of life. The emergence of the psychiatric disorder was apparently precipitated by her mother's suicide threats prior to Ada's marriage.

Conclusions

Ada's case illustrates the fact that obsessional thinking and behaviour can be found to have important meaning which can serve as a guide to psychotherapeutic interventions. It also demonstrates how unresolved conflicts of early life and the associated immature defence mechanisms may provide a psychotic core to later neurotic psychopathology and may lead to the regressive use of concrete thinking in which thoughts are experienced as things. This is perhaps one reason why obsessive-compulsive disorders are so refractory to conventional psychotherapy.

It is usually not a difficult psychiatric task to differentiate obsessional neurosis from schizophrenic or depressive psychosis. However, a deeply placed developmental vulnerability can, under some circumstances, promote the emergence of florid psychotic symptoms. In the case of Ada, the regressive process had not reached the depth that might promote schizophrenic disorganization, and she had retained sufficient sanity and the capacity to doubt to allow her to keep contact with reality most of the time. Thus, her bizarre thinking was never completely delusional, although she required help from others, as in the case of her GP, to support her sane doubts.

The psychodynamic formulations helped the therapist to begin to think more effectively about possible meanings of his patient's bizarre behaviour and of the thinking that produced it. In this manner, it helped him to help Ada acknowledge her hidden hostility to her mother (and to some extent to the therapist in the therapeutic transference relationship) and the unresolved feelings of jealousy of her childhood. As a consequence, her need for primitive defences diminished and the worst of her symptoms subsided. Her unconscious feelings of guilt lessened, and the "structure" of her self-punitive conscience (the "harsh superego" of the obsessional) was modified and was transformed into a more healthy and tolerant form.

Genuine feelings of gratitude for the therapist and pleasure at his happiness at becoming a father had been used by the patient to ward off the hidden negative feelings about her mother, father, and the rival baby. As she became more conscious of these primitive feelings and less afraid of their assumed dangerousness, her relation with the therapist became more realistic and stable.

The nature of Ada's mother's pathology and its place in Ada's early development remained uncertain. If the mother's opposition to the marriage was an expression of her own unresolved possessive jealousy it is possible that this made it difficult or impossible for her to help her infant daughter manage her own normal emerging feelings of aggressiveness towards the new baby. Had this been the case, it would suggest that Ada had been unable to differentiate her own self-image and associated aggressiveness from that of her mother. It might also suggest that her obsessional dread that she would stab her children (of the present day) was founded on a fear that she would suddenly lose her own sense of identity and, in a process of identification, behave like the "murderous mother" inhabiting her inner world. Such complex processes will receive more detailed attention in later chapters, in particular in the case of Patient E in Chapter 16.

This account of Ada's treatment is of necessity an incomplete one, and it ends at a point where aspects of her mental life remain unexplored and the work of termination of the treatment has yet to be accomplished. Although the therapist's work has not focused on the transference relationship, it has helped this chronically ill obsessional patient profoundly.

Although in some ways limited both in its aims and strategies, such psychodynamic psychotherapy conducted on a once- or twice-weekly basis is sometimes nearer to the "real world" of mental health provision for the seriously ill in a climate of scarce resources than more intensive psychoanalytic treatment. As such, it might be regarded as an offspring of the latter, rather than a competitor, in the current "market-place" of scarce resources—a subject to which we will return.

CHAPTER TWO

Obsessional symptoms following adolescent psychosis: "Brenda"

As has been seen in the previous chapter, obsessional symptoms have an intimate psychodynamic relation to psychotic mental processes and may conceal a "psychotic core". In this chapter we shall consider the meaning of a patient's psychotic symptoms and obsessional behaviour.

Brenda

At the time of the presentation of Brenda's case to a work discussion group, she had been attending a weekly psychotherapy session with a female psychotherapist for twelve months. Six months later the therapist reported on the progress of the case.

Brenda, now aged 38, first developed psychotic symptoms when she was 14 years old. For some time before, she had shown increasingly abnormal behaviour, characterized by clinging to her mother, attempting to control her attention by incessant talking, insisting that she wanted to become a little girl again, and demanding to be fed by her mother like an infant. At times when she was alone with her

26

mother away from the family home her behaviour was relatively normal, but when they returned home to the rest of the family she quickly became disturbed again. This state continued for three months, at which point she became violently aggressive. She slept only fitfully, pulling her hair out, refusing to wash, and threatening to kill the family dog. She spoke in a confused manner about the voice of the Devil commanding her to kill her mother. She heard sinister noises coming from the walls and ran out of the room to escape from dangerous influences that she believed were emanating from the television.

She was admitted to a psychiatric ward, under a compulsory order, in an acute psychotic state. With medication and nursing care, her symptoms soon subsided. After some weeks, she recovered and was discharged to the care of her family. A few weeks later, her symptoms returned in full force and she was readmitted. She spent three of the next five years in and out of an adolescent psychiatric ward. Whenever she was considered well enough, she was discharged, but soon relapsed and was readmitted. The diagnosis of schizophrenia was established, and she was maintained on a moderate dose of neuroleptic medication. After five years, she remained sufficiently free of symptoms to live outside hospital in the parental home, and for the next five years she attended hospital as an outpatient. Despite periods of work training, she was never able to take a paid job.

Chronic psychosocial disability—
attempts at rehabilitation

From the age of 24, Brenda remained at home, pursuing a fragile social life almost confined to her sisters and their children, but also with a small circle of friends, most of whom were abusers of drugs and alcohol. She neglected her personal hygiene and became sexually promiscuous. Since she did not herself abuse either drugs or alcohol, she regarded herself as superior to these friends, describing herself as "the only normal one in the gang". She began to eat excessively and became very obese.

At the age of 28 she became engaged in a psychiatric rehabilitation programme. She was assigned to an individual contact worker who was a physiotherapist, with whom she had regular supportive conversation and body-movement exercises. She refused to accept a place in a social-skills group and would only tolerate one-to-one contact with helpers. However, with the support of the community treatment team she was able to move from the parental home to an apartment of her own. Here she gradually developed a pattern of compulsive washing and arrangement of the rooms of her apartment in a way that will shortly be examined.

Psychotherapy begins

Although the past psychiatric record was incomplete in many respects, it seemed likely that individual psychotherapy was not attempted or that she was unresponsive to the attempt. It was not until she began to trust a particular contact worker who was particularly interested in her that she began to talk about her emotional conflicts, and it was on this basis that she was offered a formal weekly psychotherapy session, which she readily accepted.

Personal history

Brenda cooperated well with her therapist, and, as she began to speak more freely than before about her past life and present experiences, a coherent picture of her life, external and internal, emerged. She is the fifth of eight children, by three different fathers, of a seriously dysfunctional family. Her mother appears to have had some artistic talent and perhaps had been sexually promiscuous herself. Brenda was often ill-treated and may have been sexually abused by her alcoholic father. This man abandoned her mother when Brenda was 6 years old, being succeeded by a stepfather who was more stable and kind to her. She was regarded as a nice and conscientious child, emotionally very close to her mother and very helpful in the care of her younger brothers and sisters. She was overweight and this led to her being teased by school friends, but she was interested in her school work and gave no cause for concern to her family. However, it was noted in the original psychiatric record that a school nurse had been worried about her home circumstances when she was about 10 years of age, but this warning sign that all was not well had not apparently led to any investigation. Despite the evidence of psychiatric disturbance in some family members, at the time of her first break-down it was recorded that the family regarded themselves as per-fectly normal, and that Brenda's illness was entirely an inherited disorder.

Because her psychotic experiences no longer had their previous intensity, she was able to describe them to the therapist without undue anxiety. She described the terrifying perceptual experiences that used to begin when she was watching the television during her first breakdown at the age of 14. Words and numbers on the screen would suddenly approach her and enter her body. Inside her body, they would swell up and seem to be about to explode.

Obsessional rituals and organization of personal spaces

During her first breakdown at the age of 14 and the subsequent five years, she neglected her personal hygiene, often refusing to wash for days on end. From the time that she moved from the family home into her own apartment, this behaviour gradually changed into its opposite, washing her hands and her body in a repetitive and compulsive manner. She began to regard any of her clothes that had had contact with her mother as having become contaminated, and she consigned them to the washing-machine, where they had to be washed three or four times in a ritual sequence. When she visited her mother in the family home, she extended this treatment to her own shoes which in consequence required frequent replacement.

She transformed the kitchen of her apartment into a sort of decon-tamination centre, devoted exclusively to such ritual washing. She would allow no one else to enter this room, which entirely ceased to fulfil its normal function. As the result of this transformation of the kitchen space, there was nowhere to cook, and thus she was never able to eat warm food in her own apartment.

She also transformed a large cupboard into a storeroom, to which she consigned anything that her mother would give her. She knew that she was angry with her mother and that this was the reason why she found the gifts unacceptable and wished to throw them away. However, she could not bear to do this, and she did not know why. Eventually she decorated her bedroom in pink colours and felt happy when she thought about it and very comfortable when she was inside it.

The course and outcome of the psychotherapy

The therapist focused her attention on the exploration of Brenda's quite conscious guilt-laden anger with her mother. This centred on her feeling that her mother had never noticed Brenda's unhappiness and had failed to protect her from her drunken father's ill-treatment in her early childhood. Although the expression of these aggressive feelings gave her considerable relief, they had none of the intensity of the murderousness that had emerged in the psychotic breakdown during her adolescence.

During the early stage of the psychotherapy, she reported that her psychotic experiences sometimes returned, when she would begin to think that sinister influences were emanating from some external source. When this happened, she felt that she was becoming mad but would soon realize that the event was located in her imagination, whereupon her anxiety would subside and the experience would fade away.

The development of a strong positive transference led to a revival of the separation anxiety that had led to her desperate clinging to her mother at the onset of her psychosis. Regressive responses to unplanned breaks in the therapy took the form of brief episodes of promiscuity and bulimic overeating. During one unexpectedly long break in the therapy, she put on a massive amount of weight, and when the therapist on returning asked her how this had come about, she replied, as though stating the obvious, "Well, you went away, didn't you!"

These bulimic episodes gradually decreased, and after many large fluctuations her weight eventually returned to a normal level. Her obsessional activities greatly diminished. She slowly gave up her compulsive washing, she lost interest in the compartmentalizing of her apartment, and she began to use her kitchen for cooking. For the first time in her life, she fell in love. In this relationship she became so demanding that the man retreated, a blow to which she responded by a brief bout of increased sexual promiscuity. At this point, she told her therapist that she did not dare to leave her old patterns of living because to do so exposed her to too much pain.

Discussion

The meanings and mechanisms of Brenda's symptoms

Brenda's psychosis represented the breakthrough of her long-hidden desire for exclusive ownership of her mother and its associated unresolved violent conflicts of love and hatred, excluded from consciousness since her childhood. Her wish to be her mother's only baby could explain the main premonitory feature of her coming psychosis, the desperate angry clinging to her mother.

Her defences against having to acknowledge these wishes as belonging to her own self took the form of denial, splitting, and projection of them into a "container" (Bion, 1967), the commanding figure ("internal object") whose hallucinatory voice she could not clearly identify—"maybe the Devil". Her violent jealousy was deflected from her siblings to the family dog.

This implies that her long-standing defences against the violent aggressive feelings released by separation from her mother had begun to collapse and had led to a state of intrapsychic emergency necessitating the mobilization of the unconscious defences of splitting and projection, in a desperate attempt to protect her "good" mother and siblings from her murderous jealousy.

The nature of her obsessional behaviour

Brenda's compulsive washing and decontamination rituals were the expressions of her unconscious fear that unless she could rid herself of destructive impulses, in the symbolic form of dirt, her murderous feelings would destroy her "bad" (internal) mother. So she had to hold on to the gifts that symbolized the love and care of her "good" mother. If she angrily discarded the gifts as representing her bad mother, she would at the same time lose her good mother (as in the case of Ada's recipes, Chapter 1).

To preserve her good feelings about her mother, she had to decontaminate her "dirty" mind, symbolically represented by the "contaminated" clothing. She could not accept her mother's gifts, because this would involve recognizing her good mother and at once destroying her. This unconscious dilemma implies a failure to differentiate "good" from "bad", and thus love from hate, sufficiently to recognize and tolerate the fact that these "part" mothers are the same person.

Thus she can neither recognize the "whole object" of the depressive position [see Glossary] nor integrate the opposing feelings, and she must employ specific procedures to control (and thus preserve) the (maternal) object. For Brenda, to throw away her mother's gifts would mean unconsciously that she had irrevocably destroyed her mother, while to retain them means that this has not actually happened, and that the possibility of repairing her remains (Rey, 1994).

In unconscious phantasy, the obsessional retains the belief that the (primary) object is still alive and might possibly be rescued. In the melancholic (psychotic depressive), the belief is lost, hope is replaced by despair, and in identification with this destroyed object the patient experiences himself as without hope or as being in a state of death. In manic states, the object is felt to be dead, but this belief is negated by the defensive devaluation of the object, now regarded as worthless. The psychosexual hyperactivity often occurring in manic states may express an omnipotent belief of the patient that he has life-giving properties, a theme to which we will return in Chapter 15.

"Anality" and obsessions — Freud and Klein

The foregoing type of explanatory interpretation is based on the concept of unconscious phantasy and the theory of part-object relationships [see Glossary]. It requires familiarity with the idea that at early stages of development the infant has not yet developed a mind—or "mental apparatus"—with which to think about feelings, but experiences mental events as ("good" or "bad") objects or substances inside the body. Klein (1935) saw obsessional mechanisms as a primitive ("manic") defence against destructive wishes towards the "bad object", called into operation by the failure to differentiate good from bad, and love from hate, a differentiation sometimes called "normal splitting".

The concept of ambivalence of feelings at the anal stage of psychosexual development, elaborated by Freud (1912b, pp. 106–107), has been widely accepted as the basis for explaining the essential features of the obsessional character. It serves to make sense of the ritualistic patterns of behaviour, the decontaminating sanctions and ceremonials, the indecisiveness and procrastination, and the accumulation and hoarding of objects ("material") and their repetitive expulsion. Some aspects of obsessive doubting can be seen as the expression of unverbalized anxiety over damage felt to have been done, a self-

questioning exercise in damage control—"Did I do something destructive, or only think it? I must not throw this object (rubbish,
material) away, because it may contain something valuable and irreplaceable."

In psychoanalytic theory, faeces—an actual bodily product, which
generates (anal) sensations in the baby—becomes the prototype of the
internal (expellable) object and serves as an agent of primitive mechanisms of mental defence. In the course of mental development, faeces
can be represented by symbolic transformation into derivative forms
of varying levels of conceptual abstraction, well-known examples of
which are dirt, stones, and money (Ferenczi, 1916). Faeces can also
acquire the unconscious psychological equivalence of other part-
objects (such as baby and penis) by the process of "symbolic equation" (Segal, 1981c).

At a later stage of development, faeces can actually be controlled
by the infant to influence his caring figures or to attempt to secure
peace and safety in his inner world by expelling bad objects and
retaining good ones. Thus faeces and defecation can eventually be
used as gift to the "good" mother ("primary" caring figure) or as an
aggressive (or "sadistic") weapon of attack on the "bad" (frustrating)
mother. The common "battle of the bowel" is fought over the question
of who is going to be in charge of the contents of the infant's body. In
this sense, defecation is the first bodily activity that the infant can use
independently of his need for the life-supporting figure. Food can be
refused, breath can be held, screams can continue only for a limited
time before instinctual life-preserving needs assert themselves.

At the developmental level of thinking in which Brenda is functioning, body and mind are not yet properly differentiated and thus
she has no capacity for the conceptual, abstract thinking that could
give rise to the thought, "I attack my hated, bad, frustrating mother
in my mind, and wish to get rid of her from my mind—but if I do so
I shall lose the mother on whom my life depends." Therefore she is
compelled to repeat the obsessional decontaminating drama indefinitely. In everyday language, she (her hating self) treats her mother
like shit, rejecting her love with contempt, while at the same time she
(her loving self) retains the symbols of her caring mother in the hope
that she can undo the damage that she is unconsciously doing all the
time.

Brenda's promiscuous sexual behaviour can be partly understood
as a defence of avoidance of separation anxiety. Since attachment and

dependency on another person who might be felt to be emotionally important brings the inevitability of separation, loss, and the release of never-integrated aggressive feelings, the first defence is to avoid such dependent attachment, by making all objects replaceable and interchangeable. She thus denies the emotional specificity of an object and quickly replaces it with another if separation ever threatens, as was seen when her therapist was unexpectedly unavailable. At the same time it is possible that she may unconsciously be preserving her attachment to her mother by identification with an image of her mother as a promiscuous person. Such promiscuity might refer not only to Brenda's view of her mother's past social behaviour in the dysfunctional family, but also to her resentment of her mother's "infidelity" to her by having other babies (symbolized by the family dog), and to her longing to have the love and attention that she felt, perhaps with justification, had been denied her in her childhood.

The most obvious explanation of Brenda's bulimic behaviour is that she uses food for comfort, and this can be regarded as equating food with mother. In this sense, her eating could be considered as an "oral incorporation" of her "good" mother. Her expulsive rejection of her mother's gifts and incorporation of her in a bulimic manner might represent an attempt to ward off depression, as previously described (and see also Chapter 16, Patients I and J).

Brenda derives much pleasure by gazing at the reflection of her face in a mirror, which she sees as round and attractive. She wishes to lose her obesity but does not want in the process to lose what she calls her "baby cheeks".

In the course of normal development, the infant looking into a mirror comes to recognize himself as separate from his mother, but as Winnicott (1971) has expressed it, "the precursor of the mirror is the mother's face". The playful looking between mother and baby from the early weeks of life plays an important part in identity formation (Lacan, 1997; Wright, 1991). Perhaps there was an original failure in this respect, leading Brenda to create a wishful scenario in which, in a double identification, she is both the mother looking lovingly at her baby and is herself the baby.

Compartmentalizing

In the "accumulation-room" of her mind, her good mother survives Brenda's destructive attacks but exists in a sort of suspended animation; in the "decontamination-room", the continuing destructive attacks are undone; and in the "pink room" of an idealized infancy her baby wishes are fulfilled in fantasy. This compartmentalizing serves as a form of splitting, keeping her conflicting feelings and incompatible views of her mother out of contact with each other. They are receptacles that do not serve as "containers" [see Glossary, "containment"], in the positive integrative sense, nor are the aggressive feelings totally banished from consciousness by repression as is the case in truly neurotic disorders.

Her perceptual disturbances —
the invasive television words and numbers

Just as the projection of her murderous thoughts transforms them into commands coming from outside, so there are other thoughts (which she experiences as *things*) that she projects into the television set. These now return to invade her in the form of words and numbers, penetrating her body and swelling up inside her in a frightening manner. We do not know whether the words and numbers have some specific significance, nor whether the invasive process may have an unconscious sexual reference. Bion (1957) has described this process whereby returning projected elements may be felt to swell up inside the body and threaten to take over control in various ways. In the case of Brenda, this experience could also have a sexual meaning.

Retention and compartmentalizing as an attempt
at reparation and restoration of the damaged mother

Brenda's pattern of expulsion and retention is a characteristic feature of obsessional behaviour. Its original prototype can be seen in the oscillation of faecal retention and expulsion encountered in some emotionally disturbed children. Klein sought the roots of this behaviour in unconscious phantasies having their origin in infancy.

These processes are experienced at first by the infant in bodily terms of feeding and eliminating, only gradually achieving the status of primitive thoughts. By the process of symbolic transformation into progressively higher levels of conceptual abstraction, a range of patterns of behaviour can result, extending from the most primitive level of the eating of faeces (coprophagia: see Chapter 16, Patient I), which is not uncommon in severe dementia but is sometimes seen in severely disturbed infants and sometimes in the most extreme schizophrenic regressions. At a higher level of symbolic abstraction, unconscious phantasies find expression in obsessional hoarding and eliminating behaviour of various degrees of severity, increasingly detached from their original physical form, although sometimes leaving a residue in patterns of defecation. At the highest level of symbolic abstraction, they find expression in the form of such well-known character traits as orderliness, parsimony, and obstinacy. These can be regarded as sublimations of more primitive processes, of varying degrees of success in their defensive purposes and social value.

It will be recalled that Brenda obstinately refused to wash when she was psychotic and clung to her mother like a desperate infant, and that when she had recovered from the episode and moved from the family home to her own apartment this behaviour underwent a reversal, with the onset of obsessional washing of her body and cleansing of her clothing, now felt to be contaminated. During her active psychosis, she clung out of fear of destroying her mother; however, when separation actually happened, she continued to cling. But now her clinging took the symbolized form of obsessional washing, and later of an even more highly symbolized form, the expulsion and retention of her mother's gifts.

The future of the psychotherapy?

Her past insistence that she should be her mother's only baby implies an intensity of sibling rivalry that she has so far managed to bypass completely, both in her external life, by adopting an attitude of superiority, and throughout her illness, by avoiding all but dyadic relationships. On the other hand, it was her insistence on such exclusive relationships that eventually led to the individual psychotherapy that she needed. Thus, her overwhelming need to be special to a mother figure might be regarded as an understandable, but previously unheard and not understood, demand of an emotionally deprived and traumatized child.

There are many possible sources for the intensity of her unconscious hatred of her mother. Some may be an inherent part of the (oedipal) developmental process, of being forced to share her with father and siblings; others, the consequence of actual traumatic experience and relative emotional deprivation in an overcrowded and dysfunctional family.

At the time of the last discussion of her case, it was clear that much remained to be learned about the details and significance of the probable early sexual trauma and of the separation process. The positive transference was strong, but it remained to be seen whether it would prove possible, or necessary, to reach and work through the negative feelings towards the "bad" mother in the therapeutic transference to a sufficient extent to allow a successful termination of the therapy and the likelihood of her maintaining her very considerable improvement.

The psychotherapy had helped Brenda very much. Further progress will depend to some extent on Brenda's capacity to tolerate the pain that thinking about her self and her past releases in her. The denial and splitting that isolated her hatred for her "bad" mother allowed her to preserve her love for her "good" mother, but at the price of social isolation, the need for obsessional control of dangerous thoughts, and psychotic regression. It has yet to be learned whether further progress will involve the emergence of further negative feelings in the transference when separation and eventual termination of the therapy becomes a focus.

Postscript—two years later

Two years later, the therapist reported that Brenda had made steady progress. She had regained and retained a normal weight and had begun to develop a satisfactory social life. Her relation with her mother was much improved, her obsessional washing had completely ceased, and her apartment had assumed a normal structure and function.

Conclusions

Brenda was regarded by her family as having been a pleasant and conscientious child with a warm and close relationship to her mother. Coming from a severely dysfunctional family of eight children by three different fathers, it is difficult to form a reliable impression of what her life might actually have been like. However, her capacity to form a warm relationship with the psychotherapist suggests that, despite the severe damage to her personality, her infantile life might have been sufficiently secure to have protected her from a deeper schizophrenic regression.

Psychotherapy has shown how Brenda, once a caring mother-figure to her younger siblings, had remained in part an angry, traumatized, and emotionally deprived child. She had broken down at the time of a younger sister's early adolescent pregnancy (see the case of Grace, Chapter 13), an event that may have provoked the memory of earlier births of siblings who displaced her. Little information was available about the nature of her treatment as an inpatient from the age of 14 to 19 years or as an outpatient from 19 to 24 years, but it seems that her obsessional symptoms developed at a later date when she began to respond to rehabilitative help. This would suggest that her unconscious destructive feelings, which had found psychotic expression in her adolescence (displaced to the Devil as agent and the family dog as victim), were coming nearer to consciousness and being managed by more typically neurotic means. It is interesting to consider the possible implications of the fact that Brenda's bulimic tendencies represented an underlying oral pathology that was absent in the case of Ada (Chapter 1), whose symptoms derived primarily from the level of anal (expulsive-retentive) organization. It is also interesting to note that Brenda's murderous feelings displaced to the family dog were apparently quite direct, in contrast to the developmentally later (anal) ambivalence of Ada's behaviour towards the puppy.

If more could be learned about her treatment over the ten years following her psychotic breakdown, it might be possible to learn on what grounds the diagnosis of schizophrenia had been made. Although her recurring psychotic episodes eventually subsided, she had been left with a severe psychosocial disability. Her eventual response to rehabilitation measures, and to the individual attention to her body and her mind (in the form of "supportive conversations" and bodily movement with the physiotherapist), did not suggest an ongoing psychotic process. Although we do not know whether her treatment over the ten years was bad or good, her case serves as a reminder of the hazards of making adult diagnoses in adolescent patients (see Laufer & Laufer, 1984).

Brenda had led a frustrating and in many ways empty life in which unresolved hatred had paralysed her capacity for emotional intimacy. Her obsessional symptoms helped her survive psychologically, by warding off emerging feelings and impulses of murderous jealousy towards the mother of her childhood, until the time that individual psychotherapy became available. It is one of the achievements of the psychotherapy that Brenda has begun to acknowledge some good in her mother, to understand her mother's own traumatized and problematic life, and to be able to think effectively about herself.

CHAPTER THREE

Obsessions in schizophrenia: "Alec"

The relation between obsessive-compulsive symptoms and depressive illness has long been recognized, but the relationship with schizophrenia is less common and less understood in psychiatry. There is some evidence that long-standing obsessional symptoms may serve to protect against the emergence of a schizophrenic illness (Bychowski, 1966) or may result in a more benign psychosis.

The descriptive psychopathology and phenomenological studies of psychiatry can be complemented by psychodynamic formulation, which is a tool of psychoanalysis. The concepts of unconscious conflict between impulse and defence, involving such mental mechanisms as displacement and symbolic transformations, provide meaning and detailed understanding of the mental forces involved in obsessional and schizophrenic states, and of the relationship between them.

Alec

Alec, aged 40, had recently begun twice-weekly psychotherapy when his therapist brought his case for discussion in a small group. After this initial consultation, he was discussed at intervals of several months until the termination of treatment four years later.

The first attempt to get help for him came from his family, who insisted that he visit his GP. He was then 32 years old, the only son, with an older and a younger sister. His father, a schoolteacher, had died some years previously, when Alec was 19 years old. The family were concerned about his physical condition, but even more about his mental state. He had long been preoccupied with obsessive rituals, phobic anxieties, and brief motor inhibitions of a catatonic-like kind and these had lately become worse.

Ever since the death of his father, Alec had been living in the family home in a remote village. He led a reclusive, eccentric existence, shunning all social contacts. For a short period he worked for the local council as a road-sweeper. However, he had eventually had to give this up. He believed that the sweepings might contain live insects or vegetation that was not dead, and he refused to collaborate in their extinction by sweeping, which he regarded as an act of murder. So real was this fear that he had begun to water the sweepings with warm water in order to prevent the souls of the insects from freezing to death during the night.

Alec had many bizarre eating restrictions. For the two previous years, he had led a life of extreme asceticism, divesting himself of all possessions, declaring his ambition to shun all human contact and to become a hermit in a hut in the forest. He was very close to a metabolic crisis because of his increasingly restrictive vegetarian diet, which had resulted in a recent drop in weight from 88 to 55 kilograms.

Psychodynamic assessment

During the assessment interview, conducted in the presence of his mother and younger sister, he was agitated, repeatedly making alarming and dramatic gestures as if stabbing them in the abdomen with a knife. He was preoccupied with complex delusional ideas centring on bizarre hypochondriacal preoccupations about the interior of his body. He was also in a state of extreme anxiety, arising from his struggle to control violent aggressive impulses towards his mother and sisters.

The diagnosis of chronic schizophrenia was made, and he was advised to accept admission to hospital and anti-psychotic medication. He firmly declined this advice and continued to do so throughout his treatment, with the exception of one brief hospitalization under circumstances to be described.

He seemed to be a person of superior intelligence, demonstrating strong protective motivations, such as his concern for the protection of living things, however misplaced and delusional. For this reason, he was offered twice-weekly individual psychotherapy, which he accepted. Although he was clearly extremely disturbed, he seemed to be well contained within his supportive family, and although he would not acknowledge that there might be anything abnormal in his thinking and behaviour, he accepted that his family believed that he was ill.

After two months he broke off treatment, but resumed a year later, at which point the therapist brought his case for discussion.

Personal history

The therapist recounted the history of the patient's childhood from information gathered from the family and from the patient during the early part of the therapy. Alec was said to have been a lively and active infant, apparently unaffected by a brief separation at the age of 9 months when his mother was treated in hospital for a gynaecological disorder. There was no report of him having been disturbed by the birth of his sister in his second year.

However, in his fourth year his behaviour changed dramatically. He became very aggressive and was often involved in destructive activities, setting fires inside the house, smashing windows, and tormenting his infant sister. He developed a compulsive interest in opening and closing doors, an activity that could eventually be understood in retrospect as the first overt manifestation of the magical thinking, obsessions, and compulsions that later came to dominate his world. After entry to primary school he settled down, but with the passing years he became an odd and solitary child with few friends. When, at the age of 7 years, his mother had a brief period of illness, he became extremely agitated, imploring her not to die.

He showed a remarkable thirst for knowledge, reading widely and voraciously. He was regarded by his teachers as rather eccentric but endowed with extremely high moral and ethical standards. Until mid-adolescence, his school performance was outstanding, and he attributed this success to what he believed was his scholarly father's contempt for weakness, which made him determined to be the best.

At the age of 11, his obsessional preoccupation with the opening and closing of doors, which had emerged at the age of 4, returned in considerable intensity. It was not clear how much this may have worried his parents, but the fact that his obsessional traits of character were beginning to develop into a clear obsessive-compulsive neurosis may have gone unnoticed. When he moved into secondary school, his performance changed in a catastrophic manner. From being top of the class, he quickly dropped to the bottom and eventually graduated with the lowest grades, a failure he later attributed to excessive masturbation.

His father, who had been very protective and supportive towards his eccentric son (a closeness described by Alec as "almost tele-pathic"), could not tolerate the boy's failure in adolescence, and he withdrew his interest. This change was made worse by the onset of a serious illness that was to cause the father's death a few years later. At the same time, Alec felt his mother's behaviour to be inconsistent and confusing, alternately supporting and rejecting him.

Despite his confused and conflicted state, the patient somehow managed to complete his compulsory military service, leave home, find a job, and move to an apartment of his own. At the age of 19, he was shocked and depressed by his father's death, but he managed to function reasonably well for the next three years. A series of brief, unsuccessful attempts at heterosexual relationships increased his sense of abandonment and isolation. He became more withdrawn, confused about his sexual identity, and tormented by the compulsive intrusion of violent obsessive sexual and aggressive fantasies.

Onset of psychosis

Alec finally had to abandon his job and return to the shelter of the family home. Before long, he developed auditory hallucinations in the form of voices telling him what to do. He felt supported by these voices and followed their guidance about dietary restrictions. He devoted himself to vegetarianism, a step that eventually led him into a world of somatic delusions and malnutrition.

For the next twelve years he lived on his own near the family home, helping a little in the garden. Because he consistently refused the help of the social services, he was entirely dependent on his family's goodwill and financial support. A dread that he would in-advertently cause a fire to break out in his apartment (a fear perhaps connected dynamically with his childhood fire-setting in the parental house) led him to compulsive repetitive checking of gas and electricity fittings and moving in and out of the front door for several hours before finally managing to leave.

His dread of his intrusive fantasies of stabbing led to an intense fear of knives and a phobic avoidance of them, and he became increasingly preoccupied with diets and his bodily functioning. Despite all this torment he did not appear to have seriously contemplated suicide. In the two years prior to his referral to his general practitioner, his asceticism had reached extreme proportions, as already described.

The course of the psychotherapy

First phase (prior to breaking off)

The psychotherapy first began a month before the summer vacation on a twice-weekly basis. Alec was clearly very relieved to disclose his anxieties and dietary practices. His chief anxiety, which he called "knifing anxiety", arose from the recurring obsessive impulses to stab his mother and sisters with a knife. Although he recognized these impulses as being his own, he experienced them as being highly unwelcome intrusions ("ego-dystonic"). When they threatened to get out of his control, he managed them by immobilizing himself in a catatonic-like manner, when they would gradually recede.

He spoke of his dietary practices and some of his reasons for following them. One reason was that if he ate normally he would become fat and this would result in him taking up too much space in his environment, thereby depleting the space that others were entitled to occupy. His main aim, however, seemed to be to eliminate sexual and aggressive forces, to avoid the "murder" that eating entailed, and to make his body thin. A thin body was essential because whenever he put on a little weight and then looked into a mirror, he would experience a brief perceptual distortion in which he began to see a female body.

Although his sexual fantasies and desires were heterosexual, at these moments he believed that he was really a woman. This confusion of gender identity found expression in dreams and delusional fantasies. Sometimes he dreamed that he was a woman, which both pleased and alarmed him. At other times he could not decide whether the objects that he was finding sexually exciting were female breasts or male buttocks. He also told the therapist that in a previous life he had taken his father's place and had intercourse with his mother, making her pregnant. Sometimes he said that he had been pregnant and that the baby inside him at that time was his father.

Alec was intensely preoccupied with his bodily functions and products. He presented his views in detail, in a didactic and patronising manner that led the therapist to feel that he was being given an enlightening lesson by a powerful and omniscient guru.

He argued that a "true" human being needs nothing but air and water, which is why he had been a vegetarian for many years and had eaten nothing but fruit and vegetables for the previous two. Occasionally he would add a portion of soil in order to purify his "inner space". He would also save up his urine in bottles and conceal them in hidden places, and he would sometimes use the urine to wash his hands, in order to purify them.

He explained that previous years of meat-eating had caused the lining of his bowel to thicken to such a degree that it obstructed the exchange of life-giving substances. His aim has been to reduce the bowel lining to microscopic thinness in order to restore the necessary permeability. He wanted to be in the category of "sensitive" people, whom he felt had this thin bowel lining. This talk about his method of acquiring "sensitivity" was accompanied by a pressure of talk about his father, whom he described as a wise and saintly man. Although his father was in reality a much-admired public figure, Alec's account was a highly idealized and "sanitized" view which excluded any possible negative feelings. Alec also at times expressed a very different view of his father as being a harsh and authoritarian character, but he saw no contradiction in these (split or "pre-ambivalent") images. The therapist was later to find that the good real relationship he eventually formed with the patient was also overlaid by a similar idealization of himself (the therapist) in the transference.

At times he would become completely immobile for a few seconds on entering or leaving the room, and on crossing the floor to his chair. He explained that this inhibition of movement was necessary in order to control impulses to kick the therapist, and thus to control what he called his *kicking anxiety*. He would also stop suddenly in the action of seating himself in the chair or in a semi-stooped position during the process of seating himself, which he called *"sitting anxiety"*.

When he ate at a café, he felt impelled to avoid payment at the check-out counter. This generated *"stealing anxiety"*, and in order to control it he would regularly attempt to pay twice for his food. The disclosure to the therapist of these obsessive-compulsive counter-measures brought him a certain measure of relief and reduced the intensity of the behaviour.

As all this material poured out in the first month of the psycho-therapy, Alec came to feel less agitated and confused. He was able to eat a little more, with the result that he gained a considerable amount of weight. However, the therapist felt that Alec was actually becom-ing more anxious, and so he was not entirely surprised when he cancelled further sessions, immediately before the summer vacation. Alec explained that since he was too attached to his mother, he had decided to "liberate" himself from her. He assured the therapist that he would return to therapy when he had achieved this aim.

Second phase—on return

A year later, he reappeared looking thin and ill. He had been living the life of a hermit, existing on a diet solely of porridge and milk. He explained that this was necessary in order to control his *"chewing anxiety"*. This required him to restrict himself to food that could be mouthed or sucked but did not require chewing.

He was now more overtly psychotic, preoccupied with what seemed to be an entirely new delusional system, centring on cosmic forces and the activities of extraterrestrial beings. He said that he welcomed the diagnosis of psychosis, explaining that since his mis-sion was to save the world he was glad to be regarded as psychotic, since the Saviour who will come to rescue the world is said to be crazy.

For the first and only time, Alec accepted admission to hospital, where he remained for a month. Once again, he refused the medi-cation that was offered, and the psychiatrist involved respected his wish. The psychotherapy was then resumed, and it continued on a basis of three sessions weekly and was terminated three years later. The psychiatrist had no further need to intervene supportively in the case until after the termination, from which time he assumed the responsibility of six-monthly reviews for monitoring Alec's continued eligibility for welfare assistance.

The delusional content

It was clear that the more obvious sexual and aggressive elements that characterized Alec's earlier mental state had now been displaced by a new preoccupation with the interplay of cosmic forces of destruction and preservation. He explained that the world was soon to be destroyed, and he reacted to the thought of this coming apocalypse with panic.

However, the panic did not last long, because it was extinguished by the realization that he would be saved this fate, and that he himself was a saviour with the Messianic mission of saving the "chosen" people. Spaceships inhabited by friendly extraterrestrial beings were hovering near the earth, and they were under the command of Jesus and of Alec's father, whom he insisted was still alive. Jesus and his father would shortly send the signal that would launch the "day of judgement" when the chosen would be saved, by surviving on another plane of existence, or reincarnated into a perfect life. Alec explained that he must simply wait until the message came from the extraterrestrials announcing that the apocalyptic destruction had started. Then the drama of his personal survival would begin.

The further course of the psychotherapy

The therapist allowed sufficient time after each session to reflect on it, to consider what countertransference feelings he might have been experiencing, and to record the session in great detail.

To attempt a detailed presentation of the course of the psychotherapy and of such relevant technical issues as the detail of the therapist's method of conducting the treatment would be beyond the scope of this study. But the necessary abbreviation and condensation might convey the impression that the therapeutic task was easier than it actually was, or that the outcome was a perfect one. In reality, the therapist found his task difficult and demanding, although in a different and less difficult sense than with many borderline patients he had treated. The therapist eventually felt that the therapeutic encounters with Alec had been fascinating and highly rewarding, and he was satisfied that the outcome, although far from perfect, was in many ways a very successful one.

Progress

The early sessions were surrounded by rituals, which included lengthy visits to the toilet before the beginning of many sessions, and these would often consume much of the session time. Alec would also stop at the entrance of the therapy-room to drink slowly from a bottle filled with "specially pure" spring water. The therapist described his own therapeutic interventions as more or less fruitful efforts to translate the patient's communications into emotional language. He focused on the defensive nature of Alec's grandiosity and omnipotent controlling behaviour, his envious hatred of his loved and admired father, the fact of the father's death, and the way Alec had created cosmic fantasies in order to escape the inner conflicts and mental pain evoked by reality.

It was clear that in his initial denial that his father was dead, Alec was defending against his negative feelings about him, and that these negative feelings had entered the transference relationship. It seemed likely that this had contributed to his decision to leave the therapy after two months of the psychotherapy, immediately before a summer vacation, and thereby to free himself from feelings of dependency on his mother/therapist which were too disturbing to face at that time.

Growth of understanding is slow and painful

Alec gradually became able to tolerate his recognition of the painful sense of isolation and rejection that had marked his childhood and adolescence and the underlying intensely bitter envy and jealousy of his younger sister. Early, quite conscious, memories of his sadistic pleasure in tormenting her began to upset him. He remembered how he used to hit her in order to make her cry and then take great pleasure looking at her crying face. He would feel very triumphant when he succeeded in reducing both his younger and his older sister to tears, because he could not bear it when they became the centre of attention. As he came to feel this sense of responsibility, his relationship with them greatly improved. Although he became more anxious and depressed, he slowly resumed a normal diet and recovered a healthy weight.

He learned that an old school acquaintance had achieved considerable worldly success, and he recognized the intense envy that this knowledge aroused. This allowed him to experience some of the envious hostility that he harboured towards his professionally successful therapist. He dreaded the further pain and fear that what he described as "becoming a person" would bring, having to depend on another human being rather than to confine himself to the pseudo-independence that his psychotic thinking offered him. Despite these misgivings, he knew that he had been undergoing an enormous change for the better, and he described the way he had been discovering this fact.

He explained: "You don't become another person just like that, all of a sudden. It comes gradually and unnoticed. You really don't know when it happens. Somehow and sometime you just realize that it has happened, without you knowing it and that things are now very different." He continues: "I had to become crazy in order to survive. I had to stop thinking in order to stop existing. It was the only way. I made myself God, but God became lonely and I had to admit that I needed other people."

He realized that his suffering had been inevitable, and that the psychotherapy had brought him integration and the possibility of existing in the real world. He began to use the term "I" more frequently and came to a stable recognition that the extraterrestrial dramas were the product of his own imaginative thinking. Recollection of his feelings of inadequacy, inferiority, and social isolation, at their most intense during his father's terminal illness, caused Alec intense distress and depression and repeatedly led to a temporary revival of the defensive omnipotent thinking.

Alec had come to refer to the therapy as "the humanizing process". As he continued to cooperate with the therapeutic enterprise, his delusional system weakened and he accepted the "guiding" voices as being located in his own mind. His dependence on the support of cosmic and spirit guides disappeared, and he relinquished his self-appointed role as guiding tutor to the therapist.

Transference and countertransference

The process of mental integration was by no means straightforward and linear. Periods of progression and regression often alternated as his thinking in the areas of conflict became less psychotic, less fear-laden, less wish-fulfilling, and less anxious. The therapist had a constant struggle to keep in touch with his own feelings and to attempt to differentiate his personal emotional reactions—such as disgust, despair, anger, and excitement—from those that he considered his patient to have expelled from his own mind.

Alec began to recognize how much he had depended on the guidance of his father throughout his childhood and adolescence. He realized that he had been unable to mourn his father's death. He began to experience powerful aggressive feelings towards the therapist, representing both the "oedipal" rival father in the transference and also the representative of sanity who had caused him to relinquish his defensive encapsulation and face so much pain and anxiety.

In some sessions the therapist felt himself to be in real danger, as for instance when the patient suddenly overturned a table with great violence. As Alec became able to talk about the impulse to make a murderous attack on the therapist, his impulses and the associated *"violence anxiety"* diminished and finally disappeared.

In this way Alec gradually discovered that his therapist was not so vulnerable as he had feared. He also realized that his own omnipotent violent feelings were not so dangerous as he had believed. Meaningful and emotional talk with the therapist had begun to replace pressure for mindless action, a process first described by Freud (1917e [1915]) as "thing-presentations" being replaced by "word-presentations".

Understanding grows, obsessions recede

The improvement in Alec's mental state was accompanied by increased awareness of his aggressive feelings. He realized that the more he allowed other people to mean something to him emotionally, the more envious and aggressive he would feel towards them. The knifing anxiety had been aroused by thinking of his mother and took the form of intrusive imagery of stabbing her in the abdomen. After one particular session, he experienced a surge of "violence anxiety" as he left the room. He recounted the event:

"As I left the session the picture of myself stabbing my mother came into my mind. It was terrifying, but I let it happen, and the image finally passed away. I suppose that's the way it is. If the stabbing impulse remains unconscious, as you have said, it's more difficult to change it. It just sort of dissolved. But it is followed by terrible anxieties. But I suppose that's the way it has to be for a while".

The therapist thought that these feelings had been aroused in the transference during that particular session in which Alec had become aware of his feelings of dependency on the therapist. He felt that this dynamic might also help to explain Alec's precipitate departure at the beginning of the treatment. Alec's new-found ability to confront the impact of his destructive feelings (similar in effect to the behavioural technique of "flooding") proved to be an important turning point in the treatment.

Gradually Alec's phobias and anxieties lessened. His growing understanding of the meaning of his compulsive phobias had in this way enabled him to continue to confront them, which eventually led to their disappearance. As his *"knifing anxiety"* receded, so did his *"sitting anxiety"*, a development suggesting that the latter had been motivated by the imminent awareness of his "exclusive" place having been preceded by a "rival" patient.

As the psychotic qualities of his thinking receded, Alec was able to understand them to some extent as the product of a vivid imagination, a capacity that had brought delusional fulfilment of wishes as well as the terrors of the imminent destruction of the world. He could now begin to appreciate the symbolic nature of much of his formerly concrete thinking and to speak with the therapist about the process of repairing his own mind. He was able to recognize constructive and reparative elements inside his mind rather than in the terrestrial and extraterrestrial worlds. He showed a stronger capacity for reality-testing coupled with an increased ability to use the therapist's views and thus to appreciate his "guidance". With his increasing insights, the splitting of his self-image diminished. He then remarked that previously he had only been able to see himself as "God, or a germ".

Alec finally breaks off—
a retreat from the demands of separation

After three years of therapy, Alec was working effectively in a sheltered job, was socially much more capable, and showed no signs of psychotic functioning. However, it gradually became clear that he was beginning to withdraw from the prospect of a painful separation from his therapist which an orderly termination of treatment would involve.

The ending of the therapy was neither tidy nor entirely satisfactory. As the summer vacation approached, Alec began to cancel sessions and to seek advice from a variety of practitioners of alternative therapies. He expressed his dilemma to the psychotherapist: "I really don't dare to go further, but I can't go back—I can no longer get crazy."

After the vacation, he reported that he had fallen in love and had survived a painful rejection that followed. The therapist was sure that this event had really happened and that it was not simply an enactment of rivalrous feelings aroused in the transference by the separation, but was more like the distress of a normal adolescent.

Following the summer vacation, he continued to cancel appointments with the therapist at the last moment. He eventually decided to terminate the therapy on the grounds that he could now get on with his new life. He agreed to visit the psychiatrist at six-monthly intervals for the review of his disability pension.

The therapist believed that whatever might be his unconscious motivations, Alec was making a considered decision based on his unwillingness to face the painful feelings that the working-through of a separation would entail. Although his therapist felt that, in this respect the therapy had failed, he believed that his patient had now sufficient insight and ego strength to return to therapy should he feel the need at some future date.

Follow-up, three years later

The psychiatrist, now involved in further surveillance, reports:

"Since he broke off the therapy Alec has kept irregular contact. He has continued to make steady progress, his obsessive-compulsive symptoms have not reappeared, and he is no longer aggressive with his mother and with his sisters. His relationship with them is transformed, and he is on good terms with them. However he has not freed himself from his dependent attachment to his mother, and behaves at times like a clinging child, a feature that might lend support to the psychotherapist's view that he broke off treatment in order to avoid the experience of separation from the therapist himself. Despite this he has created a reasonably normal and happy social life, which includes occasional country 'nature' walks with an environmentally concerned group. He lives in his own apartment and is in sheltered employment. He has once again fallen in love with a young woman, but it is as yet uncertain how he might respond if he should in future experience rejection. Alec says, with considerable insight, that he realizes that he needs people, but that experiencing this need for others is very painful. He has clearly failed to resolve his ambivalent feelings about the therapist, and this certainly seems to be a reason for his avoidance of further contact with him."

One year further on

The psychiatrist reports again:

"The patient's relationship with his mother has changed in that he now appears more independent and has adopted a more distant relationship to her. This seems more like a cutting-off, a 'severance', rather than a true step towards mature autonomy. He expresses himself as grateful to the therapist, but sometimes still feels very angry with him for taking away his comforting imaginary life. He now knows that these were 'crazy ideas'. He explains that he needed them in order to allow development to take place. The 'crazy ideas' gave him a sense of being a unique and very special person. As he relinquished this claim to 'specialness' he was forced to realize how the delusional ideas had helped him escape from a life of isolation and loneliness. Nonetheless they had cut him off from human contact and created a different type of loneliness."

The English saying "not the only pebble on the beach" conveys the recognition that pseudo-independence may be comforting so long as you do not realize that other people (pebbles) exist, and that you need them, that you can learn from them, and that they can help you.

Discussion

An attempt can now be made to understand the nature of Alec's mental illness and to provide an explanation of the process whereby his psychotic symptoms appeared, and in the course of psychotherapy eventually disappeared. It will also be necessary to consider how the resolution of the psychosis has left him with emotional problems which may or may not be resolved in the future. This is a frequent outcome of "aim-restricted" psychotherapy, which succeeds in resolving the psychosis—with or without the help of medication—when the integrative capacities of the patient, or the conditions and motivation for further commitment to the painful task of working through the separation process or, at times, an underlying personality disorder (Grotstein, 2001), are insufficient.

What precipitated the psychosis?

Alec's inability to mourn the death of his father in a healthy manner suggests that his illness was a psychotic response to bereavement, a pathological mourning reaction in a pre-existing obsessional and schizoid personality. His inability to mourn could be explained by the intensity of his feelings of love and hatred for his much-admired, and unconsciously envied, father. In contrast to his relation with his siblings, for whom he at first felt only hatred and sadistic desires for vengeance, his love for his father was strong. His wish to protect the memory of his father from his envy and his cold (oedipal) hostility found symbolic expression in his providing warm water for the insects who might freeze in the cold.

In the normal or neurotic individual, such opposing feelings may be kept apart by (unconscious) repression of the negative feelings, and if these repressed feelings are intense, a pathological bereavement process may follow. However, such a process does not seriously compromise the sense of identity of the person.

If, by contrast, there is a pre-existent predisposition to psychosis, the consequences may be more profound and disruptive. In such a case, the good and bad feelings have long been widely separated by the primitive defence of splitting (usually more powerful than the more mature defence of repression) and the sense of personal identity has been only weakly established. It was this vulnerability that made it possible for Alec to develop his shifting delusional beliefs—based on his looking in the mirror—that he was female, was pregnant (in identification with his mother), and was omnipotently powerful (in identification with an idealized image of his father). Alec, unconsciously usurping his father's intellectual and sexual potency, came to regard himself as a superior being with no need of human contact and thus no fear of ever acknowledging his hatred or his dependency needs. Such a shifting kaleidoscope of partial and multiple identifica tions can help explain the states of perplexity and confusion that are a feature of the mental life of many psychotic patients.

Childhood precursors of later disturbance — sibling jealousy

It is not known what Alec was like as a baby, or whether the apparently undisturbing separation from his mother at the age of 9 months had any unobserved, or unobservable, consequence. However, he showed evidence of disturbance in his early childhood, in the form of obsessive rituals involving the closing and opening of doors. These rituals followed the birth of his sister, and it seems likely that they were a defence against the conflicted feelings aroused by his jealousy of the sister and associated oedipal rivalry. His failure to manage this traumatic experience left him with an "undigested" complex of feelings, to which he was unconsciously attempting to give symbolic expression in the door-closing activity, magically controlling access to his mother's body, symbolized by the room. It was the failure of the defensive encapsulation of these feelings that led to the outbreak of Alec's impulses to stab his sister and to knife his mother in the abdomen.

The murderous intensity of his envy and jealousy of his younger sister (and also of his three-year-older sister) emerged in the course of psychotherapy. When Alec eventually began to realize how cruel he had been to both of his sisters and how much pleasure he had derived from tormenting them, he called this behaviour "satanic". In classical psychoanalytic theory, such "anal-sadistic" behaviour would have been at its height during his second and third year, about the time of his mother's pregnancy and the birth of his sister. Its severity would have been partly determined by the vicissitudes and quality of the earlier "oral" relationship with his mother.

Alec's "chewing anxiety" could now be understood as the expression of an unconscious fantasy of eating his mother in a cannibalistic manner, a dynamic that will be exemplified in later chapters.

*Partial identifications with mother's body
and its symbolic equivalents*

His psychotic fantasies of being pregnant imply that these easily remembered experiences of cruelty towards his sister may have had earlier precursors, such as when, in his second year of life, he perceived his mother's enlarging abdomen and formed a conception of his rival as inhabiting the maternal body. The phase of smashing of windows and of fire-raising in the home might have symbolized a wish to invade the mother's body, as also might the compulsive checking, many years later, at the door of his apartment to prevent fire breaking out in the interior.

Alec's need to keep his body thin and emaciated, which he explained as partly to prevent himself from taking up too much space, can also be considered as expressing his feelings about the new baby, with whom he is at that time identified, taking up too much of his mother's mental and physical space.

Thus the behaviour of taking over control of opening and closing doors can be considered as the first overt manifestation of his later obsessive-compulsive symptomatology, used to counteract his impulses to invade and destroy his mother's baby. As such it served as an emergency method of escaping the helplessness of the rivalry situation and of protecting the mother, on whose survival his life depended. This obsessive symptom of closing and opening doors receded during his later childhood, only to return in force with the impact of more mature sexual feelings in early adolescence. The symptoms also emerged, in symbolic derivative form, during the psychotherapy when he made a ritual pause on entering and leaving the therapy-room and would often drink the draught of "pure spring water" from a bottle at the threshold in order to purify his body, a ritual that represented a cleansing of the inside of his mind of reflective thinking and disturbing feelings as he entered and left the therapy-room.

Omnipotent thinking and megalomanic developments

As the overt psychosis revived the unresolved conflicts of his early life, he was confronted by the terrifying belief that the world was about to come to an end. This is a very common feature of evolving psychosis and characteristically leads to a change in identity, the individual commonly acquiring the delusional belief that he is a Messiah, or has omnipotent powers and a special mission of salvation.

There are many variants of this central omnipotent belief, which are often aimed at avoiding a terror of losing the personal sense of identity. The loss of identity is often described in such terms as ceasing to exist, disintegrating, or falling into nothingness. In object-relation terms, the experience can be considered as a re-edition of a primordial fear of infancy, a dread that aggressive feelings will destroy the mother, on whom life depends. In other words, fantasies of world destruction may have their origins at the time when the mother is the whole world for the baby, and the baby is flooded by destructive feelings towards her.

In order to avoid the catastrophe of damage to his mother, Alec assumed a new identity, a further extension of his already-formed identification with his idealized dead father. The conflicts about his father were thus compounded by the revival of his deeper, and developmentally earlier, conflicts with his mother. In his new role of omniscient "guru", Alec now, with a great sense of triumph, succeeds in converting his sane self into believing that his omnipotent delusions are the truth. He has been robbed of the normal process of identification with the father which modulates infantile entanglement with the mother, a process called the "name of the father" by Lacan (1997).

Concrete thinking and body products

For a long period before the outbreak of his psychosis, Alec had pursued eccentric ritualistic dietary practices, as has already been described. At that time, he would often save his urine in bottles, which he deposited in concealed places, and use it to wash his hands. A possible explanation of this strange behaviour might be found by considering it as an attempt of a very primitive and concrete sort, to escape the perils of dependency, separation, and loss.

Unconsciously identifying himself with his own urine, he creates a container for this partial self, thereby inventing a derivative symbolic version of a "symbiotic" union of a baby inside the containing maternal space (symbolized by the bottles). In this "part-object" form of thinking, loss of his own urine from his body could be felt as loss of his original union with his mother, a bodily version of the dreaded "end-of-the-world" (mother) catastrophe. Drinking pure spring water as he enters the session, could in a similar manner, illustrate his claim that he has no need of the therapist's provision.

His belief that the lining of his bowel had become thickened because of years of eating meat might be seen as a complex metaphorical expression, an indirect and disguised recognition of the fact that his withdrawal has isolated him from life, making him emotionally impermeable to human feelings and to his own dependent needs. The need for it to become permeable might imply the possibility of being able to take in and digest the emotional "food of life", which, in the transference is offered by the therapist. The meaning of Alec's behaviour in relation to the toilet of the consulting-room and of idealizing the health-promoting properties of his faeces (symbolized by the soil that he would sometimes eat) and his urine (saved in bottles) can be sought in the light of these unconscious phantasies.

He idealizes his faeces (eating soil) and urine as good self-provided nourishing and cleansing (maternal) milk, a statement of pseudo-independence and an escape from the perils of attachment, separation, and loss. Saving his urine in bottles is a different way of maintaining a symbiotic fantasy, and it is also a denial of need. Thus, trying to make his bowel lining more permeable can express his sane wish to accept his emotional needs.

The "chewing anxiety" that led to his restricting his diet to food that does not require chewing can now be considered as the consequence of his fear of the destructive power of his oral-aggressive impulses. The meaning of his bizarre delusional beliefs about the inside of his body and his bodily processes can also begin to make sense. Processes that belong to his mind are being thought of as belonging to his body. His rituals of purification of the inside of his body now reveal themselves as attempts to purify his mind, to "sanitize" it, and to remove the dirt that symbolizes dangerous aggressive feelings. Such dynamics have something in common with severe anorexia nervosa, which will be considered in later chapters.

Conclusions

In the study of this case, I have explored some of the many possible meanings of Alec's symptomatology and the importance of investigating the content, origins, and functions of his delusional beliefs.

Knowledge of such basic psychoanalytic concepts as repetition-compulsion [see Glossary], whereby unresolved conflicts of the past press for expression in present behaviour and symptoms, of regressive and shifting identifications, of primitive mechanisms of defence, and of symbolic, "primary-process" thinking provides effective keys to understanding and guidance for therapeutic intervention.

Meanings and understandings —
by therapist and by patient

Readers unfamiliar with the concepts of "part-object" processes may find difficulty in comprehending or appreciating their clinical usefulness in work with psychotic patients. I hope that the many further clinical examples of "part-object" processes that appear in later chapters will help to clarify the subject.

It is important to recognize that in the first instance such knowledge is for the use of the therapist. His task is to impart only that which is within the patient's grasp at a particular moment, and which he feels will be useful to the patient. Alec's psychotherapist had a sensitive understanding of this requirement and a wide experience of psychotic patients, and this played an important part in the successful outcome.

Alec's future

The psychotherapy has been regarded by his family as having been profoundly helpful, and the psychiatrists concerned judged it as an impressive outcome. Alec's abandonment of the psychotherapy seems to have been, at least to some extent, a considered choice. In such a situation it is important that the psychotherapist should try to review with the patient what has been achieved and what has not, and what remains to be achieved in the future. It is also important that the door to further psychotherapy should be left open, and that the psychotherapeutic history of such a patient should be in some way recorded, so that in the event of him having further trouble at some future time and possibly some different place he will not be exposed to treatment that might be useless or harmful.

In the case of Alec, I have aimed to present the theory and the clinical evidence for the usefulness of psychoanalytic concepts in

discerning meaning and providing effective guidelines for psychotherapy in sufficient detail for readers to make up their own minds
about these claims and explanations. I shall continue to follow this
course throughout the book.

Alec's case illustrates the fact that it is important to avoid premature generalizations about the suitability or otherwise of a psychotic
patient for a trial of psychotherapy. It also illustrates the great benefit
that well-conducted psychotherapy in skilled hands can bring to even
severely and chronically ill psychotic patients.

Alec has not simply "recovered" from his psychosis, but has
achieved new growth and integration of his arrested personality development. Despite the intensity of his feelings of hatred, his hidden
capacity for warmth and his desire to protect his valued objects from
his destructiveness implied that he had some capacity to function at
the level of the depressive position. This is true of many obsessional
patients and, however difficult treatment may prove to be, can be
considered as a good prognostic feature.

CHAPTER FOUR

Paranoid schizophrenia—
command hallucinations: "Brian"

Some psychotic patients who have lived in a chronic state for long periods of time have never had the opportunity of a psychodynamic exploration which might have led to a better understanding of their situation. With others, an attempt has been made but, for various reasons, has failed. The following case illustrates both some of the complex factors that may be involved in such a situation and how a psychotherapeutic approach in the appropriate setting with the right psychotherapist can help the patient.

Brian

The case of Brian, aged 43 years, was brought to a large discussion group after he had had three years of weekly psychotherapy. Only a single session of discussion was possible, at which time a prognostic formulation was agreed in the group and recorded. Three years later, the therapist provided a follow-up report.

Brian had been disabled for more than twenty years by an illness diagnosed as chronic paranoid schizophrenia, and he was maintained on a moderate dose of neuroleptic medication. Attempts at rehabilitation had failed, and two attempts to engage him in psychotherapy some years earlier had been quickly abandoned because of his completely uncooperative attitude. At the age of 37, he had been admitted to a day hospital that specialized in the rehabilitation of chronic schizophrenic patients, and he had been allocated to a rehabilitation programme that required him to live in the ward during the week.

On arriving at the ward, he at once withdrew to his room and spent much of the day in bed. A new treatment plan was formulated, focusing on a change in medication to a more modern anti-psychotic drug, and a further attempt at psychotherapy was launched. An experienced female psychotherapist began to see him on a twice-weekly basis, and after three years he was sufficiently recovered to be discharged from hospital care, free of all medication, to live in an apartment of his own and to seek employment. He had become known as a "miracle case", a remarkable example of the effectiveness of psychotherapy in a well-functioning psychiatric milieu.

Doubts about stability of recovery

However, the therapist was sceptical about miracles. She felt she had not yet understood Brian sufficiently to be confident about the nature of his dramatic recovery, and she feared that he might not maintain it. She was worried that the "miraculous" result was too good to be true, that he had begun to have some depressive feelings, and that he might not manage to retain his improvement. As her report proceeded, it became clear that her misgivings about the future might be justified. Although many areas of his mental life had been explored during the course of the psychotherapy, the reasons why he had fallen ill in this particular way, and the meaning of his hallucinatory experiences, had not yet been fully understood.

Evolution of the psychosis

Brian was an apparently normal, intelligent, somewhat reserved young man until he left school and began to attend university. Although he had done quite well scholastically at school, his performance at university deteriorated and he began to fail his examinations and finally refused to take them. He subsequently withdrew increasingly into an isolated existence in his room in the family home, sleeping much of the day and watching television much of the night. He began to fear that intruders would break into his room, and he persuaded his father to change the lock on the door.

First hospital admission

When, at the age of 20, Brian became suspicious of food and stopped eating, the parents persuaded him to see a psychiatrist, and he was admitted to hospital. No detailed psychiatric records were available from that first admission, but a diagnosis of a schizophrenic episode, with paranoid thinking and auditory hallucinations, was established. He was treated with neuroleptic medication and made a quick recovery. After a few weeks he was discharged to the care of his parents, on maintenance neuroleptic medication, but he remained withdrawn and socially disabled.

He acquired an apartment of his own near the parental home, was awarded a disability pension, and attended the hospital at intervals to monitor his medication. Exploratory psychotherapy was attempted on two occasions. Both these attempts were unsuccessful, owing to his inability, or unwillingness, to engage in a process of reflective thought about himself. In these therapy sessions, he showed a complete lack of interest in the therapist's existence. He avoided eye contact and was almost totally silent, giving the impression of utter boredom, verging on contempt for the therapists, who finally abandoned their task.

Ten further years of chronicity

For the first five years he continued to lead an isolated existence, supported by the disability pension and the constant attention of his mother. He passed the time watching television, visiting his parents and his brother, and walking around the district, mostly at night. Increasing anxiety finally compelled him to return to the shelter of the parental home. He emptied his apartment of every removable object and sold all his property, telling his parents that it was all infected.

Psychotic terror

For the next five years he lived in a state of considerable anxiety in a room in the basement of the house, finally becoming acutely disturbed, withdrawing to his room, shouting at hallucinatory voices, and barricading the door. He later explained that the most terrifying hallucinatory experience was of lethal beams coming through the window. These rays moved and intersected at various points in the room, and he was forced to move continuously to avoid these intersections, because he would die if he should be exposed to them. Much later, he was able to explain to the therapist that he had believed that the rays were the work of his parents, who were trying to murder him.

Second hospital admission

His parents finally summoned the police to break down his barricaded door and forcibly remove him to hospital. He remained there for four months on heavy medication, at the end of which time he was again discharged to the care of his parents.

Acute recurrences

There he continued his isolated existence, sometimes becoming so agitated and withdrawn from reality that his parents were forced to have him re-admitted on a compulsory order. He usually improved quickly and stayed only for a few weeks. Neuroleptic medication was adjusted from time to time, and the diagnosis of chronic paranoid schizophrenia was established.

Some personal history

Brian was the youngest of four children of a troubled family, the eldest son having suffered a transient psychotic illness in early adulthood. At the age of 8 years, Brian became ill with pulmonary tuberculosis, and he was first treated in hospital and then nursed at home by his distraught mother. She took almost total control over his life, keeping him in bed for some months and then indoors and out of all contact with his friends for two years, a pattern of protective behaviour exceeding medical requirements.

Family dysfunction

In a family consultation, the younger sister, herself a social worker, said that her father had been devoted and very well intentioned, but he was often too busy with his own business affairs to exercise any authority in the family. It was the mother who dominated the family, with her personal, restrictive, philosophy that all problems should be dealt with entirely within the family.

His sister still remembered her bitterness and jealousy at the exclusive attention that Brian had had for the years when he was forcibly isolated when suffering from tuberculosis. So extreme was the mother's attitude, said his sister, that all the children suffered, because there was always one to be cared for in this exclusive and overwhelming manner. The sister had no doubt that all her siblings suffered from this apparently well-intentioned care. She explained that the siblings had never been able to talk to each other and that even today these tensions inhibited their relationships. They all still had a deep sense of loneliness whenever something went wrong, and they did not know how to communicate in anything but a superficial and impersonal manner. Her mother would never share anything, but would always respond to difficulties by taking over and insisting that she could deal with the problem on her own and that there was no need to upset Brian by calling in outsiders.

When Brian eventually recovered from tuberculosis, he was unable to regain his former level of intimacy with his friends or recover his lost self-confidence. Although he was able to join in some activities, he could not make up for the retardation of competence in social, physical, and sporting activities. However, his parents saw no reason for any special concern about him during his adolescence, until he eventually withdrew from his university examinations and retreated into isolation.

The psychotherapy

It was only due to the patience and firm commitment of the therapist that the therapy did not quickly follow the course of previous attempts. For the first year, the patient demonstrated the same behaviour as he had twenty years before. For some months he barely uttered a word in the sessions, appearing remote, contemptuous, and apparently bored. Every few minutes he would glance at his watch, and on one occasion the therapist counted forty yawns in forty-five minutes.

A crucial understanding

During this long silent phase, the therapist functioned in an intui-tive way, guided by her belief that Brian had never entirely lost hope that one day he would emerge, or be rescued, from his half-life. A moment eventually arrived when she felt that he might be able to listen to her and to think about himself. She pointed out to him that they both knew that he wanted to get well, to come alive, to leave his bed, and to enter the world. She told him that she believed he was waiting to wake up one day and find himself completely well, but that in following this course he would miss the opportunity of small improvements that would gradually lead to health. For the first time, he showed a sign of interest. He nodded his head in affirmation, and from that time onwards the intervals between consulting his watch gradually lengthened and eventually ceased.

Collaborative exploration — searching for meanings

It was now clear that the therapist was gaining Brian's trust and interest. He began to speak about his psychotic experiences and his anxieties, preoccupations, and details of his past life. As he returned to memories of the past, he showed moments of confusion in which he was unsure whether he was experiencing a hallucination or a memory. He began to dream, and often on waking he was uncertain for some hours whether he was awake or asleep.

Terrifying hallucinations

He spoke of the years of isolation that began with the onset of pulmonary tuberculosis, and his feelings of exclusion and social and physical incompetence. He dated the onset of his disturbing experi-ences to when he was 12. At this time he had not learned to swim, and while bathing with some school friends he found himself unable to follow them when they swam off into deep water. At that moment, he had a terrifying hallucinatory experience. He saw a spherical object emerge from beneath the surface of the sea, which he subsequently believed to be a "monster from the deep". It had many tentacle-like arms and began to approach him. In terror of being sucked into the sea and drowned, he ran off and hid. When he recovered, he made no mention of this to his friends or family. The hallucinatory monster continued to appear from time to time, and this contributed to the patient's further withdrawal from contact with others.

He had a further terrifying experience two years later. He was standing outside the house with his father, who was talking about the Vietnam War. Suddenly Brian heard the crack of bullets whistling past his head. Panic-stricken, he rushed inside the house and hid. He re-emerged some time later and returned to his father, who continued as though nothing had happened. His father apparently completely ignored his son's precipitate disappearance and did not seek reasons for his sudden flight.

By the age of 15, his periods of confusion between fantasy and reality and his visual and auditory hallucinatory experiences had become more persistent. Despite this disturbance, his high intelligence and areas of ego strength facilitated his entry into university. However, he was unable to concentrate during examinations, withdrew from his course, and suffered the first psychotic breakdown, as already described. He later explained to the therapist that his lack of capacity for concentration had been the consequence of voices shouting at him, saying that he was stupid, no good, and that he must not try to concentrate on such impossible work. There was no doubt that he was describing command hallucinations in the form of one or more people shouting at him in a propaganda-style manner. He did not recognize the identity of the voices, but it seemed probable that they talked about him (in the third person).

These auditory command hallucinations, beginning at the age of 20, soon became a permanent feature of his mental life. They were particularly active whenever he tried to do something to help himself, or to oppose his passivity. He described the effect as draining all the power out of him, just as he had experienced the enforced isolation of his childhood illness. The "monster-from-the-deep" hallucinations continued to haunt him.

Rapid progress in the psychotherapy

The therapy continued without major overt disturbance, and his hallucinatory experiences gradually receded into the background. Medication was slowly and carefully reduced. After two years it was discontinued at his own insistence, and after a further twelve months he was able to leave hospital and to live in an apartment of his own.

However, despite the therapist's crucial interpretation of his waiting to be suddenly "cured", no deep understanding of his inner world had been achieved, and the nature of past traumatic experiences and the meaning of much of his psychotic thinking remained obscure.

Pursuit of psychodynamic understanding

The hallucinatory engulfing monster—a "mental object"

It was Brian's inability to keep up with his peers, following his long period of social isolation, that initiated the "monster" fantasy, which had some of the qualities of a nightmare or day-dream. His mother's previously over-protective behaviour would probably have played an important part in undermining whatever self-assertive strength he might otherwise have been able to draw on. Brian's dread of drowning represents a terror awaiting many severely schizoid patients, who fear being overwhelmed by unmanageable feelings and losing the sense of personal identity, of disintegrating, or of ceasing to exist.

This combination of a wish to withdraw and a dread of drowning could be considered in several different ways. It implies weakness of the ego function of reality-testing, impairment of the ego boundaries between inner and outer reality, and regressive "perceptualization" of thinking (visualizing his thoughts). In object-relation terms, it could be considered as the activity of a dangerous internal object, a fantasy representation of an overpowering mother pulling him back into the womb.

The hallucinatory commands

The commands to abandon any attempt to struggle or to help himself were auditory hallucinations, operative at a different level from the visual perceptions of the "monster". In the terms of classical psychoanalytic theory, they might be considered as the expression of a punitive superego dedicated to making him feel useless and stupid, or of a distorted representative of an envious father or sibling who could not bear him to succeed. In object-relation terms, they could be seen as a "psychotic organization" dedicated to preventing life and growth (Steiner, 1993).

His terror could thus be understood as the consequence of these fantasies suddenly becoming real to him. In the episode of the bullets whistling past his head, and perhaps other, undisclosed, episodes of auditory hallucination, he felt himself faced with catastrophe in a different form from drowning. Although further evidence might be needed, it seemed likely that his dilemma concerned emotional closeness to his mother, which threatened engulfment, and to his father, which threatened violent death.

The discussion ends and the following
prognostic formulation is recorded

"If Brian's depressive feelings, as reported by the therapist, should emerge more clearly and prove capable of exploration, it may be possible to help him work through the process of mourning for past losses, characteristic of the depressive position. If it proves impossible to help the patient work through depressive pain, a regressive process may develop at some future time, with the loss of some of his gains and the re-emergence of psychotic symptoms. Although this may prove disappointing for all concerned, such a development would not necessarily signify the failure of the therapy and the inevitability of its termination. The patient now faces an uncertain future. There is evidence that he has a considerable degree of health and sanity. Much will depend on the possibility of continuing the psychotherapy until such time as he can function independently, and until the therapist and the caring staff are satisfied about the quality of his improvement. However, continued support without deeper exploration may prove to be all that is necessary to help him maintain at least some of his impressive gains."

At this point the therapist decided that she wanted to continue with the psychotherapy and, armed with a new way of understanding him, to focus on the exploration of his feelings of depression. She decided that it was important that investigation of the family dynamics had not so far been possible, and she suspected that the protectiveness of the parents towards Brian (as disclosed by his sister), and perhaps also towards his psychotic brother, had been excessive to a pathological degree. She felt that the family system may have been like a fortress, supporting its members at the cost of isolation from social life, and that the little boy who fell ill at the age of 8 may already have been insecure in his important attachments, and unable to form a relationship with his father of sufficient strength to help him in the task of psychological separation from his mother's influence.

Three years later

A follow-up report three years later showed important developments.

Shortly after the seminar discussion, Brian had broken off the therapy, declaring himself very satisfied to have achieved his goal, namely of being able to take care of himself so that he could cope after the eventual death of his parents. The possible influence that the therapist's experience of the discussion might have had on the transference and thus on Brian's decision to break off the treatment remained unknown. At the same time, he also broke off contact with the community contact nurse.

He settled back into his apartment and to an apparently comfortable existence, but after some months, following the suicide of a friend, he had a brief psychotic episode. He was admitted to another hospital, was given a small dose of neuroleptics, and was discharged recovered in a fortnight. He resumed a greatly improved social life, recapturing old friendships, fishing, walking, and helping on the family farm. He began to explore heterosexual relationships, but when he found himself emotionally interested in a young woman, he suddenly lost his feelings and withdrew. This behaviour could perhaps be understood as a repetition of his premature withdrawal from the psychotherapy, at a point where separation feelings and oedipal conflicts were threatening to emerge in the transference. It was for this reason that the therapist had told the patient that he could return to therapy at some future date if he felt it advisable.

Therapy for the family

Brian's new and happier life had brought great relief to the family, and they finally sought help for themselves. They became engaged in family therapy in which his two sisters participated, and which they all found very helpful. The therapist learned from the family therapists that they had found that the mother, an only child, had had a

disturbed childhood, but that the reason for her apparently pathological overprotectiveness had yet to be understood.

Discussion

Transference and countertransference

Although there had been no opportunity to examine the nature of
transference processes in detail, there was sufficient evidence to suggest that the therapist had at first filled the role of container of certain
projections by the patient. The initial silence and apparent contempt
to which she was exposed could be partly understood as a reversal
of the experience of humiliation that Brian felt in relation to others
whom he deemed superior. On an "all-or-none" basis, he found it
essential to be especially superior and aloof as a defence against his
feelings of worthlessness.

Such projective mechanisms may serve the purpose of expulsion
of intolerably painful thoughts, and sometimes for the purpose of
communicating them. It is interesting to consider that Brian may have
been unconsciously attempting to communicate the state of his inner
world to the therapist by paralysing her, as he was himself paralysed,
and preventing her from using her mind, a technique that had succeeded, to his detriment, with the two previous therapists. This might
also have been a defence against the dangers of depressive feelings or
the expression of the self-contempt which had been reinforcing his
previous withdrawal.

Although detailed transference work may prove difficult or impossible in this type of work, it may not be essential to detect it nor to
spell it out to the patient (see Chapter 18). What is important, however, is for a therapist to realize that there may be hidden and subtle
processes going on between himself and the patient. For instance, the
patient may believe that the therapist is merely gratifying his own
wishes to put the patient in the wrong, or to triumph over him and to
make him feel small and humiliated.

With the psychotic patient, these misconceptions may include the
belief that the therapist is trying to drive him mad, or that the therapist is himself mad. If the therapist is aware of these hidden possibilities, he will be on his guard to consider that the patient may not
be understanding his communications in the sense that they were

intended. The therapist will then give priority to exploring whether the patient hears something quite different from what the therapist was intending to convey.

In the case of Brian, the therapist's capacity to listen patiently without needing to explain or explore instantly may have served as the equivalent of an interpretation, thus strengthening the patient's capacity for testing out the reality of his psychotic suspicions. It seems likely that he believes that emotional contact is dangerous both to himself and to the object of his feelings. Such a belief of being dangerous and endangered might have had its roots in his mother's extreme attitude in protecting him and others from infection during his childhood.

With the onset of the bodily changes of puberty, many adolescents fear that their burgeoning sexual and aggressive capacities are dangerous (Laufer & Laufer, 1984), and this may take the form of being threatened by a monster, in dreams, fantasy, or fiction. At the extreme, this can lead to "developmental" breakdown with psychotic features. Brian's monster seemed of a more primitive and seductive kind. However, it seems likely that his premature withdrawal from the therapy expressed his fear of sexual intimacy, and that this was the reason for his premature withdrawal from heterosexual relationships three years later.

The murderous (internal) parents

The delusions centring on the hallucinatory crossing beams of light and of the gunfire attack illustrates the multiplicity of possible symbolic referents that may be involved in the construction of psychotic explanations. These could be regarded as deriving from different levels of his past development and his present thinking. At a "whole-object" level, these could be regarded as expressing his unconscious murderous hostility towards his (oedipal rival) father and his need to keep his parents apart [see Glossary, "combined parent figure"]. At another symbolic level, the light beams might represent his need to keep apart the elements that might produce dangerous thoughts.

Many more possible meanings might occur to the reader. However, it is not essential for the therapist to be familiar with all these possibilities, and certainly not essential to assume that he knows in advance of the difficult work that may be involved in finding out.

Understanding of the patient—understanding by the patient

As already pointed out, it should be clear that the acquisition of important understanding by the therapist certainly does not guarantee that he will succeed in conveying this to the patient in a useful way, or that he should necessarily try. However, the better his understanding, the more he will succeed in judging how much new information the patient is capable of assimilating at any particular moment.

If this were a neurotic illness, much might be sufficiently explained in terms of oedipal rivalry with father and siblings, and of the "examination anxiety" as the expression of a fear that his hidden guilty thoughts would be exposed. However, a psychotic predisposition implies a deeper, and chronologically earlier, developmental failure in establishing a firm sense of identity and of becoming able to integrate aggressive feelings and impulses ("pre-symbolic" affects) into his self-image, and thus to recognize them as his own. An associated failure of development may have left him profoundly tied in a "primary" identification with his mother and also unable to make the necessary constructive identification with his father, which would put in train his capacity to work himself free from the very physical ("incestuous") and biological tie to the mother.

The onset of Brian's psychosis in late adolescence was most likely the expression of the failure of defences against forbidden sexual and aggressive wishes. Were this true, the unconscious construction of the hallucinatory gunshots, and the disparaging voices (by the mechanisms of projective expulsion and symbolization of unwelcome thoughts), could be considered to be the outcome of a desperate defensive attempt to avoid the outbreak of violent feelings towards his father and their anticipated consequences ("castration anxiety"). Projection of his aggressive feelings and (introjective) identification with the "bad" father might then create an inner scenario, a reversal in which he (as father) is the target of his own childhood aggression (the abusive voices) and is prohibited from exercising any potency, assertive or sexual.

Remaining passive and helpless could then be considered as keeping his father, and thus also his parents, paralysed in his own inner world. The contempt for the therapist's approaching him with superior knowledge is suggestive of a paternal transference of psychotic quality, a transference that may have to some extent been worked through by the therapist's persistence and continued support, allowing him gradually to feel that she was trying neither to collude with his passivity nor to humiliate him.

Conclusions

Many important questions about Brian's psychopathology remain unanswered. At the time when the therapist brought his case for discussion, the psychotherapy was continuing and he was free of symptoms and apparently functioning well. Up to this point, the psychotherapy had been a remarkable success. The most obvious positive therapeutic factor probably lay in the therapist's persistent support of the healthy aspects of her patient's personality and her toleration of the countertransference stresses to which she was exposed for such a long period. This reliable consistency may have helped him to oppose his powerful tendency to withdraw. Her recognition of his "all-or-none" attitude to change seems to have been of crucial importance. In these respects, the therapist could be regarded as facilitating a process of identification, leading to a strengthening of Brian's ego functions and helping him to distinguish dream from reality and events belonging to his own mind from events of outer reality.

However, neither he nor his therapist had achieved a deep understanding of the reasons why he became psychotic in that particular way. The discussion led to a new understanding of the psychodynamics of his case and the meaning of his previous hallucinatory experiences and delusional thinking. The therapist found this extremely enlightening, but her change of therapeutic tactics may have led Brian to break off treatment. Whether her new understanding of the case led her to adopt a more psychodynamic–interpretive approach and thus had adverse consequences is an open question. It is even possible that Brian was not capable of further change, or at least not yet ready for it. It might also be considered that although the intervention of the seminar discussion led to more knowledge, it also led to the loss of the patient to further psychotherapy. Although the follow-up report showed what seemed strong evidence of consolidation of his gains from the psychotherapy, this must remain an unanswered question.

This case raises other important questions. One might ask why did Brian's brother experience a psychotic episode and not his two sisters? The difference of genetic endowment, of pathways of identification, and the possibility of a transgenerational impact of parental psychopathology are starting points for pursuing this complex question. His vulnerability to hallucinatory perceptions might well have a biological basis, but, in our present state of knowledge this possibility does not seem to have any clinical significance.

We might also wonder what might have been Brian's fate if a psychoanalytic approach had been available to him twenty-five years ago. If the understanding of a comprehensive "need-adapted" approach (as elaborated by Alanen, 1997) had been available and if it had been possible to implement it at that time, an attempt to involve the family at the earliest possible moment would probably have had the highest immediate priority and the whole case would have been seen from a psychotherapeutic perspective from the beginning. It was, for Brian, a tragedy that he had lost so many years of his life, but the late arrival of effective help proved better late than never.

CHAPTER FIVE

Hysterical psychosis: "Claudia"

reud based his theoretical constructions on a series of patients
with the diagnosis of hysterical neurosis, formulated his theory
of the Oedipus complex as the core of neurotic illness, and
specified as the basis of the psychoanalytic method of treatment the
interpretation of the meaning of the patient's free associations and
repressed, immature sexual phantasies.

This work was sometimes taken as evidence that such disorders,
although disabling, could be understood without difficulty and could
be expected to respond well to psychoanalytic treatment. Subsequent
experience persuaded psychoanalysts that this was certainly not always the case. Many psychoanalysts today would reassign Freud's
hysterical patients to the contemporary diagnostic category of borderline personality disorder and consider that such patients may be very
difficult to help with the psychoanalytic method.

The term "hysteria" as a diagnostic category can refer to a very
wide range of symptoms, including states of dissociation, conversion
to bodily symptoms, phobias, amnesias, fugues, and hallucinations.
Seeing visions or hearing voices is not necessarily a sign of mental
illness, as exemplified in the experiences of some mystics, the be-

reaved, or the "imaginative" person. But when such experiences are considered to be symptoms of mental illness, they are classified as fantasies, pseudo-hallucinations, or hallucinations, and the associated irrational thinking is classed as delusional mood, overvalued ideas, or delusions.

The familiar, usually pejorative, use of the term "hysteric" in the adjectival sense of "histrionic personality" refers to people who tend to express themselves in an overdramatic and theatrical fashion, whose emotional life is intense but shallow, who are often excessively suggestible, and who are prone to day-dream and are secretly preoccupied with erotic fantasies as a substitute for mature sexual relationships. If such individuals have sufficient talent and ego strength, they may eventually achieve considerable artistic success, based on an intelligent capacity for creative imagination. If not, they may develop schizophrenic-like illness and attract such psychiatric diagnoses as "malignant hysteria", "multiple personality disorder", "somatoform conversion", and "borderline personality", or simply "schizophrenia".

The relationship between hysteria and schizophrenia is unclear. Psychiatrists have traditionally regarded them as two distinct entities that may at times be difficult to differentiate, and in recent years the term "hysteria" has been excluded from the official diagnostic and statistical manual of the American Psychiatric Association (DSM 4).

Melanie Klein believed that neurotic conditions represent attempts to work through underlying psychotic psychopathology, and other analysts, in particular Fairbairn (1952), have regarded hysterical conditions as a defence against underlying schizophrenia. Although several authors have had much to say about the complexity of hysteria (Wisdom, 1961; Zetzel, 1970), the term has very largely gone out of fashion, being widely absorbed into the class of "borderline" personality disorders. However, some contemporary psychoanalysts have shown renewed interest in hysteria, and they believe that such a change has gone too far and that a revival of interest in the psychodynamics and aetiology of hysteria is long overdue (Bell, 1992; Bollas, 2000; Brenman, 1985; Britton, 1999; Mitchell, 2000; Riesenberg-Malcolm, 1991b).

The following patient illustrates some of the difficulties involved in differentiating hysterical states from psychotic ones, the associated diagnostic and therapeutic problems, the mental mechanisms responsible for the disturbance, the impact of these on the therapist, and the way in which psychoanalytic psychotherapy may help alleviate the patient's distress and confusion. The material is presented in the spontaneous way in which it emerged in the seminar.

Claudia

Claudia was 33 years old and had been in once-weekly psychotherapy for two years when her therapist brought her case to the seminar.

History of present illness

She had been in psychiatric treatment since the age of 19 years, having become depressed during the previous year, following a disappointment in love.

She had at first been treated with antidepressive medication, but this had not helped her. One year later, she had become very disturbed and had been admitted to a psychiatric ward in an acute psychotic state, experiencing visual hallucinations of a terrifying nature, associated with delusional thinking. She spoke incoherently of her life being threatened by a black man, and she heard the voice of the Devil, who, she said, was trying to force her to kill her mother and father.

Investigation excluded the possibility that organic factors were responsible for, or contributing to, this hallucinatory psychosis. Antipsychotic medication gradually restored her contact with reality, and after some months she returned to live in her own apartment. However, she quickly relapsed and was returned to the ward. Again, her condition was stabilized by nursing care and adjustment of medication, and she was discharged. From that time, her symptoms were rarely quiescent, taking the form of episodes in which she would become acutely disturbed for days or weeks on end.

Progression to chronicity

Over the next seven years, Claudia had further periods of hospitalization of several months' duration, and a diagnosis of chronic

schizophrenia with brief remissions and some inter-episode disturbance was established. Her psychotic world continued to be dramatic,
paranoid, and delusional. Further medication and persistent attempts
at rehabilitation produced only temporary improvement.

Not only did she feel that she was constantly in danger, but she
also felt that she was dangerous, herself a potential murderer. This
feeling at times reached delusional proportions, taking the form of
obsessional fears and doubts about killing small insects and other
creatures. Seeing a dead cat in the road, she would obsessively seek
reassurance from passers-by that it was not she who had killed it, and
she felt compelled to take obsessive precautions against the risk of
killing small insects, repetitively sweeping the floor of her apartment.

Eventually, at the age of 26, she was once more admitted, but she
remained too disturbed to be discharged to life outside the ward. She
spent much of the next year withdrawn in her room in the ward,
sometimes talking about her hallucinatory experiences and delusional thoughts but making little stable therapeutic contact with the
nursing staff.

Psychotherapy offered

During periods of relative normality she was regarded by the staff
as an attractive and intelligent individual, well motivated for self-
examination, and it was eventually decided that a trial of individual
psychotherapy was justified, despite the chronic nature and severity
of her illness.

She was transferred to a ward specializing in the treatment of
young psychotic patients, where she accepted the offer by a female
psychotherapist of a weekly session of psychotherapy within the
therapeutic milieu of the ward. By the time that the psychotherapy
began, she had been severely disabled for ten years and unable to live
for more than brief periods outside a psychiatric ward.

Presentation to the seminar

The therapy had been in progress for two years when the therapist
brought the case to the seminar. She filled in some details of the
patient's personal history and went on to describe the patient's psy-

chotic experiences and her own experience of what it was like working with her.

Claudia was the first of three children, succeeded by a sister when
she was 18 months old and a brother two years later. Neither of her
siblings had any record of emotional disturbance during their development, and they had grown up to be apparently mentally healthy
and successful adults. Her mother was several years older than her
husband, who was a farmer. Although no detailed family investigations had been undertaken, their marriage seems to have been a stable
and successful one.

Near–cot-death

At the age of about 10 weeks, her mother found Claudia lying on
her face in her cot in a state of severe respiratory distress. She rushed
her to hospital where she quickly recovered and required no further
treatment. Her mother found this event so distressing that she at once
gave up full-time care of her baby and returned to full-time work,
arranging for a nanny to care for the child during the day. She subsequently explained that she had been so terrified and traumatized by
the event that she was no longer able to trust herself to look after this,
her first, baby. For unknown reasons, the nanny was twice replaced
during the next year.

When Claudia was 9 months old, her mother became pregnant
again, and late in the pregnancy she left her work and undertook the
full-time care of both Claudia and the new baby girl. In Claudia's
third year, her mother was once more pregnant and gave birth to a
boy when Claudia was 4 years old. She continued full-time maternal
care of all three children for a year thereafter before returning to
work.

Claudia's mother experienced no particular difficulty in caring for
the two younger children. Although there was no detail recorded of
Claudia's development in her first years, or of overt reaction to the
arrival of her sister, and later of her brother, the eventual emergence
in the psychotherapy of the most intense envy and jealousy of them,
especially of her brother, suggests that it may have had deep roots.
Some evidence for this may be sought in the emotional disturbance
which was reported to have begun in her fourth year, around the time
of the birth of her brother.

Early precursors of later psychosis

From about the time of the birth of her brother, she was reported to have been very afraid of the dark, running into her parents' bed at night and telling them of lurid fantasies that terrified her and prevented her sleeping. The contents of the fantasies were similar to, and in some examples identical with, those of her subsequent psychosis in early adult life. She told of her fear of being bitten by snakes which she saw coming into her room, of barrels full of blood and bits of dismembered bodies, and of a black man threatening to kill her.

This disturbance continued until the age of 6. By this time, she was regarded as a normal but sensitive and imaginative child, and, by the time of her adolescence, artistically talented and intelligent. She showed no overt disturbance during her adolescence, apart from being inexplicably afraid of a certain male teacher whom she regarded as too strict, and she developed her interests in art, music, and singing.

She left home at the age of 18 and spent much of the next year working as an au pair in a foreign country. Here she had her first serious love affair, which terminated with her feeling deeply hurt and abandoned. She returned home in a state of depression, where she sought psychiatric help and eventually deteriorated ("regressed") into a psychotic condition, as already described.

Her psychotic "attacks"

The therapist then provided details of her thinking during the hallucinatory episodes. In the early months of therapy, Claudia was sometimes relatively calm and was able to provide a detailed description of their contents. As the therapy progressed, she became more often disturbed during the sessions.

Claudia's hallucinatory experiences and accompanying thoughts were vivid and terrifying. They would begin with the experience of an "evil eye" watching her. This was the eye of a dangerous black man, whom she sometimes identified as the Devil, whose furry skin she could feel in contact with her own. This black man would tell her that she is evil and would try to persuade her to kill her mother and father and strangle the therapist. Although she believed at other times that she is not evil, in her psychotic states she was convinced that she is totally and unredeemably evil.

She wanted to believe in God, who she believes is good, but He would suddenly become evil, leaving her feeling despairing and alone. She loves the warmth of the sun, but it suddenly changes and she has to escape it before it burns and kills her. As she leaves her session, she often hears a blackbird singing, and she believes that it is evil and is threatening to kill her.

When such episodes pass, she recognizes the Devil figure as the black man of her childhood fantasies, in which he kept a prostitute imprisoned in his castle, raped and murdered her, and had barrels full of blood and the cut-up body parts of his victims.

Command hallucinations

At times, the black man-Devil would command her to kill other patients, and she would sometimes act on this command, attacking them and attempting to strangle them. She was also commanded to run from the ward and throw herself to her death in front of a passing car. At those moments, she would visualize with horror her body lying cut up in pools of blood, and she would attempt to escape from the ward and run to the nearby road where she would be found, apparently struggling with the impulse to kill herself. As will be described later, this impulsive behaviour eventually caused serious management problems for the staff, who lived with the recurring fear that she would succeed in her attempts to kill herself.

Sense of personal destructiveness— oral-cannibalistic impulses

These experiences of being in mortal danger were associated with thoughts of herself as dangerously and omnipotently destructive. Claudia claimed that she was capable of setting off an atom bomb, and for brief moments she behaved as if she believed that she had actually done so.

Not only did she believe that she had the power of nuclear destructiveness, but she imagined herself as eating anyone standing in front of her, and she would close her mouth for this reason or turn her head aside to prevent it happening. This thought was so powerful that for several months she felt compelled to eat sweets immediately before her session, or during the course of a session, and would do so.

Much later she was able to tell her therapist that she had, indeed, had an overwhelming wish to eat her therapist, and that she had come to realize that the reason for this was that she loved the therapist so much that she wanted to keep her inside forever.

These and similar thoughts, such as her dread of accidentally killing insects and animals, had some of the characteristics of intrusive obsessional fantasies and countermeasures designed to protect other living beings ("objects") from her destructiveness.

The course of the psychotherapy—first phase

At the first seminar the therapist reported her work of the first two years. She had learned much about the patient's past history and the evolution of her psychosis. She had recognized that Claudia had extremely powerful feelings of envy and jealousy. Her approach was essentially a supportive one, and although she thought that Claudia had made some progress, she felt that she was still seriously disturbed. It had not been possible to understand her bizarre hallucinations and psychotic thinking. A very warm, positive contact had developed, and the psychotic attacks had lessened in intensity and frequency.

Further developments—discharge and relapse

Claudia had cooperated well in the therapy and had become less disturbed, and after two years she had been discharged to a more open and less supervised institution. However, she quickly relapsed, and it became necessary to transfer her to a locked intensive-care ward.

Psychiatric management—the restraining belt

Here the medication was temporarily increased, and she was confined to her bed under the restraint of a fixation belt. However, the therapist was able to maintain contact by paying frequent brief visits to her throughout her stay in the closed ward. These interruptions in the course of the psychotherapy proved so disruptive to her treatment that the staff of the open ward decided to take over this restraining procedure themselves. The patient found this a considerable relief, and as she improved she took increasing responsibility for its use, requesting it when she felt in danger of losing control of her feelings of violence and deciding when she felt safe enough to leave it.

Transference crisis and disaster

Despite the fact that the patient was being seen for only forty-five minutes weekly by the therapist, and discussed in the supervisory seminar at only six-monthly intervals, the patient and the therapist never completely lost emotional contact. However, after some time a situation of impasse developed, in which progress seemed to have stopped.

At the same time, the therapist suffered a serious bereavement and found it increasingly difficult to tolerate her patient's behaviour. Over a period of several weeks, the patient deteriorated. She was transferred once more to the closed secure ward. This time the staff of the closed ward took the difficult decision to refuse the use of the fixation belt and to encourage her to take responsibility for herself. At this point, she managed to escape from the ward, threw herself under a car, and narrowly escaped death. Badly injured, she was admitted to a general hospital, where she remained for several weeks, during which the therapist once again maintained contact with her.

Discussion in the seminar

At this point the therapist discussed the case in the seminar, and it became clear that while preoccupied with her personal loss during her visits to her injured patient she had been extremely angry with Claudia's apparently life-denying behaviour but had not expressed this verbally to the patient. The consequence was that the patient had become convinced that the therapist could no longer stand her and that the therapy would soon be ended. Claudia tried to send the therapist away and refused to talk to her, but the therapist insisted that the therapy must continue, and after several visits Claudia relented.

The turning point

The therapist's insistence on continuing the therapy proved to be a turning point. The patient now felt more safe with the therapist and less afraid of her murderous fantasies of strangling her. The therapist was better able to deal with the patient's negative feelings, now expressed more openly during the session in the form of threatening to attack her, to strangle her, and to smash up the furniture of the room. These were so violent that the therapist was left in no doubt of their genuineness.

From this point onwards, Claudia made slow but steady progress. She talked more freely in the sessions about her fantasies and their associated impulses and found increasing relief in exploring their meaning with the therapist. This went on for many months, and she gradually began to accept the metaphorical meaning of many of her dramatic, often visual, images. An example may convey a little of the intensity of this process.

In many sessions, she would suddenly appear to be terrified, staring anxiously at the walls of the room. After a while, she would relax and withdraw into silence with a happy smile. Gradually she was able to tell the therapist what she had been experiencing. She had been frightened because she could see that the walls of the room were covered in holes into which screws were fixed. She was then able to withdraw her attention from this frightening scene and go into a day-dream in which she was sitting comfortably inside the dome of a mosque. With the help of her therapist, she was gradually able to recognize the symbolic nature of these visualized thoughts as sexual fantasies from which she was escaping into a day-dream of living symbiotically inside her mother's breast or (pregnant) body.

Incestuous fantasies or sexual abuse?

After some time in therapy, she began to experience fantasies of happiness, associated with masturbation. The dangerous/evil/dark sun was joined by a golden sun, and she embarked on a sexual relationship with another patient. She dressed attractively and had another brief affair with a much younger man in the town. This experience led on to her discovering incestuous feelings towards her father and a memory of having had a repulsive taste in her mouth.

Claudia talked of feelings of love for the therapist, but when she did she felt that the black man increased his power over her and this drew her more strongly to thoughts of death and murder. She slowly became more conscious of her conflicting feelings for her father. The therapist suggested ("interpreted") that although she loved her father, she had never forgiven him for creating the babies who had displaced her, thereby taking her mother out of her exclusive possession, and she had unconsciously hated him for it ever since. This made great sense to Claudia, and as she pondered over this interpretation she felt the power of the black man beginning to wane.

At this point, her negative feelings began to find expression in the transference. She began to experience the return of violent hostility towards the therapist, threatening to strangle her and accusing her of abandoning her between sessions. Although the therapist had no doubt that Claudia's rage and murderous impulses were genuine, as on previous occasions, and not consciously a dramatization, she did not now find this situation alarming. She stood her ground and did not immediately try to defuse the situation by explanations, because she felt that these were long-split-off feelings that were emerging and that Claudia might easily banish them again.

In the process of working through these ambivalent feelings in the transference, she went to see her father and screamed "I hate your penis!", and it required much attention by the staff to alleviate the parents' distress. This explosive action, however upsetting initially to the parents, helped Claudia to differentiate her incestuous fantasies about her father from reality. The experience of a repulsive taste in her mouth seemed to be the expression of memories or fantasies of fellatio, rather than of an actual event. Although in this account the possibility of there having been actual sexual abuse may seem to have had little attention, it was actually given a great deal of thought by the therapist and by the staff, who had had much contact with the parents over a long period and had formed a very positive view of the father. They thought that this was not an "incestuous" family and that it was unlikely that sexual abuse had ever occurred. Claudia herself regretted her outburst and made it clear to the therapist that she had never seriously believed that she had been sexually abused.

Termination of the therapy—outcome

By the time the therapy was terminated after eight years of once-weekly therapy, Claudia was very much improved. After some time, it had proved possible to give her control of the key of the restraining belt so that she could decide when she felt safe enough to undo it. As the therapy drew to a close, she was well enough to go on a holiday abroad with some of the staff. She took the belt with her but did not need to use it. It had now lost its significance, and she discarded it completely.

She had recovered loving feelings for her mother, from whom she had felt emotionally distant for many years, and had a more normal adult relationship with her father. She had acquired a new sense of security and confidence and a much improved capacity for relating to other people. In moments of emotional stress, she would sometimes find her imaginary preoccupations reviving, but they would quickly recede, especially when she could talk to her friends about having a vivid imagination. In this respect, these episodes had come to assume something of the form of intruding obsessional images which could be banished with little difficulty.

When Claudia came to see the therapist one year after the ending of the treatment, it was clear that her improvement had continued. She was enjoying life and being with other people, and her musical and artistic life was flourishing. She had made some male friends and was seeking more intimate relationships.

Claudia and her therapist had worked hard and long, and the therapeutic milieu had provided the support without which the therapy could never have survived. Although she has not yet achieved a fully secure capacity for autonomous functioning or psychosexual maturity, she is happy and functioning well and for three years has been living a relatively independent life in her own apartment. She has no regular medication and has access to the staff, with whom she has occasional contact.

Claudia has understood her past hallucinatory visions and associated recurrent delusional beliefs as imaginative expressions of angry and resentful feelings towards her parents and siblings that had been buried since her childhood. The important role of envy and jealousy had received much attention, and the negative transferences had been identified and, to a great extent, worked through.

Discussion

The multiple possible meanings of Claudia's self-destructiveness and the role of the "near–cot-death"

The therapist's capacity to tolerate the patient's self-destructive behaviour throughout a time of personal mourning proved to be the decisive factor in the treatment. Claudia's self-damaging behaviour and its resolution could be understood in several ways. As a form of testing out the strength of the caring staff and the therapist, Claudia thereby achieved her unconscious aim—the ultimate proof that her destructive wishes and impulses were not so omnipotently powerful that they would drive the therapist to abandon her. In this sense, the event could be considered as a transference enactment of the original "abandonment", when her frightened and guilty mother withdrew from her at the time of the near–cot-death and handed her over to a succession of carers. This repetition, which could have caused her death, had the happy consequence of liberating Claudia from the grip of the complex of internal object relations and unconscious phantasies that had remained dormant and encapsulated since infancy, and had been revived by the experience of traumatic rejection in a love relationship at the age of 19.

This "new beginning" (Balint, 1968), although extremely dramatic, did not take the form of an instant, Damascus-style, conversion, or relief by exorcism from demonic possession. It was followed by a long period leading up to the termination of the psychotherapy, during which separations aroused the experience of hallucinatory voices commanding her to kill herself, as a proof that she was strong and, by implication, not dependent on the therapist/mother for her life.

These reactions might be compared with the history of her first year of life, where her mother's abandonment helped to force her into a pseudo-independent attitude. This development was accompanied by an unstable sense of self and a vulnerability to identifying with the "bad" (departing) mother under the specific stress of separation from primary caring figures—the parents, staff, and therapist.

As a dramatic expression of the explosive murderous aggressiveness towards the "bad" mother/therapist and jealousy of rival siblings, Claudia's suicidal behaviour can be considered as the expression of an identification with the bad mother. This was an act of "aggression turned against the self", of murderousness converted into apparent suicide, in a drama that very nearly proved fatal.

A further and most important possible motivation for creating the drama concerns the transference and countertransference. If the original trauma at the age of 10 weeks provoked a primitive fear of dying, reinforced by the immediate departure of her mother and subsequent losses during her first year, this might have persisted in the form of "memories in feeling" (Klein) or "nameless dread" (Bion, 1967, p. 116). There was no record of her becoming at all disturbed in response to the birth of her sister at 18 months, but following the birth of her brother at the age of 4 years she began to experience fear of the dark and lurid fantasies. As far as it was possible to ascertain, these fantasies were similar in content to those associated with her later hysterical attacks/psychotic episodes during her eventual hysterical/ schizophrenic psychosis.

It was such links with present and past that led Freud to comment that the hysteric suffers from reminiscences (1895d, p. 17). Claudia's "reminiscences" were the dramatic symbolic expression of her timeless inner world, populated by persecuting imaginary figures (internal objects), dramas that episodically had assumed delusional conviction.

The themes of her dream-like dramas concerned her imminent danger of being murdered by a black man, sometimes felt to be the Devil, who also murdered prostitutes, cutting up their bodies and storing the dismembered parts in containers. At the same time, Claudia also felt herself to be dangerous, as witness her obsessive search for reassurance that she had not killed the dead cat she saw in the road. Her wish not to be a murderer found expression in her concern for the safety of her endangered objects, leading her to obsessive sweeping of the floor of her apartment as a precaution against crushing insects underfoot. We have already met, in Chapters 2 and 3, other examples of this obsessive precaution, where Freud's view of the likely symbolic meaning of the insects or vermin as unwanted siblings has been mentioned.

Reflections on the symbolic meanings
of dream and hallucinatory expressions

The triadic oedipal dynamic centred on the image of the father's penis (the snakes) which had caused the unwelcome pregnancies, containing by projection her own "evil" wishes. The confusion between love and hatred finds expression in the experience that her loving God suddenly becomes evil, and the warmth of the sun suddenly changes into a destructive fire. This was reflected in the transference where her feelings of love for the therapist were immediately followed by increased activity by the destructive Devil.

It is a characteristic of destructive infantile envy that the good object is hated because it is not the possession of the subject, and because it is good, not bad (Joseph, 1986). In this sense, envy, as a dyadic process, is more primitive than triadic jealousy. Claudia's envy of her therapist and rivalry with other sibling/patients emerged clearly and were an essential part of the therapist's interpretative activities.

A search for understanding the genesis of these dangerous inner images and processes can be sought by considering the way that early, primitive, mechanisms of defence have structured her inner world and populated it with persecuting figures. These mechanisms have enabled her to survive the destructive emotions and impulses generated by the enforced separation from her mother during her preverbal (and "pre-oedipal") phase of development where she was maximally dependent on caring parental figures. The oral and anal symbolism of teeth, bombs, blackness, and rape can account for some of the imagery. Recognition of the logic of "primary-process" thinking, dominated by displacement, condensation, and symbolic expression, can help explain the construction of her frightening hallucinations. Siblings are represented by vermin, her "promiscuous" (oedipal) mother as dismembered prostitutes, the black rapist as a father image containing her own destructive infantile invasive wishes.

The failure of containment [see Glossary] in the mother–infant dyad (Bion's "maternal alpha function") has led to the continuation of projection into non-human containing images, as in the barrel full of blood and dismembered bodies. The container is itself contained, in that the Devil/father owns a castle, which contains the barrels that contain the dismembered body parts (see Appendix A). The image of the father's penis, represented by the snakes, contains her own biting teeth. The meanings of other hallucinatory or illusional expressions could be considered in the same way. When she leaves the session, the destructive feelings mobilized by the separation threaten to become conscious, so she (unconsciously) projects them into the singing blackbird outside the room, which then becomes a sinister persecutor, an agent of the Devil/black man.

In a theoretically ideal process of psychotherapy, these conglomerate images/objects would be eventually disentangled, with the acquisition of normal assertiveness, proper use of the mouth and vagina, and the capacity to welcome a "good" penis. Although the expression of these processes takes the concrete form of imagery of parts of the body, it is their function that is the object of the therapeutic work.

Such a disentanglement could then be described as finding the normal penis, mouth, vagina, eyes, and other sense organs for the first time, and the therapy as an attempt to—"render unto Caesar the things that are Caesar's . . ." (Rey, 1994).

These conglomerate images can be understood as symbolic equations (Segal, 1981c), and it is the concrete and spatial nature of their interactions that require the spatial connotations of such terms as "projection into . . .", "a penis that is a snake containing biting teeth", and so on. Other functions appropriate to the thoughts seeking expression, such as of poisoning or strangling, would require the selection of a snake with these specific qualities.

What is the relevance of such "part-object" thinking?

Attempts to "decipher" the symbolic content of the patient's psychotic thinking in these "part-object" terms can help reveal the nature of the patient's preoccupations and impulse/defence conflicts The foregoing exploration of the meanings of psychotic imagery raises the question of its relevance for the therapeutic process. It also raises the question of what use the therapist made of the new knowledge arising from the seminar discussion, a subject that we will return to later.

The therapist felt that the seminar discussions had helped her escape from what was in some ways a very long-standing impasse. She had realized that the patient was idealizing her in the transference and was defending against negative feelings, but the discussions gave her the confidence and courage to begin to interpret this to the patient and to confront and successfully work through the upheavals that followed, of which Claudia's self-damaging suicidal behaviour was the most momentous.

Claudia's case illustrates the serious problems that may confront the caring staff with such patients, who soon earn the diagnosis of malignant hysteria, hysterical psychosis, or schizophrenia. The ingenious, though controversial, use of mechanical restraint proved to be successful in helping Claudia along the path to self-restraint because it was implemented as an adjunct to the psychotherapy, which was focused on understanding why it was necessary.

The function of the fixation belt is not entirely clear. At a simple level, it offered her a direct, non-chemical restraint for her murderous impulses, freely available and under her own control, for use until she was eventually able to take responsibility for herself. Insofar as it might have reminded her of absent therapist, it could be considered as a "transitional object" (Winnicott, 1958).

However, restraint is not containment, and in retrospect it might be considered that the repetitiveness of Claudia's self-destructive behaviour might have had an unrecognized transference and countertransference significance. If it were true that ever since the "cot-death" episode she had had a powerful unconscious fear of death, it is possible that she was trying to evoke this fear in caring figures as a form of communication in countertransference form, arousing in them the dread that she was about to die. If such a process is not recognized, as Rosenfeld (1987) has shown, it may lead to an impasse or to an escalation of the behaviour, as if the patient were trying to say, *"What have I got to do to get through to you!"*

The part played by the mother in establishing a vulnerability to subsequent hysterical illness is uncertain. Some psychoanalysts consider that exposure of the child to a mother who herself has dramatizing tendencies may make it difficult for the child to move from the experience of concrete image and action into the realm of normal imagination and verbal thought—in Lacanian terms, to move from imaginary to symbolic function. This difficulty may be compounded if the relationship with the father fails to help her free herself from the identification with the mother.

Brenman (1985) considered the possible influence of the mother of the hysterical patient on her daughter's eventual disturbance. He suggested that a mother with a tendency to being overwhelmed by anxieties may convey a sense of catastrophe to her baby, and instead of containing and transforming the baby's fear of death into manageable form may thereby communicate back to the baby that the fear is unbearable. This "hysterogenic" dynamic may generate in her infant a hysterical character marked by a persistent fear of death and a vulnerability to overwhelming anxiety.

Whether or not this view is correct, it is interesting to note that Claudia's siblings showed no evidence of hysterical personality characteristics, nor was there any evidence that Claudia's mother had these characteristics. It is tempting to conclude that it was the overwhelming fright of the "near–cot-death" incident that led an otherwise normal mother to "abandon" this particular baby, leaving

Claudia with an untransformed fear of death (Bion's "nameless dread") which marked her dyadic pre-oedipal development and, in epigenetic fashion, was transferred to her subsequent triadic oedipal phase.

The attempt to make a love relationship in her adolescence released the encapsulated destructive feelings and accompanying depressive feelings and catastrophic anxieties and mobilized the immature defences of splitting and projection. This led to her being plunged into a confused nightmare-like drama of love and hate, of envy and jealousy, and ultimately of life and death.

By identification, she enacted symbolically the role of both parents (as mother being the victim of her own envious feelings, as father being the jealous destroyer), projecting her "excluded onlooker" self (the "evil eye") into the split internal object/images of God and the Devil. Her unconscious incestuous sexuality could be understood as a failure to renounce her ("symbiotic") infantile wishes to re-occupy the "containing" space of the maternal body (as symbolized by the fantasy of the mosque), and the subsequent transfer of her oral wishes for the maternal breast and nipple to the paternal penis.

Since the practice of fellatio has become socially recognized as a normal form of sexual forepleasure, the determining of its role in cases of child abuse has assumed great importance. The differentiation of memory from fantasy in this sphere may be difficult or impossible, as the "recovered-memory" controversy illustrates. "Part-object" theory, as outlined above, can help to illuminate the pathological instances in which early oral conflicts carry over to later developmental levels, creating a "nipple/penis confusion". A comparable dynamic may be active in eating disorders, as we shall see in the next chapter.

Conclusions

Hysteria or schizophrenia?

The case of Claudia illustrates the difficulty presented in assigning a diagnosis to such a psychotic illness. We have already considered some of the usefulness of the term "hysteria". The same might be true of the term "schizophrenia syndrome", despite its unsatisfactory nosological status, because, from a psychiatric point of view, there is no viable alternative (Murray, 1979).

The psychiatric classification of histrionic personality disorder (DSM 4) specifies such defining criteria as excessive emotionality and attention-seeking behaviour beginning in early adulthood, associated with self-dramatization, theatricality, and exaggerated expression of emotion. By contrast, psychoanalysis is more concerned with psychological processes than with specific disorders (Bateman & Holmes, 1995, p. 213), seeking to explain the meaning and origins of such traits of character, and dramatic productions, and why they have become necessary for the individual's mental economy. At least some "hysterics" have good reasons for their behaviour, and they need to find the attention that they seek and to be helped to understand and contain their emotions, which may certainly not be "excessive" in terms of their inner experience, as in the case of Claudia.

Some psychiatrists might classify Claudia's disorder as "psychotic disorder, not otherwise specified (n.o.s.)", others would elect for "schizophrenia", yet others might retain the outmoded term "hysterical psychosis". Like "schizophrenia", the term "hysteria" is so saturated with prejudice and preconceptions that it may be important to take into account the perspective of the user.

From a psychodynamic perspective, Claudia could be considered to have suffered from an episodic regressive psychosis of schizophreniform type, but one that did not have the depth of developmental pathology nor the biological vulnerability required to produce the more fragmented states of prototypical schizophrenia. Although a biologically determined perceptual instability might possibly have contributed to the disorder, it seems more likely that it was the early psychologically traumatic experience and its repercussions that determined her ultimate fate.

The dramatizations, phobias, convulsions, conversions, and amnesias of "hysteria" so familiar to psychiatrists, and so profoundly illuminated by Freud, cannot be easily subsumed under a simple diagnostic label, despite attempts to refine the diagnosis. This may be some merit in the term "hysterical psychosis", and attempts to eliminate it and the term "hysteria" may never prove entirely successful. The term "hysteria", as Lewis (1975) observed, will long outlive its obituarists. The same may prove to be true of the term "schizophrenia".

CHAPTER SIX

Anorexia, psychosis,
and the question of sexual abuse:
"Dorothy"

D isturbance of eating is a common symptom associated with a wide spectrum of psychopathology. At one end, it merges with normal food preferences which may be motivated by ethical and other psychologically mature considerations. At the other end, it may be a symptom of severe depression, or of a delusional belief that food is poisoned. These latter typical psychotic expressions are readily identifiable, as are the common transitory and non-psychotic preoccupations of adolescent girls and, much less commonly, of boys.

In between the extremes are found the disturbances classified as anorexia nervosa and bulimia nervosa, where the psychopathology is serious and treatment difficult. These disorders may display hysterical and obsessional characteristics, perceptual disorders in the form of voices, pseudo-hallucinations (where insight is retained), hallucinations, delusional mood, delusions, and frank psychotic disorder. Sexual abuse, real or imagined, is a frequent theme.

The concepts of unconscious phantasy and part-object relations provide conceptual keys to the understanding of the meaning, origins and significance of these disorders. They can help explain the psychotic potential of some patients with severe anorexia nervosa and the transition to a state of overt psychosis in others, as in the following patient.

Dorothy

Dorothy, aged 18 years, had just begun university education when she first sought psychiatric help for depression. Her case was brought to the seminar when, at the age of 23, she had been treated in a psychiatric ward for two years. She did not respond to the antidepressive medication that was prescribed, and she was unable or unwilling to talk openly about herself to the psychologist who tried to explore her emotional difficulties. Although she was noticed to be very thin, she talked only about depression and made no reference to her severe eating conflicts or her associated hallucinatory experiences, because, as she later told her psychotherapist, it was easier than talking about food.

However, her hidden eating inhibition rapidly increased, and she was soon admitted to a psychiatric ward in a state of severe emaciation. The diagnosis of anorexia nervosa was made, and she was treated along conventional lines, with medication, supervised feeding routines, and personal supportive contact. Under this regime her electrolyte balance returned to normal and she gained a little weight, but her mental state deteriorated. It slowly became apparent that her grasp on reality was fragile, and that she was preoccupied with a bizarre fantasy life and episodic hallucinatory perceptions and delusional thinking. She began to speak in a confused way about being spied on by a video camera and of voices commanding her to kill herself. After six months, the admission diagnosis of anorexia nervosa was changed to schizophrenia when the extent of her psychotic states of mind became evident, and she was transferred to a ward where the staff had special experience of young psychotic patients.

First period of psychodynamic treatment

On the ward she consistently refused to participate in any group activity, and although she spoke freely with her assigned personal nurse she insisted on exclusively individual relations with all other staff members as well. For the first six months, her eating was intensely supervised by a special nurse in a room apart from other patients, and she regained a reasonably normal weight, although her menstruation, which had long been suppressed, did not return. On a treatment regime that included minor neuroleptic medication, supportive contact with a psychiatrist, and art work conducted by an occupational therapist, her mental state greatly improved.

Art work

The art work took the form of regular sessions of free painting and drawing, sometimes in the presence of the occupational therapist, and it was clearly important to Dorothy. She slowly gained the confidence to be able to paint freely and dramatically and had begun to talk to the occupational therapist about the pictures that she was creating. These were mainly abstract expressions of violence (usually painted in red), destruction (pictures of shattering and disintegration), depression (black), and hope (yellow and green). Other crudely but powerfully executed themes depicted the separating and violent breaking apart of various elements, and primitive monsters and volcanic eruptions.

Dorothy pursued this activity with a good deal of anxiety, but it gave her some sense of satisfaction and temporary relief from her usual state of tension. It quickly became clear that she had a vivid dream life, and she began to paint her dreams. A frequent theme was of frightening black shapes and of a mouth with huge teeth which she said that she feared might eat her.

The occupational therapist, who had no formal training in art therapy, refrained from suggesting possible meanings of the emerging themes and made no formal psychotherapeutic attempt to explore them and their personal symbolic significance. She simply listened to Dorothy's talk about the themes, recognizing the relief that the patient was finding in having someone trustworthy to be with her, as a mother might to a small child with night terrors.

Dorothy gradually became able to eat a little with the other patients, but only with considerable anxiety, sitting alongside one of her special nurses. Her progress was punctuated by recurring psychotic episodes of hallucinated voices urging her to kill herself, and the belief in being spied on which necessitated transfer to a closed

ward for a few days, where adjustment of medication and reassuring
support quickly relieved her.

Discharge, suicide attempt, relapse

After two years of this supportive and rehabilitative regime,
Dorothy was deemed sufficiently stable to be discharged to continue
treatment as an outpatient. She returned to resume her university
training. For a few weeks she seemed to be coping well enough, but
she then suddenly made a serious suicide attempt. She was readmitted to the ward, where the treatment plan was reviewed, and she was
referred to the seminar for a psychoanalytic opinion.

Discussion in the seminar

The purpose of the referral was to clarify the psychopathology of her
illness and to determine whether she might be suitable for individual
psychotherapy of a more intensive and exploratory nature. An experienced psychotherapist who was prepared to consider offering her
regular psychotherapy sessions attended the event.

It was clear that although the treatment had helped her recover a
measure of stability, it had not identified or resolved the dangerous
pathological core of her disorder. The modalities of milieu support
and low-dose neuroleptic medication had reduced her level of anxiety to such an extent that the plan to leave hospital and to resume her
university studies had seemed a realistic one. Although this might
have proved sufficient for a less disturbed individual, it proved insufficient for her.

Dorothy had gained a certain amount of understanding of her
disorder, as being the consequence of childhood problems carried
over into her adult life. However, what insight that she had gained
was, as is often the case with intelligent anorexic patients, largely
intellectual and thus of little use to her when she was confronted with
the disturbing emotional immediacy of her inner world. The art work
had helped her to give graphic expression to her inner world but had
not gone far enough. Powerful conflicts had found graphic expression
but had not been sufficiently understood nor emotionally worked
through.

The psychotherapy begins—more history emerges

Six months later the psychotherapist presented the case again, recapitulating the history in the light of more information that had emerged in this first stage of therapy, and reporting the progress and process of the therapy in some detail. She continued reporting at six-monthly intervals until the termination of the therapy two years later.

Developmental history—family dysfunction

Dorothy is the first child of a middle-class couple and has a sister ten years younger. She was an accidental pregnancy and unwanted baby, an event that forced her mother into an unwanted marriage. Her mother's relation to the maternal grandmother was a troubled one. Eventually it emerged that there had been much conflict and unhappiness in both Dorothy's parents' and grandparents' generation. Dorothy's mother was the eldest of two sisters and had often told Dorothy how the maternal grandmother had preferred this younger sister, who was actually her mother's half-sister. Dorothy's mother had never known the biological grandfather and had been brought up by Dorothy's grandmother, who had herself been pregnant in mid-adolescence.

Her parents' relationship was a complicated and troubled one. Although well-meaning and supportive towards her in the period of her illness, they proved unwilling to cooperate in any investigation of family relationships or to provide any detailed account of Dorothy's early development, for reasons that became understandable only later.

Social isolation—anxiety and unhappiness

Dorothy was an intelligent child, learning to read very early, but was isolated and lonely at school. Outside class hours she was the target of teasing and bullying by her schoolmates, and she frequently escaped by seeking refuge for long periods in the school toilets. She became very attached to her maternal grandmother, the only person in whose love she felt she could trust, and was deeply upset at the age of 14 when this beloved figure died.

She finished primary school successfully and went on to high school, where she continued her studious but isolated and unhappy existence throughout her adolescence. In classes, she survived by being clever, doing her homework well, and pursuing an interest in music and singing, at which she had some talent. She sought solace in a private life of day-dream, an imaginative activity that played an important part in the subsequent evolution of her psychosis. When she graduated from high school, she decided to become a schoolteacher and entered university, where she found no difficulty with the intellectual requirements. However, her social inhibitions continued, increasing her sense of isolation and ushering in the depression and anorexia for which she sought help and which spelled the end of her university career.

Rejection of feminine body

She hated her feminine body and had controlled her developing bodily shape by restricting her food intake from the beginning of puberty. She later told the therapist that she actually wished to remain at the age of 10 (the year of her sister's birth), and to have none of the bodily signs of puberty. Her eating behaviour seems to have been disturbed long before her entry into university. From the age of 13, she had insisted in eating all her meals in her own room. It was accepted that she was extremely thin, but no one seemed to be concerned about her episodic vegetarianism and eating habits. Her menarche was delayed, was scanty and irregular during adolescence, and finally ceased, not returning until late in the subsequent psychotherapy.

Dorothy's account of her inner world

During her first two years of hospital treatment she had come to trust the staff sufficiently to be able to speak in some detail about her personal life, but it was not until she was securely engaged in individual psychotherapy that she was able to divulge details of her most disturbing hallucinations and their personal significance.

Vivid early memories

Dorothy gradually began to speak freely about her childhood. Her earliest memory was of being left alone lying on a carpet, calling for her mother who did not come. She had been aware of this memory ever since her childhood. It was accompanied by an intensely distressing feeling of abandonment and helplessness, and she was certain that the event happened before the age of 3 years, because she visualized it as taking place in the house where she was born, from which the family moved when she was 3 years old.

Rage in the mouth

The next memory, from about the age of 4, was of being shut up alone in her room as punishment for outbursts of rage against her mother. She remembers vividly the feeling of loneliness and being told by her mother that she must swallow her anger. This memory was an intensely physical feeling, coupled with a hallucinatory vividness in which she experienced her rage having to be swallowed in the form of a slimy green object. It was about this time that her mother told her that she bitterly regretted having become pregnant with Dorothy and that, if she had not, she would never have stayed together with father. Hearing this story, Dorothy felt completely unwanted, and it was from that time that she felt it her duty to keep the parents together.

Memories of sexual abuse

Dorothy often visited her paternal grandparents during the daytime, when her parents were at work. She liked these occasions, because very often her grandfather would take a nap after lunch, taking Dorothy into bed with him and reading her stories from children's books. Her memory of these happy occasions was painfully interrupted later in her adolescence when, at a family party, she became acutely anxious when her grandfather arrived and she suddenly remembered that during these pleasant interludes he had often undressed her and caressed her body.

In her subsequent psychotic episodes, she had moments of feeling very ugly and filled with shame, having a painful feeling of big hands placed all over her body, and of being unable to push them away. The memory she found most difficult to divulge to the therapist was of her grandfather on one occasion inserting his penis into her mouth, a memory that filled her with shame and disgust. It is important to note that these memories were apparently conscious, but suppressed, when she began the psychotherapy, rather than having been "recovered" during its course, a feature providing some evidence for her account being substantially true.

Dorothy feared that if she were ever to lose control of her violent hatred of her mother, or to speak openly about her paternal grandfather's sexual intrusiveness, the family would disintegrate.

The comforts of fantasy—the imaginary companion

At about the age of 7, Dorothy created a fantasy of a cocoon made of silver threads. It was always there for her to withdraw into, and sitting inside it she felt calm and safe. After she had created the imaginary cocoon, she invented a companion to protect her in school, naming her Doris. This companion was a bright, strong person, confident and universally popular.

Dorothy had always been frightened of the dark, in dread that a monster would appear under her bed. In creating Doris, she now had a protector whom she could import into her bed, and her fears diminished. To make Doris more real, she persuaded her mother to draw her own (Dorothy's) outline, while she was lying on the floor, on a big piece of paper which she then fixed to the wall of her bedroom, thereby reinforcing her wishful belief in Doris's constant presence. She did not tell her mother the real purpose and importance of this procedure.

The good companion becomes bad

At about the age of 10, during the course of her mother's pregnancy, she began to realize that Doris was becoming "evil" and was escaping from her control. She found herself locked in a struggle with this malevolent figure, who she felt was trying to force herself into Dorothy's body in an attempt to take control of her. Sometimes at night Doris would even make an alliance with the monster under the bed in order to scare and control Dorothy. The only safe place then was the space of the hallucinated cocoon, which Dorothy could usually manage to get into, although often with great difficulty.

Sibling jealousy, voices, and the undermining of reality

Dorothy was on the threshold of puberty when her mother became pregnant. She had been an only child until her sister was born when she was 10 years old, and she developed violently hostile feelings towards the intruder. As she struggled to control her aggressive impulses towards the baby, Dorothy found support in the form of voices that reassured her that she was strong and able to control her feelings. From that time onwards, she was convinced that the video camera and the "eye of God" had the power to observe her angry thoughts, and she believed that the voices were real.

Hallucinatory voices command her death, and she obeys

It was not until the ending of the first period of treatment in the ward that the voices had assumed a life-threatening form, and that she had made the suicide attempt. As already mentioned, she had been discharged from the ward, in an apparently stable state of mind, and was looking forward to resuming her training to become a teacher, when in a "get-together" exercise she was placed in the middle of a group of students and required to talk about herself. Suddenly she felt as if she were 8 years old, back in her old school class with the hidden camera spying on her. At this point, the voices commanded her to kill herself. She returned to her apartment, took a large drug overdose, and survived only because of being accidentally discovered.

Her psychotic world

As soon as her psychotherapy began, Dorothy described the deathly quality of her hallucinatory experiences. She explained that there was an evil eye in the sky belonging to "them", who were in control of a video camera placed in the room where she was. Sometimes she could see them, sometimes she could only feel them. Their purpose was to control and report any angry or negative thoughts, which were forbidden. She did not know who "they" were, but she could identify the voices as female.

These voices commanded her to be strong, telling her that she was not ill, that she must commit suicide, and that if she could not do this she would be a contemptible coward. At these times, she felt herself to be the "centre of the world", the only human being alive, the evil eye having changed all other people into robots. These robot-people were all totally devoid of feelings, and so they could not get emotionally close to her. As a consequence of being the only person in the world, she had all the responsibility for them. She had some sense of control over the robots and believed that if she lost this power the world would fall into pieces, and she would have to try to rebuild it all by herself.

Obsessions

During her adolescence she had developed obsessional patterns of thought and behaviour which served her in her struggle for self-control. These took various forms. When her level of anxiety would rise, she would try to distract her attention from the frightening voices and spying camera by silent spelling in a special way. She would begin by imagining a random series of numbers. These would then change into the group 2 2 2, at which point her anxiety would increase. She then would struggle to change them into 1 1 1, and if she succeeded her anxiety level would drop and she would become calm again. She had had a similar ritual using letters and visualizing her own writing, which had a sloping style. If in her imagination her writing began to lie flat on the line, she would struggle to bring it to an upright posture and to achieve thin, vertical, upright letters. Success in doing this would bring a similar sense of temporary relief from anxiety.

Another obsessional pattern was seen in her counting the seconds as she approached the red light of a pedestrian crossing, and regulating the pace of her walking so that she should arrive at the light at exactly the time it turned green. This served the purpose of escaping the situation of having to wait, with the fear that she would be responsible for a traffic accident.

Eating inhibitions—oral-cannibalistic fantasies

The investigation of Dorothy's eating inhibitions revealed powerful unconscious cannibalistic fantasies and omnipotent magical thinking, amounting at times of stress to delusion. She had been an inconsistent vegetarian since early adolescence, but for as long as she can remember she had felt, at times of stress, that to eat was destructive. As she began to make progress in the therapy, she told the therapist that at such times she had believed that if she ate some people would die, and if she starved they would survive. At such times, she would be frightened at the prospect of eating meal, although when less anxious she was sometimes able to do so.

The cannibalistic monster invades her inner space
and tries to steal her identity

At these times, she felt oppressed by the presence of the "monster" who had been a resident in her mind since the time of her early childhood fear of the dark. This monster threatened to get inside her body and to take over her identity, so that she would herself become the monster. She felt that it was the monster who was eating both the food that she swallows and her insides. This was clearly not a metaphorical expression of recognizing some quality she felt to be monstrous in her self, but a literal, though transient, belief of a dangerous object invading her body and taking over her identity.

Progress in the psychotherapy

The first six months of psychotherapy were stormy, marked by sudden eruptions of hallucinatory commands to kill herself, which necessitated a temporary increase in medication, intensive supervision on the ward, or transfer to a locked ward for a few days.

Transference and countertransference

Dorothy made a quick and very positive attachment to the therapist, who developed warm and protective feelings towards her. The recurring psychotic outbursts disturbed and puzzled the therapist until she began to realize that they were often precipitated by unplanned breaks in the routine of sessions, during which Dorothy was forced to wait for the therapist and to share her with other patients. At this point, the patient remembered a frightening dream that she had had immediately before the suicide episode some months previously:

She is looking at a flyover-type bridge for carrying traffic over a slummy
and dilapidated part of a town. She realizes with dismay that the bridge is

*made of metal sections and that they are being held together by the power
of her own mental effort, which if it failed would lead to the collapse of the
bridge.*

This dream suggests that immediately before the suicide bid she had
had a degree of awareness of the danger that lay ahead and that she
was struggling desperately to maintain her denial of the time-related
feelings of waiting, sharing, and jealousy which were provoked by
the unplanned breaks in the routine of therapy (symbolized in the
dream by her repeated bridging over the gap). With great mental
effort, she links the sessions together to prove that no separation has
taken place. The defence against these negative feelings had up till
this point been confined to her refusal to share the dining-room where
the other patients ate.

*Idealization of the therapist breaks down —
the negative transference*

The idealizing ("all-good") transference to the therapist was
clarified in the seminar discussion, and as a consequence the therapist gradually succeeded in bringing negative transference material
into the open. During the following six months, the therapy entered a
new and dramatic phase, characterized by the emergence of violently
aggressive feelings and murderous impulses towards the therapist.
Dorothy was assailed by impulses to attack the therapist physically,
but she managed to confine the expression of her feelings of rage and
hatred to words. The therapist felt confident that she was now reaching a better understanding of what was going on between her and the
patient. She felt that the violence being expressed was entirely authentic and represented the emergence in the transference of long-
controlled feelings of hatred towards her mother and grandfather.
The therapist did not feel seriously threatened, so was able to avoid
defending herself by premature explanations, thus allowing the patient to work through the feelings.

*Progress — dismantling of defences
and establishing the capacity to doubt*

Over the next twelve months, the power of the voices began to
recede and Dorothy developed an increasing capacity to resist their

commands. Her delusional preoccupation with the spying video cameras decreased and eventually returned only briefly when under emotional stress. Her reality sense strengthened under the influence of the therapist's consistent acceptance of Dorothy's rage and searching for its meaning without explaining it away prematurely. Dorothy eventually said to the therapist: "The camera used to be the truth for me, but now it is only very occasionally so, at times when I am most anxious."

It took a long time before she was able to believe that other people could not hear the voices, which she had always firmly located outside her head. She recalled that she had often believed that the therapist could read her thoughts, and she felt in constant danger that this would cause the therapist to be so disgusted that she would reject her. So strong had Dorothy's delusional convictions been, and so deep her lack of trust, that she used to be furious at the staff, whom she felt were pretending neither to hear the voices nor to believe in the reality of the spying video camera.

Working towards termination—the beginning of mourning

After two and a half years of psychotherapy, the therapist proposed to Dorothy that it should be possible to end the individual therapy in twelve months' time, and to consider the option of a subsequent period of group therapy with the support of the milieu staff if necessary. This suggestion released an outburst of indignant fury at the therapist for giving Dorothy what she felt was such a short time to work towards termination. However, she soon became reconciled to the idea and began to face her feelings of the coming loss of the therapist. Alongside this, she began to mourn for all the many other things she had lost as the result of the emotional deprivations and misfortunes of her childhood and the isolating consequences of her illness.

Robots—Dorothy's frozen feelings

The therapist felt increasingly often in deep emotional contact with Dorothy, a state that was punctuated nonetheless by moments in which she felt completely out of touch. She came to suspect that her experience might be the expression of a countertransference process in which she was responding to the projection of a part of Dorothy previously projected into other people, whom she then had experienced as robots, as described earlier, completely without feeling. Dorothy had stifled her own capacity for loving warm feelings, and the warmth offered by the therapist/mother, for a very long time, and it was she who was the mechanical robot, a state she ascribed to others. Her statement that she lived in a world of robots was clearly a metaphorical one, but she behaved as though she believed it to be true. As she worked through her feelings of anger, she began to show genuine emotional warmth towards the therapist, but punctuated by periods of withdrawal.

As her rage with the therapist/mother began to emerge, the fear of losing control over her unfeeling robot state found expression in the dream of the bridge. At first she expressed this literally—if she loses her power of control over the robots, the world will fall to pieces and she will have to try to rebuild it all without help. When the thoughts assume dream form, their several possible meanings become more clear. She must keep the family together (whose union she has unconsciously attacked) and keep herself free of feelings lest her rage lead to her mother disintegrating, and her therapist hating and abandoning her.

The therapist reported: "I have a very odd feeling in therapy when I am made a robot. I recognize it, when Dorothy becomes mentally and emotionally distant."

As the termination phase began, the therapist reported once more:

"Some weeks ago Dorothy told me that she was beginning to think it might be possible for her to end the therapy. She feels that the world has somehow changed in recent months. The video camera has disappeared, and instead, there have been good spirits around her, especially when she is alone at night. She is joining in personal contacts more and more, trying to learn to stay with them, and is beginning to have feelings of warmth and enjoyment. A year ago she moved into an apartment of her own. It is a special building in the town, where nine young psychiatric patients live in separate flats, having some community life, but also with the possibility of being alone. It has been a difficult but important separation process from her parents. She has used a lot of time in sessions talking about her feelings in relation to that."

The depressive position — emergence of reparative feelings

Her eating behaviour slowly returned to normal, her weight reached a normal level and her long-suppressed menstruation returned, albeit irregularly, and her medication was reduced to a minimum. She returned to developing her artistic interests, reconciled to the fact that she would never become the famous opera diva that she had once hoped to be, but now with the belief that she might be capable of training as a teacher.

Her relationship with her parents and her sister improved, and she began to consider what deprivations her mother might have experienced in her own childhood. Dorothy gradually concluded that she had to some extent treated them unjustly in her mind, and that the traumatic memory of her mother's revelation that she had not wanted the pregnancy had damaged her capacity to appreciate her mother's real care and affection for her. She felt that despite the reality of her own suffering and deprivations, she knew that they had done their best in a situation in which she may have been difficult to help and a cause of concern for them.

She felt that she had come to terms with the sexual abuse, which she regarded as having been extremely disturbing, but as not the main factor in causing her illness. She eventually met her paternal grandfather at a family social event and was able to speak to him in a calm but superficial manner. She maintained her view that it was essential to the family that they should keep their secrets and that any exploration or confrontation on her part might have devastating effects.

She accepted that she might find group therapy helpful in the future, and she had enough insight to understand why she did not relish the prospect.

The voices recede — hallucination becomes imagination

Her psychotic preoccupations did not completely disappear but gradually receded into the background, so that she might not be aware of them for days on end. During the termination period she would sometimes faintly perceive the voices, but more as a memory of the past, and when this happened it helped her realize that she was in a state of stress, and this helped her to turn her attention to deal with what was worrying her.

She had now acquired a very much firmer sense of differentiating events belonging to the inner world of her own mind from happenings in the outside world. She was able to understand her hallucinations as imaginative fantasies returning occasionally under stress. She now recognized the fantasies as being meaningful imaginative events within her own mind. This was dramatically illustrated when she arrived at a session in state of excitement, telling the therapist of a discovery she had made that morning. Being moderately myopic, she needed to wear contact lenses, which she removed overnight. That morning on waking she had seen a row of spiders walking along the far wall of her room. She suddenly realized that she was not wearing her contact lenses, that she could not have seen anything clearly at that distance, and that this was a hallucination, perhaps connected with a dream which she had not remembered, or with some feeling that she had had on waking.

The therapy ends

The therapy ended at the agreed time, without further upheavals and on a note of sadness. Under other circumstances, the therapy might have continued for a further period, with the aim of a fuller resolution of her sexual conflicts, acceptance of her feminine body, and a deeper understanding of her mind. However, ideal treatment goals must accommodate to life goals, and Dorothy seems to have sufficient insight and sufficient available long-term support to negotiate the ending and continue her development.

Some months after ending the three and a half years of psychotherapy, the therapist met Dorothy again and found her functioning well and beginning to become involved in the group therapy.

The future

Dorothy is now better equipped to deal with future stress and is less likely to regress into psychotic solutions. How much progress she will make in group therapy, and whether she will seek out further individual psychotherapy at some future date remains to be seen. Her problems have not been fully resolved, and she may have some way to go before she can achieve a reliable and secure sense of personal autonomy and independence. However, although she remains a vulnerable personality, any serious return of her past psychosis seems unlikely. Even if she were to encounter life stress sufficiently specific and severe to produce a regressive reactivation of any residual psychotic processes, she has sufficient insight to seek help from the professionals and, hopefully, from her family, who now understand her sufficiently to act therapeutically towards her.

Discussion

The causes of Dorothy's psychosis and the nature of the helpful psychotherapy may not be difficult to understand. It is the tale of a sensitive and imaginative child who has felt profoundly rejected and unwanted. Her mother, herself having experienced emotional deprivation in her own childhood and having felt forced into an unwelcome marriage by an undesired pregnancy, was unable to help her infant daughter form a secure attachment to her or to manage Dorothy's feelings of rejection and jealousy. The birth of the rival sister when she was 10 and entering puberty brought Dorothy the realization that further growth would bring the possibility of pregnancy. This established the unconscious phantasy of becoming her mother with the hated and dangerous baby in her womb, and perhaps of becoming pregnant by oral means.

Emotional communication with her parents became extremely limited, and her interpretation of this was that nobody listened to her, by which she meant that she believed that they could not, or would not, take her distress seriously and try to help her with it, but merely regarded her as wicked. Her fears that her guilty aggressive and sexual thoughts would be detected found expression in the fantasies of the spying video camera, and the all-seeing eye of God.

Sexual abuse

The construction of Dorothy's persecutory fantasies is likely to have been a complex process. It is not clear whether they developed entirely as a consequence of her grandfather's sexual intrusiveness, or perhaps also of a guilty undisclosed enjoyment in the experience and in being treated as "special", or whether it had had antecedents in a prior sexual curiosity of her own. The "disgusting" oral sensations evoked by rage could be explained as her reaction to the traumatic experience of enforced fellatio. This traumatic experience, so often reported in anorexic adolescent girls (albeit sometimes with no basis in reality), could also help to account for her episodic anorexia. Her memories were not "recovered" in the course of psychotherapy, but, rather, were divulged to the therapist, with shame and embarrassment.

In this respect Dorothy's account of sexual abuse was not typical of the "false-memory" syndrome that sometimes develops in the course of therapy. Such false memories are sometimes accepted as totally real by misguided therapists, occasionally with the devastating consequences that have recently become well known. Such situations may be complicated by the influence of fantasies preceding or following the reported event, with the result that the question "did it or did it not actually happen" may never find an answer. Research in a large children's hospital confirmed that in over 25% of anorexic adolescents seeking help for their anorexia the actual reality of sexual abuse was firmly established (Magagna, personal communication). The true figure, depending on the definition of sexual trauma and the means of gathering information, is probably higher (Lask & Bryant-Waugh, 2000).

Dorothy's early memories of feeling abandoned by her mother at the age of 3 years, of experiencing overwhelming rage as a "green slimy thing" that she had to swallow, and later of enforced oral intrusion by her grandfather's penis are her accurate account of her subjective experience. However, such "narrative truth" does not necessarily represent "historical truth". Early memories may be difficult or impossible to confirm or to locate correctly in time and can often be understood as a dramatic condensation of different events—real, imaginary, or both. Such "screen memories" may come to have important significance for the individual, even though the associated events may not be historically true.

The foregoing considerations have profound implications for the assessment of sexual abuse. If Dorothy's early memory of feeling completely abandoned at the age of 3 and of disgusting sensations in the mouth were to be taken as authentic, and as preceding the apparently real abuse by several years, the abusive event might have an even more traumatic effect and might help to explain the psychotic quality of her subsequent illness. It would imply that she was already vulnerable by virtue of her infantile experiences and their associated enduring unconscious phantasies. It is well known that if a person with a particular pre-existing psychopathology and vulnerability experiences a traumatic event, the consequences may be complex and severely damaging. In many instances psychotic developments may follow (Garland, 1998).

Dorothy feared that disclosure of the abuse would lead to disintegration of the family. This view may have been correct, because the family refused to cooperate in any exploratory meetings. Eventually the paternal grandfather became estranged from the maternal relatives, and an atmosphere of secrecy, so characteristic of actual sexual abuse, discouraged the milieu staff from pressing any further enquiries. This is a very difficult decision to make, in the light of the possibility that the abuser may be continuing his behaviour with others.

A reflection on Freud's much-misunderstood discovery

Such a line of thought might help illuminate the widespread misunderstanding of Freud's renunciation of his original belief in the frequency of abusive practices by trusted adults. In discovering the existence of unconscious phantasy as an explanation for many attributions of sexual abuse to innocent adults, he did not deny the reality of actual abuse. The power and pervasiveness of such fantasies may help to explain the frequent difficulty, at times impossibility, of establishing the facts of alleged abuse and can result in catastrophic consequences if "false recovered memories" are taken as being reality. In the attempt to distinguish "narrative" truth from "historical" truth, such complex processes as belief, lies, "screen memories", and "deferred action" (the re-editing of traumatic events into less painful and more remote forms) must be considered.

Projecting into the imaginary companion— command hallucinations

The transformation of the "good" Dorothy into the "bad" Doris may partly be explained as the result of the attempt to expel a bad part of the self by projective identification into an internal (imaginary) object. A large proportion of normal children have an "imaginary companion" who protects them from imaginary dangers and supports their self-confidence. However, this is normally a transitional phenomenon, relinquished by the age of 8 or 9 years (Bender, 1970; Magagna, 1995; Nagera, 1969). This process may generate those command hallucinations where imagined supportive thoughts or remembered helpful voices change into self-destructive hallucinations. This process of infiltrative transformation is an unconscious defensive one, and the destructive parts being projected are split off from consciousness. Thus the hallucinations can only be considered as belonging to the self, or of being the outcome of sub-vocal speech in this special sense (Roth, Kerr, & Howorth, 1996; Szasz, 1996). Compare Dorothy's hallucinations with those of George (Chapter 14) and Winnicott's successful treatment of a hallucinating child (Winnicott, 1958, p. 112).

Double identification and the roots of her anorexia

The revival of space-centred modes of functioning influence the perception of bodily space in many different ways. Of crucial importance in the pathogenesis of psychotic disturbance are the changes occurring in the individual's body at puberty. The new body image, with its new and real capacities of strength and fertility, can generate great anxiety in an individual whose previous preoccupations have been safely limited by the child's body (Laufer & Laufer, 1984). If an earlier developmental deficiency has already been established, the conditions exist for psychotic breakdown in later adolescence. Disturbance of the sense of identity is a common accompaniment.

With the onset of menstruation the girl, confronted with the reality of her capacity to procreate babies, is moved more firmly into identification with her sexual mother. Because her mother's procreative activities have remained a past unconscious reality for her, this fateful change evokes various infantile feelings and phantasies. In the case of Dorothy, the most primitive of these have already been described.

Dorothy had felt herself to be the victim of a cannibalistic monster, which she believed had the power to invade her body and eat her from inside. At other moments, she believed that she was herself being transformed into the monster. The instability of such partial identifications can help give meaning to episodes of bizarre thinking, of severe attacks of panic, and of states of transient confusion. Dorothy's unconscious memories of the changes in her pregnant mother's body can be caught up in this shifting kaleidoscope of partial identifications. In identification with the pregnant mother, she fears that she will be devoured from inside by her own primitive devouring wishes; at other times, she becomes herself the devouring cannibalistic baby.

This "double identification" (Rey, 1994, ch. 4), can help explain her dread of developing a pubertal female body, with the possibility of a real biological pregnancy. The baby that she would have would devour her from inside, and so everything must be done to avoid this catastrophe. Vegetarianism and excessive exercise in pursuit of thinness, and attempts thereby to remove any trace of developing female breasts or to eliminate an illusional or delusional lower abdominal (suprapubic) "bulge" of early pregnancy, are features common to most severely pathological anorexic women.

Thus it can be considered that the anorexic who refuses food may be doing it to save her own life, by avoiding the fate of being eaten from the inside by a growing baby. Depriving this baby of nourishment will reduce the risk, and, when in identification with the pregnant mother, she may also be trying to save her mother's life. This phantasy offers a meaning for Dorothy's story of having thought from an early age that if she eats then someone will die, whereas if she starves someone will live, and that she starves to save the family. A comparable statement made by a psychotic anorexic patient on actually becoming pregnant was "I must eat the baby!" whilst at other times she would say "I must eat *for* the baby!" (Jackson & Williams, 1994, ch. 4).

Psychoanalysts have long recognized that the fears of the prepubertal girl of developing a body like her mother are based on a fantasy that she will *become* her mother and will thus lose control of her own body. Because of the "incredible wealth of meaning bestowed by the unconscious ego on the entire period of orality" (Bychowski, 1966), there are many different but related aspects for which writers may claim priority. Focusing on oedipal conflicts, control of the combined parents, identification with the mother's body, and other themes can all throw much light on the psychopathology of some patients. However, in the case of the severely anorexic and potentially psychotic individual, the concept of a primitive, pre-oedipal kaleidoscope of multiple shifting projective and introjective identifications can add to understanding. This was well expressed by Bychowski (p. 195), describing his treatment of a severely anorexic-bulimic young woman:

> Further material clarified the symbolic meaning of "becoming bloated" through overeating as a symbolic acting out of mother's

pregnancy. The wish to destroy this pregnant stomach of her mother, out of which was to emerge her little sister, turns against her own bodily self after the introjection of her mother. Thus, when she overeats, she says, she tries to kill herself as well as her mother.

This profound understanding is echoed in the report of a patient whose treatment was supervised by Rey (1994). The rival baby is indeed living inside the mother's body ("stomach") but is also the container of the projected oral-aggressive/biting part-self. Thus the appropriate therapeutic aim of helping the patient reclaim her body from the identification with her mother may require attention to the manifestations of violent primitive sibling rivalry. As in the case of hysteria, lateral relationships of dependency and rivalry with siblings and peers may sometimes be more profound and important than "the limited vertical parent-child axis of explanation" (Mitchell, 2000, p. 40).

Obsessional defences

The view that Dorothy has needed to control the anxiety mobilized by unconscious destructive wishes towards the displacing rival baby can shed light on the meaning of her obsessional rituals. We have seen that when she is anxious she visualizes a random series of numbers which then escape her control and assume the group of 2 2 2, at which point her anxiety increases. She then begins the struggle to compel them to change to 1 1 1, and when she succeeds her anxiety is relieved. She has a comparable system of thought in the struggle to force her naturally sloping writing, which begins to lie flat, into a vertical and thin form.

It takes little imagination to consider the multiple symbolic meanings that may be involved in these obsessional methods of reducing her anxiety. What she cannot bear is the thought of having to accept that she is a potentially fertile female, symbolized by the number(s) 2 and the supine posture, and she therefore struggles to create a male ("phallic") identity for herself, represented by the thin vertical numbers and writing style. Since symbolism is by nature overdetermined (can generate multiple possible meanings), the reduction of 2 to 1 might also express the wish to be the only child of her mother and to eliminate the mother–new baby nursing couple. In a more general way, the number 2 can represent sharing, containing new experience, and self-reflective thinking, whereas the number 1 can represent a solipsistic and narcissistic pseudo-independence. This behaviour can be seen from the point of view of creating a soothing (self-comforting) state of mind (see Ogden's remarks on autistic shapes: 1989, p. 242). The number 2 can be divided, 1 cannot. Such a struggle to acquire a masculine-phallic identification may help to explain the ruthless pursuit of thinness so characteristic of the anorexic who dedicates herself to strenuous running and other extreme exercise.

The symbolism of the ritualistic behaviour with the traffic lights can be considered in a similar fashion. Being forced to wait at a red traffic light implies that her unimpeded progress would be suddenly obstructed by passing vehicles to whom she must give priority. This triadic situation might well activate her violent sibling rivalry and associated guilt, leading to the fear that she will cause a lethal collision (traffic accident).

In the case of the anorexic patient, whether psychotic or not, the frequent combination of high intelligence and defensiveness may lead the patient to acquiring a degree of intellectual insight, but this may well be of little or no use, more a matter of "knowing about" than "knowing". In such circumstances, it may be that access to the disturbance can be found in the dream life, Freud's "royal road" to the unconscious. From the perspective of treatment, another "royal road" is to be found in the therapeutic transference, where the disturbing patterns of internal events and relationships may repeat themselves in the relation with the therapist. If this happens, they may be worked through both intellectually and emotionally and may ultimately be deprived of their pathogenic influence.

Dorothy's self-starving was not primarily a matter of seeking attention, or of enviously attacking the nurturing mother ("biting the hand that feeds") as appears to be the case in some non-psychotic anorexic patients. It seemed, rather, to be an attempt to preserve herself—identified with her pregnant mother—from the consequences of puberty, the biological inevitability of breast development, and the possibility of having a baby inside her body.

Since this imagined baby was the unconscious symbolic representative of the earliest (sibling) intruder into her exclusive ownership of her mother, a baby containing her own projected destructive wishes, it would make a biting attack on Dorothy from inside. This imagined attack may present as a hypochondriacal symptom. Under extreme circumstances, such a patient might starve herself to death

without the possibility of it being recognized that she is unconsciously trying to preserve both her own life and that of her mother by
preventing the baby from growing and become dangerous [see Glossary, "identification"].

Conclusions

Bulimia, anorexia, and other eating disorders are very common, and
many are well enough understood in terms of personal conflicts and
social factors. It is in the more severe cases where psychotic roots may
be found, and it is in these cases that the concepts of unconscious
phantasy and identity disturbance and deep-seated disorder of body
image and sense of self, described in this book, offer keys to understanding. Dorothy's case shows how the capacity for reality-testing
can be undermined by the proliferation of comforting fantasy; how
self-created imaginary figures can become transformed by projective
and introjective processes into dangerous internal entities (objects);
and how a capacity for vivid imagination can, under adverse conditions, deteriorate into delusional thinking. Dorothy's illness demonstrates how adolescent psychopathology, itself the revival of the
pathology of childhood and of infancy, may find expression in psychotic, rather than simply neurotic, disorder. At the same time, it can
be seen that Dorothy showed none of the truly bizarre thinking and
mental fragmentation that characterizes more deeply schizophrenic
states.

Her periods of anorexia could ultimately be understood as the
expression of disturbing oral fantasies, illustrating how difficult
may be the task of differentiating between memory and fantasy and
of establishing the reality or otherwise of remembered sexual abuse,
so commonly alleged in anorexic adolescents. The consequences of
actual abuse or of imagined abuse can be so serious that premature
conclusions can be dangerous. Where there is evidence of potentially
pathogenic oral fantasies in early life, as in Dorothy's case, it suggests
the possibility that the child who falls victim to either the fantasy or
the reality of sexual abuse may have been already deeply vulnerable
to either fate.

Considering the severity of Dorothy's illness, its deep roots in the
distant past, the disturbed family background, the history of sexual

abuse, and her near-fatal obedience to command hallucinations, the therapy must be counted as a considerable achievement on the part of the therapist, the patient, and the psychiatric milieu.

In the therapy, Dorothy found a figure who listened carefully to her and to whom she could become emotionally attached and could work through her feelings of guilt and destructive rage in an immediate fashion in relative safety. This enabled her to reappraise her fears of the omnipotent power of her anger in the light of her adult intelligence and the therapist's knowledge and understanding. In Bionic terms, the therapist has succeeded in functioning as a "container" of Dorothy's pathogenic conflicts, which her mother had been unable to do, and has helped the working-through in the transference and countertransference to the extent that Dorothy's need to use excessive projection as a defence greatly diminished. Eventually, the inner devils that haunted her lost their power because they were no longer needed to function as containers of her own unwanted and expelled destructive jealousy.

Dorothy was fortunate in finding a therapist with whom she was well matched. This is an important, often underestimated, factor which contributes to a successful outcome. The positive transference that she formed to her therapist recaptured for Dorothy the feelings she had had for her beloved grandmother. This was an important factor in helping Dorothy work through and contain within her own mind the thoughts, feelings, and memories that underlay her symptoms, thus resolving her psychotic pathology and reaching a happier and more stable life.

CHAPTER SEVEN

Paranoid schizophrenia—
space–time factors: "Conrad"

S ome psychotic conditions are characterized by the regressive revival of "sensorimotor" forms of thinking, in which some mental events are experienced in bodily terms and are tied to primitive concepts of space and time and to belief in omnipotent power. In the course of psychotherapy, such psychotic thinking may sometimes be understood as an unconscious defence against the mental pain that sane and self-reflective thinking can bring.

Conrad

Conrad was 24 years old and had been in twice-weekly psychotherapy for two years when his case was brought to the seminar. Supervisory contact was subsequently continued during the following three years.

At the age of 15, Conrad had developed an acute psychosis characterized by persecutory delusions and outbursts of violence. He believed that his food was poisoned, that the KGB were trying to murder him, and that his country was under threat of an imminent missile attack. He was admitted to a psychiatric ward for children and adolescents, where neuroleptic medication soon brought his agitation under control and his delusional thinking receded. He remained in hospital for several months, during which time he was often verbally aggressive towards the staff and other patients and occasionally made unprovoked assaults on them. Although temporary increase of medication was often needed on such occasions, his aggressive outbursts gradually subsided and it eventually proved possible to discharge him on a small maintenance dose of medication.

Soon after his discharge, his psychotic state returned. He talked incoherently, behaved aggressively towards his mother, and seemed to be in a state of panic. He was listening to voices that told him that Hitler was still alive, that his life was in danger, and that a catastrophic world war was imminent. He made a violent attack on his father and was taken to hospital by the police. He was once again admitted on a compulsory order, and his symptoms were again brought under control by medication.

Conrad's illness proved resistant to conventional psychiatric treatment, and after a series of relapses he passed into a fluctuating chronic state in which he withdrew from contact with his friends and family, sometimes revealing evidence of continued delusional thinking. He spent most of the next four years in hospital, on a moderate dose of neuroleptic medication. Although he was able to return to live in the family home during less disturbed periods, his sense of reality remained extremely fragile. He frequently became preoccupied with religion, wanting to renounce his family name, and he announced that he had decided to become a priest.

All rehabilitation proved unsuccessful, and attempts to decrease the medication were followed by exacerbation of the psychotic symptoms. The diagnosis of paranoid, or perhaps hebephrenic, schizophrenia had long been established, and his prognosis was regarded as poor.

At the age of 19, he was transferred to an adult psychiatric unit and was granted a permanent disability pension. For the next three years, his state improved to the extent that he was able to remain living in the family home, and his recurring psychotic relapses could be managed by increased medication and support for the family.

At this point, he was included in a research project (which followed the Finnish "need-adapted" model) whose intensive activities included the possibility of individual psychoanalytic psychotherapy for young schizophrenic patients. He was taken on for twice-weekly psychotherapy sessions as an outpatient within a well-functioning psychodynamically oriented hospital and community-based psychiatric team.

At the time of the discussion seminar, he had had no episodes of acute disturbance, was maintained on a lower dose of neuroleptic medication, and had not required further admission to the ward.

Personal history

It was some time before a comprehensible picture of his family background could be gathered. Conrad's birth and early childhood were described by his parents as having been normal, but there was no detailed history available of his early cognitive, emotional, and motor development. Until the onset of his psychosis at the age of 15, he had lived with his parents and two younger brothers in a small country village, where he was accepted as a rather odd, eccentric child, somewhat clumsy in his movements and gait. He had performed adequately in school and had made a few stable friendships. He was reported as having been very fond of a much-admired uncle, who had died during Conrad's childhood, and of his grandfather. The latter had died when Conrad was 13, and he was said to have been extremely upset by these losses.

Psychotherapy begins

Although the outline of the antecedents and onset of the psychosis were already known, further details were slowly gathered from his family and from Conrad himself during the early phase of the psychotherapy.

Conrad had long had an enthusiastic interest in the navy, and in particular in the performance of the latest destroyers. One day he joined some friends to look over a destroyer that was on a public-relations visit, and on returning home he complained of nausea and seemed agitated and confused. He subsequently developed a low fever, and cerebral pathology was suspected. However, the fever quickly subsided, and he was kept at home from school while medical tests, which included detailed neurological investigations, were performed. No abnormality was found, and his return to school was planned. However, soon after receiving a visit by some schoolmates, his psychotic symptoms erupted

Conrad was at first quite secretive about his preoccupations, but he seemed to gain some relief from disclosing them. Although it was clear that he was hallucinating, it was some time before he was able to admit to the therapist that he was hearing voices talking to him. However, he was rarely able to say more than this, and it was not clear whether he could recognize the identity of the voices, the content of their speech, their history, or their intentions towards him. At one point, he held his head in his hands and shouted—"there are earphones on my brain!" He declined to enlarge on this belief, but it was clear that he was experiencing broadcasting of his thoughts.

At another time, he divulged that he was hearing the voice of the mother of a girl to whom he had been attracted prior to his first breakdown, and that she was speaking in critical and abusive tones to him. However, he quickly changed the subject and declined to talk further about this experience.

As he became able to talk more freely with the therapist, the reasons for his state of terror at the onset of the psychosis became clear. He said that his life was in danger because spies from the Russian KGB were plotting to kill him, and that they had poisoned the school food. He explained that the terror began when during the visit to the naval vessel he tried on the diver's equipment and was examining the breathing apparatus. When he applied the oxygen mask and inhaled, he believed that it was porridge, and not air, that he was breathing. This, he believed, was the work of the KGB, who had introduced poisoned porridge into the breathing apparatus. This made him feel nauseated and ill, but he told no one about this frightening experience.

However, he soon began to feel a little less desperate because he began to realize that the poison, which might include the AIDS virus, could be expelled from his body through his sweat and semen, and that this was a life-saving process under the control of "the Americans", who were trying to protect him. They were also trying desperately to save the world from the apocalyptic catastrophe that was about take place when the full force of the destructive aggression of the Russians would be unleashed.

The therapist encouraged him to talk about these experiences and the background life events surrounding their dramatic manifestation.

It soon became evident that Conrad was unable to differentiate clearly between his inner world of memories, fantasies, dreams, wishes, and fears and external reality. His thinking, in areas not connected with his delusional system, appeared to be normal enough, but in relation to his persecutory and apocalyptic preoccupations it had assumed a concrete and omnipotent quality.

When he heard reports that the government was considering reducing the country's defensive missile strength, he became extremely anxious and spent many hours trying to warn the military authorities of the folly of their proposals. Over the course of a year, these panics and his associated harassing of the authorities gradually became less frequent, as he began to feel that the worst danger was past and that the politicians were right in their judgement that anti-missile defences were no longer essential.

His delusional beliefs also had a powerful omnipotent and wishful character. For example, he insisted that his beloved grandfather was not dead. At times he experienced the therapist as an exclusively benevolent figure, and he often insisted that the therapist was, in fact, his grandfather, or a friendly (deceased) uncle. The interplay of his psychotic and sane thinking was striking, and in any one session he might say both "I *want* you to be my uncle" and "you *are* my uncle".

The control of time and loss

One of the most remarkable features of Conrad's thinking was his claim that he had the capacity to make time stand still, and it was clear that this represented the omnipotent fulfilment of a wish. He held it with delusional conviction and presented it to the therapist as a fact that did not require him to provide evidence. It emerged that he believed that he had many ways of controlling time. He had discovered that he was able to pull the Earth in a westerly direction, with the consequence that there would cease to be a linear flow of time. The rotation of the Earth is arrested, and the stars stand still.

Some time later, when he was beginning to realize that his therapeutic sessions were important to him, he demonstrated how his thinking in this respect was tied in a literal way to "primitive" concepts of time and space. As the end of a session approached, he rose from his chair and walked over to a table where a clock was installed within the view of both patient and therapist. He removed the cover and pushed the minute hand of the clock backwards by thirty minutes, and then denied that he had any wish to prolong the session. This form of behaviour, characteristic of the thinking of a small child (see Rey, 1994, p. 173) was carried out in such a spontaneous manner by Conrad as to leave the therapist in no doubt about its authenticity.

Fear of feelings

When Conrad began to trust his therapist a little, he made it quite clear that he was very afraid of making contact with his feelings. After leaving one session, he returned and approached the therapist in the corridor in a threatening manner, shouting:

P: "You must stop doing that! You hear me? Stop, I say, or I won't come back!"

T: "Stop doing what?"

P: "We agreed to talk about feelings. We didn't say anything about *feeling* them! Do you understand me? You must promise me not to do that any more, promise me that you'll stop doing it!"

In the following session the therapist explored this experience and Conrad, clutching his chest frantically, explained: "If you feel the feeling, I mean the feeling in itself, it's dangerous. If you feel the feeling, your heart might break and you will die!" This desperate outburst left the therapist in no doubt that Conrad was dreading actual destruction of his heart.

The perils of emotional attachment—
loss of self by fusion with the object

Another fear of emotional closeness was that he would lose his sense of identity by fusing, being engulfed, or merging with the therapist. He would sometimes seem to be deliberately mimicking the therapist's changes of posture during the session, crossing and uncrossing his legs, or making small changes of movement when the therapist did.

At one point he shouted: "I don't want to *become* you!"

He was able later to explain that he felt it necessary to keep his distance from other people. Attachment, it was beginning to appear, brought the dangers of painful loss, but also of fusion. He explained that he must take the precaution of never coming closer than a metre and a half from anyone else, including the therapist, at the beginning and end of sessions. At times he ended the session by getting up from his chair and making sudden gestures of pushing the therapist away from him.

He did not seem capable of understanding this simply as a metaphorical expression of his need to preserve an emotional distance from others; rather, to him, it was a literal, space-centred experience. His mimicry of the therapist's posture also seemed to be the expression of a wish to *become like* the therapist whose qualities he had come to admire, but which, in his concrete thinking, brought the fear that he would lose his own identity and *become* the therapist.

In one session, he was imitating the therapist's body movements and repeating his comments (in a manner that resembled the "echolalia" sometimes encountered in the chronic schizophrenic patient), when he suddenly started to shout aggressively:

P: "I don't want that! I don't want to look like you!"

T: (*momentarily disconcerted*) "You don't want to look like me, but what is it that you *do* want?"

P: "I want your help!"

T: "But when you feel that you get it, you fear that you will be unable to differentiate yourself from me!"

The patient made no further comment, but he visibly relaxed.

Death by abandonment

Conrad's intolerance of psychological pain may have had deep roots, and many factors might have been involved in its consolidation. It was evident that it was not only loss of identity that he feared, but also loss of any sense of safety and support. This took the form of dread of abandonment, and his behaviour after leaving certain sessions left no doubt of the severity and literalness of this fear. When the therapist remarked that Conrad seemed determined never to talk about his family and in particular about his relation to his mother, he replied: "That's private! If I talk about that I will be left outside this building, the trains will stop running, and I won't be able to get home!" He added: "I will freeze to death in the snow and the hospital staff will find me and flush me down the toilet!" At that point he muttered softly that he had had a thought that his mother might leave home and never return; however, when the therapist asked him to say more, he dismissed it as "just an idea!"

Although he had no realistic reason to fear breakdown of the train service, he began to shout out at strangers at the station, demanding that they should drive him home if the trains stopped running. This bizarre behaviour startled passers-by, and when he followed it with incoherent babbling when the train did arrive, the conductor refused to allow him on board.

As he made progress in the therapy, Conrad's thinking appeared at times to oscillate between a partial awareness of his confusion of inner and outer reality and the continuation of his frightening concrete thinking. On one dramatic occasion, when the therapist was trying to explore his dread of abandonment, Conrad jumped up, ran towards the door, recoiled, and left the room by means of squeezing through the small window of the therapy-room. He repeated this behaviour occasionally in later sessions and was finally able to reveal the meaning of his bizarre behaviour. He explained that at those moments there was an evil presence, whom he called "the master", waiting outside the therapy-room, ready to throw him to his death in outer space.

The therapist interpreted this belief as an expression of his fear that as he left the room he would be struck by the thought that the "bad" therapist was really glad to get rid of him because he found him such a difficult patient. Conrad responded by relapsing into silence.

The therapist's understanding of Conrad's dread of being exposed to intolerably painful feelings of loss, and of losing his sense of personal identity, made much of his bizarre behaviour comprehensible. Emotional attachment threatened the triple fate of loss of identity, total abandonment, and death.

Adolescent fears of sexuality

Later in the therapy, when he had begun to talk a little about his past life, Conrad explained that his problems began when he lost all his happiness at about the age of 12 years. Before that, he said, he had had an active and sociable life which centred on a youth club that he had attended for many years. He did not seem to be clear about the nature of the change that had ushered in his unhappiness, but its connection with the onset of his puberty, and associated disturbing feelings and thoughts about his sexual feelings and his parents' sexual life, seemed likely. Some confirmation was provided when asked about his sexual feelings. Conrad said:

P: "There is no sexual intercourse. Sex does not exist!"

T: "But if there is no sexual intercourse, how has it come about that you exist?"

Conrad appeared to accept the paradox, and he replied:

P: "Well, there may be a thing called sexual intercourse, but nice people don't do it. Refined people don't do it".

T: "What do you mean by 'refined'?"

P: "Really rich people don't do it."

T: "If that is the case, how do they reproduce themselves?"

P: "Well, there aren't too many really rich people, are there?"

This was conveyed with apparently complete seriousness.

Madness, sadness, and sanity

At times he would behave in a session in a manner so bizarre as to make the therapist suspect that he was enacting a caricature of a popular conception of a "crazy" person. Although normally rather clumsy in his movements and posture, at these times this became grossly exaggerated, and he talked for minutes on end in an incoherent babble. The therapist suggested that he was being like a baby who had not yet learned to control his bodily movements or to talk coherently. The patient seemed interested in this comment, but the behaviour continued. At other times he would ask: "Am I crazy? Sometimes I think I am a psychiatric case, mostly I don't". The therapist was puzzled by this apparent insight into the difference between sanity and madness and was even more surprised to hear the patient mutter, almost inaudibly, "Maybe I am, but maybe it has advantages", and "Maybe I can get well, but if I do what will become of us?"

In one particular session, the therapist could make little sense of his incoherent talk and was taken aback when, immediately before leaving the room, Conrad leaned over and, in a different voice and a different tone and absolutely coherently, said: "It's very sad really. It's just as sad for both of us!"

Relationship with mother

Although the identity of "us" was not immediately clear, a clue was provided much later when the ward staff interviewed Conrad's mother. In the first years of therapy, the mother treated the patient as a pre-school boy who needed her assistance in every respect. She took care of his clothing, cut his hair, and tied his shoelaces. The staff's expectations of a higher degree of autonomy obviously raised anxiety in her about losing her protecting and care-giving role. Even after allowing for the possible effect of anxiety, they found her talk frequently disconnected or even momentarily incoherent. These observations raised the possibility that Conrad, although psychotic in his own right, might at certain times be unconsciously expressing, in the form of a charade, his experience of certain characteristics of his mother.

In the sessions, Conrad was frequently verbally violent towards the therapist, sometimes threatening to kill him. At one point, he stood over the therapist and seemed about to make a violent attack on him. The therapist, who was accustomed to experiencing anxiety with some psychotic patients, felt quite undisturbed. He thought that in making these sudden moments of threatening behaviour, the patient was motivated by his envy of the therapist's composure, on the one hand trying to destroy it, on the other testing out the therapist's capacity to tolerate, contain, and understand it.

As well as his recurring incoherent and apparently meaningless babble, Conrad often behaved outside the sessions like a chronic deteriorated schizophrenic, wandering aimlessly about the hospital and shouting incoherently at staff and other patients. The therapist thought that this behaviour might have several meanings, one of which might be that the patient was expelling his own capacity for reflective thinking by projection, arousing it in other people. In forcing others to see him as a completely "crazy" person, he was able to escape the perils of thinking and to maintain a role of irresponsible mindlessness.

For Conrad, time was the great enemy, to be defeated by his belief in his omnipotent power of controlling it in order to achieve everlasting life. In a rare moment of thoughtful self-reflection, in which he was clearly unconvinced by his own wishful thinking, he had remarked: "Time does not exist. Time brings age, and age brings death. I am not a man, I am a little boy."

By reversing the hands of the therapist's clock at the end of the session he seemed to be thinking in a primitive space-centred manner, in the context of *metric* time (the distance between divisions on a clock face) and not functioning on the more abstract level of *psychological* time, which relates to emotional attachment, separation, and tolerance of more mature experiences such as waiting for, missing, and recovering an object of primary value. At such moments, Conrad was expressing his omnipotent belief that he could arrest time and make it go backwards, so that he would not have to face the fact that the ending of the session was emotionally important to him and aroused painful feelings.

Capacity for symbolization—playfulness

However, his reversing the hands of the clock seemed to have had an element of playfulness in relation to the therapist. This suggested that he had now acquired some degree of recognition that his action represented a wish, rather than a belief in his omnipotence. Thus, in controlling the clock he was actually enacting a metaphor that, at least in that session, he no longer believed was reality. Such momentary fluctuations of the capacity for symbolization, with partial comprehension of metaphor may be characteristic of the recovering patient (see Searles, 1965a). An example was seen in the case of another psychotic patient who was explaining that all his feeling were located in his left leg. When asked to clarify his statement, he became confused but resolved his perplexity by insisting that it was literal and true, but at the same time was "figurative" (Jackson & Williams, 1994, ch. 2; see also Britton, 1998).

As Conrad's reality sense gradually strengthened, his capacity for symbol recognition improved, and at times he seemed to be acting the role of his psychotic self, or, as previously suggested, behaving like a version of his mother, rather than actually being psychotic. Although there seemed to be considerable evidence for this conjecture, the therapist soon gave up attempts to interpret them to the patient. He found that, when he tried, the patient would respond with rage, would run from the room, or would sometimes begin to retch and appear to be about to vomit. He concluded that Conrad was experiencing his therapist's interpretations as an attempt to force him to take in material that he had expelled by projection into the therapist, such as his bad feelings about his mother. The transactions concerned emotional thinking, but his experience was of being forced to incorporate intolerable things. This process seemed to be dynamically related to his earlier belief that his food and the air were poisoned.

The therapist came to believe that the familiar procedures of psychotherapy, focusing on the exploration of the past and of personal conflicts, could not be addressed until Conrad had developed some degree of tolerance of reflective thinking. This required the therapist to remain constantly in touch with his own personal feelings, and to tolerate much uncertainty, anxiety, and confusion. He could not always decide whether or not moments in which he could not think clearly or had become confused were the result of his own limited understanding or of a transference–countertransference process. Were the latter explanation to be correct, it would imply that the patient was unconsciously communicating his own anxiety and confusion or, as already mentioned, making an envious attack on the therapist's mental capacities.

Self as dangerous and endangered

When Conrad began to make such statements as "Sometimes I think I'm crazy", he was demonstrating the split between his psychotic and non-psychotic selves. He had moments of sufficient sanity and contact with reality to be able to doubt such concrete thinking, as in the case of the imminent destruction of his "mother" country by Russian missiles. However, when he felt threatened by the approach of disturbing feelings, he immediately displaced the disturbance into the outer world and became acutely anxious about the fact that his country was, in reality, reducing the strength of its anti-missile defences. However, his dedication to the expulsive avoidance of doubt, with its associated capacity for sane thinking, was so effective that for a long time the therapist had to perform this function for him. It was only when the split between his psychotic and sane selves began to lessen that he could begin to tolerate doubt about his delusional beliefs, and to accept the necessity to accept the painful experience of thinking about himself.

Exploring the past

A psychotic patient may not be able to think about the past until he has developed a sufficient capacity to differentiate between the past and the present. It may be a long time before his tendency to confuse memory with perception diminishes. This is a very different situation from that to be found in neurotic disorders, where the patient can differentiate past and present, and the technical problem is of discerning when the patient (and perhaps the therapist) is talking about the past as a defence against attention to the immediate present, and vice-versa. With a psychotic patient, the immediate problem may be to decide whether the patient is talking about dream or reality. It was not until Conrad had acquired some capacity to think about his fears, and to relinquish his omnipotent control of time, that he could begin to tolerate the therapist's interest in events preceding the onset of his psychosis. It seemed that Conrad had fallen in love with a girl who had no interest in him, and that the combination of the arousal of sexual feelings and the sense of rejection had precipitated the regression into psychosis. The content of his frightening delusional experience, in which he apparently equated food (porridge) and semen, began to make some sense.

This intrusive substance could now be considered as the symbolic representative of intolerable emotional thoughts about sexual intimacy which had been expelled from his mind and were undergoing a process of "re-entry", but now in a concrete fashion, into his body. As dangerous elements inside his bodily space, they could now only be expelled in a bodily manner, by sweating or seminal ejaculation.

Sadness and depressive remorse

With increasing capacity for doubt came depressive feelings. He began to express feelings of sadness, with momentary tearfulness, and spoke with remorse about having been so harsh to his therapist and other people for so long. These moments were followed by an increase in his psychotic talk and an incoherent babbling in the session that made it very hard for the therapist to think and concentrate.

This seemed clearly to be Conrad's near-conscious intent. Nonetheless, he was able to talk about such feelings, although at first he preferred to talk in a lecturing fashion about the defensive powers of the latest naval destroyer. The metaphorical meaning of this preoccupation became clear when the therapist suggested that this was his way of defending himself against any display of sad feelings, which he regarded as weakness. Somewhat to his surprise, the patient agreed and stopped his lecturing.

The outcome of the psychotherapy

At the time of writing this report, Conrad had been in twice-weekly psychotherapy for five years in all. Although he was still a disturbed person, needing the continuation of the treatment, possibly for a considerably longer time before he might hope to function independently of psychotherapy, medication, and social support, his improvement was dramatic. His bizarre behaviour and incomprehensible talk had ceased, as also had his aggressive shouting. He was stabilized on a small dose of neuroleptic medication, and a trial of reduction of this was being considered. The psychiatric staff found him very much improved.

Whereas at the beginning of therapy he was extremely paranoid and aggressive with dominating delusions and severe acting-out, he was now free of all such symptoms and behaving normally. He had left the family home and, with the help of community nurses and social workers, had been living in his own apartment for two years. He attended his sessions as an outpatient, and for the first time he had begun to participate in a hesitant way in some social activities.

His motor clumsiness had greatly improved, and his posture and walking gait were almost normal. The therapist had previously observed that Conrad seemed sometimes to walk more on the tips of his toes than is normal. When Conrad began to feel brief moments of depressive sadness, he placed more weight on his heels in a normal fashion, and eventually his gait became normal most of the time.

The consequences of Conrad's improvement for his mother were striking. As she became able to free herself from her overwhelming worry about him, her previously severely limited social life began to blossom, and she engaged with great enthusiasm in various cultural activities for the first time.

Discussion

What precipitated the psychosis?

The most common antecedents to psychotic breakdowns are crises in the outer or inner world, in particular those that bring disappointment in an attempt to establish intimacy in a love relationship, loss of an important loved figure, a severe blow to self-esteem, or the anxiety aroused by sexual and aggressive wishes and fantasies. In the normal or neurotic person, these common life crises can be negotiated in a non-psychotic fashion, but where there is a pre-existing vulnerability the massive regressive process of psychosis can follow, often bringing the dread of catastrophic abandonment and the threat of loss of personal identity or of personal or global annihilation.

When a psychosis has an acute onset, subsequent investigation can usually disclose premonitory symptoms that had either not been noticed or not regarded as serious. This seems to have been the case with Conrad. It was eventually revealed that for some time he had been suspicious about food, and in retrospect this could be understood as a precursor to the belief that he was inhaling poisoned porridge. His experience of rejection in love had apparently been an important precipitating factor. It was not yet clear whether this experience of disappointment in love was based on reality or on a completely delusional ("erotomanic") belief.

Prior vulnerability, predisposing factors

Although an experience of rejection in the attempt to form a heterosexual relation may have played a part in precipitating the psychosis, it remains to be considered why these stresses should have produced a psychotic disorder of such severity. To seek an answer, we must consider the nature of Conrad's early relationship with his mother. Emotionally depriving or traumatic parenting of one sort or another in the early life of the psychotic person is common and can usually be recognized, and in such cases it can often be found that one or both parents have borderline or psychotic personalities.

But when well-intentioned mothering goes badly wrong, the truth may be very much more subtle and complicated. Some mothers, for example, are regarded as "overprotective" when they are actually sheltering their child out of a recognition that he has been deeply vulnerable from infancy. Others do their best, but withdraw emotionally out of the schizoid conviction that their love may harm their child. In such cases, further information—for instance, that emerging in the course of family therapy may reveal pathology in the previous generation and illustrate how powerful the transgenerational transmission of pathology, conscious or unconscious, can sometimes be. On occasion, difficulties arise simply from mismatch of the personalities of mother and baby (Stern, 1985).

Such considerations may throw light on what appears to have been a pathological tie between Conrad and his mother. However, she was eventually able to explain that since his childhood she had devoted her life to keeping the extent of his disability a secret in the small village in which they lived. It was because of her wish to protect him—and perhaps herself—from social stigmatization that she had not sought help earlier. This wish to conceal his eccentricity might also throw some doubt on her reporting that he was a normal infant. Although this has remained an unresolved question, it is clear that her devotion to her son eventually proved to be a great burden to both of them.

It was only when she began to see a stable and dramatic improvement in Conrad's functioning that she began to feel free from feelings of anxiety and guilt, and to discover a new capacity for the enjoyment of life.

Organic factors?

It remains unclear why she had felt her child to be so vulnerable since infancy. Although he had long been rather clumsy in his movements, extensive neurological investigation had never shown any sign of organic cerebral pathology. Nonetheless, despite the apparent complete absence of any sign of minimal brain damage or of primary infantile autism, it had sometimes been suspected that he might be suffering from Asperger's syndrome. If sufficient relevant information were to be discovered about his early physical and mental life, this view might eventually prove to have been correct.

The remarkable improvement—even at times complete disappearance—of his postural clumsiness might be explained by the fact that Conrad was becoming more able to contain his unconscious fear of his destructive feelings towards his mother and, in a symbolic manner, was demonstrating that he had less need to protect her. If this were to prove to be the case, it would imply that he was symbolically equating the ground with his mother, a variant of his endangered "mother-country". In psychiatric terms, this clumsiness might qualify as a "hysterical conversion" symptom, or perhaps as a psychogenic elaboration, or overlay, of an innate minor organic defect of the type sometimes found in the early history of autistic or schizophrenic patients.

But however much such biological factors may contribute to the final disturbance in such cases, and even if the diagnosis of organic pathology or autism were to be proved to have been correct, Conrad's response to psychotherapy demonstrates that organic pathology may contribute to the development of psychotic disorders, but is not necessarily a contra-indication for psychotherapy. However, this diagnostic category has undergone a considerable expansion of its boundaries in recent years, in both psychoanalytic and psychiatric writing, with the result that it may be difficult to be sure of the reasoning of those using it. The diagnosis of Asperger's syndrome sometimes seems to be applied to psychotic processes that are merely difficult to understand or are believed to be beyond the reach of psychotherapy. The presence of organic factors does not necessarily disqualify the patient from the potential benefits of psychoanalytic psychotherapy, a fact demonstrated by many psychoanalytic psychotherapists in recent years (see Meltzer, 1975; Rustin, Rhode, Dubinsky, & Dubinsky, 1997; Spensley, 1995; Tustin, 1990).

Air, porridge, and other substances—
the hidden meanings in delusions

Conrad's break with reality began with the belief that the air that he was inhaling had been deliberately and murderously contaminated with poisonous porridge and that he could only survive by means of the expulsion of sweat and semen. These substances are not, in his mind, consciously connected with the functions to which they refer, of breathing, eating, masturbation or copulation, physical activity or excitation. Air, porridge, semen, and sweat have one thing in common—namely that they are substances that are either incorporated in the body or expelled from the body, or both. It should be remembered that in Kleinian writing the terms "breast" and "penis" refer not so much to the actual organs as to the manifold functions that they serve, as "part-objects" [see Glossary]. The type of *"pars pro toto"* thinking (synechdoche) that equates such part-objects (body parts or substances) simply on the basis of their similarity in one single respect can be understood in terms of "predicate" thinking (Arieti, 1974), "symbolic equation" (Segal, 1981c), or "symmetrical" thinking (Matte-Blanco, 1998).

On the basis of this one property of passing in or out of the body, these thoughts are all experienced as physical objects involved in bodily events felt to be actually happening in a frightening or reassuring way in the immediate present. These thoughts do not have the property of "coming to mind", a process whereby the processes and functions to which they refer or symbolize can be thought about, but are, rather, experienced as things being expelled or invading the body. This failure to differentiate part objects and processes has been sometimes considered as a regressive revival of a fixated state of confusion in infancy. Rosenfeld (1987, p. 273) has expressed this succinctly: "In confusional states love and hate, and good and bad objects, become confused, creating an overwhelming and almost insoluble problem for the developing infant, one which is invariably revived in most psychotic states."

This "part-object" way of thinking about the origins and meaning of such psychotic thinking can lead the therapist to ask himself such questions as, "We breathe air, and ingest food, but in what state is the air and food, good or bad, and what part of the subject has been projected into these good life-giving substances to make them bad in the inner world?" He might wish to find out whether Conrad experienced the porridge as good or bad or both and to learn how it came to be that way, and the reason why the KGB should wish to kill him, or the Americans to save his life. How is it that the expulsion of semen has become such a life-saving activity? If the porridge is poisonous, how did this come about and did it mean that he believed that his mother was trying to kill him?

"Container" theory can offer possible explanations

In such a view, Conrad's mother had been unable, for whatever reasons, to help him integrate his destructive feelings—in Bion's terms, a failure of her "alpha-function". This necessitated the

unconscious defensive encapsulation of these wishes, which was sufficiently successful to enable him to survive in a non-psychotic, albeit
eccentric, manner, until the developmental demands of adolescence
aroused his sexual feelings and with this the wish for intimate heterosexual closeness. His primitive fears that his aggressiveness towards a
desired mother-figure was omnipotently destructive threatened to
break through his long-standing defensive structure and required the
unconscious deployment of further emergency defensive measures.
He expelled these "poisonous" wishes into the food, the part-object
symbol of his (internal) mother. His emerging sexual feelings for an
adolescent girl, contaminated by his unconscious phantasy about
their dangerous, and perhaps incestuous, nature, required them to be
expelled in the form of semen, which would then save his life and
presumably that of the object of his desires. At an everyday level, this
might imply that he had tried to abolish his dangerous sexual feelings
by compulsive masturbation.

The same approach could be applied to the attempt to understand
Conrad's belief that Hitler was still alive. Such a real-life destructive
character offers a suitable container for his own belief that he is ruth-
lessly destructive. He had no conscious awareness that he believed
himself to be so dangerous, in the sense that a neurotic patient might
come to describe himself as a "little Hitler", in full awareness that he
was making a metaphorical statement about destructive qualities of
which he was consciously aware. A non-psychotic patient might, in
similar circumstances, have gradually responded to the interpretation that he was hiding his oedipal rage with his mother and his
murderous rivalry with his father, and that these feelings had been
released from repression by his first attempt in adolescence to form
an intimate emotional and sexual relationship.

A psychotic patient such as Conrad, by contrast, finds himself
plunged into a terrifying world of events felt to be happening in the
immediate present, a world populated by mental elements that have
undergone a projective scattering, a "diaspora", into various containing objects, along with their associated substances and functions. This
process could be observed during the course of the psychotherapy.
When dangerous destructive feelings threatened to emerge into consciousness, sometimes into memory or into the therapeutic transference, he would project this part of himself that he unconsciously felt
to be omnipotently destructive into the image of Russian missiles.

Attacks on thinking/linking

Confronted with the developmental demands of puberty, Conrad's unresolved dread of the destructive consequences of emotional intimacy and penetrative sexuality threatened to erupt, necessitating the reinforcement of expulsive–projective defences. His difficulty in maintaining a grip on sane thinking could usefully be considered as the consequence of an increased submission to the "propaganda" of a "part-self" dedicated to prevent painful thinking, influencing his mind by "attacks on linking" (Bion, 1967), and conceived by various writers as a Mafia-like "destructive narcissism" (Rosenfeld, 1987), "psychotic organization" (Steiner, 1993), or "controller" (P. Williams, 1999).

Conrad's omnipotent belief in the lethal nature of his unconscious destructive wishes may have led him to the conviction that an attempt to form a heterosexual relationship would mean destroying his mother and being murdered by his father. This view would help to explain the episode when his claustrophobic anxiety led him to escape death in the hands of "the master" by escaping through the window of the therapist's room. A further possibility is that he was, at the moment of leaving, unconsciously equating his occupancy of the therapy-room with his mother's body and dreading confrontation with the father/master who would discover this trespass (cf. the case of George, Chapter 14; see also Rey, 1994, p. 25).

Conclusions

Agents of change and the decline of Hitler

There have been many factors involved in the improvement brought about by the psychotherapy. The therapist's psychoanalytic knowledge and consistently containing behaviour has gradually undermined the influence of Conrad's psychotic self, mitigated the harshness of his primitive superego, facilitated a beneficial identification, and led to a growth of personality and to the integrative level of functioning of the depressive position. This has been a painfully slow matter of gradually learning and, from Conrad's point of view, a dangerous but ultimately relieving process of risk-taking. It has profoundly reduced the intensity of his use of the primitive defence mechanisms of splitting and projection mechanisms and thus very largely abolished their psychotic consequences.

Conrad's attempt to survive the unresolved disruptive forces in his inner world led to the disabling of his capacity for reflective thinking and his return to an omnipotent world where time does not exist. In stopping time, in the wishful belief that this would protect his mother from death and himself from annihilation, he no longer needed to believe in a "lifetime" that would inevitably in due course bring the loss of his mother into the world of outer reality.

Conrad no longer talks of Hitler, and he has recently said that he realizes that he has a personal problem of a guilty conscience and that he can trust his therapist to help him deal with it. This is a dramatic illustration of the concept of the recovery of a lost, unintegrated, part of the self and of how this process has strengthened Conrad's ego functions and, in particular, his capacity to distinguish between internal and external reality.

CHAPTER EIGHT

Chronic paranoid schizophrenia—schizoid thinking: "Ellen"

L ittle is known about the long-term outcome of patients who have been deprived of adequate treatment, or have failed to respond to it, and have drifted into a chronic state. Suicide is not uncommon, but violence towards others is relatively rare, despite the media reporting of dramatic, often tragic, cases. Some paranoid patients manage to achieve an adjustment in which their distress is reduced to a manageable level. Their delusions may exert a protective function for them, and many have retained sufficient insight to realize that other people regard them as eccentric or mad, and they have learned thereby to keep their delusional world to themselves. The following patient illustrates some of the psychodynamic processes leading to such states and the meaning of such delusional beliefs.

Ellen

Ellen, a 57-year-old divorced mother of two children, had her first schizophrenic breakdown at the age of 28, spent a large part of the next thirty years in psychiatric care, being admitted on seventeen occasions, usually on a legal order, with the diagnosis of chronic paranoid schizophrenia. She had never been engaged in psycho-therapy and was currently in a supportive contact with a social worker.

At the time of the case discussion, Ellen was living in her apartment on neuroleptic medication and intensive outpatient support. Her case was discussed on one single occasion in a large group of hospital staff.

The psychiatric record at the time of her first breakdown provided little detail about her mental state, other than that she was deluded and hallucinated in both auditory and visual spheres. She talked aloud to hallucinated voices and reported seeing her mother, who was actually dead, as an angel with a beautiful halo. She believed that her persecutors repeatedly insulted her by calling her a whore and that they were trying to rob or murder her.

This first breakdown had occurred in the year after her mother's death from cancer. It had been preceded by a period of some weeks when her husband thought that Ellen had seemed depressed and withdrawn. She finally became acutely disturbed after a car accident, in which she was uninjured; she was then admitted to a psychiatric ward. Inpatient treatment with neuroleptic medication reduced the intensity of the hallucinatory voices, and after some months she was judged to be sufficiently well to leave the hospital. However, she soon relapsed. Over the next ten years, she was admitted nine times, often in connection with major life crises, including divorce, loss of the custody of her children, an abortion, and two disastrous relationships with men who treated her badly. With adjustment of medication and general support, she usually recovered sufficiently to be discharged within a month or two. At the age of 40, she made a serious suicide attempt.

No record was available of her history for the following ten years, but it seems likely that she had not required hospital treatment. The next recorded admission occurred at the age of 50 following the marriage of her daughter, which she did not attend. This time she was admitted under a legal order when she was found to be suffering from serious loss of weight and severe anaemia, the consequence of her obedience to hallucinatory voices commanding her to stop eating staple foods. The most recent admission followed the birth of a grand-daughter and the death of her father. This provided an opportunity for the social worker to learn more about her mental condition, which was permeated by her tormented psychotic world.

Personal and family background

Ellen was an only child, and little detailed information was available in the original psychiatric record of thirty years previously. There was no record of a developmental history having been undertaken, nor detailed information about her family and the mental health of relatives. However, it was recorded that some information had been provided by relatives of her mother at the time of her first breakdown. At the age of 11 years, her mother and her schoolteachers were sufficiently worried about her to suggest a consultation with a psychologist, but her father, who was regarded by relatives as being unduly possessive, refused to allow this. The next record showed that she trained as a milliner at the age of 16 and worked in the trade until her marriage at the age of 21. She seemed to have coped successfully, at the ages of 22 and 24, with the birth of her children. Nothing is known about her condition during her mother's illness, which culminated in her death when Ellen was 26.

In the last few years, Ellen was reported to have been relatively stable and had not required readmission to hospital until a few weeks before the seminar discussion took place. She had been pursuing an apparently orderly, though limited, social life, making brief superficial contact with others while walking or shopping. Always polite and well-dressed, she was regarded in the neighbourhood as a pleasant, well-spoken, but reserved and somewhat eccentric individual. She has apparently preserved her skills in millinery and is always to be seen wearing one or other of a series of attractive hats of her own making. She proved to be quite ready to talk freely to the therapist, who soon learned details of her psychotic experiences.

Ellen is preoccupied with a number of fixed delusional beliefs and of experiences that feel completely real to her. She is convinced that she is the victim of persecution by other people. She believes that men have been repeatedly breaking into her apartment. On several occasions in the past, she had summoned the police, and when they arrived she had explained that the intruders had opened the drawers of her cupboards and had put knives and sexually provocative lingerie in them. When she found that the police would not help her, she barricaded the door of her apartment, but a "morphine man" gained entry by using his ability to shrink himself and penetrate through the keyhole. She complained that another man had cut her teeth and inserted something dangerous into them.

Her most recent hospitalization had followed a series of disturbing experiences. She believed that her neighbours wished to rob her, and she noticed that they had model ships in their window. She concluded that this meant that they knew she had some bonds in shipping companies and wanted to steal them from her. She became disturbed by the sofa in her apartment and suddenly realized that intruders had been putting the sofa to some sexual misuse.

Trying to understand Ellen

Despite the lack of historical details of a clear time relationship between traumatic life events and the onset and relapses in her psychotic illness, there is much to suggest that they have been precipitated by the loss of relationships of importance to her and the associated blows to her self-esteem. The first breakdown occurred soon after her mother's death, and other breakdowns have followed further losses. The fragmentary references to a disturbed relationship with her father might suggest sexual abuse, in fact or fantasy. However, to acquire deeper understanding of the meaning of her delusional preoccupations, and of their personal significance, requires consideration of the mental mechanisms that have generated them.

One reason why she becomes anaemic is that she submits to command hallucinations that she should not eat.   We do not know if she had ever been asked such questions as whether she recognized the voices, how and where they started, where they are located, or what their intentions towards her might be. It is not yet known why the voices think it necessary that she should starve herself.

She sees model ships in a neighbour's window and concludes that he is planning to steal her shipping bonds.   Her thinking is literal and concrete, and in this example the two items of thought—the models and her shipping company bonds—have one obvious thing in common, namely ships. She ignores the essential ways in which they differ, and she equates them as belonging together on the basis of this one characteristic. The model ships do not *remind* her of—that is, *represent* or *symbolize*—shipping bonds; instead, they *present* an immediate actuality. For her, the ship is a *sign*, not a *symbol*, and it is this impairment of her capacity for symbolic thinking that accounts for its concrete, non-metaphorical nature.

She complains that a man cut her teeth and inserted something into them.
This does not sound simply like an indirect reference to an uncomfortable visit to a dentist. We would need to find out who she thinks the man was and what was inserted, but the oral-biting and possible sexual implications suggest that she is thinking of an assault of some sort by a man, a memory of an event that actually happened, or a fantasy of such an event, or both. Whatever she might believe has been inserted into her teeth, it seems likely that she is referring to thoughts in her mind about undesirable aggressiveness which she is experiencing as events within the space of her body. These thoughts and associated feelings in relation to people and events intruding into her inner reality have been subject to the processes of (projective) expulsion from her mind and subsequent (introjective) re-entry.

Men are constantly intruding into her apartment. She barricades the door, but a "morphine man" shrinks himself so that he can penetrate through the keyhole.   In this belief, the oral symbolism of the invasion of her teeth assumes a more genital sexual character, which may arouse many questions. In considering the different possible levels of meaning of this material, we might wonder whether memories of her past abusive partners are threatening to penetrate her mental defence, and whether she is equating her safe apartment room with both her own body and her mind. In which case, the intruding elements might refer both to an intrusive penis (little man in keyhole) and certain thoughts that she has denied, split off, and projected, which now constantly threaten re-entry.

She repeatedly summons the police to report that men break in and put knives and sexually seductive lingerie in her cupboard drawers.   In this example, thoughts of sexuality and dangerous aggression are contained in the (mental representation of) the knives and lingerie, and these in turn are contained in the cupboard drawers. Thus banished from her conscious mind and subjected to symbolic transformation, these thoughts are now returning in unrecognizable form as delusional beliefs. Thoughts have become things, "idea-objects" contained in spaces.

Thoughts about the sofa in her apartment begins to disturb her.   She starts to believe that people are breaking into her apartment in order to put the sofa to some abuse or misuse. She attempts to deal with this by loosening the legs of the sofa so that it would collapse under any weight. This does not succeed in preventing the abuse, so in desperation she throws the sofa out of the apartment, along with other items of furniture also in some way contaminated by the intruders. This leads to her forcible hospitalization by the police. Psychotic patients not infrequently eject the contents of a room by throwing them out of the window. This behaviour might at times be understood as the consequence of concrete thinking, in which the room is being equated in unconscious phantasy with the mother's body, or with the patient's own mental space which is felt to be in urgent need of relief by the expulsion of painful thoughts.

Her thinking is typically action-centred and tied to spatial modes. Here again, the object (sofa) and what it represents are equated, and it seems likely that it is "mental furniture" that she is desperately struggling to keep out of her mind. These "idea-objects" must be expelled in order to keep her mind free of intolerable thoughts and feelings. The banished thoughts—memories or fantasies or both—concern illicit use of a sofa. Since her father was an upholsterer, this sequence could be considered as "soft" evidence of incestuous abuse by her father. But this might be quite incorrect, so more confirmation would be required.

Discussion

These psychodynamic reflections raise the question as to why a young woman who has had the capacity to learn and practise a skilled trade, to sustain a marriage, and to nurture two children should fall victim to a devastating mental illness that has ruined her life. No information is available to suggest that biological factors were relevant to her case.

A speculative reconstruction

Although the psychiatric records offered little detail, it was recorded that some information had been provided by her mother's relatives at the time of her first breakdown. At the age of 11, her schoolteachers had been sufficiently worried about her to suggest a consultation with a psychologist, but her father refused to allow this.

Although these fragments of information do not allow of any firm conclusion, they do allow a tentative reconstruction of potentially pathogenic factors in her childhood along the following lines. She was already a vulnerable child by the age of 11 years, a disturbed child in a perhaps disturbed family. Her relationship with her father was disturbed and disturbing. She dealt with negative feelings towards her mother by denying them and constructing an idealized view of her "angelic" quality. Such a history might raise suspicion of sexual abuse at the hands of her father, or, at the least, the existence of pathogenic incestuous fantasies in her mind.

However, the evidence that might confirm or disconfirm this suspicion was not available, and the truth might have been quite different. Even if this reconstruction were proved to be correct, it would not help to explain her vulnerability to later psychosis, rather than to neurosis or personality disorder.

Ellen's sanity

Psychoanalytic theory claims that psychotic patients are only partially "insane". This implies that Ellen has two distinct aspects of her personality, a psychotic and a non-psychotic one, and that in the former her thinking is characteristic of the paranoid–schizoid position. This concept has important implications for understanding and treatment.

Ellen is able to live in society because she can usually follow social conventions and avoid any but superficial emotional contact with people. Although she does not realize that her beliefs are delusional, she realizes the impact they have on other people and keeps them to herself until such times as her paranoid experiences become unbearable and erupt in an explosive manner. Although it is not known whether she has the capacity to doubt the actual reality of her experiences, she is sufficiently sane to realize that others might entertain such doubts.

Conclusions

Although the long-term outcome of chronic schizophrenia has been shown to be less often disastrous than had previously been thought (Bleuler, 1978; Ciompi, 1984), such disturbing relapses in an otherwise relatively stabilized case are common. A paranoid psychotic state such as that which Ellen suffers is typically so intolerable, and sometimes terrifying, that the individual searches for explanations of what he is experiencing. Although the ones he achieves may help to relieve his perplexity and confusion, they bring further disturbing consequences and anxieties in their train. These delusional explanations are like old friends, and it requires much skill and training for a therapist to acquire better explanations and to use them in a way that might help her. It also requires sensitivity and patience on the part of the therapist and psychiatric staff to help the patient acquire sufficient trust to be able to begin to doubt his own delusional explanations, and to consider that the therapist's explanations may be more helpful than his own. This is the focus of much of the work of cognitive-behavioural therapists with psychotic patients.

Psychiatrists encounter many such cases of chronic paranoid schizophrenic disorders in their everyday practice. Most psychiatrists would agree that florid paranoid beliefs have a particular meaning for the individual and would recognize the symbolic references to sexuality in Ellen's delusional world. However, not all would agree that the explanations of her preoccupations might be further understood by psychoanalytically informed investigation, nor that such an investigation might have been useful in the past. The many examples of Ellen's delusional thinking that were presented in the course of the case discussion at first seemed bizarre and unintelligible. However, when the characteristics of schizoid thinking were considered, they became more understandable in terms of her personal psychotic logic.

This type of understanding can provide clues as to what her inner conflicts might be, can provide material to attempt a reconstruction of the pathogenic and traumatic aspects of her earlier life, and can suggest what interventions might have helped her in the past, or even in the present day. In this way, study of the psychodynamic psychopathology can add depth to the descriptive psychopathology.

Ellen has received humane psychiatric care and generous social help over a period of thirty years, consisting of the provision of sympathetic support when requested and periods of asylum in times of crisis, where nursing attention and a temporary increase in anti-psychotic medication has quite quickly relieved her and made life once again tolerable. However, it has never proved possible to persuade her to maintain her medication for very long.

She has received conventional "understanding" care, but her mind has not been understood, and thus her basic pathogenic conflicts have not been recognized. By the time her paranoid symptoms had been established and consolidated, it is possible that she was beyond the reach of conventional psychiatry, but it is a sad commentary on her life that the concern expressed by her teachers when she was 11 years old came to nothing. Her latest admission to a psychotherapeutically oriented ward brings the hope that even at this late stage it may prove possible to help her.

Postscript

The single seminar discussion apparently gave a new impetus to the work of the ward. Two years later, the therapist reported that Ellen was doing very well. She remained on the ward for a year, responded well to rehabilitation procedures, and returned to live in her own apartment. She has worked well and realistically as an outpatient in the day centre and has accepted the need to maintain her medication for the foreseeable future. On the ward, she was included in a psychotherapy group which she attended for a year and found very helpful. She has regained contact with her children and repaired her relationship with them. Her treatment has been a very good experience for the staff, and Ellen expresses herself as profoundly grateful for the help and understanding that she has received.

CHAPTER NINE

Paranoid violence: "Duncan"

The term "schizophrenia" has sometimes in the past been regarded in popular usage as "split personality", and cases of sudden and dramatic shifts of identity are a phenomenon familiar to fiction writers. "Jekyll and Hyde", the *"Doppelgänger"*, the "alter ego", and more complex variants such as "demonic possession" or "multiple personality disorder" (MPD) are a perennial source of fascination for the reading public. The term "split personality" is not used in psychiatric practice, where such cases are likely to be classified as hysterical disorders of dissociative type, or in the case of MPD as the expression of borderline personality disorder.

The psychoanalytic concepts of splitting and identification are helpful in understanding many psychotic and non-psychotic disorders. The following case, presented by a female social worker and discussed on a single occasion in a large group of hospital staff, illustrates the dynamics of one type of violent behaviour in a psychotic patient and leads to reflections about his possible future.

Duncan

Duncan, now aged 22 years, was admitted to a psychiatric ward on a compulsory legal order at the age of 20. For some time he had become withdrawn, apathetic, and suspicious. He had told his mother that people were planning to kill him, but that he could not find out who they were. Recently he had become verbally threatening to her, in a way that was completely foreign to his normal character. When first admitted to hospital, he was unable to tolerate being in a locked ward. He escaped from surveillance and returned to his mother's apartment, where he smashed up all the furniture with a baseball bat, threatened to cut his mother's throat, and was brought back to the ward by the police, who had found that he was carrying an assortment of dangerous weapons. On admission, he was drunk, threatening and violent. Medication and sleep soon restored his precarious stability, but he remained anxious and preoccupied with delusional thinking. He explained that the weapons were essential to protect himself from "them"—criminals whom he believed had been following him and intended to kill him.

The psychiatric diagnosis of paranoid psychosis seemed straightforward. The staff regarded him as being like two different persons, the one polite and likeable, the other—emerging when disinhibited—rather like a violently destructive and rebellious adolescent or child. The psychiatric team formed the impression that Duncan's mother was extremely overpossessive, but they were not clear whether this should be regarded simply as a sign of maternal concern and love for him, or whether some possible pathology of her own might have contributed to his disturbance.

Personal history

Duncan was the only child of a couple who had comfortable material circumstances but severe marital problems, which led to his mother leaving his father when Duncan was 3 years old. Little is known about his first three years of life, apart from the fact that his mother worried because Duncan slept badly and often seemed to be very unhappy. Her preoccupation with work outside the home led to his being cared for by his maternal grandparents. He became very attached to his grandmother, and he formed a complex relationship with his grandfather which was later to prove highly disturbing to him.

By the age of 4 years, his mother was so worried about Duncan that she took him to a psychiatrist, who judged him to be an anxious and understimulated child. The mother was offered some advice, but no further action was taken. From the time of her separation from Duncan's father, his mother lived for many years with the constant fear that the father would kidnap him.

Duncan became a quiet, polite, and well-behaved child, although solitary and with few friends in his primary school. The psychiatric record mentions that at the age of 14 he suffered a severe humiliation when a teacher informed him that he had an offensive smell, presumably the result of neglect of personal hygiene. This neglect was to be a prominent feature during later psychotic periods.

At about that time, he began to abuse alcohol and cannabis and revealed disturbingly violent tendencies when in the disinhibited state that they provoked. He was afraid of the anti-social youths at school, yet he made friends with some of them. He took to playing games with fire together with another youth. These games appear to have been potentially dangerous, although no actual episode of arson was recorded.

In between periods of substance abuse, he had remained the polite and considerate character that he had always been, apologetic about his episodic violent behaviour but slowly becoming more disturbed. Having long had severe learning difficulties, he left school early and did some occasional work for brief periods. He managed to persevere for a time in gardening work, where he was alone and at times apparently happy. His drinking continued, and he once provoked a serious assault on himself by other adolescents.

In his late adolescence, he was already showing premonitory signs of psychotic thinking. He went to the emergency-room of a general hospital, and demanded that he be given a lethal euthanasia injection. He explained that this was a reasonable request, and that he was entitled to it because in this way he could go to heaven and be reborn as a great Indian guru.

Progress on the ward—the beginning of trust

On the ward, Duncan slowly began to trust the staff sufficiently to speak about himself and his experiences. He spoke of his feelings of weakness, his sense of inferiority, and a sense of feeling himself to be

more a woman than a man, apparently in a metaphorical rather than a
delusional manner

He explained that the reason that he found staying in the ward so
intolerable was because the other patients—unlike himself—were
"crazy". Once again he ran from the ward to his mother's apartment
to retrieve his weapons, so that he could hope to live outside the ward
in the dangerous world. It seemed that he was claustrophobic inside
the ward and acutely paranoid outside it.

Nightmares

He talked freely with the social worker, to whom he disclosed
that he had long been very afraid that his mother might die and that
he had recently had repeated terrifying nightmares. He recounted
two of these that had filled him with disgust, fear and horror. In the
first:

> He is visiting his grandmother in hospital. On his way he is accosted by
> strangers who threaten to shoot him in the head. They hit him on the head
> with a bottle, but he manages to escape. He runs away over ground
> littered with rubbish and descends into a sewer where the dirt and filth is
> even worse.

In the second:

> He has lost his motor bike and is searching to find another. He comes to a
> stairway where there are several drunken men. He feels safe because they
> are friendly and have a friendly dog with them. He carries on descending
> the stairway and is confronted by a horrifying sight. He sees a pack of
> dogs who are in various states of injury, dismemberment, and mutila-
> tion, some with skin burned off, and some with eyes and limbs missing.
> He continues to descend, and suddenly he meets an enemy who is some-
> how familiar and starts to fight him. He awakens with feelings of horror
> and dread.

Grandfather—a confusing role-model

His mother told the psychiatric team a story of his early childhood that threw light on the origins of his disturbance. Whereas his

maternal grandmother took a helpful maternal role for him from the beginning, Duncan's relationship with the grandfather was much more complex. This man had been a heroic figure in the wartime resistance of his country, and Duncan admired him very much. However, by the time Duncan was born, the grandfather had become addicted to alcohol, and during periods of drunkenness he was extremely violent in the home. Later, when drunk he was cruelly aggressive to his grandson and often beat him severely. Whether his mother and grandmother were able to protect him was not clear.

At the time of the case discussion, the staff felt that they were gaining the patient's trust and were feeling cautiously hopeful about gaining a more firm, cooperative relationship with him. The staff thought that he had a wish to understand himself, and they decided that attempting to impose a total ban on drinking would be unrealistic for the moment. So they encouraged him to use antabuse (disulfuram) in the proper manner, and they persisted in their policy of firm refusal to allow him to break the structure of the daily treatment routine, accepting his fury when he could not get his own way. With firm encouragement, Duncan recovered his capacity for personal hygiene and had begun to wash in a normal manner, a striking contrast to his usual neglected and unwashed state. The staff were feeling hopeful about him and regarded the task of helping him overcome his substance abuse as a first priority.

However, the staff's optimism was tempered by the fact they felt that they had not understood him sufficiently, that he remained under police surveillance, and that control of his drinking might not prove sufficient to help him achieve stability.

Discussion

There may be many ways of explaining the nature of Duncan's "dual" personality and many factors involved in determining his aggressive behaviour. Since there was a lack of detailed information about his early life and development that might have helped clarify some obscure aspects of his case, attempts at achieving a satisfactory explanation of the nature and origins of his disorder are inevitably tentative.

In the case of Duncan, it is possible to make a provisional reconstruction of the pathogenic elements in his early development, which might allow a deeper understanding of his later difficulties and might contribute to assessing his prognosis and informing future interventions.

The dual care by mother and grandmother in the context of a deteriorating marital relationship provided a difficult start and would help explain why he was so disturbed after the parents separated. It is possible that his sleep difficulties were associated with disturbing dreams, in which case the current nightmares could be considered as later derivatives of these early precursors. Not only did the patient have this very insecure childhood, but it was compounded by the subsequent influence of the more enduring father-figure, his maternal grandfather. The grandfather, like Duncan, seems to have also had a dual identity. Sometimes he was very good and admirable, and at others frighteningly violent and punitive. If Duncan already was having difficulty in integrating aggressive feelings of his own, this difficulty can only have been made worse by his having to survive his grandfather's episodic drunken brutality.

Duncan's loss of contact
with his own primitive aggressive feelings

Another consequence may have been that Duncan lost the possibility of discovering and integrating his own aggressiveness, a quality that is essential for normal social and sexual relationships. Such a failure may deprive him of this constructive aggressiveness, which is condemned by his superego as "bad" but in fact is a mixture of "bad" and good" qualities.

Thus one task in psychoanalytic psychotherapy, with both psychotic and less disturbed patients, is to help them reclaim such lost and immature parts of the self that have in early childhood become identified (by the superego) as bad, because they are too threatening to the objects upon whom life depends. In a psychodynamic sense, these aggressive parts of the self are actually a mixture of destructive and potentially constructive qualities. A further, and potentially more psychotic, development may follow if, by the use of projective identification, the encounter with an aggressive relative comes to serve as a container for the child's own primitive aggressive feelings. This use of the defence of projective identification can thus lead the child to a blurring of the distinction between his self and the aggressive caretaker, and the child is unable to recognize his own unconscious aggressiveness because it is now experienced as being located in the overtly aggressive other person. Many further adverse consequences may follow, including the repetitive enactment in the real world of an unconscious phantasy or memory in the form of a brutally aggressive or sadomasochistic drama.

The disowning of personal aggressiveness by means of splitting and projective identification can lead to an increasing conviction that the world is a dangerous place, populated by dangerous people, and that constant (paranoid) vigilance is necessary to forestall imminent attacks. The more that actual violence is encountered, as in the crucial assault that apparently contributed to Duncan's destabilization, the worse the conviction of the world being so completely dangerous.

An even more disturbing process may ensue if these defences begin to break down under some specific internal or external stress. Under these circumstances, the projective processes may become reinforced by behaviour that is unconsciously designed to force another person into behaving in an aggressive manner towards the subject. Since society has no difficulty in providing suitable candidates for this projective drama, escalating violence and eventual murder can result.

Shifting and unstable identifications

It seemed very likely that Duncan had provoked the violent assault on himself, possibly in a drunken or drugged state. To be certain whether this behaviour was motivated simply by a wish to prove his manliness or by a complex process of identification with his drunken grandfather would need to be discerned in therapy.

Duncan's extreme lack of self-confidence and normal masculine self-assertiveness left him with profound feelings of inferiority. His wish to be re-born as a great guru may reflect the power of his buried wish to be special to his mother, and perhaps the residue of a rivalrous little boy's normal need to feel superior to his admired father, a process sometimes appearing as megalomania in more deeply schizophrenic patients. Duncan was effectively deprived of a father with whom he might have negotiated a normal competitive process leading towards a constructive masculine identification, and he had to cope with the grandfather, who was confusingly inconsistent in his admirable and brutally aggressive qualities.

These dual and unstable identifications may help to account for the startling contrast in Duncan's behaviour. Helpful identifications find expression in his normal pleasant behaviour, and harmful ones determine his periods of violent behaviour. Thus he behaves like his admirable grandfather most of the time, and in certain circumstances switches to behaviour very similar to the grandfather's drinking and violence.

Duncan as victim

However bad and harmful his grandfather might have been in these periods, it is possible that Duncan's memories of him have been to some extent distorted by the projection of his own feared aggressiveness. Should Duncan ever achieve sufficient integration of his own masculine assertiveness—the reclaiming of "a lost part of himself"—he might eventually come to perceive his grandfather as somewhat less of a monster.

Such a speculation might receive indirect support if more information were available about these early traumatic episodes. It is not known whether his mother or grandmother attempted to shelter Duncan from his grandfather's violence. We must also consider how vulnerable the patient might already have been when he encountered these traumatic events. From his early infancy he showed signs of severe anxiety, and this suggests that the experience with his grandfather may not have been a sufficient factor to account for Duncan's subsequent disturbance. It is more likely that the real world had a disturbing impact on the pre-existing disorder in his inner world. In the same way, his mother's fears that her child might be kidnapped by his father might have enhanced an already paranoid mental state.

The possibility that an earlier, more primitive, pathology lay beneath the subsequent trauma has both theoretical and practical implications. If the child who came to be traumatized by his grandfather's behaviour was already deeply disturbed, the adult disorder might be more likely to prove to be a serious and more insidious schizophrenic one. If, on the other hand, it had been the grandfather who had been primarily responsible for the disturbance, the explanation of dual identifications might be sufficient and the prognosis a good deal better.

The dreams as symbolic windows—
descent into the underworld

The two dreams that Duncan recounted made a deep impression on him, although he had no understanding of the unconscious thinking that had produced them. As already mentioned, great caution is needed in drawing conclusions from the manifest content of dreams in the absence of the dreamer's associations. However, the dreams that Duncan reported are interesting, and they may throw light on his unconscious pathogenic phantasies.

When a psychotic patient is in a sufficiently integrated state to be able to manufacture coherent dream thoughts and to distinguish dream life from waking life, it implies the beginnings of symbolization of unconscious phantasies and object relationships in the inner world. Before this level of integration is reached, the deeply psychotic patient may consider a dream to be an evacuation of some object from his mind, analogous to an evacuation of his bowels (Bion, 1962, p. 78).

Thus the dream offers a narrative in the form of a scenario that can be looked at and thus thought about and shared with others. In this way, the dream may serve as a clear and informative window on the dreamer's unconscious perceptions and thoughts.

In considering the possible meanings in the story of Duncan's dream, it is important to know that he has said that the only relationships in which he has ever felt safe and loved are with his grandmother and with dogs. He also said that the dreams were like going into hell.

In the first dream, he is going to his beloved grandmother when, as in his paranoid fears in waking life, he is attacked by strangers and hit on the head with a bottle. This dream event may perhaps express an incipient insight into the fact that he uses the bottle (drink) to prevent himself from thinking unbearable thoughts. Escaping, he descends (like Dante and the heroes of mythology) into the underworld of his unconscious mind.

In the second dream, the narrative of his journey continues and he encounters the horrifying scene of the burned and dismembered dogs. He starts to descend even further, when his way is barred by an enemy whom he starts to fight.

The dream's revelation is that he has believed, ever since his infancy, that any aggressive feelings about his mother would be (and in his phantasy have already been, and will continue to be) frighteningly destructive. As a vulnerable "internal" mother, she is not properly differentiated from a dangerous internal father.

The dream that dramatizes the unconscious phantasy is part of an internal reality that infiltrates and distorts the patient's perceptions of the real world and of the remembered past. This second dream suggests an association of his infantile aggressiveness with this dangerous, probably sexualized, adolescent play with fire. Such symbolic derivatives which connect fire-setting and urination are well known to psychotherapists of behaviourally disturbed children and adolescents. An example is seen in the self-immolating compulsions of a young schizophrenic patient (Jackson & Williams, 1994).

In the view of the dream, the dogs represent the good (internal) mother (grandmother), now seen to be suffering the fate that his primitive mental splitting defences have tried to save her (the good mother) from ever since his infancy. The danger of thinking about himself in relation to his mother is that he would then become aware of his loving feelings for her. Such a recognition would threaten to undo the splitting that has kept him in ignorance of the destructive feelings towards her.

Mutilated, dismembered, torn, bitten, and burned, and living in the repository of digestive processes (a symbolic—mental—rectum) of Duncan's mind, the dogs appear in their gentleness and kindness as the helpless and innocent victims of infantile cruelty.

Who is the dangerous adversary?

When Duncan goes on to battle with the dangerous dream enemy, he is engaged in a struggle of destructive hatred and protective love. Although the dream enemy may represent a version of the dangerous grandfather, there are other possible references that could perhaps be established in the course of psychotherapy, as seen in the account of the "Mafia"-type mental figures in Chapter 7.

Although Duncan does not yet understand it, his nightmare is telling his conscious, though sleeping, self about the breakdown of his life-long defences against infantile aggressiveness and its consequences in psychic reality. The use of alcohol and drugs has had an anxiety-lowering effect that allowed him to feel safe in the company of other alcohol abusers but, at the other times in other settings, disinhibited his capacity to control his violence. In this way, excessive drinking allowed him to bypass any risk of reflective thinking that might prove too painful for him to tolerate. The dream shows that the dog's comforting "friendliness" has been dependent on Duncan's continuing to manage to split off his destructive feeling towards his internal mother.

The final theme of the second dream suggests that the second enemy is possibly a version of the first, thus implying that Duncan has the potential to wish to fight against the forces that are keeping him trapped in the underworld of his mind. He may even have the beginnings of a vague realization that alcohol, although a friend to him (in the sense of helping him to survive psychologically), is also the enemy that releases his problematic and dangerous aggression and prevents him thinking usefully. Although he wishes to help himself, he is not yet able to accept that he may possibly be helped by the professional staff. It is likely that Duncan will find it humiliating to have to accept that he is in part a small boy who has much to learn from the parent figures, and that he may yet have to re-live in the present some of his hidden conflicts about them before they can be safely reconsigned to infancy where they belong.

Conclusions

The foregoing explanations and reconstructions emerged from a single session of consultation with the psychiatric staff. The evidence that might confirm these formulations might only be acquired during the course of psychotherapy, which had not been attempted at that time. However, the concepts used in reaching such formulations can be widely found useful in attempting to understand the meaning of psychotic thought and behaviour, and to planning therapeutic interventions.

Duncan is suffering from a paranoid psychosis, which could be regarded as being precipitated or aggravated by drugs and alcohol. The psychodynamic perspective helps in the understanding of the meaning of his psychosis, and the idea of a breakthrough of a "lost part" of his self presents the possibility of the resumption of long-paralysed emotional growth. Seen in this perspective, many psychotic patients like Duncan are much easier to understand than those with less serious disorders.

His prognosis is uncertain, and it remains to be seen whether such growth lies ahead and whether psychotherapy can be provided to help him to resume it. Psychodynamic understanding is in the first instance simply an aid to listening more effectively to the patient, and even if psychotherapy cannot be provided, the staff's use of their normal sensitivity and wish to understand the patient better can be of immense psychotherapeutic benefit. The staff's strategy of setting limits to his demanding behaviour may help to provide him with a firm role-model that will help him control his aggressive feelings.

The acquisition of important new knowledge may be like a Pandora's box. It brings painful consequences, but also hope. The psychotic patient's breakdown removes the defences against mental pain but also offers hope. Many factors determine whether that hope will be fulfilled and the psychotic breakdown will be the beginnings of a better and more integrated life and progress towards the depressive position, or whether the breakdown will represent the beginnings of a chronic schizophrenic deterioration or, in the case of Duncan, of criminal violence.

Duncan is still regarded by the police as potentially a serious crime risk, and it must not be forgotten that prolonged use of neuroleptic medication—however helpful or even essential it may be in moderate doses—may have the effect of sealing off the pathological material that is coming to the surface, and it may be some time before reduction or discontinuation of medication can be safely attempted.

The dream evidence of Duncan's capacity for intense concern is an important factor in the forensic process of assessment of dangerousness which may become necessary before he is discharged from psychiatric care. Psychoanalysts experienced in this work have made useful contributions to the understanding of the psychodynamic factors that may be involved in unprovoked assault (Sohn, 1999) and murderous behaviour (A. H. Williams, 1998). If further exploration confirms that he has a strong capacity to function at the level of the depressive position, or that he might achieve it with the help of psychotherapy, his chances of resolving his serious conflicts and integrating the potentially dangerous split in his personality are good.

Understanding of the mental mechanisms that the violent psychotic patient has been using is helpful in formulating effective treatment plans and in creating a psychiatric setting in which individual psychotherapy, if appropriate and available, can be undertaken without risk to the therapist. Although an intellectual understanding of the psychopathology of a patient is not necessarily the same as understanding the patient, it does provide a necessary foundation.

Schizophrenia—psychotherapy, termination, reparation: "Florence"

Since Freud's essay "Analysis Terminable and Interminable" (1937c), much attention has focused on the difficulties in concluding a course of psychotherapy that has been relatively successful. Klein's concept of reparation helps to explain why some patients, psychotic and non-psychotic, do not feel able to terminate psychotherapy until they have made good the damage they believe they have done to other people, either in reality or imagination, a theme that has been elaborated by Rey (1994).

Interminable therapy

Psychotherapy with a psychotic patient may need to go on for a long time if the patient is to be able to live independently without the help of the therapist (Holmes, 1997). It may be difficult to assess the quality of prolonged therapy because the therapist may believe that continuation is essential to prevent the patient from deteriorating, a doubt that may be difficult to resolve. Terminating therapy before the conflicts aroused by the process of separation have been sufficiently worked through may represent an impressive outcome for a severely ill psychotic patient, and an indication of chronic disabling dependency in another. Deficiencies in the therapist or the setting are likely to lead to the undue prolongation of treatment. Problems in the therapist's countertransference can account for the development of an impasse where little or nothing is actually being achieved (Rosenfeld, 1987).

In Rey's view, there are some patients who, although they may be doing quite well in therapy, unconsciously believe that they cannot leave the therapy until they have come to terms with their concern about a relationship with an important figure, usually the mother, who is felt to be in a damaged or distressed state. For such a patient this is an inner reality (and may also be true in actual external reality), and the unconscious wish of the patient is that the therapist should help the person ("object") recover, or at least should deal with the patient's concern, and possibly guilt. The following case illustrates some of the issues involved.

Florence

Florence, aged 34 years, had been in psychotherapy for eight years when her case was discussed in a closed seminar group of eight relatively experienced psychotherapists. Her therapist wanted to understand why it had proved impossible to terminate the therapy completely. Florence had made great progress, and the therapy was changed to a once-monthly rate. She had, however, remained dependent on continued contact with the therapist and seemed to be unable to tolerate a formal termination of the therapy.

This seminar discussion ended on a note of uncertainty since it was not clear why the patient, and perhaps the therapist, could not terminate the therapy. Neither was it clear whether the continuation of the treatment represented a necessary period of consolidation of her gains or whether it had become arrested in a relatively unproductive impasse. Two further discussions and follow-up information three and four years later helped to clarify the situation.

Onset of psychosis

Florence had had an acute psychotic breakdown when she was 17 years old, and she was admitted to a locked psychiatric ward after a serious suicide attempt involving cutting and massive drug overdose.

On admission, she was acutely anxious and confused, was found to be experiencing auditory and visual hallucinations, and was preoccupied with delusional thoughts. She believed that she was dangerously destructive and that she had an atomic bomb inside her body. At times, she refused to open her mouth because she believed that if she spoke to someone in front of her, nuclear radiation would flow from her inside and destroy the person who was listening to her.

She spoke of her terror that a "black man" would find her and kill her, and she had vivid visions of dead babies hanging from trees in the woods, and of the faces of dead babies on the ceiling of her room. She was afraid of her mother, whom she believed was invading her mind, and could read her thoughts and take them away from her. At times, she would suddenly switch into a megalomanic state of mind. In this state, she would say that she was God, and she would display her hands, saying that light was streaming out from them. She insisted that this phenomenon was evidence of her omnipotent powers, in particular of her capacity to baptize babies.

She was admitted urgently to a psychiatric ward where a diagnosis of schizophreniform psychosis was made, and an outline of her developmental history was established with the cooperation of her mother and stepfather.

Some personal history

Florence was the only child of an accidental pregnancy and never knew her biological father. Her mother left her in the care of her grandmother at the age of 2 months and returned four years later with a new husband and a new baby brother, and resumed her care. She had been well cared for by her grandmother, and her mother had kept in as close touch as her circumstances permitted. She was an intelligent and imaginative child, and grew up on good terms with her stepfather and half-brother. Although regarded as a sensitive child and adolescent, she had had no obvious sign of serious emotional disturbance until her mother was found to have breast cancer. A mastectomy was performed, and it was during her mother's convalescence that Florence made the suicide attempt.

Initial treatment

With neuroleptic medication and supportive nursing care, her acute disturbance subsided within a fortnight. She remained in hospital for several months during which the circumstances of her breakdown were explored. It was considered that the psychotic episode had been precipitated by her concern about her mother's breast cancer (from which her mother eventually was to make a complete recovery). When Florence was discharged, she had apparently recovered. Her thought disorder had subsided, but she remembered her past delusional beliefs and hallucinations as having been strange and alarming. A moderate maintenance dose of neuroleptic was continued, and further post-discharge surveillance was organized. Her prognosis was thought to be relatively good.

However, her symptoms soon recurred, and she was readmitted—again to a closed ward—as a serious suicide risk. Once again, she gradually recovered and was discharged after some months on a higher level of medication. She remained in fear of further breakdown, and since she was both intelligent and motivated to try to understand her illness she was offered once-weekly psychotherapy, which she readily accepted. The long-term commitment to her care by the psychiatric team provided the setting within which the psychotherapy could safely be undertaken.

Psychotherapy begins—the first four years

During the course of the four years of psychotherapy, Florence had several further psychotic episodes that necessitated readmissions to the ward. These episodes sometimes followed apparently suicidal behaviour on leaving the therapy session. They took the form of impulses to throw herself in front of the road traffic, behaviour that necessitated intensive supervision for long periods and frequent regulation of the level of medication.

During these periods, her psychotic thinking returned in force, but when less disturbed she realized that her thoughts were extremely strange and mysterious, but that during the episodes they were terrifyingly real to her. She felt very hurt and misunderstood if well-intentioned friends ever suggested that her problem was simply a matter of an overactive imagination or a bid for special attention.

She showed dramatic disturbances of her body image and was frequently overtaken by the alarming feeling that her breasts were disappearing into the inside of her body. Her sense of personal identity was profoundly disturbed. Florence told her therapist that she did not really know who she herself was, and that when leaving the session she felt that she lost what little sense of existence that she had. She could not at first listen to her therapist, and although she sometimes asked questions, she explained that the reason that she could not listen was that if the therapist gave an answer to the question, Florence felt that she herself ceased to exist. As her condition gradually improved, she was able to explain that she had believed at first that the therapist, like her mother, could read her mind, so there was no point in or necessity for speaking to her.

She sometimes felt that she was a boy and at other times that she was a girl. Unable to resolve this confusion, she cut one side of her hair in a close boyish fashion and left the other side to grow long. She was preoccupied with thoughts about the special significance of colours. For long periods she would wear only black, or only white clothing, and eat only dark- or light-coloured foods. She had alarming visions of black seeds, in the shape of sharp teeth.

Florence believed that she was pregnant and that it was her mother who had brought about this state. She felt that she had caused the death by starvation of children in Africa and felt that she must join Mother Teresa to help them in their plight. She felt a great desire to touch her mother's soft skin, but when she actually did she experienced a sense of severe nausea. The memory of this disturbing experience of touching her mother had sometimes led the patient to abandon eating meat and to restricting her diet to vegetables for long periods during her adolescence. She believed at times that she was suffering from cancer of the intestines, a hypochondriacal delusion typical of some psychotic and severe anorexic disorders, usually centred on cancer of the inside of the body. This has been considered as an expression of an unconscious phantasy of there being a baby inside the body of a mother with whom the patient is identified and who is vengefully devouring the host (Rey, 1994).

Sometimes she spoke of experiences she found good and comforting. For example, she thought that a bird had laid an egg in her throat, and this comforted her because she knew that the egg would eventually hatch and that the baby, felt to be herself, would fly away to a far-off happy land.

As the psychotherapy proceeded, Florence displayed clear evidence of the persistence of her delusional belief in her destructive powers, which she insisted had killed babies and apparently was continuing to do so. It was apparent that in her psychotic states of mind, her object-relating capacities were regressively replaced by shifting and unstable identifications, such as her belief that she was the pregnant mother of her childhood. It became clear that her fear of her mother, the recurring images of the dead babies, and the ever-present menace of the murderous black man illustrated that her psychotic life was the expression of her belief that she was both dangerous and endangered. The transient delusional belief that she was pregnant brought a momentary escape from the world of dead babies, as did those states of mind in which she felt able to introduce new-born babies to a protected life, by baptizing them.

From the beginning of the therapy she cooperated consistently, and she developed a strong positive transference to the therapist. As she made progress, she slowly became able to begin to accept that her psychotic thinking was abnormal and was confined to her own mind, and thus needed to be considered as a product of her own imagination. Much of the therapeutic work centred on her near-conscious feelings of envy and jealousy of the half-brother who had displaced her at the age of 4, and of her jealousy of her mother and stepfather, whose relationship seemed in reality to be a happy one. She recalled that in the months before her first psychotic episode, she had frequently insisted on sleeping between her parents, and she remembered vividly the feelings of violent jealousy that had motivated this behaviour.

Progress

The therapist gradually introduced Florence to the idea that her belief that her mother had made her pregnant was the expression of a conflict of hidden emotional thoughts and childhood memories of her pregnant mother. It was with great relief that Florence was eventually able to recognize the metaphorical nature of this belief and to exclaim: "I am *me!* I am not my pregnant mother!".

Her eating inhibitions were traced to unconscious wishes to protect her mother from her infantile devouring impulses. Her envy of her brother was considered to underlie the wishful delusion that she was half a boy, and, as she became able to recognize the meaning of her bizarre hairstyle, Florence was able to adopt a conventional feminine hairstyle. She also came to understand the nature of the fears of destructiveness that had led to symbolic expression in her delusional thoughts about having an atom bomb inside her body. She said that she now realized that she had always had to keep her bad feelings hidden inside herself, because if people knew how awful she was they would not be able to stand her and would abandon her.

During her recurring psychotic episodes, Florence's belief that her mother could read her mind reappeared, and it had been so real to her that she began to learn Chinese, rather than some other less remote language, in order to protect herself from the experience of the intrusive mother reading her thoughts.

Florence's sensitivity to threats of separation from her mother, and in the transference from her therapist, was nonetheless particularly clear. Her psychotic thinking was activated during holiday breaks in the therapy or when the subject of the eventual termination of the therapy was mentioned. She came to realize that her behaviour during earlier psychotic episodes, when she would run from the ward and stand by the passing traffic, apparently with suicidal intent, was her response to feeling enraged with her parents when they left after a visit to the ward, or with the therapist when her feelings of jealousy had been aroused in a session.

Termination of therapy is attempted

At the end of four years of weekly sessions, her psychosis seemed to have been successfully resolved, and her great improvement was recognized by the psychiatric team. Florence's belief in the literal reality of her psychotic experiences had greatly declined, and she had been able to say that she had come to realize that the "visions" and beliefs could not possibly have been true, but that she had experienced them at the time as absolutely real, although still to some extent mysterious. However, it was felt necessary to keep her maintained on a moderate dose of anti-psychotic medication. The therapist believed that her patient had acquired sufficient understanding of the nature of her past psychotic thinking to make any further relapse unlikely and that it should be possible to bring the treatment to a close.

Despite her improvement, Florence was still functioning below her intellectual potential and was unemployed, and she strenuously resisted the suggestion of working towards termination. It seemed clear that she could not tolerate the separation from the therapist that a formal ending would involve, nor face the demands of full independence. The therapist then changed the routine to a monthly session. No further admission was required in the following four years up to the time of the presentation of her case to the seminar, eight years after the beginning of the therapy, at which point the therapist brought the case to the seminar.

The seminar discussion

After the therapist had presented the details of the case, the discussion focused on two themes: the origins and meanings of Florence's bizarre hallucinations and delusions, and the nature of the inability to terminate the therapy completely. Although the therapist had understood Florence's main emotional conflicts quite well and in the therapy had worked at them and to some extent worked through them, it seemed clear that neither Florence nor her therapist had fully understood the deeper meaning of some of her past psychotic experiences.

During these last four years of monthly contact, Florence had maintained her improved social and intellectual functions and had begun to devote much time to writing. She had composed a novel based on her own experience of the psychosis and of the therapy. The therapist had read the manuscript and thought that the account was more or less accurate, but that the ending of the narrative was quite unexpected.

The novel ended with the heroine going into the forest, where she found her mother and grandmother dead, hanging from a tree. She cut them down, took them into her own bed, and brought them to life with the warmth of her body, thus providing a happy ending to her story. Although she did not succeed in her bid for publication, it apparently had sufficient quality for a publisher to give it serious consideration.

She eventually told the therapist that she now knew that she could only terminate the therapy and leave her therapist when the latter had had a baby. In view of the fact that she knew that the therapist was past child-bearing age, this enigmatic communication had perplexed the therapist.

It was at this point that a tentative explanation of the meaning of these events was attempted.

The role of pathogenic early experiences — a dynamic formulation

Florence's inability to leave her therapist could be considered to have its early "pre-oedipal" roots in the loss of her mother in infancy and the overwhelming feelings of envy and jealousy that were aroused when she returned with the stepfather and new baby brother when Florence was 4 years old. The creation of the image of the dangerous black man issues from her oedipal conflicts, one aspect of which is her destructive jealousy of her stepfather. The symbolic transformation of these early conflicts eventually came to populate her nightmare-like states of mind. Thus the black biting teeth-seeds, for instance, could eventually be partly understood as the symbolic representative of "poisonous" and "biting" words, felt by her to be literal and immediate dangerous objects associated with dangerously destructive feelings and impulses. These thoughts might help explain the nausea provoked by touching her mother's soft skin (breast).

Reparation

It will be recalled that the frightening hallucinations of dead babies hanging from trees in the forest were a main feature of her psychotic thinking, and that this content might be understood as a symbolic expression of her unconscious murderous feelings about the baby who displaced her. These feelings found delusional expression in her insistence that she was responsible for the death by starvation of countless children in Africa, and her moments of claiming that she was God could be understood as an omnipotent denial of her fears and a manic attempt at reparation. As God, she can baptize babies and no doubt raise the dead.

In Florence's novel, she has returned to the theme of her psychotic hallucinations of the drama, but this time she attempts to identify her conflicts and deal with them in a symbolic fashion. The victims of her real-life but not fully integrated destructive feelings are her grandmother, a good figure, now dead, and her mother, still alive, to whom she is still in reality deeply and ambivalently attached. In her novel, she has created the possibility of a happy ending by the exercise of omnipotent power to resurrect the dead, representing the mother and grandmother of her unconscious inner world. This can be regarded as a manic attempt at a reparation (Segal, 1981b), which can only succeed if she can become more aware of what it is that she is trying so desperately to repair.

If Florence's novel is considered as a metaphorical expression of her near-conscious awareness that further development is required before she can become truly stable and independent, its likely meaning is clear: namely that her destructive feelings about her "abandoning" mother have not yet been sufficiently worked through in the therapy and are being held in check by continuing to cling to the therapist.

The therapist may perhaps have a countertransference problem, in which she has been forced to accept the role of an overprotective mother who cannot tolerate the rage that separation will arouse in her infant-patient. Florence seems to have an unconscious awareness that before she can be free and happy, she must repair her loved objects, felt to be not dead, but kept in a state of suspended animation, awaiting the day that she will be able to repair and bring them back to life. In other words, she has the hope that her love for her mother will prove more powerful than her unconscious hatred which has not yet been fully exposed and experienced. Negative feelings have received much attention throughout the therapy, but the most immediate place in which they can become fully conscious for her—namely in the psychotherapeutic transference—still remains unexplored. It is possible that they will continue to remain so until a firm date for termination is set and the consequences are worked through. The patient and the therapist "know about" her destructiveness but perhaps do not yet "know" it sufficiently.

The requirement that the therapist must have a baby might imply that the patient wishes to give her mother a baby, to make up for the baby that she has, in fantasy, destroyed with her rivalrous hatred. It may also suggest that the patient may have some dawning awareness that the theme of her therapist having another baby may refer to the arrival of another patient, who will replace her when the therapy ends, as happened to Florence at an early age. If this were the case, it might imply that Florence is repeating a childhood wish to prevent her mother abandoning her and replacing her with another baby, and to rewrite her history rather than to come to terms with it and at the same time to lay a claim to being her mother's only child (as in the case of Grace, Chapter 13).

The urge for reparation may become very powerful in some patients who have reached the depressive position, and this may help explain why patients like Florence hold on so tenaciously to their therapy and therapist if this dynamic is not recognized and worked through.

To say that these are the "likely" meanings of the drama of her inner life is to imply that there may be further and different explanations of the material. The novel's theme suggests that Florence has made an envious manic attack on her therapist's creative therapeutic work.

There remain two unresolved questions. First, why have attempts to withdraw neuroleptic medication been unsuccessful? The ostensible reason has been that the patient might react with a revival of her psychotic thinking. But if this were to happen it would offer an opportunity to work through the remaining problems. One reason why psychotic patients may sometimes not be able to give up their delusional thinking, when they seem to have made sufficient progress to take such a step, is that the delusional material contains a hidden positive value, banished from consciousness by a harshly condemning superego and, in this sense, containing a potentially valuable "lost part of the self".

The final question is whether the patient may have actually recovered the capacity to appreciate the metaphorical nature of her imaginative thinking, but is clinging to it in order to maintain the role of very special patient, without a rival in the therapist's mind, as well as the other motives suggested above.

The therapist is now in the position of having to decide whether to reopen the matter of termination of therapy and deal with the consequences, for better or for worse. In the case of a woman with such intelligence and talent, who has had a high level of psychiatric and psychotherapeutic help for a long time and has a very supportive family, there are reasons to hope that if a further period of psychotherapy were acceptable to her and her therapist, she has a very good chance of consolidating of her impressive psychotherapeutic gains.

Three years later

Following the seminar discussion, the therapist resumed weekly sessions for a further six months, during which time she focused on Florence's unresolved feelings about her mother and its parallels in the transference. Florence's envy of the therapist, both as a successful mother and professional woman in reality and as the representative of her "abandoning" mother of her inner reality, came more fully into the open. Her relation with her mother in the present improved considerably, and she slowly came to the conclusion that her belief that her mother was so invasive was her misunderstanding of her mother's deep concern and worry about her. She finally came to understand that her past terrors had a symbolic and dream-like quality and had been revived at the age of 17 by her mother's mastectomy operation for a life-threatening cancer, by which time her own fear of having cancer had disappeared.

At the end of this six-month period, the patient decided that it was now possible to end the therapy. However, she insisted on continuing to see the therapist briefly every six weeks. The therapist complied with her request, since she believed that an abrupt termination would be beyond the patient's capacity and that the most realistic strategy was to work to adopt a slow "weaning" process. She was aware that a fuller working-through of the depressive position might involve the process of the patient's mourning of her losses, which included the many years of disability prior to her encounter with effective psychotherapy.

A further year on

One year later, twelve years after the beginning of the therapy (when Florence was aged 22), the therapist provided a detailed follow-up report. She is still seeing Florence at six-weekly intervals. Florence has made steady progress, leading an apparently normal social life and involved in creative work at a school of art, in which she gained a place in the face of considerable competition.

The psychiatrist managing the case has changed the medication from Clozapine, which had made her sleepy, to a small dose of Olanzapine, which has proved free of side-effects. On this regime Florence seems to be happy and stable, although she is still subject to brief periods of anxiety. These take the form of recurrence of hypo-chondriacal thoughts, which, although disturbing, no longer have their original delusional intensity. She has learned how to deal with them and to some extent to understand them.

When troubled by these feelings, she goes to her GP, who conducts a brief examination and reassures her. When she next sees her thera-pist, she talks about the thoughts and feelings that have been troubling her. She now understands them as mental events taking the form of disturbing bodily perceptions. Usually it is the exposure to situations that arouse deep envy that has proved to be the precipitating cause, and sometimes this can be traced to thoughts about her therapist. Recently deep feelings about her stepfather have emerged, and she has recognized her sense of disappointment that he was not able to help free her from her emotional entanglement with her mother.

The therapist considers that Florence is now, in her emotional life, functioning at the level of a fairly healthy 14-year-old. However, she recognizes that further reduction of medication will be a complicated and sensitive matter. The past psychotic episodes have been so dis-turbing and traumatic to the patient, and alarming to her professional carers, that the risk of possible recurrence has led to the decision to postpone any such attempt. At the same time, the therapist is aware that continuing the medication may have an important symbolic sig-nificance for the patient, serving as a reassuring "transitional object", independently of its pharmacological effect.

Discussion

Florence's psychotic thinking might have been considered simply as the regressive revival of the thinking of a highly imaginative child who was objectifying her imaginary experiences. However, even an unusually imaginative child does not normally experience fantasy or day-dream in such a literal fashion, such thinking in the course of normal development being confined to the sphere of psychosis, dreams, and symbolic play.

The similarity of such psychotic thinking to dreams and hyp-nogogic hallucinations—as in Freud's case of Anna O (1895d) and in the cases of Claudia (Chapter 5), Dorothy (Chapter 6), and Grace (Chapter 13)—illustrates the differences in perspectives between a psychiatric approach that strives for refinement of diagnostic classification, and a psychoanalytic one that seeks to discover the personal meaning of psychotic experience and behaviour for the individual (Bateman & Holmes, 1995). The theme of nightmarish persecution by dead babies or damaged mothers as in the case of Duncan (Chapter 9) illustrates the psychotic potential of unresolved infantile envy and rivalrous jealousy.

From a psychodynamic perspective, Florence's major conflicts could be regarded as operating at an oedipal (triadic, jealousy-centred) level, but of a developmentally earlier and more primitive (dyadic/envious) nature, focused principally on the mother. At this level, her sense of identity was not as shifting and fragmented as we have seen in the case of Conrad (Chapter 7), but splitting and projective mechanisms played a powerful defensive role. Thus, as victim of delusional destructive attacks she could be considered to be in a state of (introjective) identification with her pregnant "bad" mother, having projected her own destructive wishes into the black man/father image. At these moment, she could be considered to be in state of "double" identification, in two identities at the same time, in contrast to other identifications which may shift from moment to moment.

Conclusions

Perhaps the decline in the use of the diagnosis "hysteria" is a consequence of the wider recognition of the difficulty in differentiating severe "hysterical" disorders from schizophrenia, of the associated taxonomic confusions, and of the decline in the belief that such a condition is in some way less severe than "genuine" schizophrenia (Zetzel, 1970).

Florence's case also raises the question of how much psychotherapy is enough (Holmes, 1997), and the possibility that one of the factors involved in the highly complex subject of termination may be the patient's unconscious awareness that the "unfinished business" of reparation must be attended to before a truly constructive and stable ending to the therapy can be achieved.

CHAPTER ELEVEN

Paranoid psychosis—
delusional body image: "Elmer"

The establishment of a stable sense of identity, of a view of one's self existing unchanged over time, is a developmental achievement begun in infancy, and under normal circumstances usually consolidated by early adult life. Adverse factors may impair this process, with the consequence that the sense of self is likely to be fragile and unstable. It may disintegrate under psychological or physical stress, in which case the capacity for normal relationships, in which the self is clearly differentiated from the object (the other person), is impaired or lost, and replaced by a regressive revival of the earlier identifications. Such identifications may change in a kaleidoscopic fashion, leading to confusion or delusion in the subject and bewilderment in the observer. Psychoanalytic concepts can throw light on this disturbance and open the way for psychotherapy aimed at establishing a more mature sense of identity.

Elmer

Elmer, aged 38, suffered his first episode of schizophrenia when he was 20 years old. He was doing unskilled work in a factory when he began to fear that the machinery might come to life while he was away at lunch. He felt obliged to miss his lunch in order to keep the machinery under observation. He soon became extremely violent at home, smashing furniture and threatening his foster-mother with a knife. He accused her of trying to force him to have sexual intercourse with her, and he attacked her and shouted that he was about to kill her. He was restrained by his foster-father and was admitted to a psychiatric ward under a compulsory order.

His psychotic thinking centred on his belief in his omnipotent powers, on cataclysmic life-and-death conflicts taking place between inhabitants of outer space, and on terrifying telepathic forces seeking to destroy him. He spoke in a confused manner about seeing a film of himself going backwards in time to his childhood, of having been in a war, and of the imminent dangers of the destruction of civilization by forces of evil. Like other victims of the conflict, he had been shot in the heart, and, like them, the question of whether he would survive or not depended on the calibre of the bullet that had struck him. He sat with his legs wide apart and said that he had been "chopped up". He said that his whole body, and in particular his penis, was shrinking and that his only hope of stopping this process was for his foster-father to shrink as well. He insisted that he was pregnant, and at other times that that there was a woman inside him who had been unfaithful to him and had become pregnant. This made it necessary for him to cause these pregnancies to be aborted, by methods to be described. He appeared to be completely unaware of the symbolic character of these thoughts.

Anti-psychotic medication treatment achieved a remission in his psychosis, and he was discharged after six months, extensive neurological investigations having failed to reveal any abnormality. He soon relapsed, and for the next nine years pursued a chronic course mostly living within the hospital. Repeated attempts at rehabilitation failed; he remained disabled, on high doses of neuroleptics, capable only of severely limited function within the hospital milieu; and although no longer violent, he remained preoccupied with delusional beliefs and perceptual disturbances. Investigations had excluded the possibility that Elmer might have had a cerebral birth injury or brain pathology of other origin, and no evidence emerged that he had ever experienced auditory or visual hallucinations.

At the age of 29, he was transferred to a special unit for the intensive rehabilitation of chronic schizophrenic patients, where some details of his background were recorded and psychotherapy was begun.

Personal history

Elmer had a bad start in life. He was the younger of two children of an unhappy marriage. Although little was known of his mother's background, it was clear that she had herself had an emotionally deprived upbringing which had left her with an unstable personality. At the time of his birth, she suffered from a gynaecological illness; she separated from her husband soon after, leaving Elmer and his older sister in the care of their father. She maintained some irregular contact with her children for a few years, during which she had another daughter, the outcome of a transient relation with another man. When Elmer was 6 years old, she died from cancer of the uterus, and all three children were sent to an orphanage, and soon into foster-care. He was on good terms with his foster-parents and demonstrated no obvious psychiatric symptoms prior to the onset of the psychosis.

The younger half-sister had a different fostering and eventually lost contact with Elmer and his sister. When he talked about his childhood, the extent of his insecurity and lonely isolation became clear. He was frightened of older boys and was unable to defend himself in an appropriately aggressive way. He was bullied by his classmates, tended to be lost in day-dreams, and during adolescence took to using cannabis and alcohol more than his peers. He never succeeded in making secure friendships or in finding a place in peer groups. It seemed clear that he had escaped from painful isolation and conflict into compensatory day-dreaming in his adolescence, and perhaps in his earlier childhood. With the onset of the psychosis, his grasp on reality became impaired to the degree that his wishful and fearful fantasies assumed concrete and delusional reality for him.

The setting of the therapy

The psychodynamic orientation of the rehabilitation unit provided the setting necessary for the psychotherapy to be attempted, and he was soon transferred to a treatment home that provided milieu therapy for six young psychotic men and women.

Elmer had the good fortune to acquire a key worker who was willing and able to continue with him throughout the four years of the therapy. She was a middle-aged woman of emotional strength and long experience, and she was to play a central part in the therapy, filling a maternal role in the transference in a way that will be described.

The therapeutic benefit deriving from the milieu proved to be considerable, and the interaction between the individual therapy and the milieu therapy was complex and important. However, this chapter is confined to the explication of his inner world, of the meaning of his delusional beliefs, and of his response to individual psychoanalytic psychotherapy.

The psychotherapy

After ten years of chronicity and disablement, Elmer was taken on at the age of 30 for twice-weekly psychotherapy by an experienced psychotherapist. He brought the case to a small seminar group where it was discussed yearly during the subsequent four years of the treatment.

Elmer made good contact with the therapist and soon acquired sufficient trust to disclose important aspects of his past life and details of his delusional inner world. This allowed the therapist to build up a picture of the background of his life history and gradually to understand the meanings of his delusional thinking and the nature of the pathogenic influences of his childhood. Elmer found great relief in talking, and he soon said to the therapist: "Everyone else thinks I'm mad. You are the only one who has ever listened to me."

A favourable feature of the therapeutic process was his capacity to respond to the therapist's attitude of non-intrusive interest and curiosity, which allowed Elmer to begin to take seriously the possibility that there might be other, and better, explanations of his experience than his own delusional ones.

Delusional content—the search for meaning

It became apparent during the course of the therapy that Elmer's lack of a stable masculine identity was an expression of a profound disturbance of his sense of self and the associated processes of identity formation. Unlike the less severe identity *diffusion* that is characteristic of borderline personality disorders, Elmer showed a severe *confusion* of identity, in the form of shifting identifications. This found expression in his delusional beliefs such as that he was pregnant or in the psychotic logic of his insistence that since he had two parents he was neither man nor woman, but was both.

As he disclosed more details of his delusional beliefs, it could be seen that his basic preoccupations had not changed since the onset of the psychosis nine years before. He confided that he had special powers and was in touch with people in outer space, where space and time as we know it cease to exist, and that he lived briefly with them from time to time. Spaceships had landed on the lawn of his home and had taken him to outer space. These space people were good, since their aim was to protect the earth from terrifying destructive forces. These forces took the form of lethal radiations emanating from the walls of his room, and he has long kept an iron bar ready to protect himself from their lethal effect. The threat also came from many other quarters. Telepathic influences threatened to invade his brain, and he was under constant surveillance by cameras which he believed were actually murderous weapons (see the case of Harry, Chapter 15).

He explained that these terrifying threats to the world and to himself were relieved by the thought that the space inhabitants were on the side of life. Whenever he stayed with them, he felt safer. There were military tanks in space, and they fused together to form cold, lifeless planets. The task of the space people was to bring life and warmth into the soil of the space planets by planting pine trees so that they might gradually support life. It was vital, he said, to protect the terrestrial world from destruction and to ensure that life can go on. He said that he did what he could to offer protection by going into the forest, itself under threat of extinction, and pulling off budding leaves and eating them in order to preserve them from destruction. Believing that the earth needs what he called "biosubstance" in order to survive, he protected himself from death by carrying with him at all times, as a sort of talisman, the casing of a ball-point pen which he had filled with a mixture of urine, semen, and saliva.

He was preoccupied with the theme of war both in outer space and in this world. He said that he was in a war from the age of 7, for about two years. He experienced a woman shooting him in the heart because she was afraid of him, but she should not have needed to shoot him because he wasn't angry with her. But when he once made an unprovoked assault on another patient, he said: "I could have killed him—in war you become like a murder machine."

When people get shot in wars, whether or not they survive depended on the calibre of the bullet. In wartime there is no food, he explained, and people become cannibals.

At the same time, he was denying the existence of death: "People really don't die, so there is no such thing as the perfect murder." Showing a momentary grasp of metaphor, he said: "I am dead—I am the living dead." At other times he said that he knew that his mother was not really dead but was probably living in another country. His precarious sense of identity seemed to be confused with the image of his dead mother.

His preoccupation with his belief in the lethal consequences of aggression and methods of counteracting them was accompanied by thoughts about the life-giving powers of the penis. He explained that he is very popular with women, and so he has a great number of children. In these fantasies he seems to be both the fertilizing male and the pregnant woman, and he said that because he could give them babies it would preserve his own life.

His preoccupation with the interior of his body was illustrated when it was discovered that he had long had an inflammation of the rectum that had been resistant to treatment and that this was caused by his forcing soapy water into his rectum, along with quantities of pepper and other irritants. He explained that this behaviour was necessary because there is a pregnant woman inside his body. He must abort this pregnancy by using these irritants, as well as by swallowing mouthfuls of chemical solvent. This pregnant woman of his fantasy had been unfaithful to him by transferring her affections to another person (sometimes identified as a man, sometimes as a woman) and this was his way of seeking revenge. At other times he believed he was a woman, and he finally resolved the confusion by deciding that he was both a man and a woman, since, as already mentioned, he had two parents.

Some further samples of his psychotic thinking illustrate that his delusions represented variations on a few central themes.

• The world is threatened with extinction by destructive forces located in outer space that are invading this planet, threatening to destroy biological nature.

- Benevolent, protective forces (the good space people) are struggling to overcome them, planting life-giving pine trees in the forest. He is on their side, contributing to the preservation of life by eating the young growing leaves (in reality a recommended survival technique).

- Eating can also take a destructive form (cannibalism), but this is in the interests of wartime survival when starvation threatens the victims.

- The forces of destruction are also threatening his own life and invading the space of his room in the form of dangerous emanations from the walls of his room.

- Strongly defended aggressive objects (heavily armoured tanks) exist in space as the precursors of a cold, lifeless planet which they form by fusion of parts into a whole. This planet, and the terrestrial world, can, if the forces of life can triumph over the forces of death and destruction, be transformed into a place of warmth and life. This life-giving transformation can be brought about by planting pine trees into the earth.

- He is the possessor of a penis with great power, having created a great number of children. There is also a different penis which shrinks to diminutive size. This metamorphosis could only be tolerated if his (foster-) father's penis would suffer the same fate.

- His sense of identity and gender are fluid. He is sometimes a man, sometimes a woman, sometimes both. He is pregnant and he also has a pregnant woman inside his body, and this woman has been unfaithful to him. This baby is contained within the female body which is itself contained within his own body and must at all costs be destroyed.

- Time and space do not exist in the sphere of the space-dwellers, and his own experience also transcends them. He sees a film of himself going backward in time to his childhood, he knows he was in a cataclysmic conflict (war) after the age of 7, he is dead but not-dead, his mother is not dead. The bullet wound he suffered at the time will only prove lethal if the impact of the blow (depending on the calibre of the bullet) to his heart is too great.

The course of psychotherapy

As his self-understanding increased, he slowly abandoned such activities as the designing of spaceships, and his delusions and associated paranoid fears receded. He began to doubt the certitude of his delusional beliefs. He started to read articles on psychology and very slowly came to the conclusion that his psychotic experiences had not been real, but were "a matter of psychology". By the time that the treatment was terminated, he was able to say: "I really needed to believe all those ideas."

This cognitive achievement was accompanied by an emotional growth characteristic of integration of the split "good" and "bad" feelings, which constitute the beginnings of attainment of "the depressive position".

"Guided mourning"

When his maternal grandmother, of whom he was fond, died, he began to recognize and to tolerate his feelings of sorrow. He began to recall his feelings of grief about his mother's death and his resentment of his father for having failed to keep the family together. Although Elmer had recognized the defensive nature of his belief that his mother was still alive, he frequently continued to maintain it and, with it, the delusional belief that he can restore life to her by giving her a baby, or in a symbolic intercourse by planting pine trees in the cold, lifeless planet.

The therapist then made the unusual move of obtaining the patient's permission to examine the original hospital records of his mother at the time of her illness and death thirty years before. He went through them slowly and in detail with the patient, who responded with a flood of grief and weeping. The therapist had decided that this confrontative action, perhaps more characteristic of behaviour-therapy techniques than of transference-based psychotherapy, was nonetheless appropriate and effective in that particular context.

The patient then began to become aware of feelings of guilt in relation to his mother, and the therapist was able to help him realize that he was not responsible for her death as he had secretly feared. He had now acquired enough understanding of his aggressive wishes to be able to realize that they were not omnipotently destructive as he had assumed in his psychotic state.

Twelve months later, after a total of four years of twice-weekly psychotherapy the treatment was terminated by mutual agreement.

Discussion

Like so many psychotic patients, Elmer's delusional world had the quality of science fiction—of dangerous forces radiating from the walls, of intruding extraterrestrial beings threatening to invade and colonize his personal geographic, mental, and bodily spaces. At the same time, the projection of good objects, defensively split off from the bad, resulted in the experience of benevolent protective beings inhabiting outer space and visiting him in spaceships which land on the garden lawn. The same dynamic process issues in comparable themes in the dream life of the normal individual, where thoughts with associated affects usually take the dramatic form of hallucinated actions.

Transference and countertransference

The coexistence of the milieu therapy implies that this was a "multi-treater" enterprise, and as such it mobilized complex transference and countertransference processes involving staff members and other patients (Holmqvist, 1995). These were for the most part left for the staff to deal with, while the therapist patiently gained Elmer's trust and helped him gradually to relinquish his defences against previously intolerable feelings.

The most obvious manifestation of *transference* (rather than simply *collaboration*), assumed the form of an aggressive rivalry with the therapist and the frequency of competitive claims by Elmer to knowledge superior to that of the therapist. This theme previously had found concrete (non-symbolic) expression in his insistence that his father's penis must shrink in order to stop his own sharing the same fate. In this sense he could be regarded as competing with the father-therapist in the transference, gradually identifying with him and assimilating knowledge and understanding. The psychoanalytic use of such terms as "father's penis" or "mother's breast" may refer to the actual body part, or serve as the symbolic representative of paternal or maternal function (Lacan, 1997). Other terms, such as "phallic power", "nutritive function", "the thinking breast", or in Jungian terms, father and mother "archetypes", also seek to connote these functions.

The therapist had won the right to be seen as an admired and respected figure with the capacity not only for reflective thought, but to tolerate incompleteness and to contain his own disturbed feelings and discomfort in the interests of sanity and for his patient's sake. The therapist's management of his *countertransference* was sufficiently skilful to allow him to avoid such dangers as premature explanations of the symbolic meaning of delusions, with its attendant risk of intellectual defensiveness.

The paternal transference in the psychotherapy was complemented by a powerful maternal transference involving the female key worker. As Elmer gradually formed a deep attachment to her, the defensive split between his ("pre-ambivalent") destructive and protective feelings began to increase, and his aggressive feelings about her assumed murderous proportions.

The keyworker managed this *psychotic transference* with composure, strength, and tact, and it gradually resolved. However, in retrospect it appeared that the patient had not fully worked through the feelings involved in acknowledging her separateness (the "triadic" superstructure on the "dyadic" base). After the therapy was concluded, he was able to acknowledge how much the key worker had done for him, but he appeared to be reluctant to see her again. The therapist understood the patient's attitude as a failure to work through the separation process and mourning of the loss of her.

Understanding Elmer

The story of Elmer's life can now be thought of as that of a "broken-hearted" little boy (author's metaphor) who has lost his mother with whom he already had a precarious relationship, having not yet healed the normal developmental splitting between his loving and his destructive feelings for her. Her illness at the time of his birth and her likely personal instability offer possible supportive evidence for such a profound developmental failure, one that involved a failure to acquire a stable sense of identity. Her death soon after the arrival of the baby sister reinforced his sense of omnipotence and persecutory guilt, and left him with an unconscious legacy of dread of intimacy and a solitary and lonely life. He was unable to own and integrate his aggressiveness in the normal way that would have helped him stand up to bullying persecution by his schoolmates.

These split-off primitive phantasies, wishes, conflicts, and impulses to destroy and to protect and preserve the mother of his infancy, and the associated primitive defence mechanisms, might be regarded as the encapsulation of an infantile psychotic self (Volkan, 1995). Such a perspective might imply that the quality of parenting he subsequently received from his foster-parents may have had little influence—helpful or harmful—on the underlying process. The psychotic process might even have been beyond the reach of normal human sympathy and understanding, a situation described by Fairbairn (1952) as a static "internal closed system".

Elmer managed to keep the capsule intact by using his wishful imaginative capacity for day-dream, probably in childhood and very likely in adolescence when he was already preoccupied with spaceship technology.

Concrete thinking and the recovery of lost feelings

Elmer had recounted his story in terms that are so clearly metaphorical to the listener—dramatic conflicts of destruction and preservation (war), of a wound from which he may not recover (the bullet in the heart), of the destruction and the preservation of mother-earth and its fertilization by pine trees. He had not been able to achieve the necessary capacity for abstract conceptual thinking in this area of his experience. From a psychotherapeutic point of view, simple explanations might have been of only limited use to him. It was necessary for the pathogenic processes to come to life in a transference relationship, and to some extent worked through, before he could recognize them as his own mental products.

The primitive form of some of his symbolic expressions can be thought of as deriving from a "part-object" level of relationships and mental representations. Thus, in terms of classical psychoanalytic instinct theory, much of this material can be seen to be derived from the oral stage of psychosexual development. In object-relational terms, it can be seen that he is preoccupied with different types of devouring (in particular, a cannibalistic one), motivated by starvation, and a preservative one, motivated by protective wishes.

The leaf buds inside the forest which he eats can be considered as a concrete symbolic equation of the good (providing) maternal breast/

nipple (the part-object representative of the providing mother), just as the planting of life-giving pine trees in the earth can be considered as an expression of the procreational powers of the "paternal penis". In his omnipotent wishfulness, Elmer had appropriated this capacity from his father, giving his mother many babies to restore the damage he believed he had done to her pregnant body. He was psychologically still a small boy in unresolved rivalry with his father wishing that his father's penis should shrink to the same size as his own. He had never resolved his oedipal conflict with his father, in which he wished to be bigger than his father, but since he had never achieved a stable sense of identity (an aspect of "pre-oedipal" vulnerability to psychosis) the conflict had found expression in a psychotic rather than a neurotic way.

Elmer's fantasy of the armoured tanks that fuse to form lifeless planets is a vivid and poignant expression of the magnitude of the emotional deprivation of his childhood and the lifeless sterility of his inner world. Unable to penetrate the armour of parent figures (real or imagined), whose fusion brings no life, he has nonetheless preserved the hope that the good extraterrestrial helpers might bring a creative and life-giving transformation. Elmer's therapist achieved this transformation by putting him in touch with his lost capacity for warmth, the pain of loss, and the process of mourning.

The talisman

The "transitional object" first described by Winnicott (1971) serves to remind the infant of the existence of the good mother during her absence and eases the fears confronting the small child who is maturing through the developmental phase of separation, on the pathway towards the acquisition of a secure and separate personal identity. As such, it can be seen to have something in common with the valued charm, amulet, or fetish used in some cultures as a talisman serving to ward off dangerous influences, such as the "evil eye". In the psychotic person, the "evil eye" can also present in delusional form, as an expression of the projection of a destructive, voyeuristic, and often envious part of the self.

However, these talismanic and fetishistic objects differ from those of the transitional object, which normally loses its power as development proceeds, whereas the fetish is usually never given up and remains an essential need for the individual. This need may be a specific one, as in the case of fetishistic sexual perversion, or a more general and life-preserving one, as in the case of Elmer. A fetish may originate in early infancy as a defence against separation and subsequently as an attempt to repair a defective body image. The treatment of different objects as though they are identical, simply on the basis of one single common property, can be seen to find expression in his construction of a magic talisman from different bodily fluids contained in the casing of a ball-point pen.

Experience at the primitive level of part-object relationships is reduced to very simple and concrete forms. Thus, body products may be conceived of as being endowed magically with powerful properties, both good and bad, and with creative or destructive potentials. In the infant mind, and in the unconscious phantasies of adults, these substances can be felt to be either weapons to attack the "bad" mother—as in the case of biting teeth, burning urine, explosive faeces—or to please the "good" mother. If these infantile dangers have not been neutralized ("detoxified"), they may retain their original power and significance for the psychotic patient who has lost the capacity for metaphorical thinking.

Thus the meaning of Elmer's conviction that he will die if he loses possession of this magical object can be thought about in the following manner: his talisman is the product of a system of unconscious phantasy in his inner world, rooted in his infancy where he was exposed to the trauma of his mother's illness and eventual death; this system has remained timelessly in his unconscious mind, and at some time in his adult life he has assembled the elements of his talisman as a safeguard against the ever-present fear of death.

Thus the talisman serves to protect his "internal" mother (of infancy) whom he fears he will destroy because she was "bad", but he still retains a hope that she has survived because she was "good". If he loses the talisman, he loses the wishful delusional reassurance that she is still alive and that he has not killed her. If he were to lose that delusional reassurance, his attempts to restore her to life by methods that we have seen, such as giving her babies, will be exposed as hopeless. He will not be able to save her from his infantile destructiveness, and both he and she will die.

Thus the bodily fluids can be seen to have for Elmer the significance of omnipotently powerful substances and part-object relationships, never contained and "processed" by the mother of his infancy, and thus needing containment inside a container that he can himself control. Despite the fact that in his rational sane consciousness he must have known that she was dead, in his psychotic world she was not. This fetishistic system must have long played an important part in his inner world and presumably in the transference processes. It can also be considered that the self-comforting belief in his mother's prescience is an example of the creation of autistic objects (see Ogden, 1989, p. 55), as in the case of Claudia's obsessions.

The animated machinery

His belief that his mother was still alive might help explain the terrifying idea that inanimate machinery might come to life during his absence. Thus the animation of the inanimate machinery might have represented a nightmare-like scene of his dead mother coming to life, perhaps as a vengeful ghost. There are other possible explanations. One of these is that having failed to find a human container for a destructive part of his own mind, he was threatened with the consequence of projecting it into a container represented by the inanimate and non-human machinery, just as he also used outer space for this purpose. Such a line of thought also illustrates the fact that meanings may take many different forms, derived from different developmental and conceptual levels.

Three years later

Three years after the termination of the therapy, he was reported to be free of all psychotic symptoms and requiring no medication. He was living in his own apartment, employed in supported work, and had a reasonably satisfactory though limited social life. His therapist was uncertain about his future prospects of heterosexual happiness, because closeness to women was likely still to stir up so many complex feelings.

Elmer's abandonment of his talismanic "transitional object" (the life-preserving ball-point-pen casing) reflects maturational progress and a reduction of his unconscious fear that he is dangerous and endangered by telepathic forces. However, his failure to work through the loss of his (maternal) key worker might explain why he still fears emotional closeness to a woman.

Elmer remains a vulnerable personality, but something very much more than a restoration to his pre-psychotic level of function has been achieved, and he is likely to have sufficient insight to seek further psychodynamic help should it become necessary.

This talisman played no obvious part in the therapeutic transference but seemed simply to lose its significance for him because of his increasing sense of inner security. He found in the maternal transference with the female key worker a person who could tolerate and understand his feelings of rage towards his mother, an experience that reduced his belief in their omnipotent destructiveness. The therapist's actions in confronting Elmer with the fact of his mother's death proved to be a most helpful intervention.

Conclusions

In the case of Elmer much was achieved, and although his eventual understanding of the meaning of his psychosis and the working-through of his negative feelings towards the mother-keyworker was incomplete, it was sufficient to allow of a very much higher level of integration and stability than he had had before being overtaken by his psychosis.

This case demonstrates how a wide variety of individual psychodynamics may exist within the spectrum of schizophrenic illness. It also illuminates the nature of many common delusions and illustrates that severity of psychopathology, or even of its chronicity, should not preclude attempts to provide psychoanalytic psychotherapy, under the right conditions, for selected schizophrenic patients. If we can understand the mental mechanisms involved in the individual psychotic patient, then he is, at least theoretically, within the reach of psychoanalytic psychotherapy.

CHAPTER TWELVE

Paranoid delusions— sealing-over and working through a psychotic transference: "Frank"

Some individuals make a good recovery from a first psychotic episode, and others pursue a relapsing course which may or may not lead to chronicity. In some cases, recovery from a psychotic breakdown has been achieved by the covering-up, sealing-over, or encapsulation of psychodynamic forces. Such sealing-over may sometimes confer a sufficient stability and ego strength for an indefinite period, sometimes requiring medication on a regular or occasional basis. In other cases, the adjustment breaks down under subsequent stress and the underlying unresolved psychotic process breaks through, with the return of symptoms. However, under favourable circumstances such a relapse may present an opportunity to resolve this "unfinished business" by working through the underlying pathogenic conflicts in psychotherapy. The following case illustrates the improvement that may follow such an attempt.

Frank

Frank, 34 years old, was first referred to the psychiatric services at the age of 27. He was brought from the apartment where he had been

living by his parents, who had been worried by his increasing withdrawal, suspiciousness, and irritability over the previous year, a
change in character that had recently led to his losing his job.

He was found to be seriously out of touch with reality, preoccupied with his own thoughts, laughing inappropriately, and at times
adopting catatonic postures. He believed that somebody was interfer-
ing with his thinking and that something terrible was happening to
his head. (Frank always referred to his head and to his brain, located
inside his head, but did not use the word "mind" until the therapist
introduced it later in the therapy.) He said that the room was full of
radiation, coming from some apparatus or machine implanted in the
wall, probably the Russian KGB or the American CIA. Foreign spies
were trying to get official secrets from him. The radiations were intruding into his head and melting down his brain.

These radiations were sometimes associated with a high-pitched
tone, a noise that was being transmitted in order to torture him. His
persecutors were sending secret messages about him and to him, all
in code. The registration numbers of passing cars were encoded messages, and he was preoccupied with trying to decode them. Television
announcers were also referring to him in an indirect and coded manner. He was afraid of being murderously attacked in the street. When
he saw a book with a red cover, a man with a red coat, or any red
object he concluded that they were all signs connected with the Russian plot against him. Other people could read his thoughts and were
talking about him, "broadcasting" his private thoughts.

Despite the severity of these symptoms, it was found possible to
manage his case with neuroleptic medication in a day hospital unit,
while living in the parental home. Here he stayed for a year, attending
the procedures of rehabilitation with little benefit. He spoke less of
his symptoms but remained socially withdrawn and unemployable.
At this point he was admitted to a residential treatment unit for
psychotic patients, where weekly individual psychotherapy was begun on a weekly basis.

First phase of treatment—two years

The psychotherapist's approach was a reality-oriented supportive
one ("ego-strengthening"), without a specific exploration of possible
transference manifestations This involved eliciting details of his life

history and discussing the difficulties in his relationships with other people, and in particular with his parents and sister. Although Frank cooperated with the therapist and attended his therapy sessions regularly, it was many months before he was able to tell her that he had at first believed that she could read his thoughts and therefore that he did not need to talk spontaneously about himself.

Personal history

The therapist gradually acquired a coherent picture of his early family life and development both from Frank's own account and from corroborating information derived from family interviews carried out by the staff of the treatment unit.

Frank was the younger of two children of a couple who were both schoolteachers with musical interests and high intellectual aspirations for their children. His mother, who seemed to have considerable emotional problems of her own, was devoted to him. He experienced his father as possessive, dominating, and demanding, and Frank had no sense of emotional contact with him. He was intensely jealous of his sister, who was very much his father's favourite, while he was regarded as a "mother's boy". He had no enduring relationships with playmates or companions, and his play was solitary, centring on model cars, a preoccupation that persisted into his adult life in the form of repairing old cars. He later said that in his childhood his cars were his only real friends. He spent much time watching television science-fiction dramas, usually seeing himself as an important astronaut. This fantasy life continued into his adolescence in the form of day-dreams and often felt very real to him.

The family as fortress

The professional staff's interviews with the family left the strong impression that it was in some ways a considerably dysfunctional one. Both parents appeared unwilling to explore whatever personal emotional difficulties they may have had. Frank's mother tended to avoid social life, and the combination of his father's domineering ways and his mother's social anxieties led to the family becoming a tightly knit and inward-looking group. The children pursued their studies and musical interests, with little or no social life, and the family was like a fortress sheltering its occupants against the outside world. His father strongly discouraged Frank from participating in competitive sports.

Frank's performance at school was above average, but he made few friends, and despite some talent in engineering he failed to achieve the advanced professional qualifications that he sought. On leaving school, he worked for a year in the engineering industry, remaining at home until he went into compulsory military service. Here he was relatively successful, had officer rank in a specialized unit, and did a brief period of exchange in the U.S. military. On leaving the service, he worked for a further year and then returned to university to make a further attempt at a higher qualification. He held himself aloof and emotionally distant from his contemporaries and had no significant friendships and little conventional social life. However, his musical talent flourished, and prior to his breakdown this led to his being in demand to play contemporary music in amateur groups. His main interest outside his job was repairing old cars, a preoccupation that filled most of his spare time. His avowed aim was to restore a car to such an impressive state that it would make him more attractive to girls.

His sister left home in her late adolescence and went to live in another country where she established a satisfactory personal life and had considerable success in her musical activities. She lost contact with her family and did not regain it until her brother began to make progress in the first phase of treatment.

On the treatment unit, Frank's psychotic thinking soon became less prominent. He participated very little in group activities and often displayed an attitude of arrogance and superiority in relation to the staff and other patients. He spent much time outside the treatment home observing the way people behaved, searching for role models that might provide the information that he felt he needed in order to become a man whom girls might notice. At times he wondered whether he was actually a woman and not a man, and although this concern did not extend to somatic delusion of bodily change, it was typical of his tendency to concrete thinking in areas of conflict. When, for example, he saw a man dressed in what he regarded a masculine fashion, he would adopt similar clothing, only to find himself becoming angry and resentful and feeling that he was being expected to actually *become* that person, and thereby risk losing his own sense of identity in the process.

The course of the psychotherapy

The therapist found Frank a likeable person but a difficult and frustrating patient. He cooperated well, in the sense that he attended his sessions regularly, but for many months insisted on expressing his own views to the exclusion of those of the therapist. The therapist finally had to protest in order for there to be a space for her and her own views. He flooded her with talk and explanations of his own and, if she did not totally agree with any of his statements, would respond angrily. Frank criticized his father bitterly, blaming him for saying that women and sex were dangerous before marriage, thereby depriving him of opportunities for helpful masculine sexual experiences.

The therapist found herself sympathizing with the patient's past and present difficulties with his father, and she felt very angry about what she saw as the father's lifelong intrusive and controlling behaviour towards Frank. She concluded that the father had failed to help his son detach himself from a severely over-dependent relationship with his mother and had failed to recognize his son's underlying low sense of self-esteem. She considered that by pressing Frank exclusively in the direction of academic achievement and strongly discouraging any interest in competitive sports and other social activities, the father had seriously undermined his son's self-esteem and his confidence in living in the world of social reality. She believed that it was the father's attitude that had driven Frank to seek comfort in daydream and solitary activities and was an important factor in predisposing him to his psychotic illness. For this reason, she was puzzled by his response to her attempts to help him become more independent of his father. On one occasion, Frank asked for the therapist's support in making some decision without first consulting his father. He seemed grateful when the therapist complied but quickly became increasingly furious with the therapist, for he suddenly perceived her to be setting herself up as a superior arbiter of what he should or should not think. Although the therapist recognized this event as an expression of transference of feelings about his father and pointed it out to the patient, Frank seemed uninterested in her comment.

Recovery and discharge

However, the course of the therapy gradually became more calm, and many of his conflicts about family and social relationships were discussed at length and apparently clarified, although it was not clear how much use Frank made of the therapeutic milieu. After eighteen months, he was apparently completely free of psychotic symptoms, had been withdrawn from all neuroleptic medication, and gave the impression of feeling well and relatively secure. At this point, the psychotherapy was discontinued and he was discharged. He was no longer psychotic, and although he seemed to be have made little use of social opportunities of the milieu, his remaining difficulties seemed to be expressions of his somewhat schizoid character rather than the reflection of any underlying serious psychopathology. It was considered that he had made a good recovery, with the reservation that he might need further support for some time. He returned to live in his own apartment, on a small dose of neuroleptic medication. The regular psychotherapy sessions were replaced by a less frequent supportive contact. He remarked to his therapist: "Maybe there really is no threat at all. Maybe the truth is that I simply *felt* threatened!"

Acute relapse—return of delusions

At this point he took a vacation in America. He stayed with some family friends and was apparently well and enjoying himself. However, soon before returning he learned that his mother had an inoperable cancer, from which she was to die three months later. His psychotic symptoms promptly returned in full strength, and he returned to his own country and the parental home. It was now obvious that although he had made some progress in the psychotherapy, the deeper level of the psychosis had remained unresolved and, instead, had undergone a process of "sealing-over", only to be reactivated by the news of his mother's terminal illness. Once again he felt himself the persecuted victim of murderous agencies, and the radiation and torturing noise had returned in full force.

Neuroleptic medication was resumed, and his symptoms quickly receded. The treatment team decided not to readmit him but resumed rehabilitation activities and saw him a few times with his parents during the terminal stage of his mother's illness.

Psychotic transference

The therapist resumed her weekly sessions, which she now found difficult and disturbing. At this point, it seemed that the psychosis was confined to the transference in the therapy sessions and that

Frank was now coping reasonably well in the outside world. He now believed that the radiation was occurring in the therapist's consulting-room, and at first he refused to enter it. He demanded that his sessions should be conducted outside the room and was furious when the therapist refused to comply. When the therapist pronounced herself as being unable to hear the noise, he accused her of being in the plot to kill him. He insisted that she was in league with the murderous agencies and was trying to make him think that he was mad. He talked throughout the session with the same pressure as he had at the beginning of the therapy, and for several sessions he did not allow her to say a word.

Over the next three months the pressure of talk continued. Frank spoke but little of his dying mother, and although the therapist knew of the support he was receiving from the psychiatric team she felt completely paralysed, unable to help him mourn for his mother, and finding the bombardment of her mind very hard to bear. She also felt torn between the wish to abandon the psychotherapy and her deep commitment to the patient. However, she held her ground, and his symptoms gradually subsided.

When his mother died, he continued to live with his father, and, following the advice that he should return to his studies, he re-entered a university course, on a moderate dose of medication and with the support of the psychiatric team. Although at first he seemed to be coping reasonably well, the therapist realized that Frank was finding the experience very disturbing and was feeling intensely humiliated by having to struggle to keep up with his fellow students. He persevered for six months, then withdrew and took a job in engineering. At first he found this very difficult, suspecting that other workers were trying to make life harder for him and talking behind his back in a derogatory manner. As he brought these feelings to the therapy sessions and talked about them with the therapist, he gradually came to feel a little more secure.

The case is reviewed in the seminar

At this point the therapist brought the case for discussion to the seminar. She thought that she had not sufficiently understood the psychosis, which had once again subsided but was probably in a "sealed-over" state, leaving Frank vulnerable to further relapses in the future. She felt that his earlier behaviour of flooding her with talk had been very important, but she was unsure of its meaning. Although she had recognized the psychotic transference that she had had to endure over the period when he accused her of being in the plot to murder him, she had not known how to handle it in the sessions and felt that she had no alternative but to endure it until the storms subsided. She also had felt uncomfortable in having had her customary level of composure disrupted by moments of feeling over-whelmingly angry towards Frank's father. Although she was certain that his father had, in reality, a very controlling and domineering attitude towards Frank, she felt that the degree of disturbance that she had felt must have had some deeper significance than simply a sym-pathetic indignation on her patient's behalf.

Discussion of the material of past weekly sessions brought to light evidence that the psychotic transference that had first appeared in Frank's belief that the therapist could read his mind had been followed by other transference manifestations that the therapist had suspected but had not felt able to explore or to use therapeutically.

Resumption of the psychotherapy

The therapist found the discussion helpful and decided to con-tinue the therapy on a twice-weekly basis, a change that Frank readily accepted. Two further seminar discussions of the therapeutic work during the next six months were followed by individual supervisory sessions (by e-mail) at intervals over the next eighteen months.

During these two years of psychotherapy after the case discussion, the meaning of the patient's psychotic experiences and thinking, and of the transference processes involved in the encounter between the patient and the therapist, gradually became more clear.

The therapist found that her increasing understanding of the func-tion of psychotic mental mechanisms and of unconscious phantasy gradually helped her to listen more effectively to her patient, and to begin to discern meaning in his previously puzzling and frustrating delusional beliefs.

Frank was able to confess that he had not been truthful with her in many ways in the past, and that when he had previously said that he no longer believed that she was in the plot to murder him he was lying. As his doubt in the literal reality of his past and present psy-chotic experiences strengthened, he began, with the therapist's help, to think for himself about himself and to listen to her carefully. This change exposed a hitherto unrecognized trait of passivity in the form of a sense of entitlement, which had found expression in his belief that it was the responsibility of the psychiatrists and the psychotherapist to "cure" him of his illness, without the necessity of his attempting to help himself. This parasitic attitude contrasted with his genuinely cooperative and constructive behaviour and could be considered as a splitting within his personality.

Frank's growing capacity for self-reflective thinking then led him to a crucial recognition. He explained to his therapist that he realized that in his childhood *he had turned himself to stone and frozen his feelings and had never felt anything very strongly since that time.*

The radiations begin to acquire meaning

His newly acquired curiosity about his own mind led Frank to make a further observation about his persecutory delusions. During the first phase of psychotherapy the therapist had been exploring the question of his envy and jealousy of his sister, of which the patient was quite consciously aware. However, he now became able to tell the therapist that when he was in the presence of a particular woman whom he regarded as successful and about whom he had envious thoughts, something very strange happened. When this woman left the room he lost all emotional feelings, and at that moment the radiations began to play on his brain. The therapist recognized that there was a connection between Frank's experiences of the radiations and his feelings of envy. Therapists are constantly having to decide whether such reported events refer to external reality and should be treated as such, or whether they should be taken up as a displaced reference to the therapists themselves. In this case, the therapist was undecided, and, perhaps wisely, she made no comment. Her suspicions that these feelings might be attached to the transference were later to be fully confirmed.

Father's controlling behaviour, Frank's incestuous feelings for his "treacherous" mother

As Frank's capacity to think and listen to his therapist strengthened, he ceased to insist that she must totally agree with him, and he gradually stopped flooding her with talk. This change was helped by the therapist's suggesting that this flooding with talk might have been similar to the way he perceived his father as "invading his mind", like the radiations, insisting that he was always right and that Frank was always wrong. As a result of such comments and explanations, Frank finally gave up his invasive talking completely.

As he talked about his relationship with his mother, Frank recalled having begun to have sexual feelings towards her during his adolescence, and that he had managed to extinguish this disturbing realization. He began to think about his parents' relationship and about his mother's bitterness in the final weeks of her life. This appeared to have sprung from her long-hidden disappointment at having failed to develop her intellectual potentials, a failure for which she blamed her husband's controlling and domineering attitude. This disclosure helped to explain Frank's belief that his failure of higher education was the result of his feeling at the time that he was studying for her, and not for himself, and that she was envious of him because he had the educational opportunities that she had been denied. When he returned to university after his military service, she was extremely interested in his academic life, which Frank interpreted as a sudden loss of interest in himself.

This belief in his mother's envy proved to have had earlier antecedents. She had interrupted her teaching career in order to look after the children, and Frank remembered vividly how much he had resented her returning to work when he was 4 years old, and how he regarded it as an act of treachery and betrayal. He felt both envy and jealousy towards the school as rival but was, however, unaware of any such feelings towards his father.

The therapist was then able to point out that Frank interpreted his experience in an oversensitive manner, in "all-or-none" terms. For example, he felt that he must be the best and brightest, or that he was contemptible. Since he could never succeed in being the star in his work, his car-repairing, or his intellectual and social university life, he lived with a severely damaged self-esteem and a background feeling of total worthlessness, and he was completely unable to experience sharing with other people. He believed that other people had the same contempt for him as he did for himself, and as he unconsciously had for his father. He felt that he was either his mother's sole source of interest and satisfaction, or that she was cruelly rejecting and abandoning him.

He expressed his own increasingly bitter resentment of his father for having been such an inadequate role-model for him in his childhood. He ventilated his fury and frustration at his father's refusal to talk about his son's illness and his humiliation at having to "surrender" his own views to those of his father. It became clear that when Frank became psychotic, his father had devoted himself to helping him, which he had clearly been unable to do in Frank's childhood and adolescence. However, when Frank's mother died his father had tried to force him to cut himself off from his maternal relatives. The father's controlling behaviour added weight to the impression that his attitude to his family may have motivated Frank's sister to escape to another country and might in the past have had pathogenic consequences for them all. It also helped to explain his mother's bitterness in her last weeks of life.

"Separation" dynamics in the transference—
the "abandoned" child

It now seemed that feelings of loss and anger regarding separation were entering the transference relationship.

Before a summer vacation break, Frank complained that he was so poor that he could only wear his old winter shoes. Since the patient was far from poverty-stricken, the therapist began to recognize that Frank was feeling left out "in the cold" and abandoned by the therapist as the "betraying" mother. She also reported that when Frank left a "good" session, feeling very positive towards his therapist, he would sometimes later feel inexplicably angry towards her during the period of waiting between sessions. He would also criticize her if she was a few minutes late in starting the session, and he would often show great reluctance to leave at the end of the session.

The therapist came to understand this behaviour as the expression of Frank's dawning realization that she had other patients and that this mattered to him. Frank told her that he remembered a surprising experience immediately before the last vacation break in the treatment. Feeling a little strange, he had examined his face in a mirror and was disconcerted to find that his pupils were widely dilated. He now thinks that he must have been very angry at the time and had not known it.

The "excluded" child

Frank now began to complain that he was being kept awake at night by the sound of parties taking place in a nearby restaurant. Since this was the first time he had complained about this nuisance, the therapist wondered if it might be possible that childhood memories of listening to noises of his parents' sexual activities at night were beginning to penetrate his defences. Some possible supportive evidence emerged when he disclosed that the persecutory high-pitched noise, which had become much less intrusive, returned when he was lying awake at night after having masturbated. The therapist was not able to investigate the possible transference implications of these events, but she suggested that the noise was the expression of his guilty conscience, a comment that Frank received in a thoughtful manner.

Therapeutic "containment" and introjection
of the "thinking" therapist

When, as in the case of Frank, a therapist succeeds in containing projections, in surviving destructive attacks, in promoting the strengthening of a patient's capacity for reflective thinking, and in persevering with his care in the face of discouragement and other difficulties, the therapist gradually becomes introjected as a "containing object" in the patient's mind—in "neo-Kleinian" terms, a "thinking-feeling breast". This is a learning process of a very specific kind and is dependent on the patient having sufficient experience of a therapist who is able to integrate his own personal feelings with his thinking capacities. This process of learning can eventually alter the structure of the patient's inner world in a permanently beneficent way. It can ultimately provide the patient with a new capacity to think about his feelings, to discover them, and to understand and deal with them constructively, rather than to evade or extinguish them by the use of psychotic mechanisms.

Frank illustrated this process when he reported that the day after a therapy session he had suddenly become aware of a strange and disturbing sensation in his head. He felt strange and alarmed. Suddenly he heard his therapist's voice saying, "what is happening?", and he quickly felt relief of his symptoms. Although he did not realize that a disturbing emotional thought was entering his mind, as was probably the case, he did realize that the physical sensations in his head had some personal psychological meaning for him and was not simply a mindless and threatening event.

Paranoia recedes and radiations transform into painful feelings

As Frank began to experience his feelings, he began to tell his therapist, in a natural and moving way, that the reason that he had, in his childhood, frozen his capacity to feel must have been because his feelings hurt too much, because that is what he was beginning to feel as the therapy progressed. He talked sadly about how much he missed his mother, and how his paranoid thinking had condemned him to a life of lonely isolation. When he now talked about the past in this simple emotional way, the radiations would disappear by the end of the session.

Achievements after four years of the second phase of treatment

After four years of weekly psychoanalytic psychotherapy, Frank was very much improved and no longer psychotic. He had achieved some working through of his feelings and had begun the process of mourning his mother, and he had resumed friendly relations with his sister after many years of estrangement. He was performing well in his job and was less sensitive in his attitude to his workmates.

His medication had been gradually reduced over the two previous years to a low level, and further reductions were planned. He was beginning to have some small success in improving his capacity for social relationships. His pathological dependence on his father was much reduced, and his musical interests were flourishing. He had become aware of how his "all-or-none" attitude contributed to his life-long inability to compete in a constructive manner or to share success with others Although he had some intellectual awareness that these attitudes must influence his feelings about the therapist, these reflections were, up to this point, devoid of any feeling in the therapy sessions. He occasionally returned to suspecting the intentions of others in a paranoid manner, but he had acquired a relatively stable belief that the problem was caused by his own distrustfulness rather than by the attitude of other people.

His experience of the radiation and the intruding noise had undergone a profound change, becoming less intrusive, more faint, and less frequent. Brain-imaging investigation were repeated at this point, and the absence of acoustic or neurological pathology was once again confirmed.

Discussion

As the result of the seminar discussions and subsequent supervisory support, the therapist gained a deeper understanding of the psychotic dynamics involved and a greater awareness of the importance of transference and countertransference processes.

In the first period of psychotherapy, she had recognized Frank's most important emotional conflicts, in particular his love and hatred of his parents, his envy and jealousy of his sister, his sense of worthlessness and compensatory sense of superiority, and his resentment of his parents' failure to help him become the secure and confident man that he would like to be. Frank had appeared to have little or no awareness of these (to the therapist) rather obvious emotional conflicts. However, this apparently successful work had not resolved the psychotic core, nor could the above-mentioned pathogenic factors explain why he suffered a psychotic disorder rather than a neurotic one or a character disturbance.

In the second period, this had become understandable as the result of his disclosure that in his childhood he had dealt with his overwhelming feelings of envy and jealousy by "freezing and turning them to stone". Unconsciously feeling that these emotions and impulses were too painful, and perhaps dangerously destructive, he had continued to expel them into (his mental representation of) various "containing" objects such as the KGB, the CIA, and television announcers. The consequence was that during psychotic episodes he was unable to know that it was his own emotional thoughts, felt to be omnipotently dangerous, that were returning to persecute him in the form of murderous agencies employing the weapons of noise and radiations (see Chapter 16, Patient H). In order to effect the freezing of emotions, it had been necessary for Frank to inhibit or destroy his own capacity for self-reflective thinking.

Perhaps the major therapeutic achievement has been the therapist's capacity to continue thinking about him, and also about herself, throughout periods of stress. Her "helplessness" in the face of the verbal battering that she endured during the psychotic transference proved, in the event, to have been extremely helpful. If she had had more knowledge at the time she might have interpreted his behaviour as a repetition-compulsion in the transference of his experience of his father and thereby perhaps reduced the time of her ordeal.

While it should not be necessary nor advisable for a therapist to endure this stressful situation longer than necessary, making premature interpretations and explanations to the patient may be experienced by him as proof that the therapist is defending herself, is lying, or is unable to stand him. In such a case, the therapist might lose control of the situation and the patient might pass into an even more serious regressive state or might break off treatment abruptly. "Containing" the patient's disturbance may be a considerable achievement on the part of the therapist, but, while it is necessary, it is not sufficient to bring about integration and stable improvement.

As Steiner (1993) has emphasized, "working-through" is a task of re-possessing the painful and frightening mental contents and integrating the lost parts of the self. Frank's regression into a psychotic transference was a useful one, providing an invaluable opportunity for the integration of split-off parts of his personality.

Winnicott (1958, p. 283) has pointed out that the "unfreezing" of feelings belonging to an original "failure state" may be "reached and unfrozen by the various healing phenomena of ordinary life, namely friendships, nursing during physical illness, poetry etc." This, Winnicott says, is the reason why some patients may recover spontaneously from psychosis, which a neurotic individual cannot do without the help of analytic psychotherapy.

Frank's unconscious use of the (potentially "psychotogenic") mechanisms of splitting and projective identification had damaged his capacity to differentiate himself from others and had led to the belief that others, who thereby contained elements that belonged in his own mind, could read his mind. This process is a typical consequence of such an expulsion being performed in a violent manner. The expelled thoughts continue to seek to return in alien and persecutory form—in Frank's case, as lethal radiations.

The future of the therapy

At the time of making this report, the therapy had reached a critical point. Frank was making slow but impressive progress, and the unfreezing of his feelings and his capacity to use the therapist's help in thinking for himself about himself was continuing.

However, he may still be vulnerable to further psychotic relapse if the psychotic core is not sufficiently resolved in the psychotherapy. This implies that he may require a good deal more psychotherapy within the safety of close psychiatric management, focusing if possible on the therapeutic transference, in which destructive envy and jealousy, incestuous wishes, and persecutory guilt may become accessible in a more immediate manner than has been possible up to the present. He has yet to face the dynamic consequences of separation from his therapist and of sharing her with others.

Postscript—enforced termination

A later report from the therapist suggested that this process is well under way. The unforeseen necessity of moving to another part of her country forced her to give a date for termination of the treatment three months hence. Frank at first strongly denied that he felt upset and insisted that he could manage perfectly well on his own. However, he was aware that this move would advance her already successful career, and his feelings of envy and abandonment quickly returned. But this time he did not lose touch with his sense of reality, despite the intensity of his feelings of mourning for his mother and for the coming loss of his therapist.

The therapist now has the task of working with the psychiatric manager to ensure that some appropriate psychodynamic care will continue to be available after her departure. In such a situation, many options may need to be considered. If another suitable therapist can be found, a continuation of the therapy may prove to be the best course, even if only to help the patient work through with the replacing therapist the feelings involved in remembering that he had realized that his first therapist was, like his mother, irreplaceable. If further psychotic regressions should occur, they should as far as possible be managed as opportunities to explore the stresses, external and internal, that have precipitated them, with only a temporary increase in medication if essential.

Conclusions

Frank's case illustrates how well-conducted supportive psycho-therapy, as in the first phase of treatment, in combination with skilled psychiatric management of medication and rehabilitative social measures, can achieve very good results in terms of restoration to the level of functioning before the breakdown. It also demonstrates how this improvement may be unstable if the psychotic core has not been sufficiently resolved.

It shows some of the consequences that may follow a "sealing-over" process. If significant psychotic psychopathology remains partly or totally unresolved after treatment of an acute psychotic episode, the patient may be left with a varying degree of instability and of vulnerability to further breakdown. Psychiatric support and medication for an indefinite period of time may be a very satisfactory outcome for some extremely vulnerable patients; however, it may represent inadequate treatment for others who, had they been given adequate help, might have proved to have the capacity to resolve their psychotic core.

CHAPTER THIRTEEN

Phobia, hysteria, psychosis: "Grace"

In psychiatric practice, phobias present as a group of disorders of varying degrees of severity. At one extreme lie "simple "phobias, which may respond to behavioural methods of treatment (Marks, 1987); at the other, more complex conditions that may prove unresponsive to all psychiatric treatment. Some of these conditions may be found to overlie a latent schizophrenic psychosis.

In psychoanalytic theory, the dynamic relationship between hysteria, obsessions, and phobias has long been debated (Frosch, 1990, pp. 341–347), and the variety of clinical courses that a phobia may take is well known to sometimes include schizophrenia. Fairbairn (1952) pointed out that conditions usually regarded as neurotic—such as obsessions, hysteria, paranoid states, and phobias—may function as defences against underlying schizoid or schizophrenic pathology (Grotstein & Rinsley, 1994).

Klein believed that neurotic disorders represented the attempt to work through the unresolved psychotic anxieties of infancy. In a seminal paper, Segal (1981e) demonstrated how schizoid mechanisms were involved in forming the phobic symptoms of a borderline patient, and she concluded that these phobias served the purpose of averting an acute schizophrenic illness.

The following patient, who was treated with success by a nurse who was a member of a psychosis crisis team, illustrates some of these issues. The case was presented in a small seminar group on three occasions.

Grace

Grace, now 30 years old, first developed psychotic symptoms at the age of 26 following her attendance at an orthopaedic outpatient clinic, where she had sought help for pain in the back. The attending specialist was delayed, and she was kept waiting for some time. Apparently in desperation, she ran to the hospital canteen, where she lay on the floor screaming, in a state of extreme panic. She was found to be acutely psychotic and was admitted under legal compulsion to a psychiatric ward, where enforced medication quickly restored her to a calmer state of mind.

She explained that the cause of her panic was the threatening behaviour of certain families in the town, who were persecuting her and her family in a sinister and terrifying fashion. They were using the radio and television to broadcast coded messages about her, were spying on her, and were controlling her every movement.

On the ward, her anxiety quickly subsided with medication and nursing care, and her persecutory delusions slowly receded. Within a few weeks, she had apparently recovered and was discharged to the care of her husband. Over the next twelve months, her symptoms recurred in a less intense fashion from time to time, disappearing when she was readmitted for a brief period, when medication was adjusted.

Eighteen months later, Grace became pregnant, and her psychosis returned in full force. Her family had been dissatisfied with her past treatment, and they arranged a compulsory admission to a psychodynamically oriented ward in another town. Here, her treatment was undertaken by a small psychosis crisis team, consisting of a psychiatrist, a psychologist, a social worker and a nurse. They decided that the nurse would undertake Grace's individual psychotherapy.

The nurse/therapist found Grace to be acutely agitated and severely confused. She believed that she was being attacked by rats, of which she had had a severe phobia since childhood. No longer complaining about the neighbours, her fears were now very much worse.

She said that rats were attacking the baby inside her body and that her husband was chopping up rats, cooking them, and feeding them to her in order to poison her. She accused her nurse of having an affair with her husband and being pregnant by him. She refused to eat and would not tolerate the nurse's presence for more than a few minutes. She refused to take off her clothes, and she lay in bed, curled up in a foetal position, fully dressed and incontinent of urine. The staff accepted this regressed behaviour and attended to all her bodily needs for several days, after which her self-caring behaviour gradually returned to normal.

The general calm of the ward milieu, combined with moderate doses of anti-psychotic medication, calmed her, and she slowly began to tolerate the presence of her therapist, who visited her every day. Grace's level of psychotic thinking fluctuated. Often she would accuse the therapist of being evil, and of stealing her husband. She hallucinated the voice of her husband criticizing her, and she defended herself against the accusations, insisting she had nothing to feel guilty about. She frantically brushed off hallucinated rats from her body, at the same time insisting that they would not harm her therapist.

The psychosis team brought the case to the seminar for supervisory discussion, and they managed the case through the subsequent eighteen months of treatment. Before long, Grace had acquired sufficient sense of trust to begin to tell her therapist the background of her illness and the story of her life.

Personal history

Grace is the second of three children and has a five-year-younger brother and an older sister who now has several children. Her mother had suffered from chronic arthritis all Grace's life, and Grace considers that her mother was always too deeply preoccupied with her own pain and considerable obesity to give her the attention she wanted. She regarded her father as being overbearing and domineering. The family corroborated some items of her account, and the therapist was struck by the fact that Grace herself made no mention of the brother's existence.

Her sister was regarded as a "difficult" child, but apparently she was always mentally healthy. Grace, by contrast, was regarded as an "angelic" child, who assumed the role of "Queen of the family". Apart from a long-standing phobic dread of rats, she had had no evidence of obsessional or other pathological features of personality. Attentive to the needs of everyone else, generous in her care of her ailing mother, of her sister, and of her sister's children, she became deeply attached to an older female cousin. It was apparently the death of this cousin that had precipitated the first psychotic episode (prior to her pregnancy). She had remained solicitous and generous towards her family, and, when later in the ward her sense of reality began to return, she displayed the same striking helpfulness towards the staff and other patients. However, the staff considered that this behaviour was accompanied by an excessive demand for attention and for appreciation of her cooperative attitude.

Extremely intelligent, practical, and ambitious, Grace had become a successful businesswoman, with a reputation of being very shrewd, perhaps to the point of hardness. She is said to have had two days' holiday in ten years' work. She had wanted a baby for ten years but had been too frightened of the idea to consider motherhood. She was quite aware, at an intellectual level, that she felt envious of her sister and other friends who had babies. She was also aware of feeling inferior to her more prosperous and socially prominent friends. At the same time, she was convinced that many young women were envious of her good looks, which, at an everyday level, was probably true, since she was extremely attractive in appearance.

Content of psychosis

Much of the content of her psychosis became clear on the ward. She dreaded that she would be forcibly subjected to an injection, and when this was not attempted she was overcome by panic, convinced that the examining doctor had a needle concealed in the head of his stethoscope. She was terrified that medication might make her lose control, but she could not say what was being controlled, or what might be the dreaded consequences.

She complained of strange sensations in her throat and had difficulty in swallowing. She said that her father was not really her father but was actually the father of one of her friends, a girl. It was not clear whether her confusion extended to regarding her father as an impostor.

Grace continued to accuse her therapist of being envious of her, and of being so jealous of her relation with her husband that she had begun an affair with him, and she insisted that the therapist was now pregnant by him. By the fifth month of Grace's pregnancy her sense of reality had increased to the point that she was able, for brief periods, to accept that she was indeed pregnant and, although the baby did not yet feel very real to her, to experience some transient sense of pleasure in her condition. However, she continued to oscillate between pleasure, fear, and the return of her delusional beliefs, at which time she insisted, with little sign of overt anxiety, that it was not a baby inside her, but faeces or rats or both.

With the supervisory help of the psychosis team, themselves helped by the seminar discussions, the therapist began to acquire an increasing understanding of the meaning and nature of the psychotic disturbance. The power and childhood origins of Grace's envy and jealousy became more clear, and it was possible to understand why these—in principle, normal—human emotions should have had such devastating consequences in her adult life.

The therapist employed neither deliberate exploration of Grace's childhood, nor conventional reassurance, but continued to offer herself as a reality figure who was able to think calmly under the pressure of her patient's excitement and fear, to withstand the projected accusations, and to maintain the analytic attitude of searching for understanding. As a thinking and caring "container", she could be tolerated by the patient, who began to listen to her and to take her comments seriously and to recognize the power of her own envy and jealousy. In this way, Grace began to learn from her therapist at a level much more effective than simply accepting explanations alternative to her own psychotic ones. As the pregnancy proceeded and her cooperation in the therapy continued, Grace's fears and fantasies lost much of their strength.

Slowly the history of her illness began to acquire meaning. The first breakdown seems to have occurred in a setting in which she had for a long time been engaged in a battle with the planning authorities to permit her to build a house on land that she owned. She was finally defeated in this struggle, which was a big blow to a person of her determination, who was used to getting her own way.

The next breakdown had followed the death of Grace's beloved cousin and her discovery that she was pregnant, at which point a massive regression plunged her into a terrifying hallucinatory and delusional world of rats, endangered babies, murderous husband, and associated confusion of personal identity. Low-dose neuroleptics were resumed, and she continued in a weekly session with her therapist.

Progress and outcome

Her therapist continued the therapy throughout the pregnancy and confinement, greatly helped by the attitude of Grace's husband, who had been extremely tolerant and supportive throughout her psychosis. The actual birth of a baby girl was uneventful, but Grace was too afraid of the baby and of herself to be able to hold her, and she was, predictably, unable to breast-feed her. Her mother proved, rather unexpectedly, to be very helpful towards Grace and the baby. Grace by now was able to talk freely with her therapist about her past fears that her siblings were envious of her (actually very real) business success and her beauty. She also began to discover something of her own long-standing unresolved rivalrous feelings towards them.

Gradually she became able to hold and enjoy her daughter. After five months she appeared to have recovered fully and was devoted to her baby; she was free of medication and able to talk freely with her therapist about her psychosis and had acquired what seemed to be a sufficient understanding of its essential meanings. Six months later the therapy was terminated, and a year later she was reported to have remained well.

Discussion

*Developmental reconstruction
and explanation of the psychosis*

Melanie Klein described the primitive wishes and nascent thoughts of infants, the way they persist as unconscious phantasies throughout life, and the way they may erupt in various symbolic and derivative forms in later psychosis. The psychotic eruption is the expression of the reactivation of the unresolved emotional conflicts belonging to early developmental phases that have undergone distortion and subsequently have never been negotiated in later life. In Grace's psychotic states of mind, the content is experienced in a typically concrete, non-symbolic way. The several precipitating factors include the frustration of her infantile feeling of entitlement to colonize and establish herself permanently in the part of mother (Earth) that she owns, a frustration represented symbolically by the refusal of building permission, the death of a primary figure, and her own pregnancy.

The application of these theories to the case of Grace can generate the following explanatory formulation as a reconstruction of the essentials of the dynamic psychopathology of her psychosis.

Grace has suffered from a hysterical psychosis, whose roots are to be found in her failure to resolve serious emotional conflicts of early childhood. These conflicts have found expression in the phobia of rats which she has suffered since her childhood. In this sense, the phobia protected her from becoming conscious of her murderous sibling jealousy and allowing her to pursue the idealized role of "angelic" child. She was able to maintain this role until life situations aroused these jealous feelings to a level where the projective defence maintaining the phobia was no longer sufficient to maintain her equilibrium. Her split-off pathogenic early conflicts centred on her envy and jealousy of her older and younger siblings, and the "oral-biting" content of her subsequent delusions attest to their early developmental foundations. This new inner state of emergency required further splitting of her ego and intensification of projection. This led to the disintegration of her sense of self and to the sense of confusion resulting from the kaleidoscope of shifting identifications. Enactment of her unrequited wishes to *be* the rival baby (the regressive period) inside her mother or feeding at her breast, alongside her wish to *destroy* it (feed it with rats) and her denial of her sense of guilt, completed the construction of the psychotic state.

Her defensive repertoire has been composed of idealization, denial (such as her rejection of the true identity of her father), splitting, and projective and introjective identification. The belief in the rats attacking the real baby inside her body constituted a delusional hypochondriasis, in less psychotic patients often presenting as a fear of cancer inside the body (Rey, 1994). Developmentally less "primitive" defences have been unavailable to her or insufficient to allow the permanent encapsulation of the psychotic "core" which was finally disrupted by stresses in her inner and outer life.

These stresses have had the symbolic significance of "separation" for her. This sometimes overused term has multiple possible referents, such as loss of an object of primary emotional importance, being forced to wait in an infantile dependent situation, being forced to share, being frustrated in her entitlement to control her mother, or entry into the triadic oedipal situation. In the case of Grace, the violent envy and primitive sibling rivalry released by "separation" seems to have been the most important unmanageable emotion. The urgency of the new situations required the mobilization of projective defences of extreme intensity, a violent pathological form of projective identification sometimes considered as a defence against exclusion and a denial of separateness (Steiner, 1993), characteristic of psychotic mental processes.

Thus Grace's persecutory experiences could be expressed as arising from a split-off part of the self—a little "rat-girl" self, full of envy of her mother's fertility and babies, wanting to attack the rival "inside-baby" with the weapons of early infancy—teeth and faeces. Having attacked the mother (primary object), she becomes identified with and then becomes herself the victim of the biting/soiling rat-self, hallucinating the invading rats, while at the same time reassuring the trusted therapist that she (the therapist) is not in danger. Repeatedly she projects the envious and jealous self (although not the biting rat-self) into the therapist, who succeeds in containing it.

This illustrates some of the many dynamic meanings of the often overused term "containment"—of withstanding verbal assaults, of persevering in the face of bizarre accusations, and finally of becoming the container of the projection of a lost part of the patient's self in a psychotic transference. This part is not all bad, as Grace has believed. The recovery of it and the integration and mitigation of its destructive quality might lead to a "feminine" softening of a character that has perhaps justly been described as "hard" in certain respects. It might also help her become more of a real person and less of a generous—and, to some extent, false—idealized providing mother to all and sundry.

The original weakness of her sense of personal identity, a characteristic of her vulnerability to psychosis, was based on the lack of a functioning internal "containing" object (mother).This made her vulnerable under specific stresses to a regressive process that revived unconscious partial identifications. Thus she was overtaken by a double identification (Rey, 1994). Identified with her mother, she becomes the victim of the biting rats. Identified with the baby, she is murderously forced to eat deadly rats, the fate she unconsciously wished on the baby whom she once witnessed, or imagined, feeding at her mother's breast. This may account for the "strange sensations" in her throat and the difficulty in swallowing ("globus hystericus").

When incontinent and assuming a foetus-like posture, she is identified with (enacting the part of) the unborn baby, who is completely helpless but totally dependent. In this way, she was expressing her envy of the rival baby, unborn and born, a wish for the total maternal care that she feels that she has never had.

Grace's psychosis contains her delusional explanations of her terrifying thoughts, and unless we can find a more rational way of understanding and explaining the psychosis, we will find it difficult to help her reach towards rational and better explanations than her own delusional ones. In the case of Grace, the "angelic" child that she once was is now revealed as being based on an identification with a loving, idealized mother whom she had never felt she had had, a deprivation that contributed to her later vulnerability. Having in this role acted from both constructive and defensive motivations, she might now become free to express her more genuine qualities of care and generosity.

Rather than being confronted by the re-entry of lost parts of the self invading her from where she has unconsciously expelled them into her mental representations of the minds of other people and vermin/babies, Grace can now to some extent reflect upon them and start to consider their meaning. Her sense of guilt and her persecutory experiences can now be sufficiently understood.

Containment and countertransference

In this sense, the therapist could be regarded as having success-fully performed the "maternal alpha-function" (Bion) that Grace's narcissistically preoccupied mother had been unable to provide for her in her early life. The therapist has been a "container" for Grace, in the sense of having accepted and tolerated the patient's disturbed feelings and impulses, but also in accepting a psychotic transference, resulting from the projection of her unconscious envious self, previously projected into the neighbours. This dynamic process and its central importance in the psychotherapy of psychosis was described by Rosenfeld (1987, p. 159):

> The psychotic patient who projects impulses and parts of himself into the analyst is expelling them. But in doing so he makes it possible for the analyst to feel and understand his experiences and to contain them. In that way the unbearable experiences can lose their frightening or unbearable quality and become mean-ingful. Through the analyst's capacity to use interpretations to put feelings into words, the patient can learn to tolerate his own impulses and obtain access to a more sane self, which can begin

to think about experiences that were previously meaningless and frightening.

The case of Grace shows that the "containment" process has far wider applications and implications than in formal psychoanalytic treatment. It also illustrates how psychiatric nurses given appropriate training and supervisory help can be particularly well placed to conduct effective psychotherapy with selected psychotic patients within a psychodynamic milieu. The therapist's capacity to manage the countertransference feelings aroused by the patient's projections, and to understand the part played by unconscious envy and jealousy, was a crucial factor in facilitating the resolution of Grace's psychosis.

The future

At the final seminar, the case was reviewed and Grace's prognosis was considered. The group reached the formulation that, despite the impressive result, it should not be taken for granted that Grace has completely worked through the conflicts responsible for her psychotic disturbance. It would be best if psychotherapy could continue, and if this were not to prove possible, there should at least be some supervisory contact from time to time, until it becomes clear that she is able to recognize her own growing child as an individual separate from her fantasies about her. If significant unconscious phantasies have remained unresolved, or conflicts repressed, there could be further difficulties in store. In such a case, Grace might reveal a remaining vulnerability when her daughter begins to become more independent, or if another child, male or female, should be born.

Grace has considerable mental health and strength. Her psychotic episodes originated from the urgent need to manage the destructive feelings aroused by separation threats, rather than an earlier and deeper disturbance of bonding and attachment. Despite her—perhaps justified—criticism of her mother, and although nothing is known about her own experience as a baby, it seems likely that her mother was able to hold her and give her a good start in life. For this reason, Grace was unlikely to be prone to the extremes of regressive disintegration that characterize the more profound examples of schizophrenic disorders.

An optimistic, if guarded, prognosis seems justified. Her sound marriage, her husband's supportive attitude, her own intelligent understanding, and her very good relationship with her therapist and the psychosis team should see her through any future crisis or lead her into further psychotherapy if necessary.

Conclusions

This case illustrates some important theoretical and practical matters:

- The psychogenesis of certain phobias, and their role in defending against potential psychotic developments (Segal, 1981e).
- The importance of internal sibling relationships in determining adult psychopathology.
- The central importance of transference and countertransference in the psychotherapy of such a patient.
- The importance of a psychodynamically informed institutional setting (in this case, a psychiatric ward) in facilitating such psychotherapeutic work.
- . The part that "excessive" projective identification may play in the genesis of such a psychosis.
- The part that introjective processes play in contributing to a patient's confusion and, in particular to his hypochondriacal symptoms, a well-known precursor of schizophrenic breakdown.
- The difference between a formal intensive psychoanalytic treatment approach and a psychoanalytic psychotherapeutic one, and the advantages and limitations of both.

We shall return to consider some of these issues in later chapters.

CHAPTER FOURTEEN

Chronic schizophrenia—
catatonic and spatial features:
"George"

C atatonic schizophrenia was once common among the chronically institutionalized schizophrenic patients of many mental hospitals. In its classical form, it presented as grossly disturbed behaviour and dramatic motor phenomena. Stuporose or semi-stuporose states, often with the assumption of stereotyped postures, sometimes punctuated by sudden outbursts of panicky and at times violent agitation, were characteristic.

However, the advent of anti-psychotic drugs, advances in the practice of psychiatric nursing, and improvements in the organization of traditional mental hospitals have greatly reduced its incidence. Minor forms may still be encountered in which the differentiation from obsessional states may be difficult. In the following case, the psychodynamics and meaning of such symptoms could eventually be understood, and the underlying psychological conflicts resolved.

George

When presented to the seminar, George was 24 years old and had been in twice-weekly psychotherapy in a treatment home for young schizophrenic patients for four years. He had had his first psychotic attack at the age of 16, when long-standing symptoms of depression changed to an acute hallucinatory psychosis with catatonic features. He experienced auditory hallucinations in the form of voices commanding him to kill himself. He said that he was Hitler and the Devil and at other times that he was Jesus Christ. He had a vision, which he thought might have been a dream, of Christ on the cross, which terrified him. He believed that other people had access to his thoughts and could read his mind.

Medication reduced the severity of the disturbance, but his delusional thinking remained unchanged in the background. He was treated in an adolescent unit for two years, both in and out of hospital, maintained on medication and having individual psychotherapy, to which he failed to respond in any significant way. He was regarded as too tied emotionally to his mother, and in an attempt to promote maturation he was eventually given an apartment of his own and encouraged to "separate". He thereupon jumped out of the window of his third-storey apartment and narrowly escaped with his life, sustaining severe fracture injuries. After a long stay in an orthopaedic unit, he was referred to the treatment home for more intensive milieu therapy and individual psychotherapy.

Personal history

The salient features of George's background had been gathered during the previous period of treatment. He is the second of five children. His mother, an anxious and somewhat controlling woman, was severely depressed at his birth, and he was breast-fed for only a short time. His sleep was badly disturbed during the whole of his first year, and he often cried inconsolably. This sleep disturbance became worse after the birth of his brother when he was 2 years old. From the age of 3, George clung desperately to his mother when separation threatened. His mother was hospitalized for depression when he was 4. He grew up to be a solitary child, a lonely schoolboy with few friends. However, he coped reasonably well with his education until the time of his breakdown at the age of 16.

During his adolescence, he began to show typical obsessional symptoms, in the form of long periods of ruminating about good and bad, right and wrong, and various other, ultimately insoluble, issues.

By the age of 14, he was frequently observed to be depressed. At this time, he came under the influence of an uncle who was preoccupied by spiritualism, and who had mystical visionary experiences.

At the age of 16, George fell in love with a girl with whom he was unable to make any real contact. He became ecstatically happy for a brief period, but he soon broke down into the hallucinatory psychosis that led to his admission to hospital. During the course of his first treatment, he had occasional brief explosive outbursts of violence in the family home, when he would throw the furniture about and, at times, attack his father.

The course of the psychotherapy

When he began his sessions, he was very withdrawn, and it was some time before the therapist felt that she was making contact with him in such a way that he could begin to describe his experiences. It would take him several minutes to come into the room. He often remained immobile in a rigid catatonic position for several minutes at the threshold, with his attention fixed on a standing-lamp beside the door. He would then slowly move across the threshold and stop, fixing his gaze on a smaller lamp inside the door. After a few minutes, he would walk across the room to the chair, sometimes assuming a rigid posture in the middle of the room for several seconds. Occasionally he would pause at the entrance and then suddenly burst in, as though penetrating an invisible force-field. He would gradually begin to touch the lamps in a careful exploratory manner. He paid careful attention to the ("male") plug that was inserted in the ("female") connection in the wall and sometimes muttered that there was something strange coming out of the plug fixed into the wall connection. At times, he would stroke the chair softly before sitting down.

His speech at first was largely unintelligible or inaudible for much of the session. Sentences consisted of words and phrases mumbled but with no apparent connection. The therapist sometimes heard him mutter something about his having looked into a girl's face. He avoided looking at his therapist's face, but occasionally gazed deeply and briefly into her eyes. The therapist concluded that he was trying to establish the fact that he was actually inside her room, and to discover that she was actually existing as a separate person. Although she could not understand where he actually felt himself to be, or in whose presence he might believe himself to be, she made such remarks as, "This is *really* my room, the same as it used to be last time", or, "This is actually *me* that you are seeing".

He seemed interested in her comment, but the behaviour did not change. He also stood in front of a mirror in the room, apparently examining his face. On leaving, he would pause momentarily in an immobile posture at the door.

The staff of the treatment home reported that he sometimes behaved in the same way as in the sessions, with regard to entering and leaving the building and examining his face in mirrors. Much later in the therapy, he confided, with some sense of discomfort, that he had often thought that the therapist could read his mind and that there was therefore no point in talking to her.

Bizarre behaviour

In the treatment home, his behaviour was at first extremely disturbed. He talked very little and often in an inaudible mumble, as he did in the therapy sessions, and he would often stand for long periods in a rigid posture. Occasionally he would, apparently accidentally, spill food or drink on the floor and then spend long periods cleaning and re-cleaning in an obsessional way, responding angrily when the staff tried to get him to stop. However, he was not overtly violent and was not particularly difficult to manage.

He gradually adapted to his new life but made no effort to relate to other residents, spending much of his time in his room. He was often observed to assume a catatonic posture for minutes on end. At other times, he jumped up and down in an inexplicable fashion and kept his shoes on in bed all through the night. He was unable, or unwilling, to explain these strange patterns of behaviour.

He slowly began to join in with the group activities, and after several months his cleansing rituals and withdrawal greatly diminished, as did his motor posturing. Although the therapist was attached to the unit, she was able to limit her contact with George outside the session, which took place in her office at some distance from the treatment home. However, during the second year of his stay he withdrew to his bed, where he lay curled up in a foetal position, refusing to eat or drink. This required the staff to feed him, and since they were convinced that he needed a temporary regression to a level of babyhood they did so. He stayed in bed in his room, sometimes feeding from a bottle, for two weeks, during which period the therapist visited him briefly in his room every day.

Discussion in the seminar

His behaviour on entering and leaving the therapist's room was discussed in the seminar, where concepts of unconscious phantasies concerning maternal and body spaces helped explain his behaviour. His entering could be understood as based on a phantasy of intruding into the body of the mother/therapist (the "maternal space"), and leaving as being expelled.

This explanation made sense to the therapist, who then told George that he seemed to feel that he was going inside some alarming space at the point of entering the door, a little like the way a small child might want to get inside mother, and leaving at the end as a child never wanting to be separated from her. The effect was quietly dramatic. George listened intently, and, although no further work was done on the topic, from that point the puzzling "obsessional/ catatonic" behaviour decreased and soon disappeared completely. He began to talk about his experiences more freely, and much of his bizarre behaviour became more understandable. He was very emphatic that the therapist's comment about entering and leaving his mother's body had had a profound impact on him.

Later in the therapy he said, with great feeling, "It was so good that you told me about going in and coming out—you understood how important it was for me!"

He was now able to tell the therapist more about his experiences at the onset of the psychosis, and this helped the understanding of what it had meant to him at the time. He told her that he had seen a girl whom he found attractive. "I looked deeply into her eyes", he said, "and I suddenly felt very strong. Then I fell in love and that was very bad."

He had very soon lost contact with reality, believing that he was Hitler and the Devil. He was unable to look in any normal way into another's eyes and would either avoid eye contact completely or would gaze in apparent fascination at the other person. He was now able to speak of hearing a male voice inside his head, making teasing and critical comments. The reason for his strange past behaviour of jumping up and down now became clear. He jumped to get rid of this male speaker by expelling him through the soles of his feet. This activity was associated with great anxiety, because he was afraid of what the speaker would look like, dreading that he would prove to be the Devil. This delusional belief was also the reason for him repeatedly hitting his head and punching his body.

This hallucinatory voice issued commands such as: "You are Hitler and you have to suffer like Jesus on the cross, or jump out of the window!" The voice was truly "diabolic", confusing him by saying "no" when he was thinking "yes", and doing the same with "good–bad" and "right–wrong". This was one reason why he had often been unable to connect words to form coherent sentences. This delusional system also found expression in a fear he had expressed that he, like the male speaker, might disappear through the bottom of his feet during the night, a fate that he had tried to prevent by wearing his shoes throughout the night.

"Perverse" fantasies

With great shame, he confided that he was afraid that he was homosexual or sexually perverted. Sexuality excited but frightened him. In the course of psychotherapy as an adolescent, he had fallen in love with an older woman (apparently his previous therapist) and was frightened by the emergence of the fantasy of penetrating into her buttocks. In this fantasy, which still excited and shamed him, he would push his face between the buttocks of an older woman and smell or taste the faeces. He had been burdened with the resulting guilt and shame for more than ten years.

He began to understand that entering the room had aroused frightening and exciting thoughts about sexual entry into his therapist, and that his perverse fantasy had the same meaning for him. He came to recognize that his therapist was different from the mother of his inner life who was the object of his intruding sexual desires, and he said: "I know you now and am happy to see you and be with a therapist, but I need a mother!"

George was greatly relieved by the exposure of his "perverse" fantasy, and his therapist's acceptance of it, and was soon able to talk about his inexplicable silences and periods of catatonic immobility.

He told the therapist that at these times he had been overwhelmed by the wish to have sexual intercourse with her and, at the same time, held a frightening belief that she was trying to seduce him. He now began to explain his behaviour at the threshold of the therapy room and the significance of the lamps, which he would touch and turn on and off: "These were obsessions covering my feelings. I concentrated as hard as I possibly could on the lamps in order to control what I was beginning to feel. If my obsessions hadn't worked I would have been terrified."

He explained that the "obsessional" behaviour of spending long periods drying the floor if he spilled anything on it was an attempt to reduce his feelings of guilt. He was now becoming able to feel his feelings rather than escape or control them rigidly.

He said: "I have so many feelings—I now feel free!—I don't know what to do with my feelings!"

Another reason for his reluctance to speak became clear—speaking was unconsciously equated with doing violence to others. He had believed (had an unconscious phantasy) that to speak to others was equivalent to expelling dangerous objects, or firing missiles at other people. It was his thoughts that were perhaps the primary danger, and the danger of words lay in the fact that they revealed the thoughts. These thoughts were dangerous to him because they might make him aware of what he was feeling, which would be too disturbing. Since he could not reliably differentiate his own mind from that of others, he believed that others would be equally threatened and unable to stand him. Not-knowing was essential to his equilibrium.

He continued: "I always used to throw my words out of myself without feelings. Then everything started to change and I took chances with my words. Now, instead of throwing them out, they are now coming from inside me with power, and now they are my own. Now I can speak, and I have so much to say!"

With this change, illustrative of Freud's dictum (1917e [1950], p. 208) that the psychotic replaces "word-presentations" with "thing-presentations" and that recovery reverses this course, George was becoming able to symbolize the act of speaking, so that he no longer needed to remain silent to avoid causing damage. The therapist's non-critical acceptance of his "disgusting" wishes and her offering him a simple way of understanding them ("getting close to mother") had greatly relieved him. His overwhelming feelings of guilt receded, and he began to learn that he was not so omnipotently bad as he had believed him-self to be.

Dreaming

George then recounted a series of dreams, whose simple manifest content suggested that he had now begun to be able to give his feelings and experiences a symbolic expression. Although the therapist did not explore the dream content very far, she felt able to discern some of the many possible thoughts that had gone into their construction. Rather than investigate the patient's associations and work with him to explore possible meanings in a conventional manner, she simply took the dreams as signs of progress, of his beginning to think for himself about himself, and she told him so.

He recounts the first of a series of dreams.

"I am a prisoner trapped in a deep pit, with a strong grill over it. I awaken in panic."

This claustrophobic dream suggests that he is beginning to think of how his "invasive" infantile wishes, leading to the feeling of living inside his object, have imprisoned him and isolated him from real life (Rosenfeld, 1987, p. 169).

"A man is imprisoned in a house. I throw a ball into the house and the prisoner throws it back."

This dream might be considered in terms of his thoughts about attempting to make contact with the imprisoned part of his self, just as the therapist has succeeded in doing. However, George's difficulty in participating in the exploration of his dreams leaves open quite different possible meanings, on the one hand concerned with play and on the other with a failure to contain projections.

"I am standing behind a big powerful man. I gaze at his strong buttocks and I am seized with an overwhelming desire to stab them with a knife."

This complex dream may be expressing different layers of thinking, in which the target of his destructive feelings, male buttocks, are finding a symbolic equation with breasts and perhaps a pregnant maternal body. Access to his associations might have revealed some specific event in the transference of the previous day, as may have been the case in the other dreams. However the central theme seems to be that his rivalrous feelings towards his father, only recently available for discussion in the therapy, were finding expression for the first time.

"I see a man inside a house, and I realized that I had to get to work on a job. I felt that I was a sinner."

He woke from this dream with a feeling of sadness and a recognition of the importance of the psychotherapy. When he told his therapist the dream, he said that in the dream he had also felt very sad and felt that the dream must have some important meaning. The therapist reflected to herself that these dream thoughts expressed a lessening of his sense of helplessness, again as a sign of progress.

This dream seemed to be very important to George, for it expressed the sad realization that he must relinquish his infantile longing to remain united in a symbiotic fusion with his mother forever (so vividly expressed by his desperate clinging to her at the age of 3 and 4 years) and to begin to take responsibility for his own mind and adult development.

Further progress

From this point, he made steady improvement. His behaviour inside and outside the treatment home became more normal. He began to attend school, making good progress for the first time. He was more able to talk normally with his parents and told the therapist that, although he had often been frightened of his father, he was no longer. He also said that he had long known that he wanted to be a baby, and that the fortnight in the treatment home when he was treated like one had meant a great deal to him. In Winnicott's view (1958, p. 281), this would be considered as an organized regression that had been waiting to happen, a healthy process completely different from a pathological one. As such, it could be considered as an "unfreezing" of an original "situation of failure", contributing to the "new beginning" that therapy had made possible.

He returned to the therapist's explanation about coming into the room as forcing himself into his (internal) mother, the consulting-room symbolizing the maternal body, and how frightening he had found the sexual thoughts and wishes for intercourse with his therapist that threatened to overwhelm him at those moments. He commented on the therapist's interpretation about intrusion and expulsion from the mother's body and accompanying sexual thoughts in his remark: "Now I know that I am coming and going. When it was outside/inside I couldn't think!"

He had now come to understand that his episodes of "catatonic" immobility at the door of the consulting-room were a deliberate attempt to distract his mind by focusing on the lamps. These episodes of immobility then ceased and did not return.

Resolution of dysmorphophobia

Although he continued to look into mirrors, this behaviour was no longer motivated by anxiety or confusion, and he seemed to be perceiving his own reflection in a realistic way. He had long been preoccupied with the appearance of his nose and upper lip, repeatedly examining this part of his face in a repetitive and apparently puzzled manner, and this concern receded and finally disappeared. This preoccupation seemed to be a delusional distortion of his body image (*dysmorphophobia*), arising from his confusing his perceptions of parts of his face with his unconscious phantasies of parts of the object's body (originally, the mother of infancy). He was seeing his thoughts and phantasies about these body parts, their function and their owners, and he was attempting to differentiate his own face from that of his mother (see the case of Brenda, Chapter 2). The precise content of these phantasies was not discovered. Such an abbreviated "explanation" of the nature of dysmorphophobia (and other related somatic delusions) would require considerable elaboration to make it comprehensible to most readers. Such important formulations as "cheeks = breast", "nose = penis", "mouth = anus" are otherwise very likely to be misunderstood (see Grotstein, 1986, p. 207).

George had experienced great relief by taking the risk of telling his therapist about his "sexually perverse" fantasies. When she responded by suggesting that this was *his way of getting close to his mother*, it had made great sense to him. Although he did not speak directly about his parents' sexual relationship, he expressed a great deal of anger towards them. He was convinced that they had tried to control him, to tell him what to think, and to prevent his playing aggressive games with other boys. Because of this, he said, he had never had a childhood. He began to understand his deep-seated fears of destructiveness, as, for instance, his fears of harming others by opposing their desires. With evident triumph he said: *"Now I can say No!"*

His past episodes of refusing to eat could now be understood as a wish to be fed as a baby, and at other times as a fear of depriving others—"if I don't eat there is more for the world". A reparative motive can be found in his previous attitude of reluctance to travel in the treatment home's bus. He explained that adding his weight to the burden of people in the bus would increase the consumption of fuel and so the bus would have less capacity to transport other patients. His wish to be the sole occupant of the (symbolized) maternal space was now accompanied by a wish that the others should not be excluded. The fact that this material was being recalled at a time when a termination of the therapy was approaching might suggest that George was considering the possibility of being able to share his therapist with her other patients. However, not all transference manifestations can be explored, nor indeed do they all need to be explored in this form of psychotherapy.

Working towards termination

A year after the final seminar discussion, the therapist made the following report:

"He has made great progress in the year and is at last beginning to make good school progress. After five years of twice-wekly psychotherapy he is due to leave the treatment home to move towards a more independent existence. He no longer seems to think in a concrete way, as was the case with jumping up and down to expel the inner bad objects through the soles of his feet. The interpretation made a year ago, about his threshold rituals on entering and leaving the session in terms of conflicts about wishing to be inside, were a turning point. However, in sessions he has tended to become withdrawn when the ending of the therapy is proposed, although he is still functioning well outside. He was recently heard by the staff to say, without apparent anxiety or confusion, and with apparent recognition that he was making a metaphorical statement about his own painful future, that maybe Jesus is going to get crucified again."

Two years later

On leaving the treatment home, George moved into an apartment of his own in a communal centre supervised by the staff. The psychotherapy was brought to an end over a period of some months, without any obvious disturbance. Two years later, he was reported to be working in stable employment in a supermarket and leading a relatively normal social life. His family were profoundly impressed by his recovery of sanity and by his emotional and intellectual growth, and he was on good terms with them.

Discussion

Speaking of the "schizoid mode of being", Rey (1994, p. 12) observes that "The fear of separation from the object and the desire to penetrate into it and fuse into a primal unity can be so intense that it surpasses human understanding."

This fusional wish seems to have been the major motivation contributing to the fragility of George's sense of identity, his impairment of contact with reality, and his differentiation of self from others. The concrete and literal quality of his thinking involved the loss of the capacity to recognize symbols and to appreciate metaphorical expressions in the area of "separation". His recovery involved the *discovery* of the capacity for the use of symbolism as a way to think about his emotional experiences, his wishes, and his associated unconscious phantasies.

The essential change lay in his developing the capacity to think symbolically about the thoughts and feelings aroused by separation, which could be called a "pushing-in/pushed-out" system, and he was only able to do this because the therapist supplied him with the concepts necessary to do so.

Sadomasochism and sexual perversion

His desperate desire to penetrate and fuse with his mother found expression in his exciting fantasies of sexual intercourse with his therapist. This "sexual intercourse", however, was not primarily an expression of a developing capacity for a mature heterosexual object relationship so much as an erotization or "sexualization", which is essentially a defence against the impact of the pain of absence. As such, it represents an infantile masturbatory fantasy of self-consolation. Such masturbatory activity in infancy can serve the function of creating an altered ego-state in which the mother's absence is not noticed or is replaced by a fantasy of her being present, supported by the associated genital sensory stimulation. In this way, the recognition that a separation had taken place between him and his mother is extinguished and the subsequent oedipal conflicts are bypassed.

Given other contributing factors, such a dynamic can eventually lead to a crystallized sexual perversion, in later life, in the form of sadomasochism or fetishism (or both), whose essential meaning may be difficult to recognize. If the pain of separation is felt to be cruelly inflicted, the desire for revenge may lead to sadistic pleasure in inflicting pain (see the case of Elmer, Chapter 11). However, when the sadistic impulses are projected into the object, the patient feels that he is the victim in a sadomasochistic drama of repeated punishment (of self and object). This form of persecutory guilt is characteristic of the paranoid–schizoid position and underlay George's delusional beliefs about, and identification with, the suffering Christ.

It is interesting to note that when the ending of the therapy was proposed, he said that Christ was about to be crucified again. However, the way he spoke suggested that his fantasy of suffering like the crucified Christ had momentarily returned, but in what seems to have been a metaphorical, rather than delusional, manner (Jackson & Williams, 1994, ch. 5). As a metaphor, it could express the thought: "There are painful times ahead."

Part-object relationships

The concept of mental representation of the maternal space and body and their displacement to other spaces allows an explanatory formulation of an unconscious phantasy of an invasive-intrusive entry into the maternal body. In this conception of the body, the bottom hole is a primitive cloaca, vagina-urethra-anus-rectum not yet differentiated as representations in the infant's developing mind. As yet, he has not developed the concepts of differentiated body parts, organs, and their proper functions, including that of his own penis.

Breasts, buttocks, cheeks, and other soft rounded surfaces are at this primitive level of mental representation symbolically equated, regarded as essentially the same thing, rather than "resembling in some respects", as also are faeces and milk. This invasive entry, thought of by George as "sexual intercourse", is an expression of his longing to fuse with his mother by entry by way of her bottom. It is the dyadic (pre-oedipal) precursor of his later triadic oedipal conflicts. The associated guilt and confusion provoked the defensive catatonic immobility.

Rosenfeld (1987, p. 169) expressed this process: "when projective identification becomes directed towards the delusional object, the saner parts of the self may become trapped or imprisoned within this object, and physical and mental paralysis amounting to catatonia may result".

Whether these sexual fantasies contain the possibility of a mature sexual development in George is as yet unknown.

Looking and gazing as invasion

George's first breakdown was associated with gazing into the eyes of a girl for whom he had discovered loving feelings. His subsequent fear of looking or being looked at could eventually be understood as one of the many forms taken by his omnipotent psychotic thinking. Looking had thus acquired the quality of a projective invasion of the mind of the object looked at, a process that helps to explain his delusional belief that other people could read his mind.

Catatonia/obsession

George's catatonic immobility has expressed different motives at different times—primarily of obsessional indecision and the fear of acting destructively. His interest in the connection of the male and female electric-light plugs show that his choice of the lamps as objects of obsessive rumination was not simply a meaningless distraction, devoid of symbolic significance as he apparently believed. Thoughts of his parents' sexual intercourse and perhaps thoughts of illumination may have been involved in the choice.

His catatonia seemed at other times to have had the motivation of conserving energy. He eventually explained this motive quite clearly.

If he moved, he would consume energy and thus would need food which required eating, and this would deprive others: "If I get something the world is depleted of energy. If I don't move I stop diminishing the total sum of energy, and by saving this amount of energy I am economizing and saving and protecting the world."

This behaviour designed to protect others—unconsciously, rival babies—from his own destructive feelings also contributed to periods of self-starvation, which he was able to explain in the logic typical of concrete thinking: if he does not eat there will be more food left in the world, so others will not go hungry.

Command hallucinations

At the onset of the psychosis, at the age of 16, George experienced the voice of the Devil telling him that he was Hitler and that he must kill himself, and it was probably in response to such a command that he nearly succeeded, by jumping from a window some time later. The psychodynamics involved in the formation of such a dangerous inner figure (a "persecuting superego") are complex, involving the mental mechanisms of denial, splitting, projection, and introjection. An impressive example of the development of such an internal object figure and its arrest *in status nascendi* has been recorded by Winnicott (1958, p. 112; see also Sinason, 1993).

Conclusions

The psychogenic seeds of George's later schizophrenic psychosis can be seen to have been active at least since the time of his birth. The confirmed record of the beginnings of his postnatal life tell of a mother suffering from post-partum depression and of an early and abrupt weaning; it tells also of a baby crying inconsolably, with marked sleep disturbance, growing into an anxious toddler and young child with severe separation anxiety, clinging desperately to his mother. The worsening of his sleep at the time of his brother's birth and his mother's depression must have increased his fear of separation from her, and her depression in his fourth year can only have increased this fear.

From the point of view of treatment, there is much to be said for regarding psychotic illness as essentially a psychogenic disorder. This perspective can help the clinician to avoid the current overestimation of the role of biological factors, however important these may be from a theoretical and neuroscientific point of view. The more biologically oriented reader may see features in George's case that might be described as autistic and thus taken to justify a diagnosis of undetected minimal brain damage at birth or of Asperger's syndrome. Even if these classifications were correct, they would not disqualify psychotherapy as a treatment mode (see also the case of Conrad, Chapter 7).

Although his psychiatric history might not have suggested that George was a hopeful candidate for psychotherapy, prognostic generalizations are not always a good guide to an individual's possible openness to change and personality growth. When a psychotic breakdown is preceded by a period of depression (in George's case, at the age of 14), it may indicate a capacity for a relatively integrated state of mind and thus a more hopeful prognosis. George's parents' determination to understand and help him was another important positive feature. A further hopeful feature emerged when it became apparent that he was developing the capacity for symbolic expression, as evidenced by his capacity to dream.

George is a happier and more stable person than the one who entered psychotherapy, and his schizophrenic psychosis seems to have been completely resolved. He remains a vulnerable individual, but his good experience of psychotherapy and the continuing availability of support from the staff of the treatment home should stand him in good stead in future times of need.

Moreover, he can now, to a considerable extent, use his mind to think reflectively about himself and about his emotional experiences.

CHAPTER FIFTEEN

Manic-depressive psychosis: "Harry"

M anic-depressive disorders are widely recognized as having a biological basis, and the frequent genetic transmission of a predisposition to the illness has been convincingly established. On the other hand, the role of psychological factors in contributing to the original vulnerability, and the nature of the stresses that might precipitate an episode of the illness in those predisposed individuals, have received relatively little attention. There have been few reports in the psychiatric literature of this matter, fewer still concerning the place of individual psychoanalytic psychotherapy in formulating treatment plans.

Psychoanalysts have made major contributions to this subject in the past (Abraham, 1911; Klein, 1935; Cohen et al., 1963; Rosenfeld, 1963; Scott, 1964; Jacobson, 1967; Pao, 1968a; Freeman, 1971). The treatment of single cases from a Kleinian perspective has been reported by Jackson (1993a), Rey (1994), and Lucas (1998). However, the evident activity of biological factors and the relative efficacy of mood-stabilizing drugs has progressively discouraged interest in the psychological factors that may contribute to the predisposition, the onset, and the perpetuation of the disorder. A recent decline of interest in psychodynamics in general in many quarters of psychiatry, and the pronouncements of some influential psychiatrists, have served to deflect attention from the way that early life experiences may have a negative or positive influence on the subsequent psychological development of a genetically predisposed individual. For example, Jamison (1995) describes her own past psychotic experiences in a vivid and moving manner, but she fails nonetheless to do justice to modern psychoanalytic thinking about the psychogenic aspects of manic-depressive psychosis and the possibility of well-conducted psychoanalytic psychotherapy with selected patients in an optimum psychiatric setting. Such a "need-adapted" setting will give full consideration to the associated use of anti-manic or antidepressive medication, and of concomitant supportive work with both the patient and the family where appropriate.

An exclusively biomedical view of the nature and treatment of manic-depressive psychosis may confine psychiatrists to supportive and rehabilitative measures that may include helping the patient learn about life situations likely to disturb him. Such an approach may achieve a great deal, but, however helpful it may be, it cannot be expected to resolve the underlying internal psychological conflicts that may be precipitating psychotic episodes. It may also obscure consideration of the benefits that a psychoanalytic approach may offer some patients, despite the difficulties presented by management and the provision of sufficiently skilled psychotherapy and psychiatric resources. The following case will serve as an illustration of these matters.

Harry

Harry, aged 45 years, was admitted to a psychiatric ward at the age of 30 in a state of acute mania. He said that he had tickets to the moon and was shortly going to leave with his family in order to escape the catastrophe that was about to overtake Earth. He was admitted to hospital on a compulsory order, where his excited and hyperactive state was slowly brought under control with anti-psychotic medication. However, after some months he became severely depressed. He gradually responded to medication with lithium and antidepressants and was eventually fit enough to be discharged from hospital. However, he succumbed to the toxic side-effects of this prophylactic medication, and within a year he became severely hypothyroid. At this point, he refused to accept antidepressants and alternatives to lithium medication. He maintained this attitude for ten years, during which time he had frequent manic and depressive episodes requiring hospitalization. When manic, he firmly maintained the belief that he had been specially selected by higher powers to save the world from evil, and when depressed he was severely self-reproachful and retarded in his thinking.

Once-weekly psychotherapy was begun at the age of 42 and was continued for 120 sessions over the next two and a half years. He cooperated well, and by the end of the first year had had no further breakdowns. The therapy was punctuated by violent emotional outbursts in the sessions and periods of uncontained behaviour outside them, particularly in connection with vacation breaks in the sessions, which will shortly be described. By the end of this first year of psychotherapy, the therapist, who was also the managing psychiatrist of the ward, succeeded in helping him accept medication with carbamazepine and to continue with it on a prophylactic basis.

At this point, the therapist brought the case to the seminar for discussion, and reported back on several occasions until the therapy was interrupted eighteen months later under unforeseen circumstances. There had been no pathological swings of mood and no need for hospital admission during this period.

Personal history

Since family interviews had not been undertaken, and few details of his early life and family circumstances had been recorded, the story of his life was largely derived from his own account. There was no evidence of a family history of manic-depressive psychosis, serious mood disorder, or other psychotic illness.

Harry grew up in small country town, with a brother two years younger who has always been mentally healthy. He believes that his parents were very intolerant of small children, and he tends to attribute much of the unhappiness of his childhood to their attitude. He was a sad and lonely child, with few friends, whereas his brother was a happy and popular extrovert. During the course of the psychotherapy, he recounted occasions of being shut out of the house, perhaps for bad behaviour, and crying desperately. At the age of 18, he left the parental home and took a job in another town. He soon became psychotic, believing that the police were hunting him for having committed a murder. He did not dare to go to work and withdrew into his own room, and for days on end he lived in a tent in the adjoining forest. He gradually recovered from this relatively brief paranoid psychosis, and at the end of a month was able to return to work.

He remained apparently stable, and he married, fathered two children, and worked satisfactorily in a clerical job until his first manic breakdown, already described, at the age of 30. Some months later he became seriously depressed, at which point lithium medication was instituted. He responded well to this, but, as already described, he passed into a hypothyroid state and refused all alternative medication, with the result that he quickly returned to his relapsing manic and depressive episodes. Over the next ten years, he was admitted to hospital on several occasions, following the same pattern of excitement and grandiose delusions in manic phases and severe self-reproach with suicidal preoccupations in depressive ones. He continued to refuse prophylactic medication, and since it seemed likely that the relapses might be a response to stressful life situations, he was offered twice-weekly psychotherapy. Although he declined this, he accepted a weekly session.

Psychotherapy begins

He soon agreed to take maintenance carbamazepine medication, and under this protective shield the therapist was able to continue the psychotherapy. Throughout the subsequent two and a half years of weekly psychotherapy, Harry cooperated well and found great relief in disclosing and expressing his conflicting emotions. He formed a strong positive relationship with the therapist and slowly began to make progress in thinking about himself.

His behaviour in the sessions was very striking. When he was in a hypomanic mood, he spoke in a delusional and omnipotent way about his Messianic mission to save the world from its imminent destruction; when depressed, he would often curl up in the chair and cry like a baby. He would always recover from this state by the end of the session and be able to say that he had a deep wish to be a baby again, and thus to have a better and happier childhood than his own miserable one. Often at home he would cry in the night, when his sympathetic wife would hold his hand until he fell asleep. When "normal", he would express his resentment towards the therapist for forcing him to explore the inner world of his feelings, and he would threaten to break off the treatment.

The therapist came to the conclusion that, beneath the sad and lonely little boy who he once was, had smouldered a violently aggressive rebel, filled with murderous feelings of envy and jealousy towards his parents and, in particular, towards his extrovert younger brother. He felt that Harry's undying grievances towards his parents must have had some justification, however complex the reality might have been at the time, but he accepted that because he had not been able to hear their side of the story, this was not the time to question it with Harry. This was his personal truth, and the recognition of this split-off part of his personality helped explain a very great deal about the evolution of his psychotic illness and his subsequent behaviour in the therapeutic transference.

The first psychotic breakdown took the form of a brief paranoid psychotic episode occurring soon after the first separation from his parents. When he began to tell the story of his life and to recover the missing feelings, it became clear that in his unconscious mind the victim of his delusional murder was primarily his younger brother. He recalled vividly an event in childhood when he threw a stone at his brother, which knocked him down and left Harry with the belief that he had nearly killed him. Whether or not his intense feeling of guilt was a response to parental criticism, it had the effect of enhancing his unconscious omnipotent belief that he was dangerously destructive.

The second breakdown was apparently precipitated by major marital conflict marked by a period of mutual infidelity, the details of which never became entirely clear. He became acutely manic and, after some months of conventional treatment, suicidally depressed. This marked the beginnings of his pathological mood swings. These did not show the regular cycling characteristic of some manic-depressive illnesses, and their relation to the specific life stress of separation became very clear in the course of the psychotherapy.

Dream life

Early in the therapy, Harry began to report vivid dreams. Although he rarely had the patience to provide associations, their manifest content was sometimes so clear that they provided useful information about his state of mind and currently emerging thoughts. An early dream with an apparently homosexual content served as an agenda of what was to come:

"I was in a changing-room of a gymnasium with another man. We were both naked. I saw that the other man's penis was pointing backwards. He was embarrassed and I found it very funny."

The therapist understood this dream as a near-conscious expression of Harry's rivalrous feelings towards his potent father (the therapist himself in the transference relationship). In the "changing-room" of the therapy, he deflects his father's potency and laughs in a mocking and triumphant way at his successful reversal of paternal power.

Harry began to express these feelings towards his therapist's knowledge and status repeatedly both inside and outside the sessions. He soon came to discover that his therapist, far from being disconcerted by these attacks, was able to withstand them and interpret their meaning in relation to the father of his childhood, still powerfully active in his inner world. It could now be understood that the lonely and depressed little boy who had been unable to free himself from his impoverished emotional tie to his mother and his associated murderous rage had sought solace in his hidden feelings of superiority to his father and brother.

Harry repeatedly returned with deep emotion to memories of his unhappy childhood, an exploration that seemed to afford him considerable relief and brought some feeling of warmth towards his therapist. The therapist accepted the reality of these feeling of sadness, but he discovered that Harry would quickly resume his pseudo-independent attitude following such sessions. This change of mood was most obvious during weekends and vacation breaks, and the therapist was able to confront him firmly with comments such as, "When I go away you get angry and tell yourself that you don't need me. You can't face your anger with me because you are afraid that I will abandon you."

It was interventions such as these that led to a gradual decrease in the patient's excitability and capacity to experience and tolerate feelings of sadness and develop feelings of warmth towards his therapist. However, his hypomanic energy was so powerful that he repeatedly enacted his conflicts in the outer world in a spectacular manner, as will be described.

As Harry spoke more about his feelings of anger with his parents, he reported the following dream:

"I have bought a big heavy camera which the salesman said was very good. I want to use it and I come to a beach. There I see a very beautiful naked girl, but it is not a sexual scene. I start to put the camera on a tripod, but it suddenly turns into a rocket launcher."

This is a complex and profound dream with multiple levels of possible meanings and rich in symbolic construction, and which might have been further clarified by the patient's own associations, However, it might be thought to express the disruptive effects of his violent intrusive envy and jealousy aroused by his emerging recognition of the beauty of the loving care that was symbolized by the therapy he was being given (Grotstein, 1998; Meltzer & Harris Williams, 1988).

The therapist-salesman offers him the weighty mental equipment to record, remember, perceive, and learn. In the mental area of new experience—symbolized by the beach, where conscious and unconscious, "maternal" and "paternal" meet, and new life emerges—his explosive jealousy threatens to erupt at the point where the separateness of his desired object/mother has to be acknowledged. This had found symbolic expression in the tripod, representing the "oedipal triad". The perceptual equipment that could act as a receptor and container of new impressions is transformed into an explosively evacuative and expulsive one. The symbolic implications of this dream are profound, and the imaginative reader may be able to detect other references than the foregoing. However, the condensation of the symbolism of non-sexual ("pre-oedipal", "symbiotic") dyadic bliss being shattered by the oedipal triadic separation experience is suggestive and reveals the depth to which this once-weekly psychotherapy was reaching in this psychotic man.

Dreams indicating progress

Harry's emerging insight was finding symbolic expression in his dream life, which provided a mental space where motivations could be discussed in the therapy rather than enacted mindlessly in the outside world. He continued to present dreams that had a very clear manifest content, and these served as a reliable guide to his progress and increasing stability.

"I leave the seashore in an armoured military landing vessel. It drifts off helplessly out to sea, but I struggle to get it back to the shore. I have to negotiate the islands of a dangerous archipelago, but eventually I manage to bring it back to land."

In this dream he felt a triumphant satisfaction and relief at his struggle against such danger, and in the following session it became clear that this dream narrative did indeed symbolize a non-manic achievement at having avoided acting out his conflicts during the interval between sessions.

"In my office I suddenly see a lot of people who are monsters with strange limbs, with legs like long stilts. My colleagues watch me closely to see how I react to the presence of these monsters."

This remarkable dream gives symbolic expression to the beginnings of the acquisition of a self-observing capacity, first projected into other people (in his inner world), perhaps preliminary to a self-questioning, "How do other people see me—what do they think of my monstrous self-elevating arrogance?"

The progress of unconscious insight continues:

"I bought a small white car and parked it outside my parents' house. I go inside, and from the kitchen I see I have parked it badly on the grass, where its wheels had sunk deeply into the lawn. Suddenly two small children appear, turn the car over on its back and start scratching it and smearing it with mud."

The small white car, a modest representative of the new form of mental transport provided by the therapy (in opposition to his manic omnipotent way of carrying on), is overturned by an infantile destructive attack when left unattended and unguarded. The symbolic elements that have gone to make up this coherent dream narrative are complex, with reference to the mother's body and breast (the car), the therapeutic session (the kitchen), and no doubt many other elements.

During hypomanic episodes, Harry's sense of mission slowly became less extreme, in that he no longer saw the earth as being in imminent danger of total catastrophic destruction, requiring flight to the moon or omnipotent salvation of an unspecified sort. Instead, he began to talk more about his mission to rid Earth of evil, by cleansing it of "greedy and egotistical people" and accusing his therapist of being just such a person. A change could now be seen to be taking place, with the theme of the unspecified catastrophe beginning to take a less concrete, more metaphorical and human form.

He then began to take large-scale action in the external world. Over a period of some months, he wrote 200 letters to the president of the United States, advising him how to save the world from such evil people. He did not seem to know exactly how the President should proceed with this task, but he was absolutely sure that his policy must combat the evils of Capitalism in order to bring about the "American dream" of peace and justice. At the same time, it must fight the evils of Communism to realize the Socialist dream of justice and equality for all. There was no doubt about the reality of Harry's confused and grandiose reforming activities in the external world, which proved to have been of sufficient concern to bring him to the attention of local state security services.

This material illustrates how symbolic expressions reveal different levels of meaning. Thus the conjunction of the two opposing political forces, as with the union of sea and shore in his dream of the beach, can represent the union of his parents which he wishes both to attack and separate and also, in the depressive position, to restore to harmony. A psychotherapist's skill lies in discovering the level of relevant meaning and ways of conveying this to such a patient.

For a while, Harry thought that the best method of achieving his ambition would be to disseminate a computer virus to paralyse all the earth's communications systems, so that a better and happier world could arise from the debris. Fortunately he had acquired sufficient sanity to be able to discuss this with his therapist as an appealing idea, rather than to be driven to such destructive anarchistic activity.

The pain of dependency and insight–
sanity as a threat

His continuing progress clearly caused him great pain, confusion, and anxiety. On occasions, when his therapist was unavoidably late for a session, he turned on him in fury, shouting, "How am I going to cope with all this? You are only trying to make me depressed! I will kill or die rather than admit that I am mad! You're just a bureaucrat ! In the waiting-room I suddenly thought you are trying to get me to kill myself! You are trying to force your own dangerous ideas into my mind!"

Reparation

Harry's extraordinarily energetic attempts to bring peace to an evil and divided world were not entirely pathological. They seemed to be an expression of an identification with the therapist's attempt to bring peace to Harry's inner world—that is, as a pathological attempt at ("concrete", "literal") reparation. But the therapist also discerned the emergence of another constructive motivation. He often impressed his GP as being in a normal and constructive state of mind and as having a genuine wish to help others in the world as he had been helped by his therapist.

He lectured his therapist about the importance of self-sufficiency and independence, and it was clear how torn he was between gratitude to his therapist, envy, and a defensive sense of superiority. He propounded his political conviction that the worker's and the idler's time is equally valuable, that the person doing humble and menial work was entitled to exactly the same financial reward as the highly trained specialist, and that "If a gift isn't free and you have to fight for it, it is worthless!" To which the therapist replied "but even a baby must suck to survive!"

The patient responded with roars of laughter but was soon able to reflect on the serious implications of the therapist's response, saying "Well, maybe all this really does have psychological meaning!"

Separation reactions

His extreme sensitivity to separation, with its associated sense of abandonment, was repeatedly illustrated in the treatment. When the therapist went on vacation, Harry left the country for the duration of the break and joined an organization called "Soldiers for Peace", in an embattled region in a foreign country. This activist work seems to have been very constructive, and Harry apparently made a modest but realistic contribution. Doing the right thing for split motives, both constructive and defensive, could not, however, bring him peace in his inner world. Harry's departure was clearly a "reversing" reaction to his therapist's absence, a reaction that he repeated during other breaks.

Acting-out

During a long summer vacation, Harry left his wife, went to another city, and started an affair with another woman. Before long, he became so excited that this woman recognized that he was ill and escorted him back to his wife and family. When the therapy resumed, the therapist was able to show him that this abandonment of his wife was an act of revenge against the therapist for leaving him. It was also a way to punish his wife, who, he felt, did not support him at that time.

Sexuality and the "primal scene"

At first he feared that his positive feelings towards his therapist implied that he was homosexual, but eventually he came to understand this as his feeling neither firmly masculine nor firmly feminine. This was one outcome of his weak identifications with his parents, as already described. Dreams of girls with a penis illustrated this developmental lack of differentiation. However, he recalled having listened in the night to the sound of his parents' intercourse and of being overwhelmed with excitement. It seemed likely that one source of grievance towards his wife was that she could not satisfy those of his desires that were essentially destructive and infantile.

Termination of the therapy

After 120 sessions over two and a half years, the patient broke off treatment. This was a unilateral decision which he made after the therapist returned from a vacation. The therapist was not surprised, since the patient had recently been talking about going to another city to undertake some advanced professional training for which he had been accepted. However, the therapist understood this move primarily as an escape from the prospect of continuing dependency, with all the sense of pain and loneliness that it involved. It was clear that the goal of secure independence and autonomous functioning was a long way off.

However, the patient declared that he would consider further psychotherapy in the future if he felt it necessary. Gratitude, resentment, and envy were all evident, and the incomplete resolution of his oedipal triadic conflicts in the transference seemed obvious.

A year later

No follow-up visits could be planned, and a year later the thera-pist learned that Harry had remained stable and was working satis-factorily, but once again had left his wife.

Discussion

There is a constant interplay between the paranoid–schizoid and depressive positions in all mental life. The manic-depressive can func-tion well in the depressive position but is also capable of regression to a deeper level of the paranoid–schizoid position, a dynamic that finds expression in the psychiatric diagnosis of "schizo-affective" psychosis or, in the case of Harry's first breakdown, of paranoid psychosis.

H. S. Klein (1974) pointed out that manic-depressive individuals have achieved a much more mature level of personality development than is the case of the schizophrenic group of illnesses. They have, in consequence, considerable potential mental health, often with power-ful unconscious constructive wishes to acknowledge and put right the damage that they believe that they have done in the inner and outer world (see Jackson, 1993a).

Manic defences

Klein's concept of "manic defences" and their reparative aspects has greatly helped the understanding of the psychopathological and psychogenic aspects of manic-depressive psychosis. Manic defences are most clearly seen when the individual has reached the develop-mental level of the depressive position, where concern for the fate of the object has begun to replace the primary concern for the self which characterizes the paranoid–schizoid position. In order to escape the pain that this concern brings, the individual falls back on the manic defences. These defences—aimed at denial of the sense of need or dependence and of the psychic reality of the guilt—lead to the instal-lation of a spurious sense of independence and a triumphant devalu-ation of the needed object who has been destructively attacked and robbed of any personal significance for the patient. These attempts to escape from pain are, Klein concluded, accompanied by wishes to spare the object and put right the damage believed to have been done. If all goes well, these motivations can promote the working-through of a process akin to mourning, where regret and remorse serve to replace feelings of resentment, revenge, and grievance and their retaliatory consequences which characterize the paranoid–schiz-oid position (see Steiner, 1993). Forgiving the offender can eventually lead to the feeling of being forgiven and to a resolution of pathological guilt.

When reparative attempts occur in the paranoid–schizoid posi-tion, they may take concrete forms, such as "becoming" the life-giving person by making a pathological identification with an omnipotent phallic object—in Kleinian terminology, a "manic penis". The same process can be seen in states other than the manic-depressive one, such as "giving mother babies", as seen in previous chapters. Manic defences, in mild form, are a part of the defensive equipment of everybody in normal life. At the other extreme, they play a central part in the development of manic-depressive psychosis in the psycho-logically and biologically predisposed individual.

In severe depressive psychosis (melancholia), the patient, func-tioning at the level of the paranoid–schizoid position, has an uncon-scious belief that he has destroyed the object of his destructive wishes. He then identifies with the dead object and passes into a state in which he functions as though he were himself dead, a psychobio-logical level of regression in which certain vital physiological activi-ties may be inhibited and potentially destructive action thus disabled. When a manic phase follows (in "bipolar affective psychosis"), om-nipotent thinking and excitement are much more intense and, if untreated, can lead to destructive, occasionally violent, behaviour and exhaustion, whereas in the depressive phase suicidal behaviour, often successful, is common. Suicidal behaviour in the depressive phase may have many different, at times coinciding, motivations. These include a vengeful wish to destroy the "bad" object in identifi-cation, or to destroy the "good" part of the self that has the capacity to register the painful thoughts and feelings.

In moderately severe manic-depressive states, as in Harry's case, depression is associated with self-centred (narcissistic) self-re-proaches of a persecutory kind. At a certain point, Harry is rescued temporarily by the use of omnipotent thinking and denial of his sense of worthlessness and passes into a state of hypomanic elation characterized by a delusional sense of self-importance, omniscience, and superiority. Sooner or later this defensive operation fails and he returns to his depressive state, now worsened by his rational recognition of the delusional nature of his previous state of self-importance.

However strong reparative motivations may be, they are not in themselves a guarantee of beneficent change. Exceptional individuals may work through the depressive position and its associated mourning process alone with varying degrees of success, as can be seen in certain creative works of art and literature (see Klein, 1929; Segal, 1981a, 1991). Some exceptional manic-depressive individuals have produced works of genius during hypomanic and depressive cycles. The remarkable constitutional liveliness and energy of the manic-depressive may have the same biological and psychodynamic basis as the creative inspiration of exceptional individuals who have the unusual capacity to generate unconscious symbols, a capacity that appears to lie at the root of creative thinking.

Manic-depressive patients seem to be endowed with exceptional life energy, both psychological and biological, but it is usually of little use to them in their reparative attempts.

Since they do not know what it is that they are trying to repair, nor how to go about it, their efforts are in vain, and the oscillating states of destructive manic triumph only make things worse, adding to the self-reproach of their depressive phases.

In the report previously mentioned (Jackson, 1993a), I addressed the difficulties in reaching an adequate understanding of this disorder and of attempting a treatment that would seek to integrate psychoanalytic and biomedical perspectives. It is not surprising that such an endeavour should present great difficulties. The risk of unmanageable excitement in manic phases, and of suicide in depressive ones, may discourage attempts at individual psychoanalytic psychotherapy and confine practitioner's interests to the treatment of minor forms of cyclothymic mood disorders.

Harry's defensive behaviour

Harry's confusing message to the U.S. president could be understood as the consequence of expulsion, by the use of splitting and projective identification, of his own unconscious greed (Capitalism) and "egotistical" claims for "equality for all" (Socialism). Irrespective of the complexities of the true nature of Capitalism and Socialism, his passionately desired "equality" expressed his infantile sense of entitlement to total possession of his mother and to the obliteration of the difference between the status and privileges of children and adults. If there is no difference, there is no envy and no separation. Having thus failed to differentiate his own relationship to his parents from their relationship to each other, he was condemned to the unconscious struggle to keep them split apart in his mind. But although separating them in hatred, he was also powerfully motivated to bring them together in a peaceful and just manner. Harry's reforming activities, so necessary in the world of external reality, were totally misconceived and misdirected. It was his world of inner reality that was in desperate need of attention and repair.

One consequence of these dominating, dichotomous, unconscious phantasies and impulses was that Harry had never been able to acquire a healthy normal identification with his mother ("maternal" aspects in adult life), nor with his father ("paternal" aspects).

The dynamics of separation— the adolescent paranoid psychosis

The striking history of pathological reactions to separation from needed persons (the representative of the mother of his childhood and his inner world, his "primary maternal object"), and its repeated reactivation in the therapeutic transference, left little doubt about the meaning and psychodynamics of Harry's illness.

His extreme sensitivity to separation could be understood as the consequence of a developmental failure to resolve his profound infantile attachment to his mother or to use his father's help to separate normally from her and to establish a helpful identification with him. Such an identification, founded on the resolution of the rivalries of power, privilege, and sexuality (the difference between the generations), would, under more favourable circumstances, have carried him through the tumult of the triadic oedipal position and established a firm sense of his identity.

The developmental challenge of separation that leaving home to work in another town forced on him in late adolescence temporarily destabilized his defensive mental organization. This separation threatened to release his unconscious murderous rivalrous feelings towards his brother, who was the victim of the murder he believed that the police were convinced that he had committed. In fact, his delusional belief was that the conviction that he had murdered was located, "contained", in the minds of the police. It was not clear whether he had also "entertained" the delusional conviction himself. This expulsive evacuation of his own frightening thoughts into the external world reappeared as a major unconscious defensive strategy in his later manic-depressive illness.

What precipitated the mania?

It was not possible to study exactly how he had defensively encapsulated this volcanic rage from the time of its beginning in childhood until the outbreak of the paranoid delusional belief, or of the effect that it must have had on his character and personal relations during later childhood and adolescence. Neither was it clear how the organization of his mental life was sufficiently effective to allow him to function in an apparently normal and healthy manner until his first manic episode at the age of 30.

As is inevitable in such a restricted form of psychotherapy, much important information was inaccessible, or at least was not sought. Relatively little was learned about his relation to his wife and children or to his parents in the present day, nor about his reputation among his colleagues in his daily work as an administrator, in which he appeared to perform very well when stable. It is likely that Harry would have been particularly vulnerable to a pathological response to the birth of his own children and to difficulties in the relationship with his wife. Harry believed that it was an episode of mutual infidelity that precipitated his breakdown, but it remained unclear whether this behaviour was the cause or the consequence of the psychotic breakdown.

The use of dreams

The severely regressed schizophrenic individual has little of the mental equipment required to generate the unconscious symbolic thinking on which dreaming is based, and it may not be until he is much improved that he can differentiate dream from reality and recount a coherent dream narrative. The manic-depressive, by contrast, may have a well-developed capacity for creating the unconscious symbols that generate meaning and allow the creation of complex and highly symbolized dream-thinking. This capacity for dreaming may be recruited into the service of the psychotherapy and, if handled effectively, can provide a vital key to understanding and estimating progress, and this proved to be the case with Harry.

The dream material was certainly not employed simply as an intellectual exercise in the decoding of symbols. Although their multiple possible meanings were explored in detail in the seminar group, the therapist used them as a basis of simple statements made to the patient at a level that he could understand.

Destructiveness, guilt, triumph, and reparation

It is important to attempt to differentiate between destructive motivations of manic triumph (over the "internal" mother and father) and constructive-reparative ones that seek to spare the object and to undo the damage felt to have been done. Failure to realize this may, on the one hand, lead to the therapist unwittingly congratulating the patient on his omnipotent thinking, and, on the other, to a failure in affirming real progress. Although it may sometimes be impossible for the therapist to be certain of what was actual reality at the time, it is sometimes important to affirm that an event has actually happened in reality. This "affirmation" needs to be associated with exploration of what the patient has made of the event (Killingmo, 1995).

Matching of patient and therapist

The therapist, a powerful and athletic man, offered an ideal figure for admiration and envy of such a desperately insecure individual. In addition, he was the psychiatrist managing the case and had extensive psychiatric experience of the use of medication with psychotic patients, a good understanding of psychodynamic principles, and experience of personal psychotherapy. The subtlety of such desirable matching provides a sharp contrast to the relative crudeness of some reports of psychotherapy research in which psychotherapy is treated as though it can be prescribed like medication, with little or no consideration of matching factors between the patient and the therapist's personality and experience.

The therapist was well aware of the underlying devastation of Harry's life while understanding that concern for the patient and an attempt simply to help him contain his excitement, however helpful it might be, would not be enough. The patient required the deeper understanding that emerged from his experience in the therapeutic transference to allow him to begin to work through his conflicts in an effective manner.

The achievements and uncertainty of the outcome

The patient's right to put life goals ahead of further pursuit of therapeutic goals deserves consideration. The news that he had left his wife a year after terminating therapy brings the account of his case to an uncertain close. However, this cannot be counted as a failure in treatment but, rather, as evidence of a considerable though limited success. Premature terminations are common with psychotic patients, and it is unrealistic to believe that a formal ending of therapy with sufficient working-through to ensure reliable and enduring stability can easily be achieved in this modified form of therapy. At the same time, it is important to realize, as already pointed out, that this therapy is not necessarily a poor substitute for more intensive psychoanalytic treatment dictated by a limitation of resources, but is an analytically derived procedure in its own right, with its own advantages and limitations.

It is also important to recognize that the person who left the therapy is a very different person from the one who entered it. He had acquired some, albeit limited, capacity to think reflectively and effectively about himself for the first time, and to consider the meaning of his overwhelming emotional experiences.

The role of anti-manic medication

One of the achievements of the psychotherapy was helping the patient to accept the necessity of mood-stabilizing drug treatment. Although medication alone cannot produce insight, the psychotherapy would not have been possible without this assistance.

Conclusions

The case of Harry illustrates the fact that it is the retreat from unbearable mental pain and from the persecution of objects felt to be damaged and revengeful that forces emotionally deprived or traumatized children to find ways of surviving. When the pain is sufficiently severe at a time when the "mental apparatus" is too immature to cope, a predisposition to later psychosis may be established.

The enraged little boy, believing that he had nearly killed his rival younger brother by throwing a stone at him, retreated into guilt, miserable isolation, and loneliness and developed a compensatory secret sense of superiority. In adolescence, he escaped from persecutory guilt into the forest, and in adulthood he escaped into mania. In the therapy, he retreated repeatedly from the perils of dependency and, perhaps finally, from his wife.

However, Harry could not escape his inner world of his unconscious phantasies and object relations. It was this that had doomed him to a ruined life, and it was psychoanalytic understanding that ultimately brought the possibility of rescue and showed him the meaning of his mental disturbance. The consequence was that he began to be able to think reflectively about his mind instead of mindlessly acting.

Important questions remain

The therapist learned a great deal from his experience with Harry. However, he was left with the regret that it had not been possible to mobilize the family in exploratory and possibly therapeutic encounters from the outset.

We cannot guess whether a different strategy would have achieved the degree of success reached by Harry and his therapist. We cannot know if Harry has acquired a reliable capacity to avoid further breakdowns and to continue to recognize the need to use the prophylactic anti-manic medication for as long as is necessary, perhaps even indefinitely. We know little of the part played by the marital conflicts in his temporary abandonment of his wife in the course of a vacation break during the therapy, nor of his reasons for repeating this behaviour after the therapy ended.

On the other hand, his persistence in the therapeutic work, although reluctant, has been impressive, and when he told the therapist that he would consider further psychotherapy in the future if he felt the need, he certainly meant it.

The treatment of manic-depressive patients, many of them much more ill than Harry, is a routine responsibility of psychiatrists. I believe that even the most seriously ill patients can often be helped by psychotherapy, provided that the necessary conditions of an experienced therapist and a containing setting of a well-functioning and psychodynamic psychiatric facility can be provided (Jackson, 1993a).

Genetic, biochemical, and psychodynamic factors must all be considered in the assessment and treatment of psychotic patients, and nowhere is this more apparent than in the case of manic-depressive psychosis. However, all but the mildest case of manic-depressive psychosis need to be treated in the setting of a psychoanalytically informed psychiatric setting, with the facility for appropriate antipsychotic medication and, when necessary, compulsory legal control. No one has recognized this better than Fenichel. Speaking of the ever-present risk of suicide in severe depression and the abruptness with which dramatic events may occur within a patient who seems deceptively stable, Fenichel (1946, p. 414) observes:

> Even though the analyst's contact with a patient is different from that of the non-analytic psychiatrist, he must never discard the caution that psychiatry teaches. The more extensively planned psychoanalytic study of manic-depressive disorders needed both for the benefit of the patient and the benefit of science, must be undertaken within institutions.

Harry had required numerous hospital admissions during the ten years prior to the beginning of therapy, but none at all for the following two and a half years, that is, up to the time that contact was lost. Considering the relatively small expenditure of therapist time involved, and the fact that profound transference work proved possible in once-weekly psychotherapy, the outcome must be judged as a dramatic illustration of how psychotherapy can help manic-depressive patients if the necessary resources can be provided.

CHAPTER SIXTEEN

Vignettes

This chapter may perhaps be of limited interest to psychoanalysts, for whom sufficient detail of the context of the observations, the history of the patient, the depth of therapist involvement, and transference-countertransference matters are the essential prerequisites for the "decoding" of symbolic expressions and for serious consideration of their meanings for the patient. It is directed primarily to non-analysts who are interested in learning more about the manifold ways in which psychotic processes may find expression and exploring ways of thinking about them.

The fifteen brief clinical examples illustrate many of the specific characteristics of psychotic thinking and their various possible meanings. I hope that digesting the previous chapters will make it easier for the reader to begin to think about these further examples of gross psychopathology and bizarre psychotic thinking. The cases illustrate a range of psychotic mechanisms grouped very roughly according to their most prominent features. All the cases (with the sole exception of Patient L) were involved in psychoanalytically based psychotherapy, usually of long term, and four were in formal four-times weekly psychoanalysis with experienced psychoanalysts. Some of the cases are taken from my own psychiatric and psychoanalytic practice,

where detailed and intensive psychotherapy of disturbed schizophrenic patients, in a secure and "containing" psychodynamic environment, was possible (Jackson & Williams, 1994). "Code-breaking"
has no place in psychotherapy, since all symbols have personal meaning for each individual. Just as in the case of dreams, the therapist
needs to have the patient's associations to and reflections on the
material before he offers his own ideas. In psychotic states, however,
this is likely to prove impossible until the patient has become relatively stable and capable of cooperating with the therapist.

So although these "snapshots" have insufficient information or
detail to serve as formal case studies, they are presented as examples
of the sort of psychotic material that may confront professionals dealing with psychotic patients. The computer acronym WYSIWYG—"what
you see is what you get"—may serve as an analogy for situations
where psychoanalytic concepts can help the psychiatrist to begin to
think about similar psychotic material that may confront him in the
course of his daily clinical work. He may have very little to work on
apart from the presenting material, and he must try to make a useful
response, eventually leading him to consider necessary investigations
and to plan the treatment of the individual patient.

The explanatory comments that I have given are intended to illustrate ways of thinking about such (often bizarre and initially incomprehensible) material without claiming certitude; since there are
other ways of understanding these patients, their cases may also serve
as material for the use of teachers leading clinical discussion groups.
They should not be regarded as examples of instant "code-breaking"
but, rather, as brief excerpts from deeper and more systematic treatment situations.

Space-centred concrete thinking

Patient A

This adolescent patient was brought to hospital by police after having
been observed to be dropping tiles from the roof of a high building
into a courtyard below. He explained to the therapist that he had to
climb up high to be as near as possible to the angels, and that every
time he dropped a tile it was aimed at destroying the Devil and
saving a soul in danger. His acute psychotic episode proved resistant

to treatment, and he relapsed into a chronic hebephrenic state. After some years he was taken on for psychotherapy, where it was found that his psychosis had followed a disappointment in love and that he had a powerful symbiotic attachment to his disturbed mother. During the course of psychotherapy, he began to swallow small, physically harmless, objects, such as a pencil eraser shaped like a heart and a small paper anchor.

Comment

The splitting involved in his need to be an angel-baby high up at his mother's breast and his oedipal condemnation of his Devil-father seems clear. This recognition allowed the therapy to make steady progress. If projective and introjective processes had developed further he might have developed even more severe confusion of identity, such as thinking of himself as "the Devil", the angel Gabriel, Jesus, or even God. His intense separation anxiety had found appropriate symbolic expression in the choice of the heart (pain) eraser and the anchor as objects to incorporate. At this infantile level, desire finds bodily expression in swallowing, either hopefully, destructively, or both (see Patients H, K, and O).

Patient B

A psychotic man with severe claustro-agoraphobia began to feel that the walls of his room were saturated with evil. As the therapist explored the patient's sense of wickedness and guilt, the patient gradually lost his claustrophobic symptoms but acquired a new anxiety which he described as "the evil getting inside me". His paranoid experience had begun to acquire meaning and had moved from the space of the room to his own personal (mental or bodily) space.

Comment

It is sometimes possible in the course of psychotherapy, or in cases where spontaneous improvement occurs, to observe the progress of representation of thought, from, for instance, an extraterrestrial event, to sensations inside the body, and eventually to thoughts inside the mind. The future for this patient may lie in the development of a hypochondriacal symptom, or a direct recognition of the existence of "evil" as his own thought, perhaps at first located by projection into the therapist or other object. Such projection may play an essential role in the formation of paranoid delusions.

Projective expulsion and its paranoid consequences

Other psychotic mechanisms produce disturbances in the perception of outer space and its contents. When internal objects and processes are dealt with by the mechanism of violent projective evacuation, the consequence may be an experience of emptiness or depletion. If the projected elements return, they may give rise to threats of invasion by another person or by extraterrestrial figures, a "boomerang" or "projectile re-entry" process. There are different psychodynamic pathways to paranoid delusional beliefs, and there are individual variations in the subject's capacity to begin to be able to doubt his own delusional explanations of the psychotic experiences.

Patient C

In a state of acute psychotic terror, this man believed that he was threatened by a giant rat sent from the star Vega. Exploration revealed that he believed that the Vegans—the choice of star perhaps suggesting his oral pathology—were subjecting him to a test to decide whether he had the capacity to decide whether the rat was a real or an imaginary figure.

Comment

This rather complex dynamic suggested that he had projected his sane self, which was capable of doubting the reality of his delusional belief, and this projection was then returning as a persecutory challenge, threatening him with the thought that he was mad. Exploration of the patient's thoughts about the thoughts of the Vegans and the rat revealed that his underlying conflict was to decide whether he was homosexual or heterosexual. This discovery opened the way to exploring what this gender confusion meant to him and how it had arisen within long-standing marital conflict against the background of an emotionally disturbed childhood.

Murderous sibling jealousy—
projection and re-introjection

Patient D

A schizophrenic woman's illness began when her sister became pregnant. As a child, she had been intensely jealous of this sister, who was born when the patient was 18 months old. The onset of the psychosis was marked by her insistence in covering her mouth with a scarf and by episodic impulses to gouge out her own eyes. This resulted in severe bruising and necessitated intensive nursing supervision for long periods. She could not tolerate her pregnant sister's presence because she believed that her sister's eyes had become dangerous and were glaring at her with murderous intent. These dangerous eyes were penetrating through her own eyes into the inside of her head and taking possession of her own eyes, making them lethally dangerous. At the same time, she believed that her sister was invading and trying to take up residence inside her body, and that her own voice would then become her "destructive" sister's voice. It was her desperate attempt to preserve herself and her objects from destruction that had led to the covering of her mouth and her attempt to remove her own eyes. She explained that her sister also gets into her through her ears and comes out through her mouth in her words. As she became able to talk about these delusional beliefs and their associated feelings, the impulses gradually declined and disappeared. However, it was only after many years of psychoanalytic psychotherapy that she was able to integrate her murderous feelings in an insightful way and to achieve a reasonably happy and non-psychotic life. As in the case of Patient I, there was a history of perinatal trauma, fully confirmed, in which a congenital hiatus hernia (also afflicting her brother) led to prolonged projectile vomiting and severely disturbed feeding.

Comment

Her case illustrated the way that pathological situations of early life, and their associated defensive/adaptive management, can become encapsulated in the inner world and may later revive under specifically stressful conditions in outer and inner reality. It also illustrates the way in which projective expulsion of unwanted feelings and intentions into an object can distort perception of the container, and lead to re-introjection of a now-dangerous object. This dangerous internal object (introject) now (in "Bionic" terms) takes possession of the patient's visual and auditory apparatus, and she believes that her endangered self has become dangerously destructive.

The Biblical injunction *"if thine eye offend thee pluck it out"* has become literally significant for her because she is experiencing jealous thoughts as material things, and her eyes and ears, which are the receptors of the original situation of jealousy and associated murderous feelings, have been transformed into dangerous projective weapons. A similar process has been seen in the case of Patient B, who felt invaded by projected "evil", and of Harry (Chapter 15), who dreamed that a camera was transformed into a rocket launcher (Bion, 1967, p. 67). Such projective-expulsive reintrojective processes can under some circumstances inaugurate an escalating and increasingly dangerous vicious cycle.

Death of siblings in infancy
as psychotogenic trauma

Patient E

A manic-depressive woman attempted suicide when hallucinatory voices commanded her to kill babies. A turning point came in her psychotherapy when she dreamed that she was watching an evil man about to blow up an old-fashioned galleon full of little mythical people. She suddenly realized that she was in league with him, and the horror and guilt at the recognition of her destructive feelings remained on waking.

The therapist had good evidence to believe that a six-week separation at the age of 20 months, on the occasion of the birth of her only sibling, was a severely traumatic experience that had broken her close contact with her mother and prevented her from subsequently coming to terms with her murderous jealousy. She made great progress, but during both of her two subsequent pregnancies the command hallucinations returned in the voice of her mother telling her that she must abort the foetus. As this experience was worked through in long-term psychoanalysis, she finally achieved stability (see Jackson, 1993a; Jackson & Williams, 1994).

During this final phase, it emerged that her mother was the only survivor of six siblings, all the previous five having died postnatally from Rhesus incompatibility. This tragic history led the therapist to the explanation that her mother's unresolved guilt about the death of her own siblings had made her unable to contain her daughter's destructive sibling jealousy, thus laying the foundation for the subsequent psychosis.

Comment

This dynamic could be understood as an example of the transgenerational transmission of psychopathology, or of the transmission from mother to child of a dangerous internal object which commanded her to kill babies.

Patient F

Following the death of his adolescent younger brother in a road accident, this young man repeatedly tried to set fire to himself inside structures such as wooden huts, in obedience to hallucinatory voices commanding him to burn himself to death (see Jackson & Williams, 1994). When eventually he almost succeeded, he was committed to a mental hospital where he was found to be suffering from a schizophrenic psychosis. He spent the next ten years in mental hospital care and was eventually taken on for psychotherapy. He made a steady but limited improvement, working through some of his grief and guilt about the loss of his brother. A turning point came after three years of psychotherapy when he remembered that his mother had given birth to a stillborn baby when he was 3 years old. When these powerful emotional memories emerged from repression it unlocked feelings of rage towards his mother for having subsequently behaved as though the tragedy had never happened. The patient eventually came to understand that his mother had been so absorbed in her grief and depression over the loss of the stillborn brother that she had been unable to attend to his own needs. After a further two years the therapy was ended, and follow-up three and six years later revealed that he was well, working, and married with two children.

Comment

The patient had unconsciously held himself responsible for the baby's death in the womb, because of the rivalrous wish he had had at the time, which was in conflict with his love for his mother and his wish for a younger sibling. These wishes threatened to break out of repression when his adolescent brother died; they were then repetitively and compulsively enacted in a complex drama in which the containing structure was the symbolic representative of the maternal womb and in which the victim of the murderous burning was himself in identification with the rival baby. The symbolic womb very nearly became his coffin.

Body image

Body image disorders, hypochondriasis, dysmorphophobia, and somatic delusions can sometimes be readily understood in terms of projective and introjective identification.

Patient G

A young man with a seven-year history of paranoid schizophrenia had been able to survive out of hospital by avoiding social contacts. He found this necessary because he was dominated by the fixed delusional belief that a videotape recording had been made of him in sexual intercourse. Wherever he went, he believed that this videotape had been passed around to people, making it impossible for him to find a place of safety, even when he sought it in foreign countries. When eventually engaged in psychotherapy, it was possible to explore the psychodynamics of his paranoid thinking.

His overt symptoms began when his girlfriend left him for another man. In order to revenge himself on her by provoking jealousy, he seduced another girl, and it was in a single act of sexual intercourse that the fateful video was, he believed, made by some mysterious means. The video was then passed around by his contemptuous peers to humiliate him and to punish him for his treachery. When admitted to a psychodynamic ward, he secretly arranged for a cosmetic operation to be performed on his (normal) nose, an attempt to deal with a psychotic belief that it was the object of attention by onlookers who were appalled by its ugliness. This attempt to relieve this dysmorphophobic symptom (a somatic delusion) was only frustrated at the last minute by the prompt intervention of the ward psychiatrist.

Comment

He had suffered a considerable degree of early emotional deprivation, and his symptomatology gradually became understandable in terms of complex defensive manoeuvres as an attempt to deal with his unintegrated infantile feelings of vengeful jealousy. In identification with the "combined parents", he projects his unconscious wishes to intrude on their intercourse in a voyeuristic manner. The symbolic equation of nose and the paternal penis was partly responsible for the delusional belief that his nose was alarmingly ugly. In his unconscious phantasy, this nose/penis had been rendered ugly by a destructive (emotionally "ugly") attack on it. Such a process illustrates Rey's view, already mentioned in Chapter 10 (Florence), that "our objects (and part-objects) are sometimes in the state that they are in because we have unconsciously made them that way" (1994, ch 14).

Patient H

Another paranoid schizophrenic man was unable to venture outside his apartment in the hours of daylight because he believed that the sight of his face would horrify passers-by and lead them to suicide. He consulted a psychiatrist who told him that he was mistaking his nose for his penis. This made him worse because the symptom quickly disappeared but was replaced by an even more disabling belief that other people could hear him swallow, which would cause them to swallow uncontrollably and to suffer the same awful consequences. During the course of a long period of psychoanalysis (with the author), the details of his delusions about his face and his swallowing were revealed. In his unconscious phantasies, he was equating his nose with the maternal nipple, and his cheeks—which he experienced alternatively as full and beautiful, and lax, empty, and ugly—with the maternal breasts.

These part-object identifications were a dramatic expression of his defences against the overwhelming feelings aroused by the memory of seeing his younger brother feeding (swallowing) at his mother's breasts. In his delusional belief that others would be ruined by hearing the sound of his swallowing or the sight of his face, he was identified with the baby and was projecting his own devastated feelings of jealousy and abandonment into other people.

He also felt persecuted by a noise emanating from the central-heating system in an apartment across the street. Although this faint noise disturbed no one else, he managed to persuade the owner to install special sound-proofing, at the patient's expense. This made no difference, so he bought a cottage in a remote country district, but he had to abandon it when the total silence was broken by the sound of a distant tractor. These remote sounds had the effect of triggering off the *"gazing-at-the-baby-noisily-sucking"* complex of memories and feelings.

He was therefore condemned to a tormented and reversing state of feeling himself to be the envious onlooker of the feeding baby, and the envied and therefore dangerous baby himself, and his own face was the stage for the psychotic expression of this drama.

He could only find refuge deep in woodlands, free from human sounds and sights, where he would gradually feel normal and begin to think sanely about himself, his analysis, and his transference relationship to his therapist. This happy state, however, did not survive his return to the human world of sight and sound, where he continued his career of projecting into objects that were unable to perform the alpha-function of "metabolizing" containers.

Comment

Although the patient's experiences were largely of an illusory nature, his beliefs were delusional and were the consequences of his "suffering from reminiscences" of a primitive part-object type. His perceptual experiences in the visual and auditory spheres were rendered abnormal by the unconscious phantasies that they evoked. The analysis (undertaken thirty years ago) was in many ways highly successful, but it did not completely remove the dysmorphophobia. The above formulation is thus to some extent a retrospective one, profiting subsequently from Bion's theories of "container–contained" (1962) and of the expulsive use of sense organs (1967, p. 67). It may help to explain why the symptom of dysmorphophobia is so resistant to psychotherapeutic treatment. If the relevant part-object psychopathological processes are not sufficiently understood (as was the case in this patient), these symptoms are unlikely to yield to psychotherapeutic interventions.

The location of objects—oral incorporation, anal expulsion, oral re-incorporation

When Karl Abraham was studying manic-depressive patients, he concluded that in their depressive phases they were experiencing the loss of an object of primary emotional significance as the loss of a substance inside the body by way of the anus, a movement followed by attempts to recover the lost or damaged object by re-incorporation (see Hinshelwood, 1994, pp. 21–24, for an account of Abraham's case). Such a dynamic can find expression in varying degrees of completeness and developmental levels of symbolic elaboration. Where regression is extreme, all symbolic capacity may be lost and the process may be seen in its most direct form, reminiscent of the behaviour of some seriously disturbed infants. More successful symbolization of loss by damage and attempts at recovery is to be seen in Patients J and K and in some of the patients described in the earlier chapters.

Patient I

This young woman developed severe anorexia at the age of 11 years and a relapsing schizo-affective psychosis in late adolescence, which had become chronic by the time she was admitted to a psychiatric ward. The psychosis focused on her delusional belief that she had harmed small children and was continuing to do so (see also the case of Florence, Chapter 10). It became clear that it was her murderous jealousy of younger siblings that had found expression in this delusional belief, and the likelihood of traumatic perinatal experience was presented by a history of foetal distress and a depressed mother. Despite anti-psychotic medication, she gradually regressed into a state of severe confusion in which she began drinking from the lavatory and smearing and eating her own faeces. With the help of antidepressants she gradually emerged from this regression.

Comment

Although such behaviour was not rare in institutionalized and deeply regressed patients in old-style mental hospitals, it must be rare in contemporary psychiatric practice and can be understood as the expression of a profound psychotic depression occurring in a severely schizoid personality. It could be called a "schizo-depressive" (rather than schizo-manic) psychosis, and in psychodynamic terms as an attempt to recover the damaged, or near-dead, object by oral incorporation, as in Abraham's case. The term schizo-depressive can be considered to include those like Patient I who regress from the depressive position into the paranoid–schizoid position, in whom the severe depression is a mixture of depressive and persecutory anxiety, and who have not followed the pathway of the manic defence, which would issue in schizo-manic symptoms. After a long period of psychotherapy on the ward, this patient managed to resolve the worst of her infantile conflicts about her mother and the associated depression and lost her more severe psychotic symptoms. In her coprophagic period, her attempt to recover the mother, whom she had in her phantasy destroyed, took the most literal and concrete form conceivable and could be considered as a regression to the core of her disturbance.

Patient J

This middle-aged woman had lost her adolescent son in tragic circumstances. She was referred to the psychiatric services by a gastroenterologist who could find no cause for her complaint that a rotting process was going on inside her abdomen. She explained to the psychiatrist that inside her was the body of her dead son, which was slowly decomposing. As evidence for this belief, she displayed traces of dirt under her nails, which she explained was the product of the decomposition of his body emerging from her body. She also showed the therapist a plastic bag containing some of her own urine and faeces as further evidence. Although she regarded her son's body inside as decomposing, she felt compelled to eat only baby food.

Comment

The history that emerged in the attempt to understand the patient's pathological bereavement reaction revealed intense sibling

jealousy in her early years. This may explain the fact that her mourning for her son had failed so badly. Her eating of baby food was the
enactment of an unconscious wish to keep the endangered baby (of
whom her own dead son was the later symbolic representative) alive.
As in the case of Patient I, the loss was an anal one (symbolized by dirt
exuding from beneath her nails and the bag of excrements) and her
attempt at recovering the lost object an oral one (baby food). This is
thus an expression of the same severe depressive psychopathology as
Patient I but in a more highly symbolized and derivative form.

Rey's view (1994), already mentioned, is that many patients bring
their damaged objects to therapy in the hope of getting help to repair
them. In psychic reality, they unconsciously keep their objects alive by
the process of identification with them, or, in the instance of Patient J,
by a phantasy of incorporating and preserving the lost object inside
the body. The concrete nature of their thinking demands that the
damaged object or situation must be concretely restored to its original
undamaged state, a literal belief in the possibility of repair or resur-
rection, which achieves nothing, in contrast to psychological reparation, which requires symbolic thinking and the working-through of
mourning and guilt. The patient could then be seen as bringing two
objects to the therapist: a dead son, and an endangered sibling of her
childhood.

Patient K

Equally striking was the behaviour of a chronically schizophrenic
man who became engaged in psychotherapy after many years of
severe illness. He had powerful and split ("pre-ambivalent") images
of his father, and he associated intense emotions of love and hatred
towards him. These emerged in the transference in due course. He
conceived a great admiration for his calm and powerfully built male
therapist, which was complicated by intense feelings of destructive
envy. He brought to one session a matchbox with a colourful picture
on the front of it of a famous Norwegian–Danish sailor, Captain
"Thundershield", a folk hero of past times. As the session proceeded,
he carefully tore this picture into small pieces and ate them. He repeated this pattern for several weeks, and then he insisted that he
should be able to sit on the toilet, defecating, while the therapist
continued the session from the adjacent room. The therapist agreed to

this request, and although he did not attempt to interpret the behaviour, his willingness to accept and contain the projections led to a strengthening of the therapeutic relationship, to the ultimate abandonment of this behaviour, and to conspicuous clinical improvement.

Comment

By means of this behaviour of oral incorporation followed by anal expulsion, the patient achieved a compromise between the wish to protect and incorporate the admired father-therapist and the wish to dispose of the hated one. He had achieved a partial symbolization of the cannibalistic wishes encountered particularly in severe anorexic disorders.

Part-object identifications

Patient L

Recently widowed in a car crash at the time when he was in severe conflict with his wife and for which, as the driver, he felt responsible, this man developed a psychotic disorder with a bizarre body-image delusion. He believed that he had a second head on his shoulders, and he identified it as that of his wife's gynaecologist. He came to believe that his wife (although deceased) was having an affair with this man, and he attempted to murder the gynaecologist by shooting the second head. Since this was a phantom head, and his belief was delusional, he suffered a severe brain injury. However, he survived, only to die two years later from the effects of alcoholism and wound infection. His last months were dominated by a preoccupation with recording his thoughts about the possible reunification of the lost tribes of Israel.

Comment

Although psychodynamic exploration was not pursued in this case (Ames, 1984), the roots of such intense and lethal jealousy might, in retrospect, have been sought in a traumatic childhood history. A regressive loss of ego functions had robbed him of the capacity to differentiate between inner and outer reality, fact and phantasy, past and present. His preoccupation of reunifying the lost tribes may have been perhaps motivated by a residual sane wish to recover his scattered mental faculties and to reintegrate the parts of his self that had been lost in a projective diaspora. Such dramatic examples of body image and identity disorder may not be encountered very often, but bizarre symptoms of this kind are not uncommon both in psychiatric and neurological practice.

Coming in and going out

There are many ways of expressing the varieties of the experience of movements in space of the subject in relation to the maternal space. Thus, as in the case of George (Chapter 14), "going into" the object (or its symbolic representative, such as a room) and "coming out" is not the same experience as "being inside the object and flowing out" (seen in autistic children: Meltzer, 1975; Tustin, 1990), or "invading the object" and "being expelled, or evacuated". The details of the experience are determined by the character of the projective and introjective mechanisms involved, the power of the associated affects, the intensity of the invasive impulses evoked by threats of separation, and the degree of recognition of separateness of the self from the maternal object.

Patient M

A psychotic patient, having begun to make significant progress in his psychotherapy, reported to his therapist that when he entered the therapist's room a bird landed on his head, and that it flew off when he left, an experience that he found interesting but confusing (Jackson, 1992).

Comment

The patient was becoming aware of the significance and importance of the therapist's existence for him, the bird representing a thought coming to his mind, a thought that was to lead him to the awareness that being in the session in the therapist's presence was different from being outside the room, that he was coming and going, and that it mattered. This conjecture received some support when he gradually began to recognize that in the time of his session the thera-

pist often succeeded in relieving his anxieties. He expressed this recognition in a striking fashion, bringing to the session a cartoon of a
therapist unravelling a black cloud in the form of a ball of string over
the patient's head. There were no doubt other symbolic implications
of his experience, but this was the one that seemed to make most sense
of the immediate situation. His experiences of coming-in and going-
out were the spatial expression of his dawning new awareness that his
therapist had an existence separate from his own and thus could be
helpful. An appropriate metaphor for the experience of the bird
alighting on his head might be *"it began to come home to me that. . . ."*

Dangerous teeth—projected and introjected—
the biter bitten

Patient N

A young woman became acutely psychotic following an experience
that she subsequently described as being like a terrifying nightmare.
In a context of increasing anxiety over several days, she began to eat a
bar of chocolate. This was a long stick of black chocolate filled with
sweet creamy material. As she began to eat it, she gradually "realized" that it contained teeth, which started to bite at her mouth from
the inside and then to eat her from inside her stomach when she had
swallowed it.

Comment

The image of the harmless chocolate bar had become transformed
by projective and introjective mechanisms into a compressed conglomerate of part-objects of oral, anal, and phallic significance symbolized by the teeth, the chocolate, and the bar. Less complicated
formulations, such as "the food seems to be felt literally by the patient
to be harming her inside" may be the most appropriate and partial
understanding at the level at which the therapist is working, but they
are less profound than a formulation that describes an unintegrated
"biting" part of the self projected into the chocolate bar, a part that
needs investigating, understanding, recovering, and integrating.

The same level of concrete psychotic thinking may be observed
when a psychotic patient swallows perfume or disinfectant in order

to bring under control variously damaging parts of the self or inner world believed to be located inside the body.

Patient O

A young woman was referred to the psychiatric service following an unsuccessful breast-reduction operation. She had felt her breasts to be too big and causing her back pain, but the operation made it worse. She began to inflict physical pain on herself, banging her head and burning her hands with cigarettes, behaviour that she said gave some relief from the pain. When she began weekly psychotherapy sessions, the mental nature of the pain became clear to the therapist, although not to the patient, and its origin in a traumatic and emotionally deprived early life was revealed. Her emotionally unstable mother had repeatedly made histrionic suicide gestures and had repeatedly threatened to abandon her and her younger siblings.

During the next six months, the patient began to report auditory hallucinations and other psychotic features, which led to the diagnosis being changed from borderline personality to schizophrenia. At the end of this period, when she had begun to make considerable progress, her therapist was moved abruptly to another job in which she was unable to continue the therapy, whereupon the patient's self-damaging behaviour returned. A second therapist made good progress with her during the next year, and the patient gave up her self-damaging behaviour altogether. At this point, this second therapist became pregnant and at the same time moved to another job too far distant for the therapy to continue.

The patient thereupon began to swallow sharp objects, requiring repeated surgical extraction and transfer to a closed ward where intensive supervision was possible. The ward psychiatrist began to see her for a brief period every day and made good contact with her, and she again began to improve. Yet again, this therapist was obliged to change jobs at short notice, and the catastrophic self-damaging behaviour reappeared.

Comment

The meaning of some forms of self-damaging behaviour can sometimes be partly understood in terms of double identification—

in the case of Patient O, an identification with the "abandoning", pregnant, mother/therapist, the unconscious phantasy expressing the attack from inside by the baby containing teeth, symbolized by the sharp objects she swallows. These objects inflict pain on the inside of her body, reflecting the original symptom of pain in her breasts. This can now be considered as a symbolic representation of the emotionally hurtful experience that she felt when displaced by the rival baby. The literal repetition in the transference, when a real baby appeared, was the last of a series of displacements, each arousing her phantasies and her wishes to hurt the displacing baby by biting it, enacted by swallowing sharp objects.

This case illustrates how important is continuity of care in psychotherapy once a transference relationship has developed, and how time must be allowed to address the patient's feelings when sudden, sometimes inevitable, changes of this nature occur. The same applies to the departure of significant staff members, which may cause repetitions of feelings linked with emotionally important figures of the past. Such considerations apply particularly in the case of the usually short rotation terms of trainee psychiatrists.

The case of Dorothy (Chapter 6) illustrates the reverse pattern, where the therapist's persistence and refusal to abandon the patient had a very positive outcome.

CHAPTER SEVENTEEN

Mostly theory

In this chapter, I present a brief outline of the origins, development, and essential features of Kleinian and "neo-Kleinian" concepts and comment on their usefulness. As I explained in the Introduction, these are the concepts with which I am most familiar and have found most illuminating in my attempts to understand the psychotic mind. I have not tried to present other psychoanalytic approaches in any detail, but although I am less familiar with them I recognize the importance of their contributions.

Beginnings

Modern psychoanalytic thought about psychosis is founded on the work of Freud, Jung, and Abraham.

Freud

Freud recognized how much could be learned from the study of psychosis by psychiatrists, and he observed (1925d [1924], p. 61) that

". . . so many things that in neurosis have to be laboriously fetched up from the depths are found in psychosis on the surface, visible to every eye. For that reason the best subjects for the demonstration of many of the assertions of psychoanalysis are provided by the psychiatric clinic."

He also forecast that through psychoanalysis it would eventually prove possible to help the psychotic patient, although theoretical gains might be all that could be hoped for at that time. Psychiatrists, he continued, would eventually be compelled to recognize that psychoanalysis holds the key to understanding the psychopathology that confronts them every day, and he wrote: "Mere theoretical gain is not to be despised, and we may be content to wait for its practical application. In the long run even the psychiatrists cannot resist the convincing force of their own clinical material."

Freud developed several models of the mind, and subsequent researchers have elaborated and added to his theories. Freud's "topographical" model viewed the mind as divided into conscious, preconscious, and unconscious levels, and his "structural" model described the mind as a tripartite organization of id, ego, and superego (Freud, 1923b). He used "instinct theory" to explain human motivation in terms of the conflicts stemming from sexual and aggressive drives, and "economic" theory to explain the megalomanic grandiosity that characterized the mental state of paranoid schizophrenic patients, illustrated by his well-known writing on the case of Judge Schreber (Freud, 1911c [1910]).

Freud's theory of psychosis (1916–17), based on a developmental view of mental life, attributed psychotic phenomena to a weakness of the libidinal tie to reality, the result of hereditary factors and of adverse experiences in childhood and puberty. Believing that psychotic patients were unsuitable subjects for psychoanalysis because they were too withdrawn from reality to be able to form a significant emotional relationship (a "working transference") with the therapist, he introduced the theory of regression from a world in which other people were recognized as emotionally important to one of extreme self-centredness. In this way, he launched the study of narcissism, normal and pathological, and of the processes whereby development gradually proceeds from a hypothetical narcissistic state in infancy to object-relatedness [see Glossary]. His concept of the superego (in some respects a precursor of later object-relation theory), as heir to the Oedipus complex, provided a basis for the understanding of guilt, normal and pathological. Freud believed that withdrawal of interest ("cathexis") from people in a real world that has brought helplessness and pain led to the investment of the self with a powerful charge of this psychic energy, issuing in a sense of omnipotent self-importance and a break with reality. Delusional explanation then followed to preserve the mistaken belief in sanity and to recover contact with the real world, "a patch over a rent in the ego".

Jung

Jung had long experience of psychotic patients in the Burghölzli Hospital in Zurich, which provided him with intimate access to psychotic patients, an opportunity denied to Freud. In contrast to Freud, whose neurotic problems have been regarded as one source of his profound understanding of neurosis, Jung had a psychotic breakdown, or at least a psychotic episode. This must also have inspired his monumental work on psychosis (Jung, 1960) and informed his development of the concept of the archetype. His use of this concept led to a theoretical divergence from psychoanalysis, whose psychological explanations in terms of the individual infant's and child's maturational tasks are more specifically tied to the early development of the individual than to Jung's focus on the "collective". Jung's theory of archetypes and the collective unconscious were the first attempt to relate these universal processes to psychotic disorders. Jung was one of the first to use individual psychotherapy with schizophrenic patients, and in recent years his archetype concept attracted the attention of some psychoanalysts who see it as in some respects related to Kleinian concepts (Grotstein, 1997; Jackson, 1962). The loss to psychoanalysis of Jung and the Burgölzli hospital (Freud, 1925d [1924], p. 251) deprived it of a creative source and context for the study of psychosis.

Abraham

Abraham trained as a psychiatrist in Zurich with Jung and collaborated with Freud in trying to understand psychosis (Abraham, 1911, 1924). He was Melanie Klein's first analyst, inspiring her early work, and his premature death robbed psychoanalysis of a person of great stature and originality. He undertook individual psychotherapy with manic-depressive and schizophrenic patients and explored the infantile roots of psychosis. His work on psychosis has remained of considerable interest and significance.

Kleinian developments

Klein

Melanie Klein sought to understand the experience of the baby and growing infant. She developed her concepts of the paranoid–schizoid and depressive positions to help describe the way the individual structures his mental world from the beginning of life. This innovation provided the conceptual keys to relate different levels of emotional development and to explore the pathogenetic potentials of varying degrees of developmental failure. She dated the predisposition to psychosis to the period of infancy, or even the beginning of life, a "maternalization" of psychoanalytic theory which had revolutionary consequences.

She saw neurotic disturbances as representing the attempt to work through underlying psychotic anxieties and phantasies, a "primitive" substrate of mental life common to everyone, "normality" being a matter of the degree of resolution of such early, essentially preverbal conflicts and associated immature defences. She modified Freud's concept of an orderly progression through oral, anal, and phallic stages of psychosexual development which led into the Oedipus constellation of triangular relationships by the third or fourth year of life. She regarded these phases as occurring at a much earlier period and in a less orderly manner, and she sought for precursors of the Freudian superego in the introjection of parental objects as perceived in a distorted manner by the infant. She developed the idea of a self that was not a whole structure but, rather, a collection of different parts, functioning throughout life with varying degrees of coherence and stability in each individual, and she sometimes did not clearly differentiate the concept of self from that of ego. Her conception of ego development has been epitomized as "we are—and become—what we do with—and to—our objects" (Grotstein, 1992).

Klein's work brought a dramatic shift of interest from neurosis to psychosis and a shift of emphasis away from Freud's sexual explanations of motivations. Klein's focus was on the way that individuals— normal or psychotic—manage unconscious conflicts between innate destructiveness and manifestations of the "death instinct" and reparativeness, manifestations of protective and preservative wishes, and the expression of the integrative forces of the "life instinct". Her model of mental development is founded on the view that the human infant has instinctively derived destructive impulses against which he struggles during the process of attachment to his mother, in the course of which emotions for which we use the adult terms of "love" and "hate" develop. Whereas Freud derived his concepts of psycho-sexual development of the child mainly from his work with adult patients, Klein attempted to understand the mind of the baby from her own experience as a mother, and from her psychoanalytic work with very young children, using their play in the way that dreams and free associations are used in the treatment of adults.

In order to preserve maternal care (the "breast–mother") and thus to survive, the infant uses biologically based (Schore, 2000b) primitive mechanisms of defence and adaptation, primarily splitting, projection, and introjection [see Glossary]. Under normal circumstances, the infant has managed to begin to reconcile his feelings of hatred and love by the end of the first year of life. By this time, his split and unintegrated feelings and sense of self, associated with severe perse-cutory anxiety, have given way to concern for the object (the "bad, frustrating, mother) whom he has repeatedly attacked in the course of developing what we describe as his "mind". The emergence of these wishes to make reparation [see Glossary] is a crucial feature of the depressive position, which persists throughout life in a dialectic and synchronic relation with the paranoid–schizoid position. The depres-sive position brings the possibility of undoing the immature tie to the object and recognizing its separateness ("the use of an object", in Winnicott's terms, 1968). This achievement brings mental pain and suffering of varying degrees (Joseph, 1989; Riesenberg-Malcolm, 1999a; Steiner, 1993), but although this may feature depressive mood, the term does not refer to depressive illness but to an achievement of maturity (which Winnicott, 1950, called "the stage of concern"). It is an expression of a natural innate morality (Milton, 2000; Winnicott, 1965, ch. 8) and is an index of mental stability.

In the paranoid–schizoid position, true reparation is not possible, and attempts to protect the endangered object are motivated by the need to avoid catastrophic loss or disintegration of self. Since the self and object are as yet undifferentiated, destructive wishes threaten both. Other "positions"—manic, obsessional (Klein), claustro-agoraphobic (Rey, 1994), and autistic-contiguous (Ogden, 1989, 1990)—have been proposed but have not generally been widely used or understood.

Classical psychoanalytic theory followed Freud's view that the infant cannot truly recognize an object as having an existence separate from himself since his mental life is centred on his own ego, a state of "primary narcissism". In contrast to this view, Klein held that the new-born baby has a primitive ego and sense of self and also has the capacity to handle anxiety by the use of defence mechanisms and to make relationships. What was regarded as an "objectless" state of primary narcissism was really a rich world of primitive part-object relationships. The baby makes a (primary) *identification* with the mother which helps him negotiate the developmental steps necessary for the formation of a personal sense of identity. It makes more tolerable the gradual change, in normal development, from a state of maximum dependency to an eventual recognition of both her and his own *self* with their own individual identities, a process of *separation* [see Glossary] and *individuation* elaborated by Mahler, Pine, and Bergman (1975).

When all goes well, the small child has acquired the beginnings of the ability to identify (differentiate) and manage powerful feelings, to distinguish self from others, and to own a rudimentary sense of identity as a person. From this secure base, the capacity to differentiate things and events of the outer world of reality from those of his developing mind is gradually strengthened through daily experience and play and from games such as "Let's pretend" (Fonagy & Target, 1996, 2000). As he slowly relinquishes the use of splitting and projection to rid his mind of emotional disturbances, his capacity for reality-testing and symbolic thinking increases as this ego-strengthening process consolidates.

When things go wrong, in consequence of the adverse influence of various combinations of biological and psychosocial conditions, these primitive defensive/adaptive processes may be subject to emergency use that distorts the normal developmental sequence. Ego development and the capacity for symbolic thinking is undermined, creating a vulnerability factor in the establishment of a predisposition to later psychosis.

Klein described how processes of projection and introjection build up from the beginning a structured inner world of enduring patterns of expectations, object relations, and unconscious phantasy. Adverse experiences in early life may create a disturbed and disturbing inner reality, which remains timelessly in the unconscious mind defended against with various degrees of efficiency. When these defences break down, the (slumbering, encapsulated) primitive processes are exposed. When the resultant distortion of the sense of reality is lost, a variety of disturbances of function appear in company of what intact mental function survives, and this constitutes the state described in psychiatry and psychoanalysis as *psychosis*.

This state of psychosis is the consequence of the emergence of object relationships and phantasies that have been unconscious and active in the inner world since early life, and thus it is not strictly speaking simply a process of (temporal) regression to an earlier level of mental organization, but a move inwards to depths rather than backwards in time. The pathogenic past has become built into the structure of the inner world, exerting its influence in the present and future. Several possible factors may help to bring about structural change and improvement in mental function, but the best understood is the working-through of pathological object relationships and their associated unconscious phantasies in a psychotherapeutic transference. Insofar as a psychotic event represents the eruption of unresolved or distorted developmental processes, it can sometimes be regarded as offering a "second chance", an opportunity to work through the "unfinished business" of early life, a *"reculer pour mieux sauter"* (Jung).

Winnicott

Winnicott made profound contributions to the understanding of early object relations, and his work supported much of Klein's. His concepts of "object-relating" and "object-use" (Winnicott, 1968) developed the interpersonal aspects of the depressive position (the "stage of concern") in a unique manner. He disagreed with Klein's views about innate destructiveness, and he regarded psychosis as an environmental deficiency disease (Winnicott, 1958, ch. 17). Winnicott's observations of infants with their mothers cast much light on the primitive stages of emotional development and primitive object relationships. He described how along the normal pathway of psychological development the child passes from a position of total dependency on the mother (or "primary carer") through a transitional phase where the mother is partly relinquished by replacing her with the use of a soft toy or equivalent, a "transitional object" (Winnicott, 1958). This capacity to find a symbolic substitute for the maternal presence influences all subsequent thinking and modes of relating. Thus, through imitation (Gaddini, 1992), immature ("primitive") identifications with the mother, and with subsequent figures with whom growth and learning takes place, gradually proceed to more mature object relationships.

Developing a personality

The degree of success or failure in passing through developmental phases of identification and of managing powerful affects, containing and differentiating them, and differentiating self from other plays a large part in determining the strength of the ego and the self. During early stages of ego development, defensively distorted object relationships in internal reality may form a point of vulnerability persisting in the inner world and functioning timelessly into adult life. In such cases, psychological stress later in life may lead to a revival of deeper levels of functioning, with associated impairment or loss of ego functions.

When the earliest stages of mental development, based on the mother–infant relationship, have been sufficiently well negotiated, and the foundation of a secure sense of identity and a firm sense of reality has been achieved, the individual is unlikely to fall ill of a psychotic disorder later in life. Less severe or later developmental failures may result in *borderline* personality disturbances, in which brief episodic psychotic states of mind may occur under stress, or in *neurotic* disorders, characterized by *inhibitions, symptoms,* and *anxiety.*

In *psychotic* mental states, however, the individual has a very different experience from that of normal and neurotic people and is likely to have a different way of communicating (Lucas, 1993) and, to a varying extent, a different use of language (Rosenbaum & Sonne, 1986). This use of language is characteristically based on *primary-process* thinking, in which displacement, condensation, and symbolic expression figure prominently, as is the case in the construction of the dream (Matte-Blanco, 1998). Other characteristics include a decrease in interest in the meanings or connotations of words, which tend to be seen as objects to be manipulated (Arieti, 1974). The impairment of the capacity for appreciation of symbolism may lead to objects being equated on the basis of similarities, so that "resembles" or "like" is expressed as "is". Thus, a thought may be experienced as a thing and be treated as such (Segal, 1981c).

In psychotic states, impairment of ego functions is particularly severe and is characterized by the revival of defective identificatory processes and impairment of the capacity to differentiate self from object and *inner reality* from *external reality*. Object relations may now be replaced by identifications, and memories, thoughts, and concepts may be experienced as immediate *perceptions*, manifested as *hallucinations* or *illusory distortions*, and misidentification of persons. In these circumstances, the capacity for rational thinking is compromised, and the struggle to understand the confusing (and at times terrifying) experiences contributes to the formation of *delusional* explanations.

Klein's developments of Freud's work has had a profound impact on the understanding and treatment of psychotic individuals and has provided a more optimistic view of the possibilities of helping them. Originally regarded in conservative psychoanalytic quarters as something of a heretic, she was gradually accepted as an innovator and, eventually, as an establishment figure of increasing importance. Other theoretical streams of contemporary psychoanalysis have assimilated many of her essential ideas, although controversy and debate continues in Institutes of psychoanalysis. In the fifty years since the publication of her seminal paper on schizoid and schizophrenic psychopathology (Klein, 1946), many psychoanalysts with a special interest in psychotic patients have made further important contributions to theory and clinical practice. In particular, the works of Segal, Rosenfeld, Bion, Joseph, Meltzer, and Rey have provided a basis for the continuing extension of knowledge and the elaboration of new and clinically relevant concepts.

The seeds of psychosis

Segal (1981d, p. 133) has summarized the Kleinian view of the origins of psychosis:

> It is our contention that psychotic illness is rooted in the pathology of early infancy where the basic matrix of mental function is

formed. By projection and introjection, splitting the object into a good and a bad one followed later by integration, introjection and identification with good objects, the ego is gradually strengthened and it acquires a gradual differentiation between the external and the internal world; the beginnings of superego formation and relation to the external objects are laid down. It is at this time also, in the first year of life, that symbol formation and the capacity to think and speak develop. In psychosis, it is all these functions that are disturbed or destroyed. The confusion between the external and the internal, the fragmentation of object relations and the ego, the deterioration of perception, the breakdown of symbolic processes, the disturbances of thinking; all are features of psychosis. Understanding the genesis of the development of the ego and its object relationships and the kind of disturbance that can arise in the course of that development is essential to understanding the mechanisms of the psychotic.

Such an unambiguous and carefully worded statement aims to define the *origins* of psychotic psychopathology. Nonetheless, it might attract the criticism that it is representative of a Kleinian tendency to downgrade the processes of later ego development by constantly referring all later processes back to their early precursors. For a discussion of such criticisms see Hinshelwood (1989, pp. 135, 251).

Bion

Bion's concepts, further developed by other psychoanalysts (in particular, Meltzer, 1994, pp. 42ff.; Money-Kyrle, 1978, pp. 434ff.; Rosenfeld, 1987; Segal, 1981f;), has had a profound influence in the understanding and psychotherapy of borderline and psychotic states. The work of Esther Bick (1964; see also Hinshelwood, 1989) and others led to the establishing of organized procedures of baby observation which has become a feature of most contemporary psychotherapy training programmes.

Bion's innovative work has made the origins and processes of psychosis more understandable for those who can comprehend his novel formulations and recognize their practical usefulness. It has also provided an important conceptual link between the world of the baby and its mother and the roots of mental health and ill-health.

Whereas Klein's model of the mind has been described as a quasi-religious one—of an inner world of internal objects, whom, like the figures of mythology and of the gods, angels, and demons of religion, we ignore at our peril—Bion's model is, by contrast, an epistemological one. He investigated the origins of thinking and the acquisition of knowledge in highly original way. His concept of psychotic and non-psychotic aspects of the self has had profound implications, and his "container–contained" theory [see Glossary, "containment"] has shed much light on psychotic processes (Bléandonu, 1994; Symington & Symington, 1996).

Bion's theory of "container-contained" (Bion, 1962) implies that the human infant has the need to find a "container", in the form of his mother or primary caring figure, to allow the development of a stable sense of self. If this fails, he may go through life projecting unwanted and insufficiently differentiated parts of his self and inner world into other "objects" (people or things) with the unconscious aim of finding a container for them.

According to this model, this projective manoeuvre has its origins at the beginning of life and serves a normal communicative function between mother and baby. In this interaction, the normal mother responds intuitively to her baby's distress, thinks reflectively about its possible causes and preserves a (sufficiently) calm presence. This "toilet-breast" (Meltzer, 1992) helps the baby to recover from what might be overwhelming, disintegrating emotional storms and gradually to form a concept of having a mind that can recognize powerful affects as belonging to itself and, eventually, learn to recognize and to manage different affects. A sense of personal existence in time is then able to develop, forming a basis for the acquisition of a sense of self, of a personal history, and of the capacity to distinguish what belongs to the self and what to the external world of things and other people. According to the Kleinian model of the mind, phantasy is the mental expression of instinct. Bion elaborated this proposition with his theory of "innate preconceptions", inherited potentials for "realizations", and ultimately for concept formation, a view that has much in common with Jung's "archetypes".

In this way, "unmentalized" sense impressions ("beta-elements")—the raw material of experience—are transformed by this maternal (metabolizing, detoxifying, digesting) "alpha-function" into "alpha-elements" which can then be used for thinking, remembering, and dreaming. By contrast, beta-elements can only be subject to projective evacuation. In this sequence, subsequent introjection may proceed to further splitting, and a (re)projective–introjective cycle may lead to the creation of strange conglomerates of mental elements, which Bion called "bizarre objects".

When maternal alpha-function fails, for any of a number of complex reasons, the process of projection of unwanted elements of the mind persists and may constitute one basis for the creation of hallucinations, pathological perceptions, and paranoid misconceptions. The typical psychotic experience of being the target of dangerous and mysterious invasive forces can be considered according to this model as the consequence of the defensive expulsion of unbearably painful thoughts and associated unconscious phantasies into an external object. Since this receptacle-object cannot perform the missing maternal transformation, the expelled elements are returned in "boomerang" fashion. When this projection finds a target in the idea of the planets and stars of outer space, the consequences often take the form of science-fiction drama, the consequence of re-entry of violently projected mental contents.

Innovative concepts

The concepts of splitting and projective identification, of psychotic and non-psychotic parts of the personality, of "attacks on linking", and of "container–contained" throw much light on psychotic processes. The splitting of ego and object, and the projective expulsion of parts of the self and the inner world into various receptacles, can help to clarify much that is otherwise confusing when what the therapist meets is a scattering (diaspora) of parts of the self and part-objects. This process can serve to redefine the aim of psychotherapy as the reclaiming of lost parts of the self (Steiner, 1989).

Bion extended in an illuminating manner the familiar and useful concept of the mind being organized into different parts. In the attempt to emphasize the concrete nature of much psychotic thinking and behaviour, authors tend to overuse the term "literally". Such concrete thinking might be better understood as the consequence of the conflict between a psychotic self who entertains such an unconscious phantasy, and a sane self who does not. This concept of psychotic and non-psychotic parts of the personality helps to clarify the process whereby an otherwise sane person can be persuaded to accept delusional beliefs. Such a person believes and does not believe at the same time, but the believing self defeats the sane self for various periods of time, so imagination (in the sense of the construction of ideas or images) comes to have the quality of reality. Another fate of the sane self is to be expelled into another person, who is then subjected to pressure to abandon his or her normal *capacity* for doubting and to accept that madness is sanity.

The failure of the normal development of alpha-transformation of beta elements in the mother–infant relationship leads to a failure to establish a sufficiently "containing" object in the inner world and may doom the individual to a life of projection, repeatedly expelling subjective elements into receptacles. Since these receptacles are unable to perform the necessary transformations, the consequence is confusion and paranoid distortions of reality.

Bion's observations (1967) that sense organs can be used for the purposes of evacuation can help explain strange symptoms such as are seen in Patients D and H and as also illustrated in Harry's dream of the camera transforming into a missile launcher (Chapter 15).

Mythology and developmental challenges

The common hallucinatory preoccupation with dangerous snakes can also be considered in part-object terms as the expression of the image of an unconscious phantasy of a dangerous penis containing the projected primitive oral-biting impulses of the subject. This image finds expression in the mythological theme of the Gorgon Medusa, the symbolic representative of the terrifying and dangerous phallic mother, whose face-genital is surrounded by snakes. The related theme of the hero's entry into the underground cave, where he encounters and slays the Minotaur and finds his way back to the outside world, can be considered at several symbolic levels. At the level of genital sexuality, it represents the conquest of the dangers of first sexual intercourse for the adolescent male, based on a confrontation with an unconscious bisexual image of the "combined parents"— "father's (dangerous) penis inside mother's body"—and the mastery of the unconscious developmental challenges of childhood and adolescence of both sexes (Campbell, 1950; Grotstein, 1997).

Hysteria and sibling jealousy

Several of the patients illustrated the role of sibling jealousy as an important factor in psychotic psychopathology of a hysterical type. The hallucinatory content of "dead babies" can be understood in terms of the murderous jealousy aroused by the arrival of baby siblings or by contemplation of those anticipated but as yet unborn, or actually dead. Less severe sibling rivalry may not have such developmentally deep roots as those encountered in psychotic disorders, and normal sibling rivalry may make powerful constructive contributions to the developing personality.

Mitchell (2000, p. xi), writing as a psychoanalyst about hysteria from a feminist point of view, notes the frequency of sibling jealousy in hysteria, and she points out that sibling jealousy is everywhere but is almost never addressed in psychoanalytic writing. She presents a vigorous and closely argued challenge to some aspects of contemporary psychoanalytic theory and practice and suggests that a "lateral", sibling, perspective should be added to the conventional "vertical" mother–child one. She writes: "Once one brings in siblings, hysteria emerges. Likewise, understanding hysteria calls forth siblings . . . psychoanalysis has subsumed them to a vertical child–parent relationship."

Many examples of the potentially psychotogenic effects of unresolved intense sibling jealousy appear in the cases reported here, and reference has been made to Volkan's important contributions (Volkan, 1997). Mitchell's observations are timely and perspicacious.

The formations and function of delusions and hallucinations

Delusions and hallucinations are complex phenomena involving a regressive shift from conceptual thinking to more primitive concrete and perceptual forms (Lottermann, 1996; Robbins, 1993). Some of the patients described here demonstrate how command hallucinations in particular may evolve on the basis of primitive splitting, projection, and introjection in part-object relations and thus become unrecognizable as elements of the patient's own thoughts and inner world. Delusions and hallucinations serve unconscious defensive purposes (see Segal, 1972) but sometimes can be seen to be consciously exploited to maintain a position of specialness or self-deception or, in Bionic terms, to maintain the propaganda of the psychotic part of the personality.

Command hallucinations

Five of the fifteen patients experienced auditory hallucinations in the form of unidentifiable voices commanding them to destructive or self-destructive behaviour. Brian (Chapter 4) was commanded not to try, Claudia (Chapter 5) to strangle other patients, Dorothy (Chapter 6) to kill herself, Ellen (Chapter 8) to stop eating, and George (Chapter 14) to jump to his death. Claudia, Dorothy, and George obeyed such commands and were fortunate to survive their suicidal actions.

As the therapy progressed and splitting and projective processes diminished, the voices lost their power, faded into the background, perhaps to be briefly revived in moments of emotional stress, and finally disappeared. None of the patients expressed any strong conviction that the voices had been their own thoughts, nor did they express obvious curiosity about them, sometimes ascribing them to "imagination".

Psychoanalytic theory generally explains the nature of command hallucinations in terms of external experiences and internal phantasies which are produced by the defensive use of psychotic mechanisms and which have the effect of disintegrating the sense of self. Concepts such as "archaic-destructive-envious superego" or "attacks on linking" provide dynamic explanations that would satisfy many psychoanalysts.

An alternative view has been proposed by Sinason (1993, 1999) and supported by others (Jenkins, 1995; Richards, 1999). Sinason pursued a line of thought introduced by Jaynes (1976), who conceived of a "bicameral mind"—a brain-mind in which the right hemisphere may play a dominating and commanding role over the left. Sinason (1993) has elaborated the clinical implications of having two separate minds in the one body by describing this state as "internal cohabitation", in which one mind may exert a powerful, usually destructive, influence over the other by providing internal "ill-advice". This occurs in "normal" people but becomes a dominating influence in psychotic conditions where the inner voice can be heard as command hallucinations. When in the course of psychotherapy this is anticipated, and allowed for, its influence over the patient's mind diminishes.

As an approach to the treatment of patients dominated by command hallucinations—in which the patient's views of the identity of the commander, its motivations, and its point of view could be investigated—might have much to offer to psychotherapists, particularly to those cognitive-behavioural clinicians who are interested in making such enquiries. However, the "two-minds" basis of Sinason's highly original theory has yet to be demonstrated.

There is much yet to be learned about the subject of hallucinations and delusions and of the therapeutic approach to such symptoms, which is currently a central concern of cognitive-behavioural therapists. Some types of hallucinations may have a different psychopathology, representing, for instance, constructions used to promote a spurious sense of independence (Pao, 1979). In such a case, they could be regarded as old friends not to be lightly abandoned. Their psychodynamic relation to the benign imaginary companion who transforms into a persecutor, as in the case of Dorothy (Chapter 6), would repay exploration.

This is also true of the way in which overvalued ideas acquire delusional status, and in which imaginative activity in "the mind's eye" acquires the perceptual and affective quality of reality.

"Real" schizophrenia—a brain disease?

The clinical material presented does not cover the whole spectrum of psychotic disorders, but it illustrates the basic mental mechanisms that are characteristic of most. Obsessional and hysterical features are prominent, and their dynamic relationship to psychosis has been examined. Chronically regressed or severely disintegrated patients were rarely brought for discussion to the psychotherapy seminars, either because they were not considered relevant to psychotherapy by the presenting psychotherapists or because they were extremely unusual and not normally encountered by them.

The term "schizophrenia" has in some respects brought more confusion than clarification. Some of the foregoing cases might be regarded by some psychiatrists as not meriting the diagnosis of "true" schizophrenia, and others will maintain the view that schizophrenia is a *"brain disease"*. On the other hand, many will regard psychosis as a common end-state of a variety of disorders, including schizophrenia. Throughout this book, I have presented the view that assertions about the exclusiveness or primacy of biological factors in an illness variously called "true", "nuclear", or "Type 1" schizophrenia are reductionist and simplistic. A comprehensive approach will consider that it is the funnelling into the mother–infant relationship of a variety of genetic, biologic, psychological, and social ingredients which determines the beginnings of mental health or the sowing of "seeds of madness" (Volkan & Akhtar, 1997).

The notion of a single "true" schizophrenia has been discarded by the authors of the international systems of diagnostic classification (DSM 4 and ICD 10) and by the widespread use of the description of "the group of schizophrenias", or of "schizophrenia and related psychoses". Within a psychodynamic perspective, typical severe and chronic "true schizophrenia" might be broken down into such classes as:

- Chronic conditions resulting from ineffectual, or even anti-therapeutic treatment.

- Conditions that have been treated too late, rather than badly (Martindale, Bateman, Crowe, & Margison, 2000).

- Patients who have been covertly psychotic since infancy (Pao, 1979).

- Patients whose lives have been embedded in severe, perhaps unrecognized, pathogenic family pathology.

- Cases with a heavy genetic loading or unrecognized brain pathology, prenatal or perinatal.

None of these aspects can be considered in isolation. All may contribute in various degrees to the individual case. Without detailed study of the individual case, it cannot be assumed that they are sufficient, necessary, or contributory factors ("causes").

It is interesting to think what the consequences would be if the term "schizophrenia" were to be discarded and replaced by a psychoanalytically informed comprehensive use of the term "psychosis". However much the term "schizophrenia" may be needed for purposes of communication between psychiatrists, for epidemiology, and for public health discourse, it might be regarded as superfluous to

290 WEATHERING THE STORMS

actual clinical work with psychotic patients. During my work in one Swedish hospital with a catchment area of 100,000, the diagnosis of first-attack schizophrenia fell from an expected annual rate of 12 to 2 over a period of four years. During this period, a psychodynamic family therapy-based psychosis team had developed its skills and found the term "schizophrenia" of little use.

The benefits and limitations
of psychopharmacology

Chemotherapy often brings great relief to psychotic patients, with the suppression of some or all of the obvious signs and symptoms of the disturbance. Any nurse or psychiatrist who, like myself, has practised during the pre-phenothiazine days when treatment was limited to paraldehyde, unmodified electroshock, insulin coma therapy, and leucotomy will have no doubt of the enormous benefit that modern pharmacology has brought to the treatment of psychotic patients, transforming the psychiatric scene immeasurably for the better.

However, these benefits may obscure the fact that these products are powerful selective toxins that are not always effective, are prone to overuse, and sometimes produce serious side-effects. From a psychodynamic point of view, they are rarely, if ever, to be regarded as curative, however beneficial the suppression of symptoms may be in clinical terms, or simply in human terms in the cutting short of distress.

One of the regrettable consequences of an approach that favours a purely biological view of psychosis coupled with insufficient attention to psychodynamic factors is to be found in the case of patients in their first attack of psychosis. At this time, the need for a skilled assessment of all the possible contributing factors—biological, psychosocial, and psychodynamic—that may be involved in the particular case is greatest. The prompt and often dramatic disappearance of hallucinations, delusions and pathological excitement brought about by anti-psychotic medication frequently leads to premature discharge, inadequate evaluation, and speedy relapse (Freeman, 1988).

The psychotherapeutic perspective recognizes the role of biological factors, but it approaches the use of chemotherapy, at least in the first instance, as an adjunct to making contact with the patient and investigating the psychological factors underlying the disturbed contact with reality which characterizes the psychotic state. At the intake stage, it may be possible to postpone all medication for a sufficiently long period to determine more precisely the patient's needs and response to a psychotherapeutic approach (Räkköläinen, personal communication). When psychotherapy is undertaken, medication is to be used in modest amounts as far as possible. In this way, patients may receive understanding in depth within the hospital milieu, and formal psychotherapy may be offered to many patients who would be inaccessible without the help of medication and who would not be sufficiently understood in an exclusively biological approach (Jackson, 1993a; Oldham & Russakoff, 1987).

What is schizophrenia?

In a far-reaching study, Robbins (1993), approaching General Systems theory (Bertalanffy, 1968) with a psychoanalytic eye, presents a "hierarchical systems approach" to the study of schizophrenia. He sees schizophrenia as the simultaneous expression of a number of independent but interlocking hierarchical systems—intrapsychic, interpersonal, family, social and cultural, and neurobiological. Such an integrated approach may help remedy the monistic and reductionist attitudes that, in Robbins' view, dominated psychoanalysis a few decades ago and is increasingly doing so in psychiatry today.

The symbolic representation of experience

It has been observed that in the realm of symbolism anything can mean anything, and that although the interpretation of dream symbolism may be the "royal road" to the unconscious it is essential for the therapist to discover the direction in which the signpost is pointing. It is the therapist's task to find out the level of meaning of a symbolic expression which has most relevance for the patient at the particular moment. In this way, consideration of the symbolism involved in creating obsessional and other pathological mental structures can be a highly informative and clinically useful activity, rather than an interesting exercise in speculation. It also requires the therapist to differentiate his own imaginative associations from those of the patient. One can always find a wide variety of potential meanings when reflecting on the "polysemic" richness of symbolic expressions.

However, if it is not forgotten that one object of such an exercise in associations on the part of the therapist is to increase his imaginative repertoire, he will be less likely to ascribe something to the patient's mind which actually belongs to his own. The reward for this activity is the improvement of the therapist's capacity to attend to the associations that are meaningful to the patient at a particular time and to choose to say something at the level that the patient might find acceptable and useful. Thinking in this manner allows for the gradual formulation of possible meanings of the psychotic thinking and behaviour under scrutiny, and it guides the therapist in his choice of interventions and then to test them with the patient and to modify or change them if he can find better explanations. This procedure might be regarded as the scientific aspect of an artistic or "hermeneutic" activity and as having relevance to the debate as to whether psychoanalysis belongs primarily to the social or the natural sciences (Bateman & Holmes, 1995).

Decline of interest in the content of dreams and delusions

Several of the patients in this study reported dreams when they were functioning at a relatively integrated level and were sufficiently able to differentiate dream from reality. Such dreams may provide a window on preconscious and unconscious thoughts, memories, wishes, and fears, sometimes linking the present in the transference with external reality and events of early life, and they may then offer the possibility of interpreting such meanings to the patient at an appropriate time and manner.

Much has been learned in psychoanalysis about the way in which a patient may use dreams in a defensive manner, but this increased interest in the form of the dream seems to have been accompanied by a decline of interest in the content of dreams (and a lack of enthusiasm for dream interpretation) and, to some extent, in the content of delusions and hallucinations. Contemporary psychoanalytic emphasis on the therapeutic transference and its expression in the immediate

present may have reduced interest in the dream as a valuable window, not only onto the present, but also onto the past, and of the
interpretation of dream symbols in terms of memories of the past,
whether retrievable or irretrievable (which include what Klein, 1957,
called "memories in feeling").

Psychosomatic expressions of hidden psychotic processes

Since none of the patients reported showed any prominent physi-
ologically based psychosomatic symptoms, I have not attempted to
address the relationships that are sometimes found between certain
psychosomatic symptoms (such as asthma and ulcerative colitis) and
psychosis (see Engel, 1962, 1980; Jackson, 1976, 1977, 1982; Sperling,
1955, 1978; G. Taylor, 1987).

CHAPTER EIGHTEEN

Mostly practice

In this study, much attention has been paid to exploring the *content* and *meanings* of delusions and hallucinations and the details of the patients' past history, remembered or reconstructed. This perspective is in contrast to much of current psychoanalytic practice, where minute examination of the transference and countertransference takes precedence over the investigation of past history. There are good reasons behind this perspective, which has yielded great dividends, in particular in respect of discovering subtle and important transactions taking place between analyst and patient from one moment to another within the session.

The past in the present— the "here-and-now" and the "there-and-then"

Bion recommended that the analyst should relinquish "memory and desire", an opinion that has sometimes caused confusion in those therapists who have taken it to mean that they should forget all about the patient's past history during the therapeutic sessions. If understood as advising the therapist to abandon conscious wishes to cure the patient, to approach each session as though it were the first, and to rely on his unconscious mind to prompt him at appropriate moments, it is an important contribution. However, in the case of psychotic patients, it is most important to have available, and to remember, detailed biographical information (Rosenfeld, personal communication).

Some situations may arise in psychosis psychotherapy where the therapist may have the opportunity to point out the meaning of symbolic material and to demonstrate the repetition of particular past experience in the transference and in the outside world in much the same way as a "mutative" interpretation may be offered to a neurotic patient (Szalita-Pemmow, 1951). Such an interpretation may only be appropriate to a patient who has achieved the beginnings of a sense of personal identity, and to a therapist who has a good understanding of what is going on in the immediate present of the transference. This is a very different matter from the premature "decoding" of symbols. Rey (personal communication) considered that if the patient is partly functioning at a particular infantile level, the therapist should provide him with the knowledge—in the form of a "cognitive structure"—to think about his experience. Such an explanatory framework can function as a "metasystem", allowing the transformation of primitive psychological processes and structures to a less concrete, more abstract, and more mature form.

It is as much of a mistake to underestimate a psychotic patient's potential for understanding the therapist's explanations of the relation between past and present and of the meaning of his experiences as it is to overestimate it.

Thus the psychoanalytic focus on the "here-and-now" of the therapy session is not always appropriate to psychoanalytic psychotherapy, where detailed attention to the transference may often be impossible. However, in both situations the therapist must attend to the possibility that in a therapy session the patient may be talking about the past as a defence against anxieties in the present, and vice-versa.

In the case of Grace (Chapter 13), a phobia, originating in childhood, protected her from a schizophrenic breakdown until the time when the projective defence proved insufficient to deal with the massive revival of the envy and jealousy provoked by her sister's pregnancy. This psychotherapy case can be compared with a psycho-analytic one (Segal, 1981e) in which the schizoid mechanisms creating the phobia were shown to have protected the patient from a schizophrenic breakdown. The analyst was aware of her patient's great difficulties in childhood but reported no detail, perhaps for reasons of conciseness of presentation or of confidentiality. However, twenty-five years later she reported that she would today pay less attention to the patient's fantasies and dreams and focus on the moment-to-moment study of the interaction in the sessions. This contrast might be taken to demonstrate one way in which the two approaches and techniques differ, and how each is appropriate to its own context. Both "here-and-now" and "there-and-then" need the attention appropriate to the particular setting (Riesenberg-Malcolm, 1999c).

Part-object psychology

The commentaries and theoretical formulations that I have offered are meant to serve as an introduction to ways of thinking about such psychotic material. Such concepts as partial objects, selves, identifications, and identities may be difficult to comprehend and unfamiliar to some readers, but I hope that the material has served to illustrate their explanatory power. Some of the explanations, formulations, and conclusions offered may seem to be (and, at times, actually to be) based on slender evidence, often dependent on reconstructions of stories of traumatic childhoods, with little corroborated detail, and thus more speculative than scientific. However justified might be such criticism, my main purpose is to show how helpful part-object thinking can be in the search to understand the meaning of psychotic phenomena, and to formulate psychoanalytically oriented treatment plans for psychotic patients, whether or not the patient will eventually become engaged in psychotherapy.

There are many different and perhaps conflicting ways of considering this material, but this is the way that I and the participants found to be useful. Although analytic thinking about psychotic illness is an intellectually demanding task, the tentative nature of many of the explanations and formulations presented does not imply a lack of confidence in the concepts and explanations but, rather, a recognition of the multiple meanings to be discovered in each individual and the polysemic nature of symbols. What may at times perhaps seem to be unbridled speculation should be considered in this light. It is the personal, individual focus that is central to this way of working, characterized by a respectful approach to the individual patient, an approach that can make an important contribution to the intellectual and emotional needs of all those involved.

Therapists' use of new knowledge

In an important study of long-term outcomes in psychoanalysis and psychoanalytic psychotherapy (Sandell et al., 2000), it was found that many psychotherapists who had not had psychoanalytic training tended to adopt what they believed was a classical, objective, and uninvolved psychoanalytic stance with their (mostly non-psychotic) patients. This was associated with an unfavourable outcome, which the authors concluded was a reflection of the psychotherapists conducting their treatment in a dysfunctionally psychoanalytic manner. Such a misconception would be even more inappropriate for psychotic patients.

In writing about this work, it seemed important to be clear about what would not help. Idealizing psychotherapy as a panacea for psychotic disturbance could lead therapists to underestimate the difficulty in helping chronic and fragmented patients and thus to disappointment and disillusionment. A facile equating of psychoanalysis and the work of the psychoanalyst with this kind of aim-restricted psychoanalytic psychotherapy could lead therapists into omnipotence and the oversimplification of immensely complex matters. Dilution of psychoanalytic knowledge could be misleading and harmful to the therapists and to the principles of psychoanalysis. Intellectualization and the defensive use of theory could create destructive impasses or damaging regressions in vulnerable patients and could lead to underestimating the difficulty in helping chronic and severely fragmented patients and to failing to recognize or manage psychotic transferences. Looking back, I believe that most of these pitfalls were avoided or overcome in these seminars. The fact that all the therapists had had some experience of personal analytic psychotherapy as part of their basic training was largely responsible for this satisfactory outcome.

For all the therapists, the input of knowledge that was, to a varying extent new, aroused great interest and "food for thought". For most it provided an important new learning experience, improved their confidence and therapeutic technique, and, for many, increased enthusiasm for this type of thinking in their future work with psychotic patients.

The important role of psychiatric nurses with psychotic patients

My own experience of working with nurses on a psychodynamically based psychiatric ward (Jackson & Cawley, 1992; Jackson & Williams, 1994) has convinced me that psychiatric nurses who are given the opportunity of skilled supervisory help or of some training in psychodynamics could provide a huge resource for psychodynamically based care and psychotherapy of psychotic patients in the public hospital service.

It is usually the nursing staff who know the hospitalized psychiatric patient best, and their psychotherapeutic potential has long been recognized in some centres and their opportunities for further training promoted (Barnes, 1967; Benfer & Schroder, 1985; Fabricius, 1994; Hughes & Halek, 1991; Jackson, 1993b; Jackson & Jacobson, 1983; Teising, 2000). Their skills can be applied at many levels, from that of "contact-person" or "primary nurse" through to formal training as specialists in psychotherapy. Alanen in particular (1997; Alanen et al., 1986), has reported impressive results with a large number of psychotic patients treated by nurses with a relatively small amount of training in psychodynamics, but with the help of experienced supervisors. Such a use of nursing skills is illustrated by the case of Grace (Chapter 13).

If the new psychoanalytic knowledge about psychosis were to be progressively integrated with developments in psychosocial, psychological, and pharmacologic approaches and adequately rewarded financially, it would offer security and the satisfaction of effective and creative work to psychiatric nurses and other members of multidisciplinary teams. If this could be achieved, nurses who have the wish and the ability to do such work well would be encouraged to stay on such units for long periods and, when they move on, to leave in a way that can be helpful to the patients. Such a development would make an immense contribution to the welfare of seriously disturbed psychotic patients.

One of the many important therapeutic functions of nurses on an admission ward is to "contain" the acutely disturbed patient by means of their informed understanding. Skilful nurses who can maintain their composure and talk with the patient about his fears may reduce the level of his anxiety and can allow lower doses of medication than might otherwise be necessary. Such an approach has much in common with Bion's "maternal alpha-function", previously described, with the anxiety-reducing interventions of "expressed emotion" interventions with families (Leff & Vaughn, 1985) and of the work of the Soteria Project (Mosher & Menn, 1976). It is recognized as an important part of the Turku research, where many acute psychotic patients require little or no medication or in the first instance only benzodiazepines (Räkköläinen, personal communication).

Of at least equal importance are nurses or nursing assistants who may have little or no training in psychodynamics, but have talent for the work and wide and appropriate life experience. When such nurses have a high tolerance of disturbed behaviour and a natural capacity for warmth, they can form a stable and invaluable nucleus for the unit and contribute to the important function of maintaining some sort of open-ended contact with appropriate patients after discharge. Such exceptional individuals may not wish to learn more about psychodynamics and may, indeed, be better off without formal training.

Surface, depth, and developmental levels

Freud's injunction that in therapy we should proceed from the surface to the depths is not necessarily appropriate when the depths are on the surface, as is often the case in psychotic disorders. Klein's view that neurotic disorders conceal deeper psychotic processes does not imply that pathology deriving from developmentally later levels of impulse and defence are unimportant. The adaptations of the prepubertal and adolescent years may all be deeply influenced, in an epigenetic manner, by developmental disturbances in the first year or two of life. In our *thinking* about psychotic disorders in adolescence and adult life, we need to consider what were the likely earliest roots of the illness, and in what way they may have influenced subsequent development. Sufficiently bad later experience can undo the stability achieved by a good beginning, and sufficiently good early experience can go far to undo the influence of a vulnerable genotype (Tienari, 1992).

Thus in our *practice* with a particular psychotic patient, we must work at the point of his most immediate anxiety (Klein), at the level at which he seems to be functioning, and in terms that make the most sense to him. Thus it may be necessary to deal with the neurotic level of the material at one time, and the psychotic level at another.

Holmes (1982), working in a psychoanalytic and Piagetian context, provided an illustration of the way that earlier deficits may be found to underlie later ones. Describing the acquisition of "imaginative competence" in certain obsessional states, he compared the developmental issues at ages 1–2 years and at 10–12 years, and with examples of non-psychotic patients he showed how obsessional dynamics in the latter ages may be used in the service of correcting a faulty capacity for reality-testing deriving from the former periods.

The fact that the focus of study in this book is on the deepest developmental roots does not minimize the significance of the branches of less deep-rooted processes. I find it helpful when confronted with psychotic material to speculate at the outset about what the experience of the patient as a baby, and of the mother–baby relationship, might have been. Subsequent evidence might then add weight to such speculations and illuminate the way in which pathogenic processes have influenced later developmental phases in an epigenetic manner and are continuing to exert their influence in the patient's present disturbance. This is often illustrated in those disturbances arising in adolescence whose basis can be found in disturbances in infancy and prepubertal life.

The symbolic transformation of primitive levels of mental processes into progressively higher and abstract forms creates a layering of mental structure and a diversification of mental functioning, leading, under normal circumstances, to a stable and flexible mental structure. When these developmental pathways take pathological forms, they remain embedded in the internal world, to be reactivated at a later date if the subject meets particular environmental stresses. Such a reactivation requires the mobilization and intensification of defence mechanisms in the attempt to manage the crisis. In the most extreme form of emergency, this process leads to that state of confusion of internal and external mental events which we call psychosis.

Psychoanalysis
and psychoanalytic psychotherapy

Psychoanalytic psychotherapy is usually based on weekly or twice-weekly sessions, and some modifications of procedures is not uncommon (Kernberg, 1999). In the case of psychotic patients, once-weekly sessions are not only more readily available, but are more appropriate for many of the severely disturbed patients that the psychiatrist encounters. For such patients, more frequent sessions, at least at the beginning, may prove overwhelming and may lead to damaging responses that cannot be contained in the sessions. On the other hand, more frequent sessions may bring a smaller risk that suicidal ideation may be carried into action (as in the cases of Claudia, Chapter 5, and Dorothy, Chapter 6). Much will depend on the therapist's capacity to contain (manage) the patient's self-destructive developments within the session and, in the case of a supportive or actively therapeutic milieu, of the staff's capacity to do so.

In formal psychoanalytic treatment, the most important intervention takes the form of *interpretation* of the patient's free associations, with the aim of helping him become conscious of the unconscious phantasies, emotional conflicts, and mental defence mechanisms which are at the root of his disability, as they are revealed in the transference. Winnicott (1962, pp. 169-170) expressed the uniqueness of this approach succinctly:

> If our aim continues to be to verbalize the nascent conscious in terms of the transference, then we are practising analysis; if not, then we are analysts practising something else that we deem to be appropriate to the occasion. And why not?"

Since the time of that observation, Winnicott's "something else" has become an important issue for psychoanalysts and psychotherapists alike. Work in which the transference is recognized but is not necessarily the central focus is today characteristic of much once-weekly psychotherapy with psychotic patients (Tyndale, 1999).

When a therapist can understand and manage his countertransference reactions to the patient, it can constitute an invaluable source of understanding and an important therapeutic instrument, and, as such, it requires regular monitoring (Lottermann, 1996, p. 81) and "calibrating". For example, a normal wish to help the patient may develop into a powerful desire to cure him, perhaps leading to frustration, guilt, and despair and eventually to hatred—conscious or unconscious—of the patient (see Winnicott, 1958). If this happens, the therapist must decide how much the feelings can be understood as a rational response on his own part, an irrational one requiring further self-examination, or a symptom of the patient pointing to the communication of pathology requiring attention. The therapist must be prepared to tolerate long periods of considerable frustration and uncertainty without resorting to premature explanations or interpretations and must therefore have a capacity for "masterly inactivity" or "negative capability". The experience of emotional assaults or erotic temptations may be both disturbing and enlightening, and ultimately therapeutically helpful.

In the course of psychotherapy—and indeed of life in general—internal and external reality are always combined, and it is the task of psychotherapy to help the patient, whether psychotic or neurotic, to think more effectively about this matter and to improve his capacity for differentiating the two worlds. It may require the emergence and interpretation of transference processes to disentangle the elements, or help in the task from family interviews (not a feature of formal psychoanalysis) or other sources of corroboration.

There is clearly a great deal of common ground between psychoanalysis and psychoanalytic psychotherapy, and much attention has been paid to this matter in recent years, the most outstanding research coming from the Menninger Clinic (Wallerstein, 1986).

CHAPTER NINETEEN

Conclusions

I have presented a wide range of examples of the thinking and behaviour typical of severe psychotic illness and have offered commentaries based on the application of Kleinian concepts. I wished to demonstrate the value of these concepts as guidelines, or navigational aids, to learning and treatment by psychotherapists, psychiatrists, and others working in the field who have different perspectives and different but related special skills.

At the beginning, I pointed out that the perspective of this book is that however much later experience may promote or obstruct normal development, it is in the mother–baby relationship that the seeds of psychosis are to be found. I quoted Winnicott's maxim that the place to study psychosis is in the nursery and Segal's assertion that the roots of psychosis lie in the pathology of early infancy which structures the budding inner world and influences later developmental levels in an epigenetic fashion. I also remarked that it was not going to be easy to write a text that would be intelligible and do justice to both psychiatric and psychoanalytic thinking.

I hope that the case material has helped to bring some life to some of the more abstract theoretical formulations of psychoanalysis. As an example, in early chapters obsessional mechanisms are described in terms of "anality", and, in some of the cases where pathology of eating is encountered, "oral" pathology can be held to be a developmental precursor. These theoretical terms can perhaps only come to a vivid living reality for those who have observed very small children closely or have actually had experience of the psychotherapy of children and of formal infant observation.

I have referred to the great importance of the fears that may be aroused in adolescents as the consequences of the bodily changes of puberty. Klein believed that the most profound unconscious anxiety of the girl from very early in life is of having her body invaded in a destructive manner. As can be seen in the case of severe, near-psychotic anorexia with onset at puberty, the invading object may contain the projections of the girl's own unconscious invasive/destructive wishes. This may help account for the relatively infrequency of severe anorexia in the male. The pubertal boy may dread both the destructive potential of his increasingly powerful body and his budding genital sexuality which brings castration fears both literal and symbolic. It is interesting to consider that the preoccupations of many adolescent males (of all ages) with fictional (and real) violence, monsters, alien beings, and the like may in part be the expression of attempts to find containers for the projection of the (perhaps universal) "monster" of the inner world. When the ego is sufficiently strong, this may help develop confidence in differentiating inner from outer reality. When it is not, overt psychotic consequences may follow. Such adolescent processes may have their roots in earlier development where the need for monsters is at least as important. Many vivid descriptions are to be found in the literature which demonstrate how overwhelming can be the terrors of very small children, and how real may be their belief in the destructiveness of their bodily impulses and of the retaliatory consequences (Joseph, 1966; Ramzy, 1966).

All the patients that have been described have suffered serious emotional deprivation or traumatic experiences in early life, and I have tried to explain the way in which such experiences, often to be heard in the history of apparently healthy adults, have contributed to a psychotic outcome. The story of early development elicited in the course of routine psychiatric history-taking may tell us little of what the baby may have experienced, or of the range of possible pathogenic effects of early traumatic experience within the mother–infant relationship and of its epigenetic effect on later levels of cognitive development and affect management. Skilful history-taking, formal infant observation, analytic psychotherapy, and research into perinatal events (see Barrows, 2000) will continue to advance our knowledge.

The primary task of the therapist is to help the patient establish the capacity to differentiate himself and his conflicted desires from those of other people and to recognize that the reality of his inner "imaginative" world is different from the reality of the external "real" world. This involves reducing his use of projective identification, withdrawing projections, recovering lost parts of the self, and recognizing and tolerating (containing) his unwanted and feared impulses and wishes. He can thereby hope to acquire a new and more stable sense of identity and a capacity to think for himself about himself and, ultimately, to be able to take more responsibility for his own mind.

This ego-strengthening process depends very much on the quality of his relationship with the therapist, and thus on the therapist's knowledge and skill, prerequisites that also apply to the case of non-psychotic patients. However, in the case of the psychotic patient, the psychotherapist faces an even more demanding challenge. As we have already seen, countertransference processes may exert powerful pressures on him to respond in non-therapeutic ways, and the more he is aware of the irrational "psychotic" aspects of his own personality, the better will be his understanding of the patient and the safer will be the patient in his hands. The therapist's reward for this self-knowledge will be a greater freedom and confidence in his work and a capacity to work more with psychotic patients in the future if he chooses. It is of great importance that psychoanalysts and psychoanalytic psychotherapists should have this personal insight and that many should wish to become involved in the field if in the future psychoanalysis is to provide the help for psychotic patients that is possible (see Quinodoz, 2001).

Psychotherapy, with or without associated medication, can often help resolve an acute psychotic episode relatively quickly, but when this has been achieved the therapist is left with the task of considering the character of the patient's underlying personality. This may be found to range from normal to severely disturbed and may be classifiable in such descriptive terms as psychotic character (Frosch, 1983), schizoid, schizotypal, borderline, sociopathic, or hysterical. Grotstein (2001) has considered this matter in terms of the multi-axial classification system in current psychiatric taxonomy, in which states (Axis 1) can be differentiated from traits (Axis 2). In this perspective, the recovery from a psychotic state may at times confront the therapist with the necessity of continuing with what might be a long character analysis before pathogenic conflicts can be sufficiently resolved and reliable stability can be achieved.

Grotstein has also pointed out that the recovered patient may benefit from help to deal with the trauma that the psychotic episode itself and the attendant therapeutic (at times anti-therapeutic) procedures have caused, and he has called this type of intervention "rehabilitative psychoanalysis". A manic-depressive patient who recovers from an episode of mania may have to face the realization that what he had thought was abundant good health has proved to be severe illness, and this may induce suicidal despair and contribute to a depressive reaction. However, he usually recovers hope.

Recent psychiatric reports have drawn attention to the need to attend to depressive states in the schizophrenic patient and have found that suicidal intent and early mortality is more common than is often realized. This seems to be particularly the case in young female schizophrenic patients with less severe psychotic symptoms at the stage where these symptoms are abating (Schwartz & Cohen, 2001). It may be that the loss of the defensive function of the regressive process exposes the patient to the intolerable feelings of despair and confusion that have provoked the regression in the first place, now augmented by the recognition of his isolation, stigmatization, and the loss of contact with his peers that his period of absence from social life has brought about, and he may not easily recover hope. He may feel confused and not understood, and "rehabilitation" psychotherapy might help him with such traumatic consequences of the psychotic episode itself and could add depth to a psychiatrist's understanding of such depression as simply an illness to be treated in conventional ways.

It is difficult to assess the quality and stability of the impressive improvements achieved in some of the patients reported and the durability of the beneficent changes seen in others. The concept of "cure" has little place in clinical work, and more dynamic criteria such as "sealing-over" or "integrative recovery" are more appropriate (Cullberg, 1991, 2001). Improvement in symptoms and decrease in distress, however impressive or gratifying, do not in themselves necessarily indicate that stable and improved psychodynamic change has occurred. What is needed before stable improvement can be proclaimed is convincing explanations of how changes have taken place, prognostic predictions, and adequate follow-up.

There has recently been much interest in considering what are the agents of growth-promoting change and in developing a theory of change (Rogan, 2000; Stern et al., 1998). It is becoming clear that factors leading to beneficent change may be much more complicated than has been generally realized. It has also been recognized that formal psychoanalytic therapy contains supportive elements, and even cognitive-behavioural ones, and that both supportive and cognitive psychotherapy may at times contain effective, albeit unspoken, interpretations (see Rycroft, 1968c).

As with the therapy of neurotic patients, an individual may feel much better but be psychodynamically worse, and the reverse. At the best this outcome might count as a highly desirable "useful false solution" (Malan, 1963). At the worst, relatives and others may suffer, and relapse or the emergence of different or disturbing symptoms is only a matter of time. What constitutes an "adequate" period of follow-up of a psychotic patient who has improved following psychological treatments is a matter of opinion. Ugelstad (personal communication) from long experience considered five years a minimum and ten a preferable period of time.

The fifteen patients studied in depth in this book all had the background of a psychotherapeutically oriented psychiatric ward, or specialized treatment institution for young psychotic adults. It has not been possible to do justice to the importance of the types of special treatment institutions in Scandinavia which provided the necessary setting for some of the cases; neither has it been possible to describe their own specialized therapeutic functions, nor the great complexity of the therapeutic and anti-therapeutic forces that are inevitably involved in such circumstances. These institutions can generally be considered as therapeutic communities specifically designed for the needs of small numbers of young adult psychotic patients, with resources for individual long-term psychotherapy.

Many of the patients discussed here have been profoundly helped by their psychotherapists, and most had been so severely and chronically disturbed that they could not have been taken on outside a containing hospital setting. Some of the therapists had sufficient psychoanalytically based training and experience of psychotic patients to allow them to work confidently with transference phenomena. These therapists refined their personal techniques of interpretative therapy over the years of this collaborative work. Other therapists could best be regarded as conducting supportive psychotherapy at the outset and as making varying degrees of use of the psychoanalytic input as the work proceeded.

In general, the case discussions were found profitable by the therapists and improved the quality of their work. Their own increased understanding of psychotic mechanisms helped them, to a varying extent, to engage their patients as partners in a joint enterprise, in which the psychotic illness, at first inexplicable to the patient, came to acquire meaning and personal significance.

Psychoanalysis as a necessary source of knowledge for psychosis treatment

For various reasons, psychoanalysts no longer take on psychotic patients for treatment as a matter of routine. Throughout this book, I have emphasized that psychoanalysis offers an indispensable contribution to the deep understanding and approach to treatment of psychotic conditions and that its integration with other approaches is of great importance. Integration does not, however, mean one discipline taking over another; rather, it is the respectful sharing of points of view with other fields of knowledge, experience, and special expertise. At the present time, the most prominent contributions to research and psychological treatments of psychosis are being made by cognitive-behavioural psychotherapists (Chadwick & Birchwood, 1994; Chadwick, Birchwood, & Trower, 1996; Fowler, Garety, & Kuipers, 1995; Garety, Fowler, & Kuipers, 2000; Turkington & Siddle, 1998). Many such workers have long experience in research methods and spend much profitable time in talking to psychotic patients in an educational and reality-testing manner. Some psychologists are becoming interested in what a psychoanalytic approach may contribute to their work, and some psychoanalysts are exploring the way that the cognitive-behavioural therapy (CBT) paradigm, as applied to non-psychotic patients, although limited in its explanatory power and widely idealized as a rational and quick-acting panacea, may be more suitable for many patients, particularly in the public sector (Milton, 2001).

In the case of severely ill psychotic patients, CBT therapists have been vigorously filling the gap left by the failure of psychoanalysis, in the last few decades, to find opportunities to expand its research methods into the field of psychosis and to apply it in the public health sector, where the vast majority of severely disturbed psychotic patients are to be found. The work of CBT therapists is a great improvement on some contemporary psychiatric practice. Cross-fertilization with analytic psychotherapy could bring benefit to both approaches.

So what is the future of psychoanalysis for psychotic patients?

I have emphasized that the sort of once- or twice-weekly psychodynamic psychotherapy in which most of these patients were engaged could, under the appropriate conditions of setting and support, be regarded as an effective method in its own right, in much the same way that group therapy has proved to be far more than an attempt to deal with long waiting lists and a shortage of trained individual therapists. This need not be a matter of making a virtue of the necessity of providing an affordable "psychotherapy for the people" but, rather, an approach that might be suitable for the majority of psychotic patients encountered in public health services. This view implies that such work would continue to depend on and be nourished by psychoanalytic theory, where its origin and theoretical base lie and to which it could make its own contributions. More formal four- or five-times weekly analysis might remain the ideal treatment choice for some psychotic patients, as well as for all psychoanalytic and most psychotherapy trainees.

Reservations

Rycroft (1985) has pointed out that the benefits deriving from the current diffusion of psychoanalytic ideas into clinical psychiatry and briefer methods of psychotherapy may be bought at a cost. He writes:

> Perhaps there is something valuable, private, but inherently esoteric about the long-term psychoanalytic encounter which eludes the contemporary vogue for short-term relationship-oriented

psychotherapies, and perhaps research into such obscurities as the genesis of self-awareness and symbolic thinking, the relationship of the self to its self, its body, its sexuality, requires greater intensity of contact and greater intellectual rigour than the contemporary psychotherapies can afford.

A succinct answer to the question of the future of psychoanalysis for psychotic patients has been given by Segal. Considering the psychoanalytic approach to psychosis, she writes (1981d, p. 135):

> What then is the value of psychoanalytic treatment? I think we have to differentiate here between the value to the patient and the value to the community. To take the patient first: it is my conviction that in the rare cases where the conditions are right, psychoanalytic treatment is the treatment that gives the most hopeful therapeutic prognosis for the individual patient, and that, when successful, it is the treatment that deals with the very root of the disturbance of his personality; and I would not refrain from recommending it to an individual patient on the grounds that it is not a social solution, any more than I would withhold kidney machines or grafts from patients to whom they may be available, just because they are not universally available. From the point of view of society, the value of psychoanalysis of psychotics lies mainly in its research aspect. Psychoanalysis is basically an investigation, a method that throws light on the actual psychopathology of the illness. It is on such knowledge that all other psychotherapeutic endeavours, such as management, group therapy, individual therapy, or community care must be based. As Alanen (1975) has made clear, psychoanalytic research can also contribute here to methods of prevention which we hope will one day take precedence over treatment. Another aspect of the research on psychotics is the light it throws on mental phenomena in general. In every analysis of the neurotic, and even more so of borderline and delinquent patients, we have to deal with psychotic anxieties and mechanisms, and it is in the treatment of psychotics that one can observe these phenomena at their greatest intensity.

As a "position statement" concerning psychotic patients, this implies: *psychoanalysis for the few, psychoanalytic psychotherapy for the many, and a psychotherapeutic approach for all.*

Conclusions

Here, in summary form, are the main conclusions that I wish to repeat:

- Psychotic experience and behaviour are events with important meaning in terms of the life of the individual, his culture, and his inner world. Psychoanalytic concepts can help these meanings to be understood in ways that can be profoundly helpful to the sufferers and to their families.

- Individual psychoanalytically oriented psychotherapy, properly applied for sufficient time in an optimum, "need-adapted" setting, is the treatment of choice for properly selected psychotic patients. A model for such an optimal "need-adapted" setting, which gives priority to family therapy interventions when it is appropriate, has been given by the Scandinavian psychiatrists and psychologists whose work I have described.

- A psychotherapeutic approach can help in the psychiatric management of all psychotic patients and can thereby enrich the work of all members of multidisciplinary psychiatric teams.

- Case-discussion seminars, even at long intervals, are an effective and economical method of providing new ways of understanding and working with psychotic individuals, especially for those interested workers who do not have access to advanced training centres.

- Psychotic patients need and deserve a detailed psychoanalytic assessment of their current mental state at the earliest possible opportunity. The professional doing the assessment should have sufficient training and understanding of the psychoanalytic theories of psychosis, as well as some personal experience of actually treating psychotic patients psychotherapeutically or of observing them for a period sufficient to achieve adequate understanding of psychotic mental mechanisms. At the least, a psychoanalytically trained person should be available in a consultative capacity.

- Psychotherapists undertaking this difficult work under the proper conditions and in collaboration with psychoanalytically informed psychiatrists will be making significant contributions to the alleviation of psychotic suffering. They will also be rewarded by increasing understanding of their less disturbed patients and of themselves.

- Even a small amount of psychoanalytically based understanding can be of great help to spouses, children, and, indeed, to future generations. It may sometimes help to stop the often remorseless process of the reverberation down the generations of unresolved pathological attitudes and mental illness.

- All the studies presented in this book have demonstrated that psychotic patients deemed suitable for psychotherapy need to be provided with it for sufficient time and in an adequate supportive setting. All these patients had been ill for a long time before psychotherapy was considered as an option. It is likely that the longer the psychosis continues untreated, the more rigid the psychotic mechanisms and social defensiveness will become and will progressively reduce the accessibility of the patient to painful and laborious change. If psychotherapy for suitable patients were begun at the earliest possible moment, it seems obvious that progress would be very much quicker, but this has yet to be established. Except in cases where time is being wasted in therapeutic impasse, five years of once- or twice-weekly psychoanalytic psychotherapy may be enough. How long is "sufficient" depends on many factors, such as the therapeutic quality of the milieu, the skill of the therapist, and the patient's personal psychological assets. Some patients may need much less, some much more, but all need the option of open-ended contact with psychotherapeutically minded staff for as long as seems necessary. The provision of such resources, and the demonstration of their effectiveness from both a human and a financial point of view is a pressing problem of enormous dimensions and multiple socio-political implications.

- However important may be the socio-economic restrictions involved in the provision of necessary resources, they are not the primary obstacle to the implementation of new knowledge in the search for progress.

- Finally, I wish to emphasize that *psychotic patients need all the help that can be provided. It is therefore important for all professionals, of whatever persuasion, to become sufficiently informed about the work of others, to acquire a respectful and informed view about the merits and limitations of such work, and for specialists with diverse disciplines and orientations to find ways of sharing expertise and points of view, thereby enriching each other's thinking and work with the same patient.*

Characteristics of schizoid thinking

I have frequently referred to the writings of Henri Rey, which have been collected in his book *Universals of Psychoanalysis in the Treatment of Psychotic and Borderline States* (1994). Rey uses the term "universal" in the sense of the primitive mental structures and mechanisms that have their deepest roots in antenatal, perinatal, and postnatal mother–baby relationships and are the substance of the paranoid–schizoid level of development as elaborated by Klein. These universals find expression in different contemporary diagnostic groupings such as borderline, schizoid, or narcissistic personality disorder, and in the psychiatric classification of schizotypal personality disorder. The following is a distillate of Rey's views on the "*schizoid mode of being*", a pure culture of features that are found in varying degrees in individuals who have not reached the level of the depressive position.

- The schizoid individual finds great difficulty in making contact with others and finds it impossible to maintain any warm and steady relationship. If he actually manages to enter into a relationship, it rapidly becomes intensely dependent and results in disorders of identity.

- The schizoid has failed to transform certain sensorimotor experiences into representations, images, symbols, and memories, a transformation that is essential for the construction of a normal mental apparatus for thinking.

- In schizoid thinking, the idea is equivalent to the object and these idea-objects are always contained or containing. The schizoid thinks not in terms of persons but of objects placed somewhere in a container, and thoughts are material objects contained somewhere and expelled into something or other, and even the containing object is itself contained somewhere. He treats people as things, to remove the dangerous affectivity.

- Schizoid elements of thought have a concrete character ("thing-presentations", as opposed to "word-presentations").

- He must control his objects (whole, part, or "bizarre") so full are they of projected sexual and destructive impulses. He is suffering from a split between his normal intelligent ego and that part arrested in the paranoid–schizoid position. In therapy, progress depends on the possibility of undoing this schizoid structure and allowing progress towards the depressive position. At that more mature level of mental functioning, symbolic transformation of concrete experience, of bizarre objects, and of sensory experience can take place, making more mature modes of communication possible.

- A frankly schizophrenic episode may be necessary to return to the point of bifurcation between normal and abnormal development— a regressive dissociation of parts that have become assembled in a faulty way. At this point, the growth of a paralysed affectivity, previously enslaved and rigidly controlled, may be resumed, and the edifice reconstructed. Cases who regress from depression have a better prognosis ("schizo-affective").

- Under the sway of persecutory anxiety and fear of catastrophic dissolution of the ego (the primitive anxieties of the paranoid–schizoid position), he splits intensely and repeatedly to get rid of bad parts of the self (and sometimes good parts of the self), and this leads to fragmentation of object and ego, and re-introjection and re-projection leads to the formation of "bizarre" objects.

- He thinks in terms of an "inside" and an "outside", and of invading the object and being invaded by others (or by the object).

- Claustro-agoraphobic panic is an ever-present threat. He cannot acquire a stable ego, because of the intensity of his invasive-projective impulses, which distort the object, rendering it dangerous, collapsed, or invasive.

- These processes occur in the early ego, and splitting is used—both in the ego and in mental representation of the object—to disperse the concentration of the destructive tendencies that threaten both the object and the subject with invasion and annihilation.

- These mental mechanisms and processes have been relegated to a minor role in the healthy adult's mental economy, but in those predisposed to schizoid and psychotic developments they have not. Because they leave a predisposition, they are often revived under later stress, which leads to schizoid or schizophrenic manifestations.

- The ultimate origin of the destructive feelings are seen (in Kleinian theory) as the operation of the death instinct. Young children and infants have a constant struggle between the urges to destroy and to preserve valued objects (originally, the providing mother or primary caring figure). This destructiveness proceeds from the operation of the death instinct from within, creating anxiety and the fear of annihilation and mobilizing early defences against these anxieties (idealization, splitting, projective identification), leading to a loss of the awareness of boundary between self and object ("fusion", "merging").

- In order to gain access to the deeper layers of the mind, we must analyse the negative transference—where Klein discovered envy (as a manifestation of the death instinct), which has been split off from conscious awareness, early in life, and thus has become obstructive to development and otherwise difficult of access in analysis.

- In exploring schizoid thinking and schizoid language, we are attempting to understand the deep and primitive structures in the personality, and progress in the treatment and understanding of the more severe mental disturbances allows for theoretical developments in the understanding of less severe disorders.

- The experiential world of the psychotic is characterized by a structuration of "space", conceived of as having actual concrete boundaries, and the maternal space may be symbolized by rooms, etc. The aim of treatment is to help the psychotic to expand his limited space and give up living inside his objects by projective identification in a parasitic way, and to cease to treat all his objects as fragile, malevolent, or persecutory.

- The fear of separation from the object, and the desire to fuse with it into a primal unity, is intense. The difficulty that the schizoid has in acquiring a stable ego is the result of faulty introjection created by the persecutory objects, themselves resulting from the invasive projection of greedy, insatiable, envious, and destructive impulses of the subject.

- In inner reality, the schizoid is neither hetero- nor homosexual, because his identifications depend on internal objects that are not properly differentiated or assimilated and on the fact of living inside a containing object.

- The schizoid functions at the level of space-centred thinking, as in dreams, and moves only slowly and distrustfully from the inanimate towards more human relationships. During the process, he may become aware of the envy that leads him to attack all that the object does for him, rendering it lifeless and useless.

- Psychosis represents the loss of the ability to test reality, including the intrusion of a new reality, as a consequence of the psychotic process. This leads to an impairment of ego-functions, which in normal development permit a clear distinction to be made between self and object. This is a dynamic mobile process sometimes active for brief periods in the borderline personality.

- The *borderline* has a distorted or impaired relation to his external objects but maintains contact with them, whereas the psychotic suspends, or abandons, relations to external objects comparable to that which happens normally in the state of sleep.

- In the case of schizophrenic manifestations, we may be seeing the outcome of an attempt to banish the dread of destructive impulses (envy, hatred), mobilized by the original threat of separation (before the depressive position). These attacks are originally directed against the mother's breast and body. In normal development, these defensive mechanisms of infancy are outgrown or are relegated to a minor position in adult life.

- When the schizoid becomes schizophrenic, he has abandoned external reality and his only reality is that of the inner fantasy world.

- By contrast, the manic-depressive has either to identify with or submit to the demands of his megalomanic ego-ideal (of varying degrees of archaic sadism) or to identify with it. Thus, this is a disorder of a higher level of integration, particularly in the sense that evidence of reparative wishes tend to be clearly discernible.

A general appreciation of Rey's work has been made by Steiner (1995), and the relevance of his thinking to psychoanalytic work with autistic children is discussed by Rhode (1995).

Infancy research and the "right mind"

Although Klein's "maternalization" of psychopathology at first drew criticism, its importance is now widely recognized, and contemporary research findings are throwing increasing light on the significance of the preverbal mother–baby relationship for the development of mental health and ill-health. The findings of workers with cognitive, psychoanalytic, neurobiological, and evolutionary perspectives are opening up this "last continent to be explored" (Bowlby, 1988). (Holmes, 1996, has provided an outline of Bowlby's "attachment theory" and refers to the work of Ainsworth, Main, Fonagy, and other contemporary workers in the field.)

The recognition of the high incidence of postnatal depression and its frequent pathogenic aftermath (Lucas, 1994; Zachary, 1985), and the impairment of the process of "primary maternal preoccupation" (Winnicott) or "maternal reverie" (Bion) that may result, all draw attention to the importance of the perinatal period for subsequent mental health.

A new focus on the management of affect, and of the regulatory function of the right brain (Cutting, 1999), is providing evidence for the biological basis of the unconscious mind (Kaplan-Solms & Solms, 2000; Schore, 2000a, 2000b; Solms, 1995). Schore (2001), in acknowledging the central importance of the concept of projective identification, has examined it from a "psychoneurobiological" perspective, regarding it as a universal innate adaptive and defensive mechanism used in the service of establishing the relationship between the neonate and his primary care-giver. The recognition that the structural maturation of the infant's right hemisphere is directly influenced by its interactions with the primary care-giver represents a major advance in the understanding of the mind–brain relationship, and a significant rapprochement between psychoanalytic and neurobiological perspectives. Recent discoveries suggest that disturbances in the mother–baby relationship may effect neuronal development, but also that neuronal plasticity may possibly allow subsequent regrowth under the influence of psychotherapy. It is also possible that the dramatic effectiveness of antidepressants in certain severe depressive states may be associated with improvement in neuronal function (Reid & Stewart, 2001).

These contemporary developments are pursuing the belief of those analysts who have long promoted the view that a true convergence of psychoanalysis and neurobiology is both possible and necessary.

The future—winds of change

In the last few years, important collaboration has grown among psycho-analytically informed professionals devoted to developing and integrating the application of psychoanalytic and other psychological methods of research and treatment in the psychoses and other severe mental illness (Johannsen, Larsen, McGlashan, & Vaglum, 2000; Martindale et al., 2000; McGorry, 1996).

An initiative begun several years ago in the United Kingdom, the Association for Psychoanalytic Psychotherapy in the Public Health Sector (APP), has grown dramatically. It has forged links with other European groups to form the European Federation for Psychoanalytic Psychotherapy (EFPP), with an active section devoted to psychosis and a membership of 12,000 in twenty-three countries.

The International Symposium for the Psychotherapy of Schizophrenia (ISPS), founded by Benedetti and Muller in Switzerland in 1954, has become a large and growing international organization. It has recently extended its boundaries to embrace new contemporary perspectives, with a new title, The International Society for the Psychological Treatments of the Schizophrenias and Other Psychoses, while maintaining its acronym (ISPS) and its dedication to preserving its psychoanalytically based origins. Expanding from its original nucleus in Switzerland into the United States, the Scandinavian countries (TIPS), and recently Australia (EPPIC), it has taken root in the United Kingdom and promises to have increasing influence in the coming years. In these organizations, as well as in the International Psychoanalytic Association (IPA), special interest is developing in the relation of psychoanalysis to the psychotherapy of psychoses. An initiative aimed at building bridges between psychoanalysis, neuroscience, cognitive science, and psychology has recently been launched by the Anna Freud Centre, London.

I believe that the integrative initiative, which Holmes (2000) has succinctly expressed as "fitting the biopsychosocial jigsaw together", is well under way and will eventually bring about the necessary socio-political changes that will provide the resources necessary for the best treatment of psychotic patients.

Website addresses

The Anna Freud Centre	www.annafreudcentre.org
Association for Psychoanalytic Psychotherapy in the Public Health Sector	www.app-nhs.org.uk
British Psychoanalytical Society	www.psychoanalysis.org.uk
EPPIC	www.eppic.org.au
European Federation for Psychoanalytic Psychotherapy	www.efpp.org
International Journal of Psycho-Analysis	www.ijpa.org
The International Society for the Psychological Treatments of the Schizophrenias and Other Psychoses	www.isps.org
TIPS	www.tips.info.com

GLOSSARY

Psychoanalytic terms can be confusing to the reader who is unfamiliar with the language. This glossary (adapted from Jackson & Williams, 1994) may serve to provide a background to, and elaboration of, the terms encountered in the book. A clear exposition of Kleinian terms is to be found in Hinshelwood (1989), and more general references in Rycroft (1968a), from both of whom I have borrowed freely. Abram (1996) has provided a valuable summary of the language of Winnicott, and detailed and comprehensive psychoanalytic references are presented by Moore and Fine (1968), Laplanche and Pontalis (1973), and Sandler et al. (1992).

Biopsychosocial This term is currently used to describe an approach to the understanding and treatment of schizophrenia, an approach that attempts to take into account all factors that may be contributing to the illness. As such, it represents a very positive development in psychiatry. However, as Robbins (1993, p. 31), has pointed out, the model was introduced by a psychoanalyst (Engel, 1962), in a context of liaison psychiatry, not schizophrenia. The term is vulnerable to being used to promote a view of schizophrenia as an organic disease, albeit one with psychological ramifications to the personality. As such, it is prone to ignore early environmental contributory factors in the mother–infant relationship and unconscious mental processes in general.

Claustro-agoraphobia This term describes a state of mind that is characterized by anxiety in closed spaces, often associated with similar anxiety in open spaces. It may sometimes be explained, following Klein, as the consequence of excessive projective identification, an unconscious phantasy of *intruding*, or *penetrating*, or *living inside* the object (the first being the mother's body), or of being threatened by separation anxiety of various forms when *leaving* or *being expelled* from the object. Some have considered such a dichotomous experience as having its pre-symbolic origins in the experience of birth

321

(Rey, 1994, p. 25). The anxiety can range in intensity from terror to the slight unease that can be felt in such situations by the normal person. When successfully transformed in the course of development, it may play a part in determining particular features of character and life-style, not necessarily pathological. Balint (1959) has written in an interesting fashion about how such anxieties can sometimes be effec-tively sublimated, often in highly successful activities, which could be called *agoraphilic*, as with acrobats and solitary long-distance ocean sailors ("philobats"), or *claustrophilic*, such as cave explorers ("ocno-philes"). Claustro-agoraphilic symptoms are commonly found in se-vere form in psychotic and borderline conditions.

Combined parent figure   The classical concepts of the oedipal triangle and the "primal scene" centred on the child's feelings of exclusion from the intimate (sexual) relationship of his parents. Klein explored the early, "pre-oedipal" origins of this combined parental couple and conceived of a more primitive scene, chronologically earlier in origin than the oedipal one, a universal phantasy in which the parents are locked together in a permanent gratifying physical union, from which the infant is excluded. His violent wishes to intrude create a dangerous, and even terrifying, situation in his mind arising from his phantasies of retaliation by the couple. In the most primitive form, the combination is felt as the mother with the father (represented by his penis) inside her.

Since the mother's body is unconsciously conceived by the infant as the container of all things desirable (good) and undesirable (bad), various phantasies concerning different contained ("inside") "part-objects" can follow. Illustrations of such phantastic scenes as "babies-inside-mother" or "father's penis inside mother" are to be found in the patients reported in this book. Growth of the personality and development of sexual and intellectual creativity depends on the degree of success that the individual has in transcending these primi-tive concepts and in reconstructing them into more "whole-object" and realistic terms. It is such considerations that lead some analysts to the reflection that one of the best outcomes of psychoanalysis is the capacity to allow the parents (internal and external) to be happily alone together.

Concrete and symbolic thinking   Psychotic thinking tends to show a literal quality and a lack of comprehension of metaphoric and sym-bolic expressions. The psychotic experience is to a varying extent a world of *signs*, indicating events felt to be happening in the immedi-ate present. Such thinking follows the laws of *primary process*, as characterizes dream life. Many explanations have been advanced to account for this concreteness, which often appears to be the consequence of an impairment or diminished use of the capacity to classify items according to their similarities. For example, a thing that *resembles* another thing in only one respect may be treated as if it were *identical* with the other (Arieti, 1974). Concrete thinking can be partly understood as the revival of the "sensorimotor" mode of thinking held to be characteristic of infancy, which in the course of normal development is succeeded by more abstract and sophisticated forms of thinking (Piaget, 1948). In this view, the future psychotic has suffered a failure of this normal developmental process and remains vulnerable to its revival, with the loss of the weakly established capacity for recognition of metaphoric and symbolic expressions. Freud described this regressive process as the original "thing-presentations" of an immature level of development replacing the higher level of organization of mental representations, "word-presentations". As he demonstrated, much highly valued witticisms depend on the exploitation of concrete thinking, often with hidden sexual and aggressive reference. Segal (1981c) has proposed a Kleinian view of the nature of concrete thinking [see "symbols" (symbolic equation)].

Containment   This term is often used loosely, and it is therefore important to be clear about what is being referred to, about whom, and in what context. In psychiatric usage, it signifies actions necessary to protect the acutely disturbed patient from harm to himself or others, usually involving admission to a suitable secure structure, typically a psychiatric hospital ward, where he will find people who will try to "contain" him. At best, this involves controlling his aggressive or self-destructive behaviour, reassuring him as far as possible by words and behaviour, and talking with him in order to understand what he is experiencing, and, if these anxiety-alleviating measures prove insufficient, administering appropriate tranquillizing medication. When the acute disturbance subsides, a further level of containment then becomes possible, facilitated by an understanding, withstanding, accepting, and enquiring attitude, whether or not the patient is engaged in individual psychotherapy. This response to psychotic disturbance is part of good clinical psychiatric practice.

In a psychoanalytic sense, the word "containment" may also be used to refer to the process whereby the therapist may at times detect that the patient is unconsciously attempting to recruit him into acting a role in his inner drama. This use of the term "containment" refers to the psychotherapeutic skill of being able to accept and emotionally and cognitively digest (*"metabolize"*) the patient's projections, in the

service of understanding him. Elucidation of the drama being unconsciously enacted by the patient in the therapeutic relationship can
help the psychotherapist to recognize, *withstand*, and tolerate the
impact of the process (in the *countertransference*). He may thereby
eventually come to *understand* sufficiently to help the patient to *work
through* and ultimately find better ways of managing the (usually
unconscious) inner impulses and desires that he is experiencing and
sometimes communicating by means of projection. These wishes,
emotions, and associated impulses have never been properly acknowledged or integrated into the patient's sense of self but, instead,
have been organized defensively into an aspect of his personality and
been subject to a form of *repetition-compulsion* throughout much of his
life.

Nursing staff can play an important part in this interpersonal
process, and it requires them to differentiate between *regressive* behaviour that is undesirable from that which represents material the
patient is unwittingly bringing to the specialists to be helped
(Jackson, 1991). The concept of containment in this sense of a potentially growth-promoting process has been elaborated in great detail
by Bion (1967) in his "container–contained" theory.

Countertransference   This term refers, in a general way, to all the feelings aroused in the therapist by his relationship with the patient. In a
more restricted way it refers to feelings aroused by the patient's
projective processes, which he uses unconsciously as a form of defence, or perhaps communication (Bion, 1967). Detecting, attending
to, and monitoring transference and countertransference responses is
a central feature of the therapist's work (Lottermann, 1996; Racker,
1953). [See also "transference".]

Delusion   In psychiatric usage, a delusion is a false but fixed belief that
is impermeable to reason and logic. Grandiose, persecutory, and
erotic delusions are characteristic of schizophrenic, paranoid and
manic psychoses, and delusions of unworthiness of psychotic depression. Psychoanalytic theory pays particular attention to grandiose
and wishful delusions, which often take the form of a psychotic
identification with an idealized powerful ("phallic") figure, as in the
common "Messianic" delusion, unconsciously contrived to avoid
the painful experience of powerlessness, loss, or helplessness or of the
feelings aroused by *separation*. Persecutory delusions, occasionally
containing a kernel of objective truth, may represent retaliatory consequences in the mind for destructive envious and acquisitive wishes.
Delusions may appear in the psychotherapeutic transference and,
depending on the circumstances and the skill of the therapist, may

bring psychotherapy to a halt or, if sufficiently well understood and managed, may provide a unique learning experience for therapist and patient. Delusions have important meaning, an important informative content, and a hidden emotional charge (Hingley, 1997; Roberts, 1992).

Dependency   It is important to differentiate between dependency developing in a psychotherapeutic transference (which leads to integration and growth of the personality and eventually to a more mature state of autonomy and "interdependence") and states of passivity or parasitism, which lead to impasse or worse.

Depressive position   [see "paranoid–schizoid and depressive positions"].

Envy   The envious wish to own the possessions or the good fortune that the object is seen or believed to have, and that the subject does not have, may generate admiration and a desire to emulate and acquire through personal effort. This constructive, life-affirming impulse represents the positive face of envy. In the case of destructive envy, sometimes referred to as primary or infantile envy, there exists a wish to deprive the object of his possession or to spoil it by devaluation or other hostile means. Klein regarded envy as an innate element in mental life, first directed at the mother's feeding breast and at the creativity this represents, and she considered it to be a basic pathogenic factor in all mental illness, in particular at the core of schizophrenic psychopathology.

In contrast to *jealousy*, which involves three parties, envy reflects a two-party situation. The envied object is hated, not because it is felt to be bad, but because it is perceived as being good, and this fact carries profound implications for mental life, in particular in states of confusion between the feelings of love and hate (Rosenfeld, 1987).

Primary (infantile) envy, according to Klein, leads to the creation of unconscious phantasies of invading and colonizing the inside of the mother's body and of appropriating or destroying its contents, commonly (as exemplified in several earlier chapters) rival babies. Normal mental mechanisms—primarily splitting, projection, and introjection—permit development to proceed in infancy into the *depressive position*, where the emergence of feelings of love, trust, and gratitude can overcome envious hatred. The combination of envy with *greed* (an excessively demanding attitude that may be difficult to distinguish from *need*) can have particularly harmful consequences for mental health. An individual may be rendered vulnerable to psychosis in later life by the varying degrees of failure and distortion of these normal developmental steps. The role of envy in predisposing to the development of psychosis has not been completely accepted by all psychoanalysts. For a clear exposition of sources of evidence in favour of the concepts of innate destructiveness, of envy, and of the theory of the "death instinct", and for an examination of the disagreements of other psychoanalytic theorists, see Hinshelwood (1989). Joseph (1986) has given a vivid description of how envy finds expression in everyday life, ranging from deeply destructive forms, conscious and unconscious, to the normal manifestations that may promote admiration and constructive emulation.

Fantasy   The term "fantasy" is used in various ways. Rycroft (1968a) has clarified the relation of this term to imagination and illusion by defining the several connotations of the term "fantasy" as being:

- a general mental activity
- a particular neurotic form of this activity
- a state of mind arising from it, and
- the fictive realm in which it occurs.

(The term "phantasy" [q.v.], spelt "ph", is used by Kleinians and has a connotation very different from, albeit related to, "fantasy".)

Hallucination   In fever, toxic delirium, drug intoxication and other organic states, and in states of sensory deprivation, things may be perceived that are not actually present. These pathological perceptions are more commonly visual and tactile than auditory. In psychotic states where the reality-testing ego function is weakened, hallucinations are a common feature. These, in contrast to those accompanying organic states, are commonly auditory. Visual hallucinations are uncommon in schizophrenia but are not uncommon in hysterical states. Because both auditory and visual hallucinations are not necessarily pathological, psychologists tend to prefer the terms "voices" and "visions". Visions are a common and usually normal phenomenon in the course of mourning (hallucinating the appearance of the lost person), in the experience of individuals reporting the seeing of ghosts, and of non-psychotic mystics. The "creative imagination" of exceptionally gifted visionaries and poets, such as William Blake and William Wordsworth, is currently attracting the attention of psychoanalysts interested in the creative process (Britton, 1998; Segal, 1991; Williams & Waddell, 1991).

Identity   One of the characteristics of maturity is the possession of a strong sense of identity, the stable conviction of being an individual distinguishable from all others, and an enduring sense of existing intactly in space and over time. Psychoanalytic theory holds that a sense of identity has its origins in infancy, where early mental development develops on the basis of processes of *imitation* and *identification* (Gaddini, 1992), together forming a process of unconscious learning that gives structure to the inner world and gradually evolves in the course of normal development into the capacity for mature object relationships.

Identification Contrary to the popular sense of this term as a process of recognition of others, identification refers to a mental process whereby the subject comes to feel himself to be the same as or identical with another person in one or more aspects. Identification may be a highly complex process and may take different forms, and the term is used in different senses. The subject can achieve this identification by either extending his identity *into* someone else (projection), borrowing his identity *from* someone else (introjection) or fusing or confusing his identity *with* someone else, at times believing similarity to mean equivalence (Rycroft, 1968a). *Projective identification* refers to an unconscious belief that a part of the self or inner world, usually unwanted, can be disposed of by relocation into the mental representation of another object. This is usually regarded as a primitive form of the mental mechanism of *projection*, often involving behaviour by the subject towards the object in a way that will allow him to confirm his omnipotent suppositions. The projectively identifying mechanism can be used for purposes of denial (of disposing of unwanted thoughts and feelings), of controlling others, or of interpersonal communication. In the last case, the therapist needs to attend to his own non-rational responses to the patient's communications, his *countertransference*, which will constitute an important source of information about the patient's state at that moment. Many psychoanalysts hold that projective identification is a primary form of communication between mother and baby (Bion, 1967), characterized by the *attunement* of normal mothers to their baby which is described by workers in infant observation research (Stern, 1985). Rey (1994) uses the term *"double identification"* to explain a psychotic process, sometimes seen in severe anorexia nervosa, whereby the patient feels herself (and sometimes *himself*) to be a pregnant mother and at the same time to be (identified with) the baby she imagines that she contains inside her body (see Chapter 6).

Imagination In the sense of the unconscious manufacture of concepts or of images in the absence of considerations of reality, imagination needs to be differentiated from hallucination, day-dream, vision, illusion, self-deception and lying (Barnes-Gutteridge, 1993; Britton, 1998; Rycroft, 1968b). This may not be easy in any particular case [see "phantasy"; "hallucination"].

Introjection   Introjection is a process of taking something into the mind (internalizing), which can sometimes be felt as a bodily event (incorporating). Such elements may then be integrated, temporarily or permanently, into the ego and felt as being part of the self, thus completing the process of *introjective identification*. Since projective identification depletes the self and distorts perceptions of the object, what is introjected may also be a more or less distorted version of the actual object.

Differentiation of what belongs to the subject and what to the object is held to be a fundamental process of infant mental development and is often a major sorting-out process in psychotherapy. Introjective identification is the basis of much normal learning, and normal projective identification underlies a mature capacity for *empathy* (the ability to imagine oneself in another person's place without losing awareness of one's identity). By contrast, *pathological* projective identification is conducted with omnipotence and violence (Bion, 1967) leading to a confusion of self and object and susceptibility to psychotic developments.

Insight   This complex concept has several referents. In everyday usage, it refers to self-knowledge or self-awareness. In psychiatry, it refers to the capacity to recognize that disturbing thoughts and feelings are subjective and can be tested against reality, a capacity that is more or less absent in the psychotic. In psychiatric practice, the assessment of insight is of central importance (Berrios & Markova, 1992; David, 1990; Perkins & Moodley, 1993). Insight can be considered as a continuum, with different mechanisms responsible for impairment in individual patients. In psychoanalytic usage, a distinction is made between emotional and intellectual insight. The latter can be used for constructive purposes or for defence (*pseudo-insight*). The term "insight" is also used to describe a psychotic patient's capacity—or often the lack of it—to realize that he is seriously ill. In practice, many patients who might seem suitable for psychotherapy may prove inaccessible for reasons of a deficiency of such insight. Such patients may never achieve this insight, or it may require a considerable deterioration in their condition before they can begin to accept the seriousness of their condition.

Interpretation   In the simplest sense, this means an explanation that the therapist gives to the patient of something that the patient has not

understood and seems ready to learn. In practice, it is usually preceded by the painstaking exploration of meaning from the material
that the patient brings into the therapy in the form of associations, of
symptoms, of dreams, or of *transference* phenomena. Interpretations
may address the transference, the elements of defence, or the content
of thoughts or may take the form of direct statements regarding the
meaning of symbols, given independently of the patient's associations. The latter activity is susceptible to misuse in unskilled hands.

Jealousy   In contrast to envy, jealousy involves three parties, and it
is the third who, feeling excluded, suffers the emotion of jealousy.
Jealousy is related to possessiveness of the other; envy is related to
comparison of the self with what the other has or is felt to be. Jealousy
characteristically has its childhood origins in the oedipal triangle
(father, mother, child) and forms part of the Oedipus complex. Jealousy may sometimes be difficult to distinguish from envy (Shake-
speare's "green-eyed monster"), and, when intense, both emotions
and the behaviour they may arouse may have highly destructive
consequences. The jealousy accompanying sibling rivalry is often
underestimated as an important pathogenic factor in some types of
mental illness (Mitchell, 2000; Volkan, 1997); several examples of this
process appear in this book.

Manic defences   Klein described a series of defensive mental operations
aimed at escaping the pain of the depressive position. These are
mediated by omnipotent thinking and belief in personal omniscience.
They comprise denial of psychic reality and devaluation of the importance of the object, associated with an attitude of contempt and
triumph. These are central characteristics of the pathological excitement and pathological sense of well-being of manic states.

Meaning   This semantically dense term has many complex referents,
such as significance, purpose, and explanation (Taylor, 1991). As
used in this book, it implies a recognition that the behaviour and
experience of a psychotic patient, however incomprehensible or bizarre, can be understood and "make sense" for the therapist if it is seen
as arising from the patient's personal history, his inner life, his conflicts, and his unconscious defence mechanisms.

The psychotic patient, for whom experience is likely to have
the quality of inexplicable *happenings* occurring in the immediate
present, is driven to search for meanings, which he finds in the form
of delusional explanations. The processes whereby the normal mind
generates meanings, conscious and unconscious, through the use of
symbolic expressions are complex and incompletely understood.

Mourning   In its normal form, mourning is a response to the loss of a loved object, following bereavement, accompanied by grief and pursuing a course that ultimately leads to recovery and a renewed interest in life. This healing process may be arrested or distorted in many ways, and since the time of Freud's classic work "Mourning and Melancholia" (1917e [1915]) the subject of unresolved or pathological mourning has received much attention by psychiatrists and psychoanalysts (Bowlby, 1980, 1988; Klein, 1940; Parkes, 1975; Pedder, 1982). Freud was the first to consider melancholia (psychotic depression) as a pathological form of mourning, and Klein extended the term to embrace losses in the inner world of object relations, losses that may be independent of external reality. The capacity to mourn in a healthy manner is an maturational achievement of the depressive position.

Object   In psychoanalytic usage, an *object* is usually a person or part of a person, or a symbol representing the whole or part-person, to which the *subject* relates in order to achieve instinctual satisfaction. In *object-relation theory*, priority is given to the individual's need for persons rather than simply for the satisfaction of instincts. Melanie Klein was a major contributor to object-relation theory, but her work can be distinguished from that of Fairbairn (1952), Guntrip (1961), and Winnicott (1958), who did not accept the concept of an innate destructive drive ("death instinct") and are generally regarded as the fathers of contemporary object-relation theory. Development of object-relation theory led to the conceptualization of *internal objects* and relationships in the inner world of *psychic reality*. These internal "mental" objects are dynamic structures that are in constant interplay with *external objects* in the "real" (external) world and contribute to the basic structures of the personality (Bateman & Holmes, 1995; Grotstein, 2000; Perlow, 1997; D. Taylor, 1991). At the beginning (in the paranoid–schizoid position), objects are perceived in a dichotomous fashion as "good" (gratifying, providing) or "bad" (frustrating, withholding), a dichotomy resolved at the developmental level of the depressive position.

Omnipotent thinking   Omnipotent thinking may serve several purposes in the mental economy, and thus may have more than one meaning. A person who, for instance, believes she can set off an atom bomb (Claudia, Chapter 5) clearly feels herself to be very important, however terrifying may be the implications for her, and such a claim constitutes a powerful defence against feelings of smallness and helplessness. The more unbearable are such feelings, the more omnipotent the delusional beliefs need to be.

Paranoid–schizoid and depressive positions   Klein asserted that the normal infant has, by the age of 3 to 6 months, reached sufficient mental maturity to be able to integrate the previously split and opposing versions of his mother ("good" and "bad"). Before this, his feelings of love and hatred are dealt with by primitive defence mechanisms, principally splitting and projective–introjective procedures. This early stage is the *paranoid–schizoid* position and the later one the *depressive* position. The latter can be regarded as a maturational achievement, the "stage of concern" (Winnicott, 1958). The first stage is accompanied by persecutory guilt, where concern is for the survival of the self, the second by depressive guilt, where concern is for the object. This guilt is a "specific sort of pain that one bears over time in response to real or imagined harm that one has done to someone for whom one cares" (Ogden, 1989, p. 72). Attainment of the capacity for depressive anxiety is considered a necessary quality for the forming or maintaining of mature object relationships, since it is the source of generosity, altruistic feelings, reparative wishes, and the capacity to tolerate the object's ultimate separateness. It is not a once-and-for-all achievement in which the paranoid–schizoid mode is left behind but, rather, a dialectic (or synchronic) relationship between different levels of integration, continuing throughout life. Increasing maturity brings a growing capacity to function at the level of the depressive position. Such growth does not bring an idealized freedom from unhappiness but, rather, brings new and different burdens, albeit of a human sort, and a potential for freedom to make responsible choices. It is not the resolution of a dilemma. "Thus , for better or for worse, one develops a feeling of responsibility for one's psychological actions (thoughts, feelings, and behaviour)" (Ogden, 1989, p. 71).

Phantasy   The term "phantasy" was originally used by Freud, and Klein extended it to introduce her new concepts. *Unconscious phantasy* is a theoretical model, referring to inferences employed to explain the nature of certain sorts of mental events, rational and irrational. In Kleinian theory, unconscious phantasy is regarded as the permanent substrate of mental life from the beginning and is the expression of innate libidinal and destructive instincts that are held to accompany and to drive all mental processes. Their reality is inferred from the evidence of dreams, the play of young children, and the symptoms of neurotic and psychotic individuals. An unconscious phantasy can be regarded as a state of activity of one or more internal object relations, a very different concept from that of *fantasy*.

As the basic building-blocks of the mind, unconscious phantasies accompany all experiences of reality and find expression through the construction and use of symbols by the ego. In the course of development, unconscious phantasy is first experienced in the form of bodily sensations, next as images ("preverbal ideographs"), and dramatic expressions, and finally as verbal thought and speech (Hinshelwood, 1989).

The "ph" spelling, "phantasy" can cause confusion with the many processes conventionally described as conscious or unconscious "fantasy", in the sense of imaginative activity. "Phantasy" has finally become something of a Kleinian trademark and is now found most consistently in the writings of Kleinian authors. The topic has been examined in detail by Britton (1998).

Precipitation   In cases of gradual onset of psychosis, there may be no obvious precipitating cause, and a gradual decompensation of mental defence mechanisms in the face of the developmental demands of normal life may prove to be a satisfactory explanation. Where the onset is more acute, an immediate precipitating factor may be found in an inability to cope with a specific life stress, often in the external world, and involving disappointment, frustration, object loss, or separation (Räkköläinen, 1977). Arousal of guilt and anxiety over envious, sexual, or acquisitive wishes may operate at an unconscious level as precipitating factors, sometimes leading to the formation of persecutory delusions of anticipated reprisal or punishment. Such anxieties tend to be so severe and threatening to a sense of coherent self that they have been variously termed *traumatic anxiety*, *organismic panic*, and *ontological anxiety* to indicate their overwhelming nature.

An external traumatic experience may sometimes precipitate a psychosis in a person already predisposed by his inner reality, in which case his experience of the trauma is very different from that of the normal victim (Garland, 1998). In some cases where there seems to have been no obvious premonitory symptoms, investigation may reveal "prodromal" disturbances of various types. One such disturbance consists in compulsive masturbation, which, as Freeman (1988) has pointed out, may have the purpose of reassuring the individual whose sense of his own gender, as male or female, is under threat, creating anxiety and confusion.

Predisposition   Biologically oriented psychiatry maintains that a main factor predisposing to schizophrenic, manic-depressive, and some other psychoses is the presence of innately determined disorders of brain function. Attention deficit as the neurological substrate of schizophrenia is believed to lead to disturbances of integration and differentiation. Psychoanalytic thinking, while accepting the contribution of biological factors to vulnerability, approaches the question of predisposition in terms of failure of adequate formation of primi tive object relations in infancy. This failure may lead to the persistence of immature mental defence mechanisms protecting the fragile core of the personality. This *defence* view contrasts to some extent with a *deficit* view held by some psychoanalytic theorists who question the Kleinian emphasis on the role of conflict in early infancy in the genesis of schizophrenia.

Prognosis   The best prognostic outlook is for the adolescent or young adult with little or no sign of previous disturbance, breaking down acutely under major stress within a mentally healthy family. A preceding period of depression may be a favourable feature. About one-third of acutely psychotic patients recover in a matter of weeks or months with or without specific treatment and experience no further attack. A similar proportion have recurrent attacks which may lead to chronicity. These first two groups are regarded by experienced psychotherapists as being likely to be suitable subjects for psychotherapy, with or without anti-psychotic medication. A further, more chronically suffering group is generally held to be unlikely to respond to a psychotherapeutic approach and is best helped with medication, cognitive and behavioural methods of treatment, and long-term rehabilitation and support in the activities of daily life. However, even such chronic patients may sometimes respond to psychotherapy in skilled hands. Even with the most refractory and chronic patients, it has been shown that the long-term outcome is better than had traditionally been thought. The degree of preservation of the sane (non-psychotic) part of the self, the possibility of early skilled treatment, and what Alanen has called the preservation of "the grip on life" are major prognostic indicators.

Psychodynamic   Although several theoretical and clinical approaches deal with the dynamics of psychological forces, the term "psychodynamic" is commonly used to define the approach founded on basic psychoanalytic concepts of unconscious mental life, conflict and defence, internal reality, transference/countertransference, repetition-compulsion, and working through in the therapeutic process. The same defining criteria apply to the designation of *psychoanalytic psychotherapy*.

Psychoneurosis   Psychoneurosis is usually differentiated from psychosis on the basis of the intactness of the sense of reality in the former. In Kleinian psychoanalytic theory, neurotic disorders represent the

belated expression of psychotic processes of various degrees that
have not been successfully negotiated in early life.

Psychosis, psychotic   The term "psychosis" refers to a broad category of
mental disorders that are characterized by severe abnormalities of
thought processes. These are associated with disturbance of the sense
of reality and often with delusions, hallucinations, and disruption of
the sense of personal identity. Psychotic elements may occur in severe
neuroses, psychosomatic disorders (Jackson, 1977; Sperling, 1955; G.
Taylor, 1987), sexual perversions and "borderline" personality disorders. Psychoses may be *organic*, if caused by demonstrable organic
disease, or *functional* if no organic pathology can be found. Functional
psychoses are regarded by some as purely *psychogenic*, requiring only
psychological understanding and treatment. At the other extreme,
some hold to the view that most psychoses are essentially *biogenic*. A
more integrated approach allows for the possibility that both elements may make a contribution in any given case. The widely used
"stress-vulnerability" model attempts to embrace both factors, but it
tends not to give weight to disturbance of emotional development in
infancy or childhood as a contribution to vulnerability to later psychotic breakdown. Nor are unconscious factors in internal reality
always considered in that model, factors that play a central part in the
stress that precipitates a psychotic disorder and help to determine
why one person becomes psychotic in the face of external stress and
another does not.

The concept of *psychotic and non-psychotic parts of the personality* in
the one individual, introduced by Bion, has provided a new perspective to the understanding of psychosis and an emphasis in psychotherapy on making contact with the *sane part* of the personality
presumed to be present in every psychotic patient. An example can
sometimes be found when the patient uses splitting and projective
identification to expel his sane capacity for doubting into another
person and then tries to force the other person to abandon his sense of
reality and agree with his delusional views. A comparable process
can work in the opposite direction, when parents and others unconsciously project their own psychotic elements into the (present or
future) patient. This "effort to drive the other person crazy" (Searles,
1965b) may follow different dynamic pathways, ranging from fully
conscious malevolence ("gaslighting"), to the delivery of uninten-
tional confusing messages ("double-bind").

The term "psychotic organization" (as developed by Steiner, 1993,
following Rosenfeld and Bion), refers to an anti-emotional/anti-
thought system in the mind, developed from a background of early
trauma and deprivation, a system that is dedicated to destroying any

thinking that might revive past mental pain. In this view, psychosis may be regarded as partly the consequence of the activity of a mental strategy directed to annihilation of any sensitive part of the self that might be capable of thinking reflectively, and of loving and caring, and as such is a destructive way of dealing with mental pain.

Psychotic anxiety refers to a dread, at the worst amounting to terror, often described as intolerable confusion, dissolution of the sense of self, or fear of disintegrating and falling to pieces or of ceasing to exist. Lesser manifestations are encountered in non-psychotic individuals who are dominated at some point by the activity of a psychotic part of the self. Klein believed that the overwhelming emotional storms of infants have features resembling, but not equivalent to, the worst experiences of psychotic adults.

Psychotic defences are immature or "primitive" mental mechanisms—primarily denial, splitting, and projection—which are mobilized to avoid such anxiety and are regarded as pathological when they are implemented prematurely and violently. Primitive mental processes are not psychotic, but are normal stages in development of the ego and the mind, but they can become *psychotogenic* under certain circumstances (biological and environmental) unfavourable to normal development. Under such circumstances, these *paranoid-schizoid* (or "psychotic") elements act as contributory factors to a predisposition to psychotic illness at a later date—usually in adolescence or early adulthood, but not uncommonly in childhood (Rustin et al., 1997).

Reality   The terms *"internal (inner) reality"* and *"external (outer) reality"*, and the capacity for *"reality-testing"* are part of the everyday language of psychoanalysis. The term *"inner world"* is sometimes used in the sense of preconscious mental processes within the subject's grasp, and as such is not the same as *"psychic reality"*, which refers to unconscious processes that are organized in the form of phantasies about object relationships. However, convenience dictates that they are often used synonymously. It is important to recognize that a patient's account of his present and past life, and in particular of the behaviour of other people towards him, should not be taken as (external) reality until sufficient evidence has accumulated. A facile and premature "jumping to conclusions", such as the blaming of parents, disregards the possible distortions produced by the patient's projections. These may find expression in the psychotherapeutic transference and help the therapist decide when a patient's reproaches directed towards parents seem justified and where they are not. The same applies to the patient's account of his early life, and it is such considerations that has led psychoanalysts to differentiate between literal and psychic reality, between subjective *"narrative"* truth and objective *"historical"* truth, and between internal and external objects and object relationships. The task of differentiation may be very difficult or even—as is sometimes the case of recovered memories of childhood sexual abuse—impossible. To opt prematurely for either side can lead to serious social and therapeutic consequences, an error incorrectly attributed to Freud.

Regression   In the face of psychological stress, the individual may revert to an earlier and less mature level of functioning. This regression can be understood as a defensive retreat to infantile stages of development, stages that are never completely outgrown and may at times have the constructive potential of a withdrawal to a safe base where mental forces can be regrouped. Regression occurring in the course of psychotherapy can have beneficial consequences (see Winnicott's concept of *"false self"*, 1960), or a bad one, *"malignant regression"*, an outcome depending on the maturity of the patient and the skill of the therapist. The contemporary belief that long periods of hospitalization accompanied by psychotherapy will inevitably cause dangerous regressions in otherwise well-functioning individuals has been firmly challenged by Robbins (1993, pp. 273ff.)

Opinion is divided on the wisdom of encouraging therapeutic regression in patients with personality disorders. In psychotic patients, the use of regression as a deliberate technique is generally considered as at the very least unwise, and at the worst dangerous, except perhaps in the hands of specially experienced practitioners. The psychotic patient is usually quite regressed enough, at least in the acute stage, and the problem is usually that of containing the regression within the institution and the therapy, and searching to understand its causes and meanings. Evidence is accumulating for the view that regression in an acute psychotic attack can be substantially alleviated by family therapy meetings on first contact (Lehtinen, 1994).

In Kleinian thinking, psychotic regression activates long-established pathological structures and modes of functioning. Grotstein (1981, p. 405) has pointed out an inconsistency in the psychoanalytic uses of the term. When we use the term "regression", he observes, we really mean *progression* of primitive processes to the surface, rather than the other way around. It is not our perceptual apparatus, nor our mental structures, that regress.

Reparation   Melanie Klein's views on the ubiquity of destructive phantasies and desires in early life have sometimes been received with scepticism by those who have not recognized or accepted the central position accorded in her theories to the power of protective and reparative feelings accompanying normal development. In her analytic work with small children, she recognized the distress and guilt that accompany destructive wishes, and she observed the growth of feelings of remorse and of desire to repair damage done in reality or phantasy to ambivalently loved figures who are the target of frustrated rage and envious and jealous hatred. Such reparative desires often take the form of obsessional activity, partly understandable as an attempt to repair, prevent, or forestall damage by magical means. In the course of psychotherapy with adults, failed attempts at reparation may often be discerned, and manic states may sometimes be found to contain similar strivings. Such *manic, or schizoid, reparation*, like other failed attempts, does not succeed, partly because the subject is unaware of the damage he believes he has done—and perhaps is still doing in external or in psychic reality—and also does not know how to go about repairing it.

The emergence of reparative feelings marks a higher level of maturity and integration, the *depressive position*, which was regarded by Klein as a moral achievement (Milton, 2000) and the mainspring of true creative processes. The application of this concept to the psychotherapy of the adult adds an optimistic note to the uncovering of hitherto unconscious, painful, facts of mental life. Reparative wishes bring the possibility of beneficent change, of putting things right when possible and of mourning when impossible, and of emotional growth. It is the task of the psychotherapist to help the patient differentiate between where his personal responsibility lies, and where it does not, and to find ways of making amends where necessary. The concept of the need to repair *internal* as well as *external* objects permits the working-through of feelings of regret, remorse, and mourning, even if the victim of the destructive attacks is long dead. The term "reparation" should be differentiated from *repair, restitution*, and *reconstruction*, which imply restoration of an original situation or, in the case of psychosis, a "patch over the ego", an attempt to restore meaning to a world of confusion and anxiety. Freud's view (1911c [1910]) that "the delusional formation, which we take to be the pathological product, is in reality an attempt at recovery, a process of reconstruction", does not refer to reparation.

Repetition-compulsion   Freud coined this term to describe what he saw as an innate tendency to revert to earlier mental conditions. This tendency bypasses the need to remember and to work through past trauma. This working-through process is in some ways analogous to mourning, insofar as attachments to emotionally charged objects and familiar behaviour patterns may need to be painfully relinquished (Freud, 1920g, 1926d [1925]).

Schizophrenia   The term "schizophrenia" was introduced to define a group of severe psychotic disorders characterized by a dissociation or splitting of the mental functions, in contrast to an earlier view of a single specific mental disease leading to dementia (dementia praecox). It has been variously considered as an illness, a syndrome, a way of living, or even a medical fiction invented to satisfy relatives, society, and psychiatrists (Szasz, 1961). It has no single agreed cause but is best considered as a syndrome or group of disorders with a range of causative factors of biogenic, sociogenic, and psychogenic origins. The term is susceptible to misuse if used simply as a label for severe or chronic symptoms in cases where considerations such as age, context, evolution, and dynamic content have not been sufficiently evaluated. The development of the detailed and complex DSM 4 classification system (the fourth edition of the *Diagnostic and Statistical Manual of the American Psychiatric Association*) has gone a long way towards refining psychiatric diagnosis: its "multi-axial" diagnostic procedure allows for diagnosis to be regularly revised in the light of changes in the clinical condition of the patient. Thus, in a case where emotional feelings are prominent, a diagnosis of *schizo-affective psychosis* is usually deemed appropriate, and unless six months of continuous illness have passed, the diagnosis *schizophreniform* should be made. Where there is a recent precipitating stress, the diagnosis *reactive psychosis* is available, and, where uncertainty remains, *psychosis n.o.s.* (unspecified) may be used.

Many clinicians consider that the term "schizophrenia" has outlived its usefulness, and they prefer to regard psychosis as a final common path of many different dynamic configurations, of which schizophrenia is the most severe and the most biologically grounded. In this sense, the generalization that *schizophrenia is essentially a brain disease* might be accepted as being appropriate for some patients. It is important to recognize that the use of such a generalization may imply that the user has the mistaken belief that biological factors inevitably put the patient beyond the reach of psychodynamic understanding and psychotherapeutic treatment modes.

The earlier notion of *"schizophrenogenic"* mother, now fully discredited, has been shown to be a gross oversimplification of subtle and complex interactions, conscious and unconscious, between parent and child.

Self   The term "self", as used in psychoanalysis, refers to the individual as an *agent*, aware of his own identity. It belongs to a different frame of reference from the term *"ego"* with which it is sometimes confused. The latter refers to a structure in the mind, parts of which are unconscious. The various adjectival forms commonly encountered, such as self-esteem, self-preservation, self-mutilation, self-observation, are usually regarded as referring to a *whole* self. However the concept of *part*-selves, which may exist in a state of identification with other (part- or whole) objects, may at times promote the question "*which* self?" or "*which* object?", particularly in the case of the psychotic person. These partial identifications may be of long standing and may have complex, condensed meanings. Rey (1994), following Piaget in regarding mental processes as having coordinates in space and time, has provided a formula to help the psychotherapist who wishes to explore the details of such a process: "*What part of the subject situated where in space and time does what, with what motivation, to what part of the object situated where in space and time, with what consequences for the subject and the object?*"

Sensorimotor thinking   In infancy thinking is initially space- and action-centred and undifferentiated from perception. Piaget (1948) called this "sensorimotor" thinking. The relation of Piaget's monumental contributions to psychotic thinking has been expounded by Rey (1994) and elaborated by Robbins (1993).

Separation   This term is widely used, in different contexts. It has roots in psychoanalysis, where Mahler et al. (1975) and others have described a universal phase of development in the second year of life ("separation–individuation") which may take a deviant and pathological course. Blos has described adolescence as a second separation–individuation phase (Blos, 1962; see also Laufer & Laufer, 1984).

Another root of the concept of separation can be found in ethology, and Bowlby has attempted to reconcile psychoanalytic and ethological models in his influential "attachment" theory (Holmes, 1996). As it is used in connection with psychosis, the term "separation" refers to the developmental demand to recognize the separateness of the mother, and to the destructive feelings that this may release. Whereas Mahler's work referred more specifically to the developmental conflicts of the toddler, the term "separation" has widely been used in an extended sense, ranging from the event of birth, the premature loss of the nipple, and the behaviour of the insecure patient during intervals between therapy sessions. "*Separateness*" refers to the usually unwelcome discovery that the needed object, originally the mother, is not under the subject's total omnipotent control and has a mind and a life of its own.

Splitting   This term is used in different senses. As a normal mental activity, it is used to describe the process of differentiation, whereby the ego strives, as part of its development, to define distinctions and differences. As a function of dissociating certain elements from consciousness, it is associated with projective identification and is a precursor of the more mature, mental mechanism of *repression*. In its pathological forms, excessive splitting and projective identification in early life may predispose to later psychosis. Splitting within the ego can create two different, coexisting, and incompatible attitudes to reality, the one more realistic, the other based on denial and omnipotent wishful thinking (Grotstein, 1986). Splitting associated with projective expulsion allows life to go on without overwhelming anxiety, but at the cost of weakening the ego, loss of potentially valuable parts of the self, and distortion of the perception of the object receiving the projection. Bion (1967, p. 69) differentiates splitting—which, when excessive leads to the "minute fragmentation" of psychosis—from dissociation. The latter, a more benign activity, characteristic of hysteria, is dependent on the pre-existence of elementary verbal thought, with a content of whole- rather than part-objects.

Structure, structural change   Freud's structural model of the mind (psychic apparatus) designated three functional groups called ego, superego, and id. The term "structure" has since been elaborated in order to include sub-structures resulting from processes of defensive splitting. These various structures can be considered as habitual and enduring patterns of internal object relations and (in Kleinian terms) their associated unconscious phantasies. They are relatively stable and tend to be subject to repetition-compulsion, in the form of pre-conceptions, expectations, perceptions, judgements, and behaviour. It is a convention of psychoanalytic thought to regard the goal of alleviation of symptoms as a limited or even dubious one, because if the structures underlying and ultimately responsible for the symptoms have not changed for the better, symptom relief is likely to be only temporary or unstable. However, this contrast to those behavioural therapies that are focused on symptom amelioration may sometimes be an oversimplification. Since symptoms, considered as maladaptive solutions of conflict, tend themselves to be habitual and enduring, they may in some cases be regarded as structures. It follows that the goal of symptom relief is not necessarily a non-psychoanalytic one (see Sandell et al., 2000).

Symbols, symbolism, symbolic equations   Whereas *signs* refer to the presence of some object, process, or condition, *symbols* refer to the idea, or concept, of such things. All mental function rests on the ability to create symbolic *representations* of the external world and to develop the capacity for abstract conceptual thinking, a capacity that is to various degrees defective in psychotic states, where the symbol is felt to be the same as the thing symbolized—"symbolic *equation*" (Segal, 1981e)—and thinking becomes more "concrete".

In some psychoanalytic theory, conventional symbols that are received from other people and are the currency of our daily life are distinguished from those that are generated unconsciously by the individual and support various mental processes, in particular the generation of emotional meanings. Received symbols become worn out and inadequate for emotional communication with self and others, leading people to resort to (sometimes antisocial) inappropriate action in the place of thought (Meltzer, 1997).

Transference   The concept of transference has evolved over a long period. First regarded by Freud as an obstacle, it has come to be accepted as an essential tool of psychoanalysis. It refers to the process of enactment whereby the patient tends to displace ideas and feelings belonging to past relationships—sometimes of very early origin ("infantile transference")—onto the therapist. In a more specific sense, it describes the re-enactment in the treatment process of unconscious phantasies and object relations going on all the time (Joseph, 1989). Different types of transferences can be described as positive, negative, split, erotic, infantile, narcissistic, or psychotic (Rosenfeld, 1987) and also delusional (Little, 1986). Transference tends to find expression in a displaced manner outside the therapy sessions ("acting-out"). "Splitting" of the transference may take the form of idealization of the therapist and hostility to others in the external world (see Dorothy, Chapter 6). The therapist has the task of deciding whether or not the material that the patient brings to the session is primarily referring to the relation with the therapist himself. Acting-out in the "total situation" of a transference (Joseph, 1985) may be difficult to detect and to manage when there is an intense idealization of the relation with the therapist and a long interval between sessions. It may be difficult to detect destructiveness when the therapist is unwittingly pursuing a course of "anything for a quiet life" and maintaining a relation of "agreeableness" (Joseph, 2000), thereby generating a "positive transference" in which negative feelings are excluded.

Borderline and psychotic patients may sometimes, for shorter or longer periods of time, fail to distinguish between the therapist as a real figure and his own phantasy objects. This "psychotic" transference may present difficulties in management, but, if managed successfully, it can be of great therapeutic benefit. [See also "counter-transference".]

Unconscious   Mental events are regarded as being unconscious when the subject is unaware of them. Some of these can be recalled to consciousness without great difficulty (*descriptively* unconscious, or *preconscious*), others, held in repression, cannot (*dynamically* unconscious). As a noun, the term refers to a functioning structure in the mind (the *system unconscious*), which constitutes the larger and hidden part of mental life and follows a logic and rules of its own. Freud called these characteristics the *primary processes* of thought (which use the mechanisms of displacement, condensation, and symbolic expression), in contrast to the rational *secondary processes* of the conscious mind, and he demonstrated how they dominate the thinking of dreams and of neurotic and psychotic symptoms. The concept of the unconscious has recently been approached from the perspective of mathematical logic, as a differentiating and classifying system (Matte-Blanco, 1998). The *collective* unconscious is a term of Jung's designed to describe the realm of archetypes (universal innate ideas), or the tendency to organize experience in innately determined patterns, a concept in some ways near to the work of Klein and of Bion. This usage has a conceptual connection with Freud's concept of a primitive unrepressed unconscious and with Klein's use of the term "unconscious phantasy".

It has recently been pointed out that the concepts of the unconscious proposed by Freud, by Klein, and by Bion are in many respects very different, an observation with considerable implications for the psychotherapy of psychosis (de Masi, 2000).

Understanding   This is a diffuse concept which can be taken at many levels, as in claims to "understand" a patient. A patient may have a gratifying feeling of being understood when he is actually being misunderstood. He may also wish to be understood, but not wish to understand. He may not possess the impulse of curiosity on which all learning depends, and if progress is to be made the therapist may first need to show the patient that he (the patient) has no interest in trying to learn why he feels as he does (Bion, 1962, p. 108; see also Taylor, 1997).

As used in psychoanalysis, "understanding" indicates a subtle process involving acts of empathy leading to a degree of recognition of the patient's inner world and personal experience. The psychotherapist's search for such understanding of a psychotic patient may place a considerable demand on him, and this is why some personal analysis and supervision can be so valuable. Understanding that is defensively intellectual can lead the worker to much understanding of the psychopathology but little of the essential emotional contact with the patient.

REFERENCES AND BIBLIOGRAPHY

Many excellent texts offer clear and accessible information about psychotic and borderline states. An authoritative account of the life and work of Melanie Klein has been presented by Segal (1979). Bateman, Brown, and Pedder (2000) give a comprehensive and up-to-date exposition of dynamic psychotherapy, and Bateman and Holmes (1995) offer a lucid introduction to contemporary psychoanalysis. Sandler, Dare, and Holder (1992) give a detailed clarification of psychoanalytic concepts. Taylor (1991) sets Kleinian contributions within a context of classical psychopathology, elaborating the varied uses of such terms as "meaning", "identification", and "knowing", and exploring the problems associated with "scientific" research in psychopathology.

Petot (1979, 1991) has produced a masterly exposition of Kleinian theory. Jackson (1991) provides clinical illustrations of the psychotherapy of psychotic patients encountered in psychiatric and psychoanalytic practice. A concise presentation for the general reader has been made by Arieti (1979). Robbins (1993) has produced a masterly presentation of different approaches to schizophrenia, and Lottermann (1996) describes an approach to psychosis psychotherapy specific to different clinical syndromes.

A useful selection of the basic works of Klein with associated commentaries can be found in Mitchell (1986), and Waddell (1999) has described the development of personality from a Kleinian perspective. Ruszczynski and Johnson (1999) and Johnson and Ruszczynski (1999) describe the work of psychoanalytical psychotherapists in the Independent and Kleinian tradition. Hingley (1997) illustrates a way in which psychodynamic psychotherapy might be combined with a cognitive-behavioural approach.

A recent overview of current work directed at integrating the many different modes of understanding and treating psychotic patients has been presented by Holmes (2000). Hinshelwood (1989, 1994; Hinshelwood, Robinson, & Zarate, 1998) has contributed outstanding expositions of Kleinian theory and practice.

344   REFERENCES AND BIBLIOGRAPHY

Further reading. Arieti (1979) provides an authoritative overview of the psychoanalytic approach to schizophrenia, and Freeman (1969, 1988) describes the psychopathology of psychosis and the role of psychoanalysis in psychiatry from an ego-psychological perspective on psychotic illness. Spillius (1988) has assembled many of the most important theoretical and clinical publications of Kleinian authors.

Familiarity with the work of pioneers of the psychoanalytic approach to psychotic states, such as Searles (1965a), Arieti (1974), Bion (1957, 1962, 1963), Boyer (1983), Freeman (1973), Frosch (1983, 1990), Grotstein (1977), Kernberg (1975), Rosenfeld (1965, 1987), and Segal (1979), is indispensable for trainees in the psychoanalytic psychotherapy of psychotic and borderline states.

Abraham, K. (1911). Notes on the psycho-analytical investigation and treatment on manic-depressive insanity and allied conditions. In: *Selected Papers of Karl Abraham*. London: Hogarth Press, 1965.

Abraham, K. (1924). A short study of the libido, viewed in the light of mental disorders. In: *Selected Papers of Karl Abraham*. London: Hogarth Press, 1965.

Abram, J. (1996). *The Language of Winnicott*. London: Karnac.

Alanen, Y. O. (1975). The psychotherapeutic care of schizophrenic patients in a community psychiatric setting. *British Journal of Psychiatry* (Special Publication No. 10, *Studies of Schizophrenia*, edited by M. H. Lader).

Alanen, Y. O. (1997). *Schizophrenia: Its Origins and Need-Adapted Treatment*. London: Karnac.

Alanen, Y. O., Lehtinen, V., Lehtinen, K., Aaltonen, J., & Räkköläinen, V. (2000). The Finnish integrated model for early treatment of schizophrenia and related psychoses. In: B. Martindale, A. Bateman, M. Crowe, & F Margison (Eds.), *Psychosis: Psychological Approaches and Their Effectiveness*. London: Gaskell.

Alanen, Y. O., Räkköläinen, V., Laakso, J., Rasimus, R., & Kaljonen, A. (1986). *Towards Need-specific Treatment of Schizophrenic Psychoses*. Heidelberg: Springer-Verlag.

Alanen, Y. O., Ugelstad, E., Armelius, B. E., Lehtinen, K., et al. (1994). *Early Treatment for Schizophrenic Patients: Scandinavian Psychotherapeutic Approaches*. Oslo: Scandinavian University Press.

Ames, D. (1984). Self shooting of a phantom head. *British Journal of Psychiatry, 145*, 193–194.

Anon (1994). Worse than the worst nightmare. *British Medical Journal, 308* (1995).

Arieti, S. (1974). *Interpretation of Schizophrenia*. London: Basic Books.

Arieti, S. (1979). *Understanding and Helping the Schizophrenic: A Guide for Family and Friends*. London: Penguin Books.

Balint, M. (1959). *Thrills and Regressions*. London: Karnac, 1987.

Balint, M. (1968). *The Basic Fault: Therapeutic Aspects of Regression*. London: Tavistock.

Barnes, E. (Ed.) (1967). *Psychosocial Nursing*. London: Tavistock.

Barnes-Gutteridge, W. (1993). Imagination and the therapeutic process. *British Journal of Psychotherapy, 9*: 267–279.

Barrows, P. (2000). Making the case for dedicated infant mental health services. *Psychoanalytic Psychotherapy, 14*: 111–128.

Bateman, A., & Holmes, J. (1995). *Introduction to Psychoanalysis: Contemporary Theory and Practice*. London: Routledge.

Bateman, A., Brown, D., & Pedder, J. (2000). *Introduction to Psychotherapy*. London: Routledge.

Bell, D. (1992). Hysteria—a contemporary Kleinian perspective. *British Journal of Psychotherapy, 9* (2): 169–180.

Bender, L. (1970). The maturation process and hallucinations in children. In: W. Keup (Ed.), *Origins and Mechanisms of Hallucinations*. New York: Plenum Press.

Benedetti, G. (1987). *Psychotherapy of Schizophrenia*. London & New York: New York University Press.

Benfer, B. A., & Schroder, P. J. (1985). Nursing in the therapeutic milieu. *Bulletin of the Menninger Clinic, 49* (5): 451–465.

Berrios, G. E., & Markova, I. S. (1992). The meaning of insight in clinical psychiatry. *British Journal of Psychiatry, 160*: 850–860.

Bertalanffy, L. von (1968). *General Systems Theory*. New York: Braziller.

Bick, E. (1964). Notes on infant observation in psycho-analytic training. *International Journal of Psycho-Analysis, 45*: 558–566.

Bion, W. R. (1957). The differentiation of the psychotic from the non-psychotic personalities. In: *Second Thoughts*. London: Heinemann, 1967.

Bion, W. R. (1962). *Learning from Experience*. London: Heinemann.

Bion, W. R. (1963). *Elements of Psycho-Analysis*. London: Heinemann.

Bion, W. R. (1967). *Second Thoughts*. London: Heinemann.

Bléandonu, G. (1994). *Wilfred Bion. His Life and Works 1897–1979*. London: Free Association Books.

Bleuler, M. (1978). *The Schizophrenic Disorders: Long-term Patient and Family Studies*. New Haven, CT: Yale University Press.

Blos, P. (1962). *On Adolescence*. New York: Free Press.

Bollas, C. (2000). *Hysteria*. London: Routledge.

Bowlby, J. (1980). *Loss*. London: Penguin.

Bowlby, J. (1988). *A Secure Base: Clinical Applications of Attachment Theory*. London: Routledge.

Boyer, L. B. (1983). *The Regressed Patient*. New York: Jason Aronson.

Boyer, L. B., & Giovacchini, P. (Eds.) (1990). *Master Clinicians: On treating the Regressed Patient*. New York: Jason Aronson.

Brenman, E. (1985). Hysteria. *International Journal of Psycho-Analysis, 66*: 423–432.

Britton, R. (1998). *Belief and Imagination*. London: New Library of Psycho-analysis. London: Routledge.
Britton, R. (1999). Getting in on the act: the hysterical solution. *International Journal of Psycho-Analysis, 80*: 1–14.
Bychowski, G. (1966). Obsessive compulsive façade in schizophrenia. *International Journal of Psycho-Analysis, 47*: 189–197.
Campbell, J. (1950). *The Hero with a Thousand Faces*. Princeton, NJ: Princeton University Press.
Chadwick, P., & Birchwood, M. (1994). The omnipotence of voices—a cognitive approach to auditory hallucinations. *British Journal of Psychiatry, 164*: 190–201.
Chadwick, P., Birchwood, M., & Trower, P. (1996). *Cognitive Therapy for Delusions, Voices and Paranoia*. Chichester: Wiley.
Ciompi, L. (1984). Is there really a Schizophrenia? The long-term course of psychotic phenomena. *British Journal of Psychiatry, 145*: 636–640.
Cohen, M., et al. (1963). An intensive study of twelve cases of manic-depressive psychosis. *Psychiatry, 17*: 103–137.
Cullberg, J. (1991). Recovered versus non-recovered schizophrenic patients amongst those who have had intensive psychotherapy. *Acta Psychiatrica Scandinavica, 84*: 242–245.
Cullberg, J. (1993). A proposal for a 3-dimensional aetiolological view of the schizophrenias. *Nordic Journal of Psychiatry, 47*: 355–359, 421–424.
Cullberg, J. (2001). "The Parachute Project". First episode psychosis: background and treatment. In: P. Williams (Ed.), *A Language for Psychosis*. London: Whurr.
Cullberg, J., & Levander, S. (1991). Fully recovered schizophrenic patients who received intensive psychotherapy: a Swedish case-finding study. *Nordic Journal of Psychiatry, 45*: 253–262.
Cutting, J. (1999). *Psychopathology and Modern Philosophy*. London: Forest Publishing.
Danto, E. (1998). The ambulatorium: Freud's free clinic in Vienna. *International Journal of Psycho-Analysis, 79*: 287–300.
David, A. S. (1990). Insight and psychosis. *British Journal of Psychiatry, 156*: 798–808.
Deahl, M., & Turner, T. (1997). General psychiatry in no-man's land. *British Journal of Psychiatry, 171*: 6–8.
De Masi, F. (1997). Intimidation at the helm: superego and hallucination in the analytic treatment of a psychosis. *International Journal of Psycho-Analysis, 78*: 561–577.
De Masi, F. (2000). The unconscious and psychosis: some considerations on the psychoanalytic theory of psychosis. *International Journal of Psycho-Analysis, 81* (1): 1–20.
Ellwood, J. (Ed.) (1995). *Psychosis: Understanding and Treatment*. London: Jessica Kingsley.
Engel, G. L. (1980). The clinical application of the biopsychosocial model. *American Journal of Psychiatry, 137*: 535–544.

Engel, G. L. (1962). *Psychological Development in Health and Disease*. Philadelphia, PA: Saunders.

Fabricius, J. (1994). Psychodynamic perspectives. In: H. Wright & M. Ciddey (Eds.), *Mental Health Nursing* London: Chapman & Hall.

Fairbairn, W. R. D. (1952). *Psychoanalytic Studies of the Personality*. London: Tavistock Publications.

Feinsilver, D. B. (Ed.) (1986). *Towards a Comprehensive Model for Schizophrenic Disorders*. London: Analytic Press.

Fenichel, O. (1946). *The Psychoanalytic Theory of Neurosis*. London: Routledge & Kegan Paul.

Ferenczi, S. (1916). *Contributions to Psychoanalysis*. Boston: R. Badger.

Fleck, S. (1995). Dehumanising developments in American psychiatry in recent decades. *Journal of Nervous and Mental Diseases, 183*: 195–203.

Fonagy, P., & Target, M. (1996). Playing with reality: I. *International Journal of Psycho-Analysis, 77*: 217–234.

Fonagy, P., & Target, M. (2000). Playing with reality: II. *International Journal of Psycho-Analysis, 81*: 853–874.

Fowler, D., Garety, P. A., & Kuipers, L. (1995). *Cognitive Behaviour Therapy for Psychosis: Theory and Practice*. Chichester: Wiley.

Freeman, T. (1969). *Psychopathology of the Psychoses*. New York: International Universities Press.

Freeman, T. (1971). Observations on mania. *International Journal of Psycho-Analysis, 52*: 479–486.

Freeman, T. (1973). *A Psychoanalytic Study of the Psychoses*. New York: International Universities Press.

Freeman, T. (1986). Psychotherapy and general psychiatry—integral or separable? *Psychoanalytic Psychotherapy, 1* (1): 19–30.

Freeman, T. (1988). *The Psychoanalyst in Psychiatry*. London: Karnac.

Freeman, T. (1994). On some types of hallucinatory experience. *Psychoanalytic Psychotherapy, 8*: 273–281.

Freud, A. (1966). Obsessional neurosis: a summary of Congress views. *International Journal of Psycho-Analysis, 47*: 116–122.

Freud, S. (1895d) (with Breuer, J.). *Studies on Hysteria. S.E., 2*.

Freud, S. (1900a). *The Interpretation of Dreams. S.E., 4–5*.

Freud, S. (1909d). Notes upon a case of obsessional neurosis. *S.E., 10*, pp. 155–319.

Freud, S. (1911b). Formulations on the two principles of mental functioning. *S.E., 12*.

Freud, S. (1911c [1910]). Psycho-analytical notes on an autobiographical account of a case of paranoia. *S.E., 12*.

Freud, S. (1912b). The dynamics of transference. *S.E., 12*.

Freud, S. (1914g). Remembering, repeating and working-through. *S.E., 12*.

Freud, S. (1916–17). *Introductory Lectures on Psycho-Analysis. S.E., 15–16*.

Freud, S. (1917e [1915]). Mourning and melancholia. *S.E., 14*.

Freud, S. (1920g). *Beyond the Pleasure Principle. S.E., 18*.

Freud, S. (1923b). *The Ego and the Id. S.E., 19.*

Freud, S. (1925d [1924]). *An Autobiographical Study. S.E., 20.*

Freud, S. (1926d [1925]). *Inhibitions, Symptoms and Anxiety. S.E., 20.*

Freud, S. (1937c). Analysis terminable and interminable. *S.E., 23.*

Frosch, J. F. (1983). *The Psychotic Process.* New York: International Universities Press.

Frosch, J. F. (1990). *Psychodynamic Psychiatry: Theory and Practice.* Madison, CT: International Universities Press.

Gaddini, E. (1992). *A Psychoanalytic Theory of Infantile Experience.* New Library of Psychoanalysis, No. 16. London: Tavistock Routledge.

Gallwey, P. L. G. (1978). Transference utilisation in aim-restricted psychotherapy. *British Journal of Medical Psychology, 51:* 225–236.

Garety, P., Fowler, D., & Kuipers, E. (2000). Cognitive-behavioural therapy for people with psychosis. In: B. Martindale, A. Bateman, M. Crowe, & F. Margison (Eds.), *Psychosis: Psychological Approaches and Their Effectiveness.* London: Gaskell.

Garland, C. (1998). *Understanding Trauma: A Psychoanalytic Approach.* London: Duckworth

Grinberg, L. (1996). The relationship between obsessive mechanisms and a state of self disturbance: depersonalisation. *International Journal of Psycho-Analysis, 47:* 177–183.

Grotstein, J. S. (1977). The psychoanalytic concept of schizophrenia. 1. The dilemma. 2. Reconciliation. *International Journal of Psycho-Analysis, 58:* 403–452.

Grotstein, J. S. (1981). *Do I Dare Disturb the Universe? A Memorial to Wilfred R. Bion.* Beverly Hills, CA: Caesura Press.

Grotstein, J. S. (1986). *Splitting and Projective Identification.* New York: Jason Aronson.

Grotstein, J. S. (1990). Invariants in primitive emotional disorders. In: L. B. Boyer & P. Giovacchini (Eds.), *Master Clinicians: On Treating the Regressed Patient.* New York: Jason Aronson.

Grotstein, J. S. (1992). Foreword. In: O. Weininger, *Melanie Klein: From Theory to Reality.* London: Karnac.

Grotstein, J. S. (1997). Klein's archaic Oedipus complex and its possible relationship to the myth of the labyrinth: notes on the origin of courage. *Journal of Analytical Psychology, 42:* 582–609.

Grotstein, J. S. (1998). The apprehension of beauty and its relationship to "O". *Journal of Melanie Klein and Object Relations, 16:* 273–284.

Grotstein, J. S. (2000). *Who Is the Dreamer Who Dreams the Dream?* London/Hillsdale, NJ: Analytic Press.

Grotstein, J. S. (2001). A rationale for the psychoanalytically informed psychotherapy of schizophrenia and other psychoses: towards the concept of "rehabilitative psychoanalysis". In: P. Williams (Ed.), *A Language for Psychosis.* London: Whurr.

Grotstein, J. S., & Rinsley, D. B. (1994). *Fairbairn and the Origins of Object Relations.* London: Free Association Books.

Guntrip, H. (1961). *Personality Structure and Human Interaction*. London: Hogarth Press.

Hansen, J. B. (1993). *Crossing the Borders: Psychotherapy of Schizophrenia*. Ludvika: Dualis.

Heimann, P. (1950). On countertransference. *International Journal of Psycho-Analysis, 31*: 81–84.

Hill, D. (1978). The qualities of a good psychiatrist. *British Journal of Psychiatry, 133*: 97–105.

Hingley, S. M. (1997). Psychodynamic perspectives on psychosis and psychotherapy, 1: Theory. 2: Practice. *British Journal of Medical Psychology, 70*: 301–312, 313–324.

Hinshelwood, R. D. (1989). *A Dictionary of Kleinian Thought*. London: Free Association Books.

Hinshelwood, R. D. (1994). *Clinical Klein*. London: Free Association Books.

Hinshelwood, R. D., Robinson, S., & Zarate, O. (1998). *Introducing Melanie Klein*. New York: Totem Books.

Holmes, J. (1982). Obsessional phenomena and the development of imaginative competence. *British Journal of Medical Psycholoogy, 55*: 147–158.

Holmes, J. (Ed.) (1991). *A Textbook of Psychotherapy in Psychiatric Practice*. Edinburgh: Churchill Livingstone

Holmes, J. (1996). *Attachment, Intimacy, Autonomy*. New York: Jason Aronson.

Holmes, J. (1997). Too early, too late: endings in psychotherapy—an attachment perspective. *British Journal of Psychotherapy, 14*: 159–171.

Holmes, J. (1998). The changing aims of psychoanalytic psychotherapy: an integrative perspective. *International Journal of Psycho-Analysis, 79*: 227-240.

Holmes, J. (2000). Fitting the biopsychosocial jigsaw together. *British Journal of Psychiatry, 177*: 93–94.

Holmqvist, R. (1995). *Countertransference Feelings in Milieu Therapy*. Umea, Sweden: Umea University Press.

Hughes, P., & Halek, C. (1991). Training nurses in psychotherapeutic skills. *Psychoanalytic Psychotherapy, 5*: 115–123.

Hughes, P., & McGauley, G. (1997). Mother-infant interaction during the first year with a child who shows disorganisation of attachment. *British Journal of Psychotherapy, 14*: 147–158.

Jackson, M. (1962). Jung's later work—the archetype. *British Journal of Medical Psychology, 35*: 199–204.

Jackson, M. (1976). Psychopathology and psychotherapy in bronchial asthma. *British Journal of Medical Psychology, 49*: 249–255.

Jackson, M. (1977). Psychopathology and "pseudo-normality" in ulcerative colitis. *Psychotherapy & Psychosomatics, 28*: 179–186.

Jackson, M. (1982). Psychoanalysis, somatisation and pseudo-normality. *Bulletin of the British Psychoanalytical Society, 7*: 28–36.

Jackson, M. (1991). Psychotic disorders. In: J. Holmes (Ed.), *Textbook of Psychotherapy in Clinical Practice*. London: Churchill Livingstone.

Jackson, M. (1992). Learning to think about schizoid thinking. *Psychoana-lytic Psychotherapy*, 6 (3): 191–203. [Reprinted in: J. Ellwood (Ed.), *Psy-chosis: Understanding and Treatment*. London: Jessica Kingsley, 1995.]

Jackson, M. (1993a). Manic-depressive psychosis: psychopathology and individual psychotherapy within a psychodynamic milieu. *Psychoana-lytic Psychotherapy*, 7 (2): 103–133.

Jackson, M. (1993b). Psychoanalysis, psychiatry, psychodynamics: training for integration. *Psychoanalytic Psychotherapy*, 7 (1): 1–14.

Jackson, M., & Cawley, R. (1992). Psychodynamics and psychotherapy on an acute admission ward: the story of an experimental unit. *British Journal of Psychiatry*, 160: 41–50.

Jackson, M., & Jacobson, R. (1983). Psychoanalytic hospital treatment: the application of psychoanalytic principles. In: P. Pichot, P. Berner, R. Wolf, & K. Thau (Eds.), *Psychiatry: The State of the Art*. London: Plenum Press.

Jackson, M., & Williams, P. (1994). *Unimaginable Storms: A Search for Mean-ing in Psychosis*. London: Karnac.

Jacobson, E. (1967). *Psychotic Conflict and Reality*. London: Hogarth Press.

Jamison, K. R. (1995). *An Unquiet Mind: A Memoir of Moods and Madness*. London: Picador.

Jaynes, J. (1976). *The Origins of Consciousness and the Breakdown of the Bicam-eral Mind*. Boston, MA: Houghton Mifflin.

Jenkins, M. (1995). "Further Thoughts on the Concept of Two Selves." Public lecture at the Highgate Library and Scientific Institute, Lon-don.

Johannsen, J. O., Larsen, T. K., McGlashan, T., & Vaglum, P. (2000). Early intervention in psychosis: the TIPS project, a multi-centre study in Scandinavia. In: B. Martindale, A. Bateman, M. Crowe, & F. Margison, (Eds.), *Psychosis: Psychological Approaches and Their Effectiveness*. Lon-don: Gaskell.

Johnson, S., & Ruszczynski, S. (Eds.) (1999). *Psychoanalytic Psychotherapy in the Independent Traditions*. London: Karnac.

Joseph, B. (1966). Persecutory anxiety in a four-year-old boy. *International Journal of Psycho-Analysis*, 47: 184–188.

Joseph, B. (1985). Transference: the total situation. *International Journal of Psycho-Analysis*, 66 (4): 447–454.

Joseph, B. (1986). Envy in everyday life. *Psychoanalytic Psychotherapy*, 2 (1): 13–22.

Joseph, B. (1989). *Psychic Equilibrium and Psychic Change*. New Library of Psychoanalysis, No. 9. London: Tavistock/Routledge.

Joseph, B. (2000). Agreeablenes as obstacle. *International Journal of Psycho-Analysis*, 81: 641–649.

Jung, C. G. (1960). *The Psychogenesis of Mental Disease*. London: Routledge & Kegan Paul.

Kaplan-Solms, K., & Solms, M. (1996). Psychoanalytic observations on a case of fronto-limbic disease. *Journal of Clinical Psycho-Analysis, 5*: 405–438.

Kaplan-Solms, K., & Solms, M. (2000). *Clinical Studies in Neuro-Psychoanalysis: An Introduction to Depth Neuropsychology*. London: Karnac.

Kernberg, O. (1975). *Borderline Conditions and Pathological Narcissism*. New York: Jason Aronson.

Kernberg, O. (1992). Foreword. In: D. Rosenfeld, *The Psychotic: Aspects of the Personality*. London: Karnac.

Kernberg, O. (1999). Psychoanalysis, psychoanalytic psychotherapy and supportive psychotherapy: contemporary controversies. *International Journal of Psycho-Analysis, 80*: 1075–1092.

Killingmo, B. (1989). Conflict or deficit? *International Journal of Psycho-Analysis, 76* (3): 65–79.

Killingmo, B. (1995). Affirmation in psychoanalysis. *International Journal of Psycho-Analysis, 76* (3): 503–518.

Klein, H. S. (1974). Transference and defence in manic states. *International Journal of Psycho-Analysis, 55*: 261–268, 1075–1092.

Klein, M. (1929). Infantile anxiety-situations reflected in a work of art and in the creative impulse. In: *Contributions to Psycho-Analysis*. London: Hogarth Press.

Klein, M. (1935). A contribution to the psychogenesis of manic-depressive states. In: *Love, Guilt and Reparation and Other Works: Writings, Vol. 1.* London: Hogarth Press, 1975.

Klein, M. (1940). Mourning in its relations to manic-depressive states. In: *Love, Guilt and Reparation and Other Works: Writings, Vol. 1.* London: Hogarth Press, 1975.

Klein, M. (1946). Notes on some schizoid mechanisms. In: M. Klein, P. Heimann, S. Isaacs, & J. Riviere, *Developments in Psycho-Analysis*. London: Hogarth Press, 1975.

Klein, M. (1957). Envy and gratitude. In: *Envy and Gratitude and Other Works: Writngs, Vol. 3.* London: Hogarth Press, 1975.

Klein, M. (1959). Our adult world and its roots in infancy. *Human Relations, 12*: 291–303. [Also in: *Our Adult World and Other Essays*. London: Heinemann, 1963.]

Kohut, H. (1977). *The Restoration of the Self*. New York: International Universities Press.

Kohut, H., & Wolf, S. (1978). The disorders of the self and their treatment: an outline. *International Journal of Psycho-Analysis, 59*: 413–425.

Lacan, J. (1997). *Écrits. A Selection*. London: Tavistock Publications.

Laplanche, J., & Pontalis, J.-B. (1973). *The Language of Psychoanalysis*. London: Hogarth Press. [Reprinted: London: Karnac, 1998.]

Lask, B., & Bryant-Waugh, R. (2000). *Anorexia and Related Eating Disorders in Childhood and Adolescence* (2nd edition). London: Psychology Press.

Laufer, M., & Laufer, E. (1984). *Adolescence and Developmental Breakdown*. London: Yale University Press.

Leff, J., & Vaughn, C. E. (1985). *Expressed Emotions in Families*. New York: Guilford Press.

Lehtinen, K. (1994). Need-adapted treatment of schizophrenia: family interventions. *British Journal of Psychiatry, 164* (Supp., 23): 89–96.

Lehtinen, V., Aaltonen, J., Koffert, T., Räkköläinen, V., & Sylvahtie, E. (2000). Two year outcome in first-episode psychosis treated according to an integrated model: is immediate neuroleptisation always necessary. *European Psychiatry, 15*: 312–320.

Lewis, A. J. (1936). Problems of obsessional illness. *Proceedings of the Royal Society of Medicine, 29*: 325–336.

Lewis, A. J. (1975). The survival of hysteria. *Psychological Medicine, 5*: 9–12.

Little, M. (1986). *Transference Neurosis and Transference Psychosis. Towards Basic Unity*. London: Free Association Books.

Lottermann, A. (1996). *Specific Techniques for the Psychotherapy of Schizophrenia*. Madison, CT: International Universities Press.

Lucas, R. (1986). On the contribution of psychoanalysis to the management of psychotic patients in the N. H. S. *Psychoanalytic Psychotherapy, 1* (1): 19–30.

Lucas, R. (1993). The psychotic wavelength. *Psychoanalytic Psychotherapy, 7*: 15–24.

Lucas, R. (1994). Puerperal psychosis: vulnerability and aftermath. *Psychoanalytic psychotherapy, 8* (3): 257–272.

Lucas, R. (1998). Why the cycle in cyclical psychosis? An analytic contribution to the understanding of recurrent manic-depressive psychosis. *Psychoanalytic Psychotherapy,. 12*: 193–212.

Mace, C., & Margison, F. (1997). *Psychotherapy of Psychosis*. London: Gaskell.

Magagna, J. (1995). L'occhio rivolto al interno. In: *Contrapunto, No. 17*. Firenze: Libreria Le Monnier.

Mahler, M. S., Pine, F., & Bergman, A. (1975). *The Psychological Birth of the Human Infant*. London: Karnac.

Malan, D. (1963). *A Study of Brief Psychotherapy*. London: Tavistock.

Mander, G. (1995). In praise of once-weekly work: making a virtue of necessity or treatment of choice? *British Journal of Psychotherapy, 121*: 3–14.

Marks, I. M. (1987). *Fears, Phobias and Rituals*. New York: Oxford University Press.

Marks, I. M., O'Dwyer, A.-M., Greist, J., et al. (2000). Subjective imagery in obsessive-compulsive disorder before and after exposure therapy. Pilot randomised control trial. *British Journal of Psychiatry, 176*: 387–391.

Marshall, R. (1995). Schizophrenia: a constructive analogy or a convenient construct? In: J. Ellwood (Ed.), *Psychosis: Understanding and Treatment*. London: Jessica Kingsley.

Martindale, B. (2001). New discoveries concerning psychosis, and their organisational fate. In: P. Williams (Ed.), *A Language for Psychosis*. London: Whurr.

Martindale, B., Bateman, A., Crowe, M., & Margison, F. (2000). *Psychosis: Psychological Approaches and Their Effectiveness*. London: Gaskell.

Matte-Blanco, I. (1998). *Thinking, Feeling and Being*. London: Routledge.

McGorry, P. (1998). Verging on reality. *British Journal of Psychiatry, 172* (Suppl. 3).

Meltzer, D. (1967). *The Psychoanalytic Process*. London: Heinemann.

Meltzer, D. (1975). *Explorations in Autism*. Perthshire: Clunie Press.

Meltzer, D. (1992). *The Claustrum*. Perthshire: Clunie Press.

Meltzer, D. (1994). *Sincerity and Other Works*. London: Karnac.

Meltzer, D. (1997). Concerning signs and symbols. *British Journal of Psychotherapy, 14*: 175–181.

Meltzer, D., & Harris Williams, M. (1988). *The Apprehension of Beauty*. Perthshire: Clunie Press.

Milton, J. (Ed.) (1996). *Presenting the Case for Psychoanalytic Services. An Annotated Bibliography*. London: Tavistock Clinic Library.

Milton, J. (1997). Why assess? Psychoanalytical assessment in the NHS. *Psychoanalytic Psychotherapy, 11* (1): 47–58.

Milton, J. (2000). Psychoanalysis and the moral high ground. *International Journal of Psycho-Analysis, 81*: 1101–1116.

Milton, J. (2001). Psychoanalysis and cognitive-behavioural therapy—rival paradigms or common ground. *International Journal of Psycho-Analysis, 82* (3).

Mitchell, J. (Ed.) (1986). *The Selected Melanie Klein*. London: Penguin.

Mitchell, J. (2000). *Mad Men and Medusas*. London: Penguin.

Money-Kyrle, R. (1978). *The Collected Papers of Roger Money-Kyrle*. Perthshire: Clunie Press.

Moore, B. E., & Fine, B. D. (1968). *A Glossary of Psychoanalytic Terms and Concepts*. New York: American Psychoanalytic Association.

Mosher, L. R., & Menn, A. Z. (1976). Dinosaur or astronaut? One year follow-up from the Soteria Project. *American Journal of Psychiatry. 133*: 919–920.

Murray, R. (1979). Schizophrenia. In: P. Hill, R. Murray, & A. Thorley (Eds.), *Essentials of Postgraduate Psychiatry*. London: Academic Press.

Nagera, H. (1969). The imaginary companion. *Psychoanalytic Study of the Child, 24*: 165–196.

Ogden, T. H. (1979). On projective identification. *International Journal of Psycho-Analysis, 60*: 357–373.

Ogden, T. H. (1989). *The Primitive Edge of Experience*. New York: Jason Aronson.

Ogden, T. H. (1990). On the structure of experience. In: L. P. Boyer & P. Giovacchini (Eds.), *Master Clinicians: On Treating the Regressed Patient*. New York: Jason Aronson.

Oldham, J. M., & Russakoff, L. M. (1987). *Dynamic Therapy in Brief Hospitalisation*. New York: Jason Aronson.

Pao, P.-N. (1968a). On manic-depressive psychosis: a study of the transition states. *Journal of the American Psychoanalytic Association, 19*: 787–798.

Pao, P.-N. (1968b). On the formation of schizophrenic symptom. *International Journal of Psycho-Analysis, 58*: 389–402.

Pao, P.-N. (1979). *Schizophrenic Disorders: Theory and Treatment from a Psychodynamic Point of View*. New York: International Universities Press.

Parkes, C. M. (1975). *Bereavement: Studies of Grief in Adult Life*. London: Tavistock.

Pedder, J. (1982). Failure to mourn and melancholia. *British Journal of Psychiatry, 41*: 327–337.

Perkins, R., & Moodley, P. (1993). The arrogance of insight. *Psychiatric Bulletin, 17*: 233–234.

Perlow, M. (1997). *Understanding Mental Objects*. New Library of Psychoanalysis, No. 22. London: Routledge.

Person, E. S., Fonagy, P., & Figueira, S. (1995). *On Freud's "Creative Writers and Day-dreaming"*. London: Yale University Press.

Petot, M. (1979). *Melanie Klein: First Discoveries and First System 1919–1932*. New York: International Universities Press.

Petot, M. (1991). *Melanie Klein. The Ego and the Good Object*. Madison, CT: International Universities Press.

Piaget, J. (1948). *The Language and Thought of the Child*. London: Routledge & Kegan Paul.

Pylkkanen, K. (1989). A quality assurance programme for psychotherapy. *Psychoanalytic Psychotherapy, 4*: 13–22.

Quinodoz, D. (2001). The psychoanalyst of the future: wise enough to dare to be mad at times. *International Journal of Psycho-Analysis, 82*: 235–248.

Racker, H. (1953). *Transference and Counter-Transference*. International Psycho-Analytical Library, No. 73. London: Hogarth Press.

Räkköläinen, V. (1977). *Onset of Psychosis: A Clinical Study of 68 Cases*. Turku, Finland: Turku University Press.

Räkköläinen, V., Lehtinen, K., & Alanen, Y. O. (1991). Need-adapted treatment of schizophrenic processes: the essential role of family-centred meetings. *Contemporary Family Therapy, 13* (6).

Ramzy, I. (1966). Factors in early compulsive formation. *International Journal of Psycho-Analysis, 47*: 169–176.

Reid, I. C., & Stewart, C. A. (2001). How antidepressants work. New perspectives on the pathophysiology of depressive disorder. *British Journal of Psychiatry, 178*: 299–303.

Reiser, M. (1988). Are psychiatric educators "losing the mind"? *American Journal of Psychiatry, 145*: 148–153.

Rey, J. H. (1994). *Universals of Psychoanalysis in the Treatment of Psychotic and Borderline States*. London: Free Association Books.

Rhode, M. (1995). Links between Henri Rey's thinking and psychoanalytic work with autistic children. *Psychoanalytic Psychotherapy, 9* (2): 149–155.

Richards, J. (1999). The concept of internal cohabitation. In: S. Johnson & S. Ruszczynski (Eds.), *Psychoanalytic Psychotherapy in the Independent Tradition*. London: Karnac.

Richardson, P., & Hobson, P. (2000). In defence of NHS psychotherapy. *Psychoanalytic Psychotherapy, 14* (1): 63–74.

Riesenberg-Malcolm, R. (1999a). *On Bearing Unbearable States of Mind*. New Library of Psychoanalysis, No. 34. London: Tavistock/Routledge.

Riesenberg-Malcolm, R. (1999b). Hyperbole in hysteria: how can we tell the dancer from the dance? In: *On Bearing Unbearable States of Mind*. New Library of Psychoanalysis, No. 34. London: Tavistock/Routledge.

Riesenberg-Malcolm, R. (1999c). Interpretation: the past in the present. In: *On Bearing Unbearable States of Mind*. New Library of Psychoanalysis, No. 34. London: Tavistock/Routledge.

Roberts, G. (1992). The origins of delusions. *British Journal of Psychiatry, 161*: 298–308.

Robbins, M. (1993). *Experiences of Schizophrenia: An Integration of the Personal, Scientific and Therapeutic*. London: Guilford Press.

Rogan, A. (2000). "Moving along" in psychotherapy with schizophrenic patients. *Journal of Psychotherapy Practice and Research, 9* (3): 157–166.

Rosen, I. (1957). The clinical significance of obsessions in schizophrenia. *Journal of Mental Science, 103*: 772–786.

Rosenbaum, B., & Sonne, H. (1986). *The Language of Psychosis*. New York/London: New York University Press.

Rosenfeld, D. (1992). *The Psychotic: Aspects of the Personality*. London: Karnac.

Rosenfeld, H. A. (1963). Notes on the psychopathology and psychoanalytic treatment of depression and manic-depressive patients. *Research Reports of the American Psychiatric Association*: 73–83.

Rosenfeld, H. A. (1965). *Psychotic States: A Psychoanalytical Approach*. London: Hogarth Press and the Institute of Psycho-Analysis.

Rosenfeld, H. A. (1987). *Impasse and Interpretation*. London: Tavistock Publications.

Roth, M., Kerr, A., & Howorth, P. (1996). Comments on "audible thoughts" and "speech defect" in schizophrenia. *British Journal of Psychiatry, 168*: 536–539.

Rustin, M., Rhode, M., Dubinsky, A., & Dubinsky, H. (Eds.) (1997). *Psychotic States in Children*. London: Duckworth.

Ruszczynski, S., & Johnson, S. (Eds.) (1999). *Psychoanalytic Psychotherapy in the Kleinian Tradition*. London: Karnac.

Rycroft, C. (1968a). *A Critical Dictionary of Psycho-Analysis*. London: Nelson.

Rycroft, C. (1968b). *Imagination and Reality*. London: Hogarth Press and the Institute of Psycho-Analysis.

Rycroft, C. (1968c). The nature and function of the analyst's communication to the patient. In: *Imagination and Reality*. London: Hogarth Press and the Institute of Psycho-analysis.

Rycroft, C. (1985). Where is psychoanalysis going? *Journal of the Royal Society of Medicine, 78*: 524–525.

Sandell, R., Blomberg, J., Lazar, A., Carlsson, J., Broberg, J., & Schubert, J.

(2000). Varieties of long-term outcome among patients in psychoanalysis and long-term psychotherapy. A review of the findings in the Stockholm outcome of psychoanalysis and psychotherapy project (STOPPP). *International Journal of Psycho-Analysis, 81*: 921–942.

Sandler, J., Dare, C., & Holder, A. (1992). *The Patient and the Analyst.* London: Karnac.

Schore, A. N. (2000a). Attachment and the regulation of the right brain. *Attachment and Human Behaviour, 2* (1): 23–47.

Schore, A. N. (2000b). Clinical implications of a psychoneurobiological model of projective identification. In: S. Alhanati (Ed.), *Primitive Mental States, Vol. 3: Pre- and Perinatal Influences on Personality Development.* New York: Jason Aronson.

Schore, A. N. (2001). Minds in the making: attachment, the self-organising brain, and developmentally-oriented psychoanalytic psychotherapy. *British Journal of Psychotherapy, 17* (3): 299–328.

Schwartz, R. C., & Cohen, B. J. (2001). Psychosocial correlates of suicidal intent among patients with schizophrenia. *Comprehensive Psychiatry, 42* (No. 2, March/April).

Scott, W. C. M. (1964). Mania and mourning. *International Journal of Psycho-Analysis, 45*: 373–379.

Searles, H. F. (1965a). *Collected Papers on Schizophrenia and Related Subjects.* London: Hogarth Press.

Searles, H. F. (1965b). The effort to drive the other person crazy. In: *Collected Papers on Schizophrenia and Related Subjects.* London: Hogarth Press.

Segal, H. A. (1964). *Introduction to the Work of Melanie Klein.* London: Heinemann.

Segal, H. A. (1972). A delusional system as a defence against the emergence of a catastrophic situation. *International Journal of Psycho-Analysis, 52*: 393–401.

Segal, H. A. (1979). *Klein.* London: Fontana/Collins.

Segal, H. A. (1981a). Delusion and artistic creativity: some reflections on reading *The Spire* by William Golding. In: E. B. Spillius (Ed.), *Melanie Klein Today, Vol. 2.* London: Routledge, 1988.

Segal, H. A. (1981b). Manic reparation. In: *The Work of Hanna Segal.* New York: Jason Aronson.

Segal, H. A. (1981c). Notes on symbol formation. In: *The Work of Hanna Segal.* New York: Jason Aronson.

Segal, H. A. (1981d). A psychoanalytic approach to the treatment of psychosis. In: *The Work of Hanna Segal.* New York: Jason Aronson.

Segal, H. A. (1981e). Schizoid mechanisms underlying phobia formation. In: *The Work of Hanna Segal.* New York: Jason Aronson.

Segal, H. A (1981f). *The Work of Hanna Segal.* New York: Jason Aronson.

Segal, H. A. (1991). *Dream, Phantasy and Art.* London: New Library of Psychoanalysis.

Segal, J. (1985). *Phantasy in Everyday Life.* London: Penguin Books.

Seppala, K., & Jamsen, H. (1989). Psychotherapy as one form of rehabilitation provided by the Finnish social insurance system. *Psychoanalytic Psychotherapy, 4* (3): 219–232.

Silcock, B. (1994). "Three tales of madness": The musician's tale. *Sanetalk* (Summer).

Sinason, M. (1993). "Who is the mad voice inside?" *Psychoanalytic Psychotherapy, 7* (3): 203–221.

Sinason, M. (1999). How can you keep your hair on? In: P. Williams (Ed.), *Psychosis (Madness)*. Psychoanalytic Ideas, Vol. 1. London: Institute of Psycho-Analysis (internet publication: www.psychoanalysis.org.uk).

Sohn, L. (1985). Narcissistic organisation, projective identifications and the formation of the identificate. *International Journal of Psycho-Analysis, 66:* 201–104.

Sohn, L. (1997). Unprovoked assault: making sense of apparently random violence. In: D. Bell (Ed.), *Reason and Passion*. London: Tavistock Clinic Series.

Sohn, L. (1999). Psychosis and violence. In: P. Williams (Ed.), *Psychosis (Madness)*. Psychoanalytic Ideas, Vol. 1. London: Institute of Psycho-Analysis (internet publication: www.psychoanalysis.org.uk).

Solms, M. (1995). Is the Brain more real than the Mind? *Psychoanalytic Psychotherapy, 9* (2): 107–120.

Spensley, S. (1995). *Frances Tustin*. London: Routledge.

Sperling, M. (1955). Psychosis and psychosomatic illness. *International Journal of Psycho-Analysis, 36:* 320–327.

Sperling, M. (1978). *Psychosomatic Disorders in Childhood*. New York: Jason Aronson.

Spillius, E. B. (Ed.) (1988). *Melanie Klein Today, Vols. 1 & 2*. London: Routledge.

Steiner, J. (1989). The aim of psychoanalysis. *Psychoanalytic Psychotherapy, 4*.

Steiner, J. (1993). *Psychic Retreats*. London: Routledge.

Steiner, J. (1995). The influence of Henri Rey's work. *Psychoanalytic Psychotherapy, 9* (2): 109–120.

Stern, D. (1985). *The Interpersonal World of the Infant*. New York: Basic Books.

Stern, D. N., Sander, L. W., Nahum, J. P., Harrison, A. M., Lyons-Ruth, K., Morgan, A. C., Bruschweiler-Stern, N., & Tronick, E. Z. (1998). Non-interpretive mechanisms in psychoanalytic therapy: the "something more" than interpretation (the process of change study group). *International Journal of Psycho-Analysis, 79:* 903–921.

Symington, J., & Symington, S. (1996). *The Clinical Thinking of Wilfred Bion*. London: Routledge.

Szalita-Permow, A. (1951). Remarks on pathogenesis and treatment of schizophrenia. *Psychiatry, 14:* 295–300.

Szalita-Permow, A. (1952). Further remarks on the pathogenesis and treatment of schizophrenia. *Psychiatry, 15:* 143–150.

Szasz, T. (1961). *The Myth of Mental Illness*. New York: Hoeber.

Szasz, T. (1996). "Audible thoughts" and "speech defect" in schizophrenia: a note on reading and translating Bleuler. *British Journal of Psychiatry*, 168: 533–535.

Taylor, D. (1991). Psychiatric contributions to the understanding of psychiatric illness. In: J. Holmes (Ed.), *A Textbook of Psychotherapy in Psychiatric Practice*. Edinburgh: Churchill Livingstone.

Taylor, D. (1997). Some of Bion's ideas on meaning and understanding. *British Journal of Psychotherapy*, 14: 67–76.

Taylor, G. J. (1987). *Psychosomatic Medicine and Contemporary Psychoanalysis*. Madison, CT: International Universities Press.

Teising, M. (2000). "Sister, I am going crazy, help me": psychodynamic-oriented care in psychotic patients in inpatient treatment. *Journal of Psychiatric and Mental Health Nursing*, 7: 449–454.

Tienari, P. (1992). Implications of adoption studies on schizophrenia. *British Journal of Psychiatry*, 18 (Suppl.): 52–58.

Tonnesmann, M. (1989). *About Children and Children-No-Longer*. New Library of Psychoanalysis No. 10. London: Tavistock/Routledge.

Turkington, D., & Siddle, R. (1998). Cognitive therapy for the treatment of delusions. *Advances in Psychiatric Treatment*, 4: 235–242.

Tustin, F. (1990). *The Protective Shell in Children and Adults*. London: Karnac.

Tyndale, A. (1999). How far is transference interpretation essential to psychic change? In: S. Johnson & S. Rusczynski (Eds.), *Psychoanalytic Psychotherapy in the Independent Tradition*. London: Karnac.

Volkan, V. D. (1990). The psychoanalytic psychotherapy of schizophrenia. In: L. P. Boyer & P. Giovacchini (Eds.), *Master Clinicians: On Treating the Regressed Patient*. New York: Jason Aronson.

Volkan, V. D. (1995). *The Infantile Psychotic Self and Its Fates*. New York: Jason Aronson.

Volkan, V. D. (1997). *Siblings in the Unconscious and Psychopathology*. Madison, CT: International Universities Press.

Volkan, V. D., & Akhtar, S. (1997). *The Seed of Madness*. Madison, CT: International Universities Press.

Waddell, M. (1999). *Inside Lives*. London: Duckworth.

Wallerstein, R. (1986). *Forty-two Lives in Treatment: A Study of Psychoanalysis and Psychotherapy*. New York: Guilford.

Weininger, O. (1992). *Melanie Klein: From Theory to Reality*. London: Karnac.

Whitwell, D. (1999). The myth of recovery from mental illness. *Psychiatric Bulletin*, 23 (10): 621–622.

Williams, A. H. (1998). *Cruelty, Violence and Murder: Understanding the Criminal Mind*. London: Karnac Books.

Williams, A. H. (1999). Psychoanalysis: an art or a science? A review of the implications of the theory of Bion and Meltzer. *British Journal of Psychotherapy*, 16 (2): 127–135.

Williams, M. H., & Waddell, M. (1991). *The Chamber of Maiden Thought*. London: Tavistock/Routledge.

Williams, P. (Ed.) (1999). *Psychosis (Madness)*. Psychoanalytic Ideas, Vol. 1. London: Institute of Psycho-Analysis (internet publication: www.psychoanalysis.org.uk).

Williams, P. (Ed.) (2001). *A Language for Psychosis: Psychoanalysis of Psychotic States*. London: Whurr.

Willick, M. S. (2001). Psychoanalysis and schizophrenia: a cautionary tale. *Journal of the American Psychoanalytic Association, 49* (1): 27–56.

Winnicott, D. W. (1950). Aggression in relation to emotional development. In: *Collected Papers: Through Paediatrics to Psycho-Analysis*. London: Tavistock Publications, 1958.

Winnicott, D. W. (1958). *Collected Papers: Through Paediatrics to Psycho-Analysis*. London: Tavistock Publications.

Winnicott, D. W. (1960). Ego distortion in terms of true and false self. In: *The Maturational Processes and the Facilitating Environment*. London: Hogarth Press, 1965.

Winnicott, D. W. (1962). The aims of treatment. In: *The Maturational Processes and the Facilitating Environment*. London: Hogarth Press, 1965.

Winnicott, D. W. (1965). *The Maturational Processes and the Facilitating Environment*. London: Hogarth Press.

Winnicott, D. W. (1968). The use of an object and relating through identifications. In: *Playing and Reality*. London: Tavistock, 1971.

Winnicott, D. W. (1971). *Playing and Reality*. London: Tavistock.

Wisdom, J. (1961). A methodological approach to the problem of hysteria. *International Journal of Psycho-Analysis, 42*: 224–237.

Wright, K. (1991). *Vision and Separation: Between Mother and Baby*. London: Free Association Books.

Young, R. M. (1994). *Mental Space*. London: Process Press.

Zachary, A. (1985). A new look at the vulnerability of puerperal mothers. *Psychoanalytic Psychotherapy, 1*: 71–89.

Zetzel, E. R. (1970). The so-called good hysteric: In: *The Capacity for Emotional Growth*. London: Hogarth Press.

INDEX

Page numbers in bold indicate Glossary entries.

Bateman, A., 8, 94, 175, 289, 292, 330, 343
Bell, D., 77
Dender, L., 114
Benedetti, G., 319
Benfer, B. A., 298
Bergman, A., 278
Berrios, G. E., 328
Bertalanffy, L. von, 291
beta elements, 283, 285
bicameral mind, 287
Bick, E., 282
biomedicine, 2
    see also medication; psychopharmacol-
        ogy
Bion, W. R., xvi, 158, 260, 285, 342, 344
    attacks on linking, 139
    concept formation, 283
    container–contained theory, 31, 264,
        324
    countertransference, 324
    maternal alpha-function, 90, 137, 216,
        299
    maternal reverie, 317
    "nameless dread", 89, 93
    projective identification:
        as mother–baby communication, 327
        pathological, 328
        on psychotic organization, 281, 334
        relinquishing "memory and desire",
            294
    return of projected elements, 35
    splitting vs. dissociation, 340
    theories of, 282–284
    Unconscious, the, 342
biopsychosocial approach to treatment of
    schizophrenia, 319, **321–322**
bipolar affective psychosis, 247
Birchwood, M., 308
bizarre object, 284, 314
Blake, W., 326
Bléandonu, G., 283
Bleuler, M., 147
Blos, P., 339
bodily space:
    invasion of, 132, 184
    perception of, 114
body image:
    delusional distortion of, 228–229
    disorder [clinical examples]:
        Elmer, 176–190, 188, 231
        Patient G, 262
        Patient H, 204, 257, 263–265, 285
Bollas, C., 77

borderline patient(s), 5, 47, 134, 208, 310,
    341
borderline personality, 77, 134, 271, 282,
    316, 322
    disorder, 76, 77, 150, 179, 280, 305, 313,
        334
Bowlby, J., 330, 339
    attachment theory, 317
Boyer, L. B., 344
brain, right, regulatory function of, 317
breast–mother, 277
Brenman, E., 77, 92
British National Health Service, 2
British Psychoanalytical Society, 320
Britton, R., 77, 130, 326, 328, 332
Brown, D., 8, 343
Bryant-Waugh, R., 112
bulimia, 30, 34, 38, 95, 115–116, 118
    see also anorexia nervosa
Burghölzli Hospital, Zurich, 275
Bychowski, G., 40, 115

Campbell, J., 285
carbamazepine, 237, 238
castration anxiety, 73, 304
catatonia, 232–233
catatonic features of chronic schizophre-
    nia [clinical example: George], 114,
        139, 219–234, 269, 287
catatonic posture, 41, 44, 192, 221–224,
        228, 232
Cawley, R., 298
Chadwick, P., 308
chemotherapy, 290
Chestnut Lodge Hospital, 6
Chomsky, N., xvi
chronic states, factors leading to, 141–149
Ciompi, L., 147
claustro-agoraphilia, 322
claustro-agoraphobia, 257, 314, **321–322**
"claustro-agoraphobic position", 277
claustrophilia, 322
claustrophobia, 139, 153, 226
Clozapine, 173
cognitive-behavioural therapy (CBT), 9,
        148, 288, 307
    role of, 308–309
Cohen, B. J., 306
Cohen, M., 235
collective unconscious, 342
    Jung's theory of, 275
community care, 310
concrete symbolism, 23

projective identification (*continued*):
psychotogenic, 218
Rosenfeld on, 232
use of
psychotogenic, 205
projective–introjective cycle, 283
promiscuity, 33
psychiatric taxonomy, multi-axial
classification system in, 305
psychodynamics (*passim*):
definition, **333**
psychoneurosis, definition, **333–334**
psychopharmacology, 3, 290–291, 298
see also biomedicine; medication
psychosexual development:
anal stage of, 32
Freud's theory of, 276, 277
Klein's theory of, 276–279
psychosis(es) (*passim*):
biogenic, 334
bipolar affective, 247
definition, **334–335**
depressive: *see* depressive psychosis
see also melancholia; psychotic
depression
functional, 334
hysterical [clinical example: Claudia],
76–94, 174, 189, 287, 301, 330
manic-depressive [clinical example:
Harry], 180, 235–254, 260, 285
organic, 334
origins of, 281–282
and phobia [clinical example: Grace],
38, 172, 174, 208–218, 295, 298
psychogenic, 334
regressive, episodic, 94
schizo-affective, 246, 265, 314, 338
schizo-depressive, 266
schizo-manic, 266
schizophreniform, 338
psychotherapy (*passim*):
aim-restricted, 54
interminable, 162–163
rehabilitation, 306
time needed for, 25, 301–302, 312
psychotic anxiety, 335
psychotic core, 24, 26, 204, 206, 207, 214
psychotic defence(s), 335
psychotic depression, 266, 324
as pathological mourning, 330
"psychotic organization", 68, 139, 334
psychotic personality (*passim*):
part, 287

psychotic thinking (*passim*):
bizarre, 83, 255
characteristics of, 255
concrete, 270
part-object, 91
roots of, in mother-baby relationship, 8
symbolism of, 292
psychotic transference, 185, 215, 216, 297
and paranoid delusions [clinical
example: Frank], 191–207
puberty, adolescent's fears during, 72,
100, 111, 114, 117, 128, 139, 304

Quinodoz, D., 305

Racker, H., 324
Räkköläinen, V., 3, 291, 299, 332
Ramzy, I., 12, 19, 304
Rasimus, R., 3
rat(s), 13, 18, 19, 89, 90, 209–216, 258
Rat Man, Freud's case of, 12, 13
reaction formation, 23
reactive psychosis, 338
reality:
concept of, **335–336**
external (outer), 127, 199, 249, 260, 330
concept of, **335–336**
internal (inner), 127, 145, 159, 173, 249,
260, 279, 280, 315, 332, 334
concept of, **335–336**
vs. external (outer), 68, 74, 124, 140,
163, 268, 278, 281, 302, 305, 316
psychic, 159, 246, 267, 330, 337
concept of, **335–336**
testing, 51, 68, 72, 118, 300, 315, 326,
328, 329
concept of, **335–336**
reconstruction vs. reparation, 337
regression, 24, 266, **336**
Freud's theory of, 274, 323
institutional, 324, 336
malignant, 336
psychobiological, 247
psychotic, 36, 37, 38, 81, 94, 132, 206,
212, 246, 265, 297, 306, 314
Kleinian theory of, 336
into psychotic transference, 205
therapeutic, 222, 227
use of, 336
rehabilitative psychoanalysis, 306
Reid, I. C., 318
Reiser, M., 2
repair vs. reparation, 337